Teaching Music
through Performance
in Choir
Volume 1

G-6534

Teaching Music through Performance in Choir

Volume 1

Frank Abrahams
Anton E. Armstrong
Joseph Flummerfelt
Graeme Morton
Weston H. Noble

Compiled and Edited by Heather J. Buchanan
and Matthew W. Mehaffey

GIA Publications, Inc.
Chicago

Dedication

To the music teachers who challenged
and inspired us.

Information from Chapter 2, **"Does It Dance?"**, is also presented in *Creating a Special World: A Collection of Lectures* by Weston H. Noble, Copyright © 2005 GIA Publications, Inc. All rights reserved.

G-6534

Copyright © 2005 GIA Publications, Inc.
7404 S. Mason Ave.
Chicago, IL 60638
www.giamusic.com
ISBN: 1-57999-514-4
Book layout: Robert Sacha
Dust jacket design: Robert Sacha
    Images from Katherine Bolcar,
    featuring Montclair State University Chamber Singers
Printed in the United States of America

Table of Contents

PART II: The Choral Conductor as Music Teacher
Repertoire Resource Guides

ACKNOWLEDGEMENTS

The following **RESEARCH ASSOCIATES** are
gratefully acknowledged for outstanding scholarly contributions to the

REPERTOIRE RESOURCE GUIDES

Chris Bartley
Doctoral Student
University of Arizona • Tucson, Arizona

Heather J. Buchanan
Director of Choral Activities
Montclair State University • Upper Montclair, New Jersey

Bruce Chamberlain
Director of Choral Activities
University of Arizona • Tucson, Arizona

Thomas Cunningham
Director of the Dartmouth Chamber Singers
Dartmouth College • Hanover, New Hampshire

Wayne Glass
Doctoral Student
University of Arizona • Tucson, Arizona

Christopher Jackson
Visiting Assistant Professor
Adams State University • Alamosa, Colorado

Lani Johnson
Doctoral Student
University of Arizona • Tucson, Arizona

G. Mikael Lindström
Doctoral Student
University of North Texas • Denton, Texas

Ming Luke
Assistant Conductor/Education Director
Sacramento Philharmonic Orchestra • Sacramento, California

J. Aaron McDermid
Doctoral Student
University of Arizona • Tucson, Arizona

Matthew W. Mehaffey
Director of Choral Activities
The George Washington University • Washington, District of Columbia.

Lee Nelson
Doctoral Student
University of Arizona • Tucson, Arizona

Russell Nelson
Director of Music
Central United Methodist Church • Asheville, North Carolina

Carmine Prezioso
French, Italian and Spanish Translations
Princeton, New Jersey

Krystal Rickard
Choral Director
Morris Hills High School • Rockaway, New Jersey

Anthony Reeves
Director of Choirs
The University of North Dakota • Grand Forks, North Dakota

The following CHORAL DIRECTORS AND MUSIC EDUCATORS are gratefully acknowledged for their repertoire suggestions for the

REPERTOIRE RESOURCE GUIDES

Frank Albinder
Choral Director
Washington Men's Camerata • Washington, District of Columbia

Heather J. Buchanan
Director of Choral Activities
Montclair State University • Upper Montclair, New Jersey

Ronald Burrichter
Professor of Music
The University of Florida • Gainesville, Florida

Bruce Chamberlain
Director of Choral Activities
University of Arizona • Tucson, Arizona

Rita Cortez
Choral Director
Lower Macungie Middle School • Macungie, Pennsylvania

Duncan Couch
Director of Choral Activities
Stetson University • DeLand, Florida

Allen Crowell
Heyward Professor of Choral Music
University of Georgia • Athens, Georgia

Patrick Gardner
Director of Choral Activities
Rutgers University • New Brunswick, New Jersey

Paul D. Head
Director of Choral Studies
University of Delaware • Newark, Delaware

Mary Jacobsen
Choral Director
West Windsor-Plainsboro High School North • Plainsboro, New Jersey

Ann Howard Jones
Director of Choral Activities
Boston University • Boston, Massachusetts

James Jordan
Associate Professor of Conducting
Westminster Choir College of Rider University • Princeton, New Jersey

Laurie Lausi
Director of Choral Activities
Cherry Hill East High School • Cherry Hill, New Jersey

Jing Ling-Tam
Director of Choral Studies
University of Texas at Arlington • Arlington, Texas

Matthew W. Mehaffey
Director of Choral Activities
The George Washington University • Washington, District of Columbia

Graeme Morton
Director of Choral Activities
St. Peter's Lutheran College • Brisbane, Australia

Nancianne Parrella
Assistant Director and Accompanist of Westminster Choir
Westminster Choir College of Rider University • Princeton, New Jersey

Anthony Reeves
Director of Choirs
The University of North Dakota • Grand Forks, North Dakota

Z. Randall Stroope
Director of Choral Activities
University of Nebraska • Lincoln, Nebraska

Betsy Cook Weber
Associate Professor of Music
University of Houston • Houston, Texas

Introduction

Heather J. Buchanan

Although the gestation period of this book was far longer than anticipated, it is with great pride that we present this first volume in the choral series *Teaching Music through Performance in Choir*. Based upon the model of the original landmark series, *Teaching Music through Performance in Band*, this book is the first in a choral series designed to support and facilitate the ongoing education and development of the tens of thousands of choral directors and music educators in the world who engage in the art and craft of choral conducting on a daily basis. Volume 1 has been written with the needs of the high school choral director specifically in mind, although the content of this book is also valuable and relevant for conductors of college and university choirs, choral music education student-teachers, and conductors of community and church choirs.

The content of Volume 1 is divided into two parts. Part I features chapters by major figures in the choral field, and Part II comprises the Repertoire Resource Guide, which includes historical, biographical, and analytical information about one masterwork (the Fauré *Requiem*) and 102 choral pieces for mixed, women's, and men's vocal ensembles. By far the most difficult task was the music selection for the Repertoire Resource Guide, and we are indebted to the choral directors who willingly shared their suggestions and music with us for this section. Choirs come in many forms and sizes, and we were mindful of the need to find a balance between sacred and secular literature, music for different voicings and ensemble sizes, music of different historical periods and genres, and music for choirs of varying levels of ability and experience. Coeditor Matthew Mehaffey gives a more detailed explanation of the Repertoire Resource Guide in the introduction to that section.

The first volume in any series is a significant publication, and we are honored that each of the major authors agreed to be part of this book. Their collective wisdom, advice, and insights provide valuable information on many different aspects of the art and craft of our profession. After fifty-seven years at Luther College, Weston Noble has justifiably earned the title "Doyen of American Music Educators and Conductors." He is internationally recognized for his work with the Nordic Choir and for his inspiring musical, spiritual, and humanitarian leadership of generations of young musicians.

Joseph Flummerfelt's career spans thirty-five years, during which time he has earned widespread acclaim for his performances with the Westminster Choir and Westminster Symphonic Choir as well as for his many outstanding collaborations with international orchestral conductors such as Abbado, Bernstein, Boulez, Mehta, and Muti, to name only a few. Anton Armstrong is one of the most dynamic and "in demand" choral musicians of his generation; he maintains a rigorous national and international profile in addition to his work with the St. Olaf Choir. Joseph Flummerfelt and Anton Armstrong represent the two great American choral schools of music—Westminster and St. Olaf, respectively.

Graeme Morton is our international contributor. A preeminent figure in the Australian choral music scene, he is renowned for his innovative work in contemporary choral music performance and has extensively toured the United States and Europe with his choirs. Frank Abrahams is a leading music educator and choral conductor whose chapter on the National Standards brings education and art together in a dynamic and creative way.

This book has been a team effort and is the result of many years of planning and hard work. Special thanks must be given to James Jordan for his encouragement; Alec Harris at GIA Publications for his patience and support; Elizabeth Dallman Bentley, our copy editor; and the singers in our choirs who have trusted, honored, and inspired us with their generosity of voice and spirit. Ultimately, this book is a testament to the dedication of choral conductors around the world whose passion for musical excellence and artistry is reflected in the hearts, souls, minds, and voices of the singers they enlighten and inspire.

PART I

THE TEACHING OF MUSIC

CHAPTER 1

Does It Sing?

Joseph Flummerfelt

For me, it all begins with *breath*—the means of opening to the deepest inner connection to a creative impulse beyond the stricture of an individual ego. A spiritual connection allowing a spontaneous flow only emerges when the ego-driven need to control has subsided.

The essential nature of song is intrinsically spontaneous. It necessarily flows from a source that is other than (beyond) the connotative specificity of language. The singer, whether vocalist, instrumentalist, or conductor, becomes a kind of channel through which the music flows. This does not imply that a music maker abdicates individual responsibility and becomes only a kind of mindless tube through which an outside force flows. Clearly, all aspects of the craft must be in place. Indeed, in making music, as in all aspects of life, the goal is to grow toward balance, a balance between controlling and allowing, between action and reaction, between doing and being. With respect to a work of art, it is the balance of surface (craft) and substance (content or meaning), the temporal and spiritual, the cognitive and the intuitive, and so on. Consider for a moment aspects of these three elements of balance in a work of art.

Concerning the surface or the craft, the conductor or music maker must continually monitor the musical disciplines of intonation, rhythmic integrity, dynamic contour, texture, balance, articulation, etc. The craft must be mastered before the meaning or the substance that informs the surface of the craft comes into play. Or one can say that the meaning or content of a work of art can only emerge if its form is fully in place.

What about meaning in music? The Bach B Minor Mass, a Brahms *Requiem*, a Haydn mass, or a Schubert song lives and continues to be a source of truth, precisely because I believe each work flows from the same creative impulse, from the deepest recesses of human experience, or beyond, call it what you will. To be sure, each of these works speaks with a different voice because of its cultural and historical context, and each of these works has a coherent voice because of its consummate technical mastery. Yet I submit that at the moment of creation each composer was connected to or became a kind of channel of the same life-giving, creative force. Perhaps the most vivid example of this is Mozart, who said that for him composing was like taking dictation.

For those of us who work in the realm of "texted" music, meaning emerges to the extent that we constantly probe beneath the surface of the notes to ask why or how it came to be. How does this melodic, rhythmic, or harmonic gesture symbolize a given textual idea? Certainly, there is no direct connotative link between a given word and a given musical idea. Music has neither the specificity of the written language, nor does it express or mean a specific emotion. For example, what is the musical formula for love or longing? Yet, qualities of a state of being can be expressed that go beyond the specific meaning of a given word.

A familiar example that comes to mind is the first entrance of the chorus in Brahms' *Ein Deutsches Requiem*, movement 1, measures 1–28.

The orchestral introduction begins on a throbbing quarter-note F pedal, and harmonic tension is gradually created until a relaxing of tension begins on the second-inversion tonic chord in measure 13. At this point, there is a gradual lessening of tension or a kind of harmonic surrendering to the opening words of text, "Selig" or "blessed." At this moment, the pulsating bass stops, and only human voices are heard. It is as if earthly time has stopped and one feels suspended in a kind of celestial space. The further miracle of this moment is that Brahms sets the second word of the phrase "sind," meaning "are they," with a V6/4 chord, which has the effect of sending the quality of blessedness into open-ended space. This seems to me a perfect illustration of the principle that song with its multiplicity of color can only emerge in the fullness of communicative power when it flows out of a deep connection to meaning. The miracle of this moment of musical symbolism is that one feels removed from the temporal dimension of time, and Brahms evokes a quality of spaciousness that for an instant leaves the dimension of earthly grounding.

For a second example of meaning, we turn to the choral entrance in the first movement of Stravinsky's *Symphony of Psalms*. In this text, the speaker cries out for deliverance from his or her mortal condition.

> Hear my prayer, O Lord, and my supplication; give ear to my cry.
> Be not silent: for I am a stranger with thee, and a sojourner as all my
>   fathers were.
> O forgive me, that I may be refreshed, before I go hence, and be
>   no more.
>
> *Psalm 38:13–14*

It is as though the speaker feels trapped in his or her condition and longs for release. This entrapment is vividly symbolized through Stravinsky's *Symphony of Psalms*, movement 1, measures 26–48.

The alto enters with a kind of wailing in which the musical line gets caught on the note E. It keeps pulling away to F, but continually falls back. Underneath this, one hears the unrelenting ostinato. Ostinato is a circular musical device that goes nowhere; the entrapment of the choral line is powerfully reinforced by this directionless instrumental writing.

For a third example, consider the familiar *Ave Maria* of Victoria, with the text "et benedictus fructus ventris tui" (blessed is the fruit of your womb) set as follows.

Here the narrow compass of each essentially conjunct line has a kind of harmonic churning that seems to me to symbolize the gestation in the womb. One may, of course, disagree with my reading of the meaning of each of the examples. That is unimportant. What is essential is that we constantly ask our musical imaginations to consider the meaning of each musical moment.

Concerning the temporal and the spiritual, a musical work exists in time, and intrinsically the manifestation of each moment comes from and is going somewhere. Each moment has a past and a future. Yet for the temporal to emerge and evolve with organic inevitability, one must be fully present and connected to the reality of each moment. Then the spirit can flow, and the surface aspect of the craft, however correct, can become alive; this way a balance is reached that allows a work to fully communicate. I stress "in the momentness" because in our horizontal, goal-oriented world, we far too often are so concerned with the forward motion of a musical line that we disconnect from the fullness of each moment. In musical performances as well as in life, both the vertical and horizontal aspects must be in balance.

The balance of the horizontal, the historical, the temporal, and the cognitive with the vertical, the spiritual, and the intuitive is, I believe, at the crux of the matter. When this balance is in play, a work sings. It sings because its progress evolves with a quality of spontaneity that is possible when one balances control of the craft with giving way to the full force of each successive instant.

A word about the balance of cognition and intuition: Some years ago, I came across a fascinating book, *The Origin of Consciousness in the Breakdown of the Bicameral Mind* by Princeton psychologist Julian Jaynes. The thesis of this book is that as humankind has evolved toward ever-increasing consciousness, and as our scientific and technological world has "progressed," we have lost touch with the "other" side or what some would call the subconscious. The mere fact that we no longer seem to have Old Testament prophets or Delphic oracles that speak to us in revelation is in large part because we have become so totally ensnared by our conscious mind that we can no longer hear these voices, which exist outside the cognitive or the conscious realm.

Well into the book, Jaynes describes a "dada" test in which the intuitive side of a subject's brain was safely sedated, and, though the subject was able to speak, the subject could not sing. Conversely, when the cognitive side was deadened, the subject could sing, but could not speak. It seems to me that this is a powerful verification of the notion that song comes from the "other" side, however one characterizes that, and it is only when we are able to release the need to consciously control it that a musical, singing performance emerges. It sings because it has a quality of spontaneity. The performance sounds as though the work were composed at that very moment. To be sure, thoughtful thinking through of how we expect to proceed with respect to tempo, qualities of rubato, and all manner of nuance must have taken place. Yet this must be internalized so that at the moment of pre-creation one is open to the ever-changing context of each moment.

Perhaps it is our fear, or distrust, or disconnection from the "other" side that is at the root of today's cultural afflictions. Humankind has believed since perhaps the dawn of enlightenment that if we proceed far enough along the linear path of the cognitive world, all will be revealed. This way of thinking is, of course, implicitly horizontal, and as we came to place ever-increasing veracity upon this plane, our distrust of or disconnection from the other side, the intuition, or what I choose to call the vertical dimension of each moment, increased. Projected onto an even larger arena, it is interesting to consider all of the religious and cultural implications of the more horizontal Western world and the more vertical Eastern world. Although further discussion of this is beyond the purview of this chapter, it does seem to me that the next chapters in the evolution of our world will be the result of a synthesis of the more vertical Eastern culture and the more linear Western culture. Clearly, we have seen the early manifestations of this in the realms of religion and art.

In musical performances, the disconnection I allude to above has manifested itself in performances in which technical virtuosity becomes the only goal, and the music student, both theoretical and historical, very often stops short of musical considerations. Meaning, which I believe can only be ascertained by allowing oneself to intuitively reflect upon the human/ spiritual impulse of each musical gesture, allows a song to happen because the synthesis of cognition, intuition, craft and content, spirit and flesh, surface, and substance are in play. The full form of a musical work of art is allowed to communicate, not to dazzle, not to impress, but to communicate. Then the listeners' lives can be touched at the deepest level and be forever changed.

Joseph Flummerfelt is Conductor Emeritus at Westminster Choir College of Rider University in Princeton, New Jersey. For thirty-three years, he served as Artistic Director and Principal Conductor of Westminster Choir College, during which time he collaborated with many eminent conductors, including Abbado, Bernstein, Boulez, Chailly, Giulini, Masur, Mehta, Muti, Ozawa, Sawallisch, and Steinberg. Choirs prepared by Flummerfelt have been featured on more than forty recordings, including Britten's War Requiem and Brahms' Ein Deutsches Requiem and Schicksalslied with Kurt Masur and the New York Philharmonic. He is chorus master for the New York Philharmonic and the founder and conductor of the professional choir the New York Choral Artists.

CHAPTER 2

Does It Dance?
Stylistic Awareness
from Polyphony
to the Classical Period

Weston H. Noble

Polyphony (1450–1600)

In the middle to late 1950s, I was asked to be the choral clinician for the Iowa fall workshops. The requested topic for discussion was the "style characteristics of choral music in the different musical periods." I was reluctant to accept this invitation because I did not know enough about the differences. From the 1930s until the late 1950s, *tone* was the single most discussed element of choral singing. The positive factors of this element are obvious. The negative factor is obvious as well: all music had a tendency to sound the same, with no differentiating characteristics of style. I accepted this assignment with trepidation—this was my challenge to grow. With the help of the great Howard Swan, then at Occidental College in Los Angeles, I became the "style authority" for the state of Iowa!

In our profession, we must have a stylistic awareness and discriminating taste in directing choral music of various periods. As in *The Sound of Music*, let us "start at the very beginning"—polyphony. The interpretation of polyphonic music involves understanding of the following factors: speech, rhythm, melody, dynamics, and tempo.

RELATIONSHIP TO CHANT

A study of music history shows us that polyphony is a direct descendant of chant, which is the direct descendant of speech. In conclusion, speech and polyphony are closely allied. Each part must be heard when it presents important material. All parts cannot be preeminent at all times. Each melodic line is not of equal importance.

RHYTHM

Rhythm is present as in all music, but in polyphony it is not metrical; it is not measured in the sense to which we have become accustomed with bar lines. The rhythm can begin at any place within the phrase. James McKelvy's edition of Victoria's *Gloria in excelsis Deo* (Mark Foster #404) is an outstanding illustration. Here you see "phrases" that are four beats, two beats, five beats, etc. The beginning and ending of each segment of each rhythm is based entirely on the text. His addition of bar lines makes it so clear to us who have "grown up" with this basic principle of rhythm. Student comprehension is all but immediate, yet when sung the melodic lines disregard the bar lines. Music sets the length of the notes (the structure of melodic lines and changes of harmony), and this may or may *not* set *regular* measures.

Remember my opening statement about polyphony being the direct descendant of chant and chant being the direct descendant of speech? Speech has a natural syllabic stress that remains the same, only it is sung. The basic principle seems simple, but it is not in actuality. We naturally remain the victims of the tyranny of the bar line—that beat one is automatically stressed if an edition of sixteenth-century music uses the bar line for clarity. Robert Shaw's edition of Victoria's *O Magnum Mysterium* (G. Schirmer, 43074c) is an excellent example of underscoring syllable stress using the clarity of the bar line. This is the first clear edition of sixteenth-century style that I encountered!

MELODY

When notes of equal value proceed stepwise, they are nearly always sung legato. The larger the intervallic skip, the greater the sensation of separation. Larger intervals often indicate word stress. The longer the note value, the greater its intensity, weight, and body. Quick notes are taken lightly. If a note is tied over a bar line, no accents of any kind occur after the bar. Tension should appear in ascending lines and relaxation in descending phrases; these are just the natural rules of speech.

DYNAMICS

Sing with good taste—**nothing** that smacks of effect. Great shades of dynamics are personal, as in the Romantic period. This is group worship with the choir "leading" the congregation. The music must express the mood of the text, but not a personal, individual text—rather, a group text. Polyphonic composers thought of steadiness of sound with the number of parts determining the dynamics. There must be an overall dynamic for the entire selection, centering on *mp* or *mf*, with little deviation for the entire piece. A crescendo or diminuendo must not be obviously recognized as such, but as an increasing or decreasing intensity of small segments following the rise and fall of the melodic line. Imitative motives should always be recognizable, with more restraint on other parts instead of a harder pressing of the motive. The musical results will be subtler this way.

TEMPO

A fluent tempo is so important, and, particularly in sacred repertoire, the tempi chosen are usually too slow. If a conductor errs on the slow side, he or she will feel that something is missing and attempt to put in or overlay "expression." This is wrong. Remember, pulse is the determinant. The note values are relevant. Long notes are not sung more slowly just because they appear to be long on the page. On the other hand, never take a composition at a faster tempo than all the details of the music can be clearly heard.

Hans David, a great musicologist at the University of Michigan, said, "rubato could be used in polyphony so long as it is *within* the phrase and not *over* several measures." It is interesting to look at the 1932 edition of Victoria's *O Magnum Mysterium* edited by John Finley Williamson (G. Schirmer, 35752c), founder of the Westminster Choir, to see just how far we have come in critical stylistic awareness. Go back to 1919 and an edition of Victoria's *Vere Languores*, edited by Kurt Schindler (Oliver Ditson, no. 13,380). It is an even "dirtier edition," full of dynamic and tempo changes. Now refer back to James McKelvy's edition of Victoria's *Gloria in excelsis Deo*. There is not one single dynamic marking or tempo alteration—it is totally clean. Bravo!

Baroque (1600–1750)

As we enter the Baroque period, one does not find the one, all-powerful church of the period of the Renaissance—Catholicism. Instead, we encounter the strengthening of Lutheranism with the counter-reformation in Catholicism. The function of music within the two churches differed.

Monteverdi's first opera employed the use of the solo song through the recitation (prose rhythm of the text) and the aria (metrical organization). The recitation (recitative) fulfilled the great desire to project words clearly, interpreting primarily from the text; when an aria was performed, the interpretation came more from the musical connotation. The Baroque period was primarily a revolt against counterpoint as composers wanted to get the words heard more plainly. True, there is some counterpoint, particularly in the music of Schütz and J. S. Bach, but it was more a "throw-back" to what had been prevalent before. Bach's sons did not view their father's compositions with unusual admiration; he was simply "behind the times."

We now see an emphasis on "dramatic expression," as determined by the word. One cannot overlook the text in the Baroque, but it does not call for the emotion of the Romantic period. In the Baroque period, one perceives choral structure that is harmonic in implication. The change from polyphony to Baroque constituted one of the most drastic changes of emphasis in the history of music, second only to the revolution as we moved from impression-ism to the twentieth-century music!

RHYTHM

Baroque music is far more metrical than polyphony. With the advent of the bar line at the close of the Renaissance period because of the complexity of the music, we find regular accentuations at regularly spaced intervals. Syllabic stress was not the dominant factor in the establishment of rhythm. Rather than starting anywhere within the phrase, rhythm is very regular at evenly spaced intervals. Yet the obvious positive advantages of metric regularity also had a negative side. Beat one became so dominant as to take away the "dance feeling." The natural accents of a given measure gave a "square feeling" due to the nature of their undue importance. Duple rhythm especially could take on a pneumatic feeling of constant regularity (like a pneumatic drill in an air hammer).

Early in my musical career I attended a wonderful evensong at St. Mark's Episcopal Church in Seattle. When I congratulated Peter Hallock, he simply said, "Well, all music must dance!" I reflected on this statement. Must a somber Lenten hymn dance? A march? I understood how well triple meter would fit into this concept, but duple? Prior to meeting Peter Hallock, I spent two six-week sessions with Robert Shaw in San Diego. I recognized that he approached rhythm in a manner somewhat foreign to me. I felt the difference as we sang with him day after day. I liked it. But what was the underlying principle? How could I verbalize it? **His music danced!** For him, rhythm was not only timing but also *spacing*.

Several years later, when sharing with an instrumental colleague, I mentioned how intrigued I was with the "Shaw feeling," but I found it so hard to verbalize. "Have you ever read anything on this type of phrasing?" he inquired. I hadn't, and he recommended a doctoral thesis housed at the Catholic University in Washington, D.C., titled *Note Grouping: A method for achieving expression and style in musical performance* by James Thurmond. Once I started reading it, I could not put it down. I had found the gold. I knew the fundamental principle to make *all* music dance! The term "Baroque phrasing" became part of my musical vocabulary. I had a core curriculum of basic principles governing phrasing that prevailed at the time. To my delight, these principles prevailed in subsequent periods of music as well. I could not teach form, not from intuition alone!

Baroque phrasing emphasizes what happens on weak beats and between the beats, quite opposite to the traditional concept of the dominating impor-tance ascribed to primary accents (or natural accents) as customarily taught. Principal beats of the measure are traditionally stressed through accents, a somewhat mechanical and unmusical technique. Rather, the principal beat should be approached from the previous weak beat! Was this difference of approach the reason the performance of one artist touches our spirit so deeply while another may be intriguing technically but seems not to have touched a deeper side of us?

Baroque principles of phrasing quickly emerged (weak to strong) as James Thurmond studied the note grouping principles of Marcel Tabuteau, the great oboist of the Philadelphia Orchestra, in detail. Nothing in life desires to remain weak if it is designated as such. Strength is the recognized virtue. Natural accents are obviously the strong beats of a given measure. Weak beats are inherently present as well. Can a weak beat become strong? If so, there are two possibilities for consideration: the strong beat before the weak beat, or the strong beat following the weak beat. It is impossible to look back and become strong, but one can look ahead and derive strength. **Weak to strong is the underlying principle of Baroque phrasing!** Interestingly, scripture states: "When I am weak, I am strong...my grace is sufficient for you, for my power is made perfect in weakness" (2 Corinthians: 9–10). Every weak note must never remain static but become strong by leading or "lifting" into the strong beat that follows. A weak note then becomes an upbeat.

James Thurmond writes in *Note Grouping: A method for achieving expression and style in musical performance*, pp. 18–19:

> After much study of the extant literature regarding interpretation, expression and musicianship, it has been found that there is an important relation between the way the **arsis** (or upbeat) is played, and the **movement** imagery present in the mind when one is listening to music. This imagery of movement, as will be seen later, actually does affect the kinesthetic nerve system and can cause the foot to tap, or incite in one the desire to dance. How many times have we heard someone say, "What a moving performance!" or "I was so moved by his playing!"? The Reverend William J. Finn, director of the Paulist Choristers, was cognizant of this relationship when he wrote, "The mystery of music is in the upbeat.

There are four basic rules in the accomplishment of Baroque phrasing, which, in actuality, are applicable to all subsequent periods. Shaw added a fifth one, which I will explain later.

Rule #1: Weak to Strong

Any weak beat must lead to a strong beat. Nadia Boulanger, the great French teacher of so many of our great musicians such as Bernstein, Sessions, Copland, Barber, and Menotti, to name a few, placed particular stress on the beat just before the bar line (i.e. four in duple meter). The weakest beat in any measure is just before the bar line. **It must be lifted across the bar line to** become strong with the energy of movement and flow of the phrase. The term "cross-bar phrasing" is also used in conjunction with Baroque phrasing. The "tyranny of the bar line" must be overcome—i.e., the undue emphasis on beat one. As beat four must go to beat one, so must beat two (weak) lead to beat three. Triple meter is somewhat different and will be explained later.

Two basic terms come into being: **thesis** (thetic) and **arsis** (arsic). "Thesis" in Greek means "to fall," a dominant point. Thus all strong beats are termed "thetic." "Arsis" in Greek does not mean "weak," as logic might imply. Interestingly, it means "to lift," to lead on to a destination—the weak beat then leading on to the strong. The same basic principle applies in shorter time values as well. When two eighth notes are present, the first one is the stronger. The destination of the weaker one is paramount. When four eighth notes are present, the first one is the strongest and the fourth one the weakest. In a faster tempo, rather than thinking the microcosm of the second eighth note going to the third (which it does) and the fourth going to the following note (which it does), one might feel the first eighth note as thetic but the following eighth notes as arsic, all three leading on to the next downbeat. Tempo could be a determinant as well as the composer's preference.

Look at sixteenth notes. Most often the first sixteenth is thetic with the remaining three being arsic leading to the next downbeat. Yet, in a subdivided passage, the second sixteenth might clearly go to the third one and the fourth to the following downbeat. Again, tempo and the composer's taste become the determinants. A function of a note might change. For example, if a measure consists of two half notes in 4/4 time, one might surmise both half notes are thetic in feeling. In this instance, however, the second half note is arsic, leading across the bar to the downbeat.

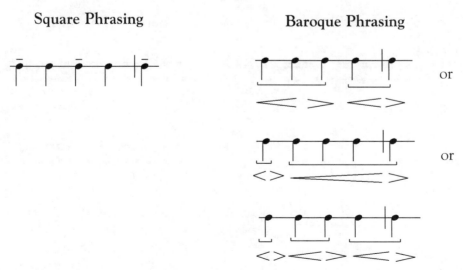

Figure 1a: Weak-to-strong phrasing for quarter-note rhythms in duple meter.

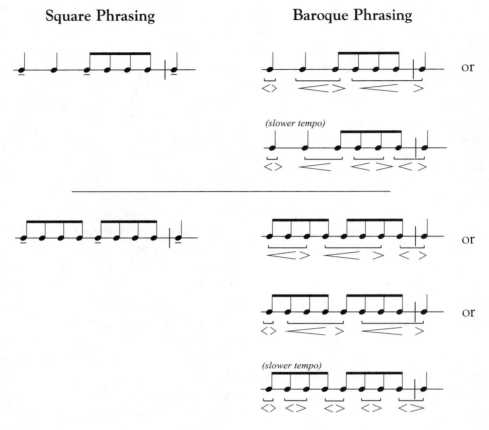

Figure 1b: Weak-to-strong phrasing for eighth note rhythms in duple meter.

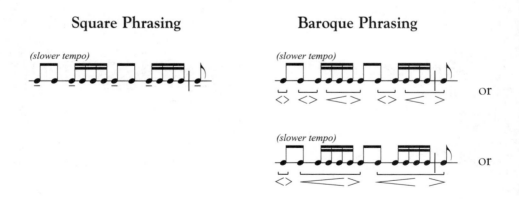

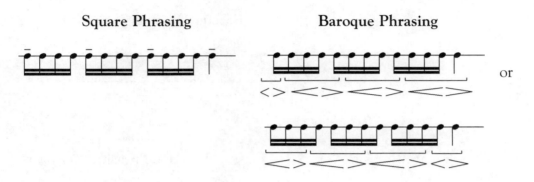

Figure 1c: Weak-to-strong sixteenth notes in duple meter.

Rule #2: Short to Long

Shorter time values always lead to longer time values. This is really a further clarification of Rule #1 in that the shorter time value is always weak and the longer time value is strong. Shorter time values can be viewed in two different ways. For example, in the case of a quarter note followed by two eighths followed by a quarter, the two eighths can be viewed as collectively as weaker. The second perception of "short to long" is more obvious, such as a dotted quarter followed by an eighth. The eighth is the weaker and must lead on to the stronger beat that follows.

Now I want to introduce a term I use: "springboard." Let us examine more closely the dot of the dotted-quarter note. Rhythmically it is an eighth note, making it thetic in relationship to the actual eighth note that follows. If it is viewed as thetic, it must have "energy"—it must have strength, it must have emphasis. It must function as a "springboard" to the eighth that follows. This can be realized by some emphasis being placed on the dot, especially by the conductor. In certain instances, Shaw would ask that an eighth rest be sounded on the dot or maybe a dotted-sixteenth to give clarity both of precision and emphasis with the following eighth note leading on to the next stronger beat. The same principle applies with a dotted eighth followed by a sixteenth, etc.

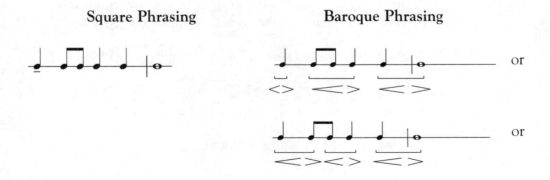

Baroque Phrasing, cont.

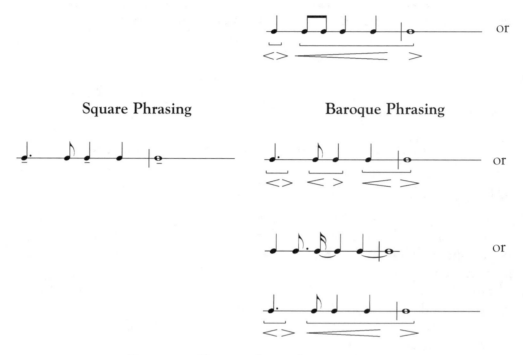

Figure 2: Short-to-long phrase groupings.

Rule #3: Repeated Notes

Repeated notes are often separated, a further subdivision of the basic "weak-to-strong" principle. As I mentioned above, a shorter time value can be viewed as a quarter note followed by two eighth notes followed by a quarter. But more often, the two repeated notes have a feeling of separation. Shaw would state this so eloquently: "Don't sing successive eighth notes as equal values—sing the second one as a point of departure." If two eighth notes are not thought of in this manner, the tempo will invariably rush, and the intensity of the forward motion within the phrase will be immediately lessened.

Figure 3: Grouping repeated notes.

Rule #4: Change of Song

If the melody line changes direction, the melodic turn determines the necessity of the notes after the turn being treated as weak, with the note preceding the turn being treated as strong, or thetic. The following weak notes are arsic in direction. In the subsequent example, it becomes immediately clear how this idea enhances the flow of the phrase because there is a new burst of kinetic energy!

Figure 4: Change of song.

Rule #5: Just Because I Feel Like It!

Who else would dare add this rule! Think how deeply he trusted his basic instinct—a challenge to all of us!

Triple Meter

Now to triple meter. Baroque realization can be accomplished in two different ways depending on the intent of the composer. In the first instance, it can be a case of beat three being led across to beat one, with beat two the realization of the downbeat (in other words, minimized); or in the second instance, it can be a case of both beats two and three being led to beat one. The difference is quite stark and should be realized by determining the composer's intent. The examples illustrated in Figure 5 illustrate this clearly.

Square Phrasing

Baroque Phrasing

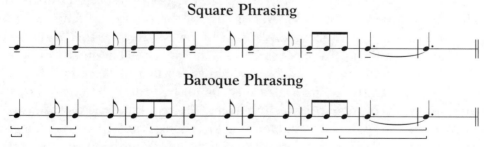

The addition of a crescendo and a decrescendo to the numerous short motivic groupings creates not only a high degree of musical sensitivity but simultaneously creates two phrases that reinforce ideal cadence structure.

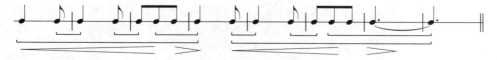

Figure 5: Triple meter grouping.

I explained my use of the term "springboard" in the discussion of Rule #2. May I take this a bit further? Rests have a definite function in most instances. Visualize a 4/4 bar consisting of a quarter rest followed by three quarter notes. The rest is most often viewed as a moment of silence. This is wrong! The rest must be felt as **thetic**, with the following three quarter notes as arsic to the downbeat; or in a slower tempo, the first quarter note is arsic, leading to beat three, which would be thetic. In other words, the rest is a springboard, and the conductor must energize the downbeat to signal it as such. If the rest is not perceived in this manner, the first quarter note will always be felt as thetic, and this is absolutely wrong! Sometimes rests in the Romantic period are treated as moments of silence to enhance the drama of the moment. One must delineate between the two possible functions of rests.

What is the function of a tie? Just to lengthen the preceding note? Absolutely not! The second note of the tie must be viewed as a springboard as well, functioning as a thetic note, with the note following the tie then being arsic in direction. The first note of the tie is arsic leading to the strong beat second note of the tie. Thus, a static moment is avoided, and the flow of the musical line is enhanced.

How does syncopation fit into this? One day in a rehearsal, Robert Shaw pointedly asked me, "Weston, in syncopation do you feel the stress on the downbeat or the offbeat?" Flustered, I gave the answer "the offbeat." He quickly replied, "Wrong. Weston, you always feel the downbeat in syncopation to get the feeling of the offbeat." In other words, in syncopation you give the downbeat of the syncopation a thetic feeling, which then gives the second part of the syncopation an energetic arsic feeling. Interestingly, in jazz it is just the opposite. I will never forget that moment with Shaw as long as I live!

How does one accomplish this realization of space between the thetic note and the following arsic note? The realization of this space results in the beginning of a new point of kinetic energy in the phrase, which is vital to fine music making. It is accomplished in two ways: first by the "schism" or "indentation" resulting in space that may be an actual moment of space, which I call "accomplished through sunlight." Or it may be accomplished in a mental sense, with the resulting space accomplished through "mist." The use of either depends on tempo, style, and degree desired. I feel the most sensitive performer mentally lifts at moments even though not directly indicated within the phrase. It is a wonderful, constant subdivision!

Directors do not have time to explain every moment when Baroque phrasing is desired. It can be beyond the comprehension of the singers as well. If the instructor sings a passage with the desired result of this type of phrasing but substitutes a "day" for every thetic moment and a "tay" for every arsic moment, the choir will sing back what was emulated, and it will follow every basic rule of Baroque phrasing. **The music will immediately dance!** The choir will respond with relative ease, simply because it feels so natural to sing this way. One might use the neutral syllables "doo" [du] or "too" [tu] in passages that are quieter and where the ranges are not as extreme. A definite mood is realized, enhancing the beauty of the selection being learned. Recordings by the Swingle Singers are excellent examples of the use of neutral syllables to enhance rhythmic groups. Bach "swings" or dances as never before in their singing. Students are obviously drawn to this rhythmic feel.

There are several rehearsal methods for gaining the feeling of a springboard. One is to have the choir members tap on the dot, rest, tie, or downbeat syncopation, or for the director to do the same. I often bob my head slightly to add kinetic energy to the springboard. Shaw would often ask us to put a sixteenth rest within a dot or tie, creating space. This is particularly true in a larger ensemble. Remember, all composers do not follow Baroque phrasing consistently. They may intentionally ask for a different phrasing to avoid monotony and to achieve individuality. One can trust the marking of Romantic composers in this regard. Prior to this period, the realization can be more complicated. In-depth study of the original score or style of the period should be considered.

Teach the rules of Baroque phrasing through the use of this simple poem: Weak to strong, Short to long, Repeated notes, Change of song. The above is Baroque phrasing in the microcosm—one burst of kinetic energy to the next, arsis to thesis. Several microcosms put together can have an umbrella feeling of arsic or thetic movement. As more and more microcosms are connected, a musical phrase is the ultimate result. Refer to Figure 6, which includes Beethoven's Fifth Symphony ("layered microcosms"). Notice how the brackets get progressively larger until a musical phrase is the result. Were you to look at a Shaw score, this is exactly how it would be marked, with each unit a different color bracket!

Figure 6: Layered microcosms.

The presence of a text gives singers a decided advantage in realizing the above poem. Because articles and adjectives (usually weaker works) naturally lead to nouns, pronouns, and verbs (usually stronger words), a well-set text enhances the 'weak to strong' principle. The string player has a decided advantage since bowings are often determined by the "weak-to-strong" approach. Woe to the built-in air for the wind, keyboard, and percussion families—there is none. It must be articulated!

I remember so well the day I began to naturally follow the above rules to a certain degree. Understanding the rules thoroughly gave me a solid vehicle for teaching rather than having an ensemble mimic back what I either sang or instructed. Shaw gave us a new definition of rhythm. Rhythm is obviously timing, but now we must add the word "spacing." There is a world of difference. May I end this section of Baroque characteristics with a Shaw quote? "Togetherness comes from a divided pulse—think of sixteenth notes!"

MELODY
Baroque melodies asks us to think of chordal structure, which is harmonic in implication. The melody is generally in the soprano line rather than in each voice.

DYNAMICS
Dynamics are terraced, not gradual changes from one level to the other. The same dynamic level is kept over comparatively long periods of time rather than changing abruptly every few measures. The effect of terraced dynamics usually comes about by the addition or subtraction of vocal parts or instrumental groupings. Bach added or subtracted from both vocal and instrumental lines and thought of these as one. Also, no great dynamic ranges are called for. Many are aware of the group Mannheim Steamroller. In 1749, Johann Stamitz invented the orchestral crescendo with the Mannheim Orchestra in Germany, which became known as the "Mannheim steamroller."

TEMPO
Baroque tempi are unhurried, with animation but without haste. Tempi are even more regular in the late Baroque—never exaggerated. Use rubato only with great discretion, and not nearly as often as within the musical phrases from the Renaissance.

Classical (1750–1820)

The first generality of the Classical period is an absence of the "sweep" of the Baroque era. Instead, we find more elegance, charm, and grace in the music. This brings into being the second generality: one always uses a lighter beat. Third, a structural perfection of the figured bass disappears. Fourth, one finds a basically harmonic approach with some contrapuntal writing. Finally, there is increased use of chromaticism by composers of the Classical period.

RHYTHM
Composers strive for unusual rhythms. One finds that multiple meters are not always indicated in the time signature. Rhythmic alterations with dislocated natural accents (commonly known as syncopation) are also present. Composers have a desire for rhythmic surprises (Haydn!). We also find rhythmic energy even in rests. Therefore, the purpose of the climax determines the length of the rest—it must be determined by the emotion of the moment.

MELODY

Longer phrases are present in the Classical period. Cadences are often either avoided or resolved deceptively. Composers also strive to bring out points of color in chords. Many interpretive markings are present that greatly assist in interpreting the score. Without question, the melody line is of utmost importance.

DYNAMICS

All dynamic devices are heightened even more. A true "orchestral crescendo" enters the music world.

TEMPO

Tempi move more to the extremes (i.e., slower *largo* and faster *allegro*). We have more frequent use of *accelerando* and *ritardando*, and one finds more abrupt stops and starts.

Resources and Acknowledgements:

Note Grouping by James Thurmond, published by Meredith Music Publishing, can be purchased through many music dealers.

The note grouping examples in Figures 1–5 are provided courtesy of James E. Richards, retired professor, University of Texas at Arlington. (Notice the dynamic markings under the examples.)

Suggested octavos for illustrations of the following principles:

Syncopation: *Jubilate Deo* (Althouse). Shawnee Press, A1835.

Rests, dots, and ties: *May You Be Led by the Highest Star* (Nygard). Hinshaw, HMC-1530.

Triple meter: *Summer Is A-coming In* (Arr. Braz). Hinshaw, HMC-1489.

Weston H. Noble is Professor of Music at Luther College, Decorah, Iowa. His retirement at the end of the 2004–05 academic year brings a fifty-seven-year career at the college to an end. An internationally acclaimed music educator and choral conductor, Noble is a recipient of innumerable music and music education awards. Since 1948 he has been the spiritual and motivational core of the Luther music program. He has been the leader and conductor of ninety-three music ensemble tours, including two tours of Europe and sixty-six of the Nordic Choir, including nine abroad. The Nordic Choir is a seventy-two-voice ensemble that has earned a reputation as one of the elite a cappella college choirs in the United States.

CHAPTER 3

Practical Performance Practice in the African American Slave Song

Anton E. Armstrong

For many throughout the world, the African American slave song, or the African American spiritual, as it is more commonly called, becomes one of their entrées into the world of multi-cultural music. This song form originated in the southern region of the United States during the nineteenth century and developed from the music of West Africa, where many of the slaves who were eventually brought to the New World originated. Before looking at slave songs, as we have come to know them in the twentieth and twenty-first centuries, we need to go back to the origins and traits of West African music.

West African Music

First of all, a very brief overview of West African civilization reveals that Africa was not the "dark continent," as it is often referred to, or the barbaric land commonly portrayed in the Tarzan movies. The heathen savage concept developed out of the slave owners' inability to understand the foreign culture; this misunderstanding allowed them to justify the exploitation of African people.

The concept of monotheism, one God, was firmly established in West African society. The early eighteenth-century missionaries found that parts of Africa already knew the Bible and the Bible stories but often incorporated it into their folklore. In fact, Christianity was already established in North Africa as early as the fourth century AD. Polytheism did exist in parts of Africa, but Western European Christians misinterpreted the Africans' respect of all aspects of nature, which was sometimes expressed as a deification of elements of nature such as trees and rivers. This point is important and must be understood because this has often been the justification for calling the African people barbaric or ignorant and thus gave credence and justification to the institution of slavery.

A close look at the role of music in West African culture reveals that music was an integral and functional part of African life, not some abstract art form. Important events like births, marriages, funerals, and simple day-to-day life activities were celebrated with music. Workers had music to aid them in accomplishing common tasks. Music was also used to spread news and gossip, satirized those in positions of power, and expressed discontent with employers and those who were in government positions. Music also accompanied the daily lives of children for playing games and other types of entertainment. In many ways, song represented the preservation of communal values, solidarity, and culture. The following quotation by Cloud and Curtis (1991) summarizes the significance of music/song for the preservation of cultural and communal values and solidarity in traditional West African culture.

> It is said you can say publicly in song what you cannot say privately to a man's face. So this is one of the ways African society [took] to [maintain] a spiritually healthy community. In this way, West African music represented the preservation of communal values and solidarity. Songs provided the chance for individuals to transcend, at least symbolically, the inevitable restrictions of environment in society by permitting the expression of deeply held feelings.

Griots, the trained musicians of West African society, were experts in storytelling, poetry, genealogy, religion, and political and social customs. These individuals, usually men, memorized and passed down the oral histories of their people through song. It is through these stories and traditions that we discover those who took on the roles of the preservers of song and story in the music and the positions of slave society. In addition to the preservation of stories and tales, "music sharing" is another slave song characteristic shared with West African song that was integral to the very form and fabric of the traditional culture.

The most common form of musical sharing is the "call-and-response," singing that allows a very spontaneous and improvised sense of choral song. One of the most famous modern day examples of this would be the B. Jester Hairston setting of *Amen*. Another example is Undine Smith-Moore's "Fare Thee Well," in which there is a soloist and/or a solo ensemble and the full chorus or ensemble response. Another distinguishing characteristic of the slave song that has its origins and roots in West African song is the use and type of rhythms and percussion. West African music is filled with polyrhythms. Drums of many sizes and timbres are used. What we often forget, especially when we look at these rhythmic patterns, is that they are often tied to the speech patterns of the native dialects. These patterns of speech, which are then translated to the rhythmic patterns in the drum, not only maintain the obvious rhythmic vitality of the piece but also send messages in many ways, and, most importantly, create the mood for the use of body movement or dance in song.

> Dance, the expressive movement of the head, torso, limbs and feet, is rooted in West African people as a very natural and instinctive part of their culture. The word "expressive" is important for the dances of the African tribes were not of the folk, social or court type of Europe. They were not based upon the technique of classical ballet. Dance and the word "expressive" refer to the idea that the dancer deals with what is felt when emotion is being experienced by the dancer himself. The beauty of black dance lies in the total lack of inhibition. Therefore, the music of West Africa, whether religious or secular, combines some element of dance to invade the emotion of the people involved. The dancers are usually accompanied on the instrument of the people, the drum. (Cloud and Curtis 1991)

In terms of movement in West African song, which later appears to some degree in slave song, we can say that part of the power and drive of African music derives from the way that African musicians play forward toward the beat. The African musician is not so much moving along with the pulse as pushing the beat to make it more dynamic. What we now commonly understand, especially with music of this form, is that the strong beats of West African music occur on beats two and four instead of beats one and three as in Western music. Additionally, African melody was built from scales that usually had between four and seven steps. What is most telling, though, is the idea and the way in which the slave and the spiritual unified a community, and this has a very strong antecedent in West African music because it is true community music. Everyone becomes involved in creating through singing, playing, or dancing; music is used to relieve the mundane aspects of life and the monotony of work; and it helps to contribute to greater efficiency by helping workers to cooperate and to alleviate fatigue or tiredness in their work. West African music was not only for the moment, but it also provided and served as a keeper of historical events and an informer of current events. Those are some very basic points about West African music and the form that it took in influencing the music of the slaves.

Evolution of the Spiritual

The creation of the spiritual came about as a response to the hardships of the slave life. We have to actually go back to the origins of the hymns that Richard Allen created in *The Hymnal* in 1801 and the founding of the AME Church and its songbook. The slave song or spiritual is truly part of an oral tradition. It must also be noted that not all slave songs are religious. Actually, there is a large genre that we have some access to but has never been classified as choral music. The corpus of music that we know is really a small amount, but we will look at the totality. The concepts of "sacred" and "secular" didn't really exist in the West African tradition, nor in American slavery, though worldly concepts soon emerged.

The slave song that is called the spiritual shows the relationship between song and the Holy Spirit, and it is said these pieces possess a lyrical quality and express a wide range of emotions, such as elation, hope, and sorrow. The spiritual emerged through the melding of numerous elements. Slaves used the Old Testament Bible stories of faith, hope, and liberation and fit them into a musical structure that at times reflected African forms such as call-and-response and polyrhythms. They then instinctively drew from their African past and also incorporated some of the music and sounds they heard in the New World, (i.e., African tonality and scales combined with the Western seven-note scale). Slave songs provided unity for the slave community and also became an instrument of communication. These songs began to replace the drum as a means of communication after the slave owners forbade their use. Most importantly, the spiritual provided the community with a coded language for use in emergencies.

Slave Song Categories

There are five categories of the slave song. I am indebted to some research by Jester Hairston in this area.

1. **Religious spirituals**: These make very direct reference to the images of King Jesus, the devil, judgment day, and heaven; these are the preaching or teaching spirituals. Some examples include William Dawson's "King Jesus is a-Listenin'" or Moses Hogan's "My God Is So High." These are examples in which the text instructs. For example, "My God is so high, and I can't get over Him. My God is so low, and I can't get under him." These songs teach the people in basic terms about spiritual beliefs.

2. **Freedom spirituals**: These spirituals make reference to Moses, the Hebrews, and the people of Israel in the sense of deliverance. Spirituals such as "Great Day," "Go Down, Moses," and "City Called Heaven" are examples of freedom spirituals—songs that talk about earthly freedom.

3. **Escape spirituals**: These are also called the "coded spirituals" or "telegraph spirituals." They are so named because the planning for escape is very clear in the messages of the lyrics. Spirituals such as "Wade in the Water," "Steal Away," "The Drinking Gourd," and "Keep Your Lamps" are examples.

4. **The shout and hollers**: The whole idea of this category of song is to serve as instruction. It is also a part of the ring-shout tradition One famous example of this type of spiritual is "Ezekiel Saw the Wheel." In William Dawson's setting, instructions are given on how to proceed with the dance. For example, the verse: "You better mind my brother how you walk on the cross, your foot might slip and your soul get lost" makes a very direct reference as to where the shout occurs and specific instructions on what to do while shouting. The first line of the text in this verse, "You better mind my brother how you walk on the cross," refers to the front of the church where the pews are pulled back to the side. A group of shouters forms a circle that moves counterclockwise while a group of singers forms off to the side to provide the music. The pews are pulled back at the circle's position. The next portion of the text, "your foot might slip and your soul get lost," refers to the shouters' and the church's belief that there are differences between sacred and secular dance. Secular dance takes the feet up off the ground, while sacred dance maintains contact with the earth. This may be a subcategory of slave songs that needs greater investigation. Many of the non-religious slave songs could be used for educational purposes.

5. **Work songs**: These songs were used as people worked in the fields. One example is Andre Thomas' "Goin' Up to Glory." Other songs have connotations with slave songs, such as "John Henry," which tell stories, but were used for work. This category has a rich abundance of songs that can be rediscovered and used by choirs throughout the world.

   The spiritual, or slave song, is the earliest community song of the African American experience. It is one that established a link and a sense of communion between participants, and also defined a concept of God for a collective whole. It should be remembered that these songs were created by the community, not by individual composers. Not until the later nineteenth century did groups like the Fisk Jubilee Singers start to share the music; only at this time did they begin to be notated.

   At the turn of the century, Harry T. Burleigh and others presented slave song melodies to some of the major composers like Dvořák, and these songs gradually became part of the concert tradition. With the rise of singers such as Roland Hayes, Marian Anderson, Paul Robeson, and the later generation of Leontyne Price and other black artists who followed, African American spirituals became the staple not only of the concert song tradition, but eventually found their way into the world of choral music.

Issues of Performance Practice

In presenting a chapter such as this, I need to say from the outset that there is no one correct way of performing the slave song. For example, those of us involved as conductors in interpreting the music of Bach or Beethoven are influenced by a variety of situations. The same may be said of the spiritual. Some might say that modern spiritual arrangers are less authentic. For instance, there were no pianos in the fields, but some arrangers use piano within a spiritual. This does not necessarily diminish the integrity or quality of the music. In such situations, we have to look at what is being offered in terms of the preservation of the songs. What I suggest in terms of performance practice is that individuals seek to at least sing these songs with greater integrity. Authenticity can always be argued—but the music, whether it is higher art music or folk music, must be performed with integrity.

Written transcripts of how these songs were performed are unavailable. At best, people have simply developed basic assumptions about the performance. There are three key issues that have to be dealt with in performance practice:

1. Dialect and the use of it.
2. Tempo and rhythm.
3. Appropriate type of vocal timbre/color.

Before we get into these three concepts, which often are at the heart of performance practice, one again has to go back and understand the cultural function of slave songs. I think my earlier description of the categories should help people as they delve into this realm of literature.

1. Dialect and the use of it: In dealing with dialect, there is a wider question: to use or not to use? There are three schools of thought on dialect: use of standard English, a hybrid approach, or use of African American dialect. There are those who believe that a more standard English should be sung. This approach may be favored by the older generation so as to not show disrespect, and this is often done throughout the world. The second is a hybrid approach, which many contemporary conductors, composers, and arrangers use. In the hybrid approach, some of the language is more dialectal, almost vernacular in nature. The attempt is to give a flavor without expecting that all people will be able to approximate the language of the slave.

The third category is the use of dialect, which is favored by those who attempt to try to bring the greatest integrity and some aspect of authenticity to the performance. Curtis (1991) writes, "Dialect is an integral facet of the composition. It should be given the same respect which is given to foreign languages." As one who has attempted to sing the slave song with more and more use of dialect, I want to speak in greater depth about this area because there are certain issues which need to be considered. I am indebted to Andre Thomas for his research in this work, too.

Phonetic decay: Let's use Andre Thomas' "Keep Your Lamps" as an example. "Keep your lamps trimmed and burning, the time is drawing nigh" is the way the words are read in the score, and many choirs sing them with articulate, proper English pronunciation. If we apply phonetic decay to the words, we would first have to decay the final "g" in the words "in burning" and "drawing" so they are sung "burnin'" and "drawin.'"

Consonants: We have to recognize that certain sounds common in the English language are absent in many of the African dialects. For example, some of the harder consonants, such as the voiced "th" in words like "*the*" and "*there*" simply did not exist in many African dialects. Rather, the use of a harder consonant or a substitute consonant eventuated—for example, "d" instead of a voiced "th." Hence the words would be sung: "Keep your lamps trimmed and burnin', *de* time is drawin' nigh" rather than "*the* time is drawin' nigh." There is also a softening of certain consonants. For example, "v" becomes "b," and "t" becomes "d." Hence, "heav'nly" sounds like "hea*b*'nly."

Diphthongs: We also have elimination of diphthongs: "Keep your lamps trimmed and burnin', de *tahme* is *drah*win' *nah*," features elimination of the diphthong, which reflects more of the speech pattern of the people of the southern United States.

Schwa [ə]: There is also more prevalent use of the schwa. For example, "hea*v*enly Father" would be softened to "Hea-*buhn*-ly" and the "r" would be softened to "Fatheh."

Clipping words: Sometimes there is a clipping of certain words. For instance, the word "plantation" may be clipped to "plan'tion" or "witness" may be clipped to "wi'ness" as seen in the spiritual "Witness": "Who be a wi'ness foh mah Lawd? Soul is a wi'ness foh mah Lawd."

2. Tempo and rhythm: We need to be careful not to confuse the music of the slave song with later forms that derived from it, such as ragtime, jazz, and gospel. Most often we have a problem with the concept of "swing," how people understand the idiom of swing, and how it is translated from jazz to the spiritual. Curtis (1991) says, "The swing of the spiritual is a part of the religious experience of African Americans. It is a feeling, not a notation, and in order to feel it, one must be aware of the history of the music or the time of the struggles." The spiritual should not be confused with jazz. Consequently, editions that use the words "in a jazzy style" are misleading. It is a body-based sensation, not the sort of swing that comes out of jazz, which is a completely different type of feel. Often, spirituals are not meant to be swung as we think of swing in terms of the triplet. A clear example is the opening of Andre Thomas' "Rockin' Jerusalem."

These are meant to be even eighth notes. The point is the swing is not to be notated as the swing we know in jazz.

With regard to the rhythm of the piece, this article reflects my views. All too often I find that people take spirituals too fast, especially in certain arrangements. There are basic inner rhythms that must be considered, and when the pieces are taken as fast as some people want to, there is a misconception that the spiritual is simply music of celebration. Too often, tempo or speed is simply used as a means of reaching a sense of energy, excitement, and celebration.

We have to remember to tie the piece to its function. For example, consider a piece like "Keep Your Lamps." You may understand the essence of that music as an escape song, but it may also have been sung as the people were coming back from the fields, chained together. If you sing it fast, the music doesn't work because the people were not moving like that. But if you imagine tired, hot, physically abused people chained together leg-by-leg, this affects the tempo and the interpretation of the piece by instilling a sense of down-troddenness. The people who sang this music were down-trodden—both literally and figuratively. This issue requires the same type of attention we would give to music from the Renaissance and the Baroque. When interpreting music from these periods, we should understand the period dance forms and the types of steps used. Hence, our tempi may be vastly different than those heard on common recordings. To understand the tempo and style of an African American spiritual is a matter of being able to know the feel of the piece and understand the truth about the origins and the history of the songs. James Weldon Johnson and his brother, J. Rosemond Johnson, authors of *The Book of American Negro Spirituals* (1925), have this to say in their book:

The swing of the spiritual is altogether a subtle and elusive thing. It is subtle and elusive because it is a perfect union. The religious ecstasy that manifests itself in swing embodies the whole congregation. Swing is responding to the baton of some extremely sensitive conductor....it is necessary to know the truth about their origins and history, to get in touch with the association of ideas that surround them, and to realize something of what they have meant and experienced in the people who created them. In a word, the passing of feeling in these songs in singing them was more important than any amount of mere artistic technique.

To delve into and understand the text, one must read and listen. In this day and age, this is a relatively easy task, with such wonderful resources as a compilation of tapes by Bernice Regan Johnson of *Wade in the Water* and other recordings readily available.

Understanding inflection and attitude of the spiritual: "Wade in the Water" and other spirituals are tied to an African American style of preaching, one that places great emphasis on vowels. A black preacher speaking that text wouldn't say "Wade in the water," but rather "W*aaa*de in the water, W*aaa*de in the water, God's a gonna trouble the w*aa*ter." Part of my thesis as conductor of African American songs is to relate the words back to the preaching style, and I think that quite often this point isn't articulated enough. For example, consider the context of the words "One day when I was a-walkin' down a lonesome road." The context in which Dawson intended this music to be sung uses the imagery of old black men who sit in church and preach with the deacons, going back and forth, not a modern-day gospelinterpretation.

You're telling a story! What is the context? How is it expressed? This is oral tradition. When we take a piece from oral tradition and notate it, we've already removed it one level from authenticity. With that said, we also have to be careful we don't lock it into one way of doing it.

In terms of interpretation, there is also the question "What do we do when we look at the words?" The clearest example I can think of is in the recording of William Dawson's "Soon Ah Will Be Done." For years Dawson had one concept of what that text meant. He notated it, and we've been locked into it. With all due respect, I believe those words can suggest another way. After seeing the 1959 movie *Imitation of Life* with Lana Turner, I was tremendously influenced by the closing scene when Mahalia Jackson sings at a funeral. She comes from a gospel background, and she sings this one as a lament: "Soon Ah will be done with the troubles of the world, going home to be with God." In the oral tradition, Dawson may have heard those words in a "salvatory" way, but there is another way it could be understood—as a lament, still praise but also lament.

In a recording my group made of this song, I chose to use a halfway point. The refrain is slower, more responsive to the pain of this world. The verses become a vision of being with God in the heavenly Kingdom, or at least released from the hell in which they lived—reflecting a sense of anticipation and joy. I also altered the tempo. I believe we have to look at the background of the songs, and look at the text. They have to be left open for the possibility that there is another way they can be examined. In some of these arrangements, including Dawson's and Hairston's classic arrangements, we tend to try to do call-and-response and preach, so it is clear that the tempo will be a little more emphatic. But people have to have spatial time and respond to that, too—they are listening to respond. In a preaching spiritual like "My God Is So High" I think you have to take into consideration that someone is preaching and others are responding. That's understanding the slave song as proclamation.

3. Vocal timbre/color: This is an area open for discussion and debate. When I perform music from certain periods, I try to understand how the people would have sung the music. I think one reason we have a certain style of sound for Renaissance music is that we believe most of the music was sung by boys, which implies a pure, vibrato-less sound. We also know the continental sound of boys singing is very different from that in Great Britain—so Victoria is going to sound different from Byrd. In this way, I think there are certain generalities (without being racist) that one can make in that African and African American singers tend to have a darker hue in tonal quality. So I believe that part of the idea in recreating spirituals with integrity versus authenticity, is understanding that the timbre and tone color need to be part of the equation, part of a respectful and successful interpretation of the slave song. When that is coupled with use of a dialect that reflects the speech patterns of that period, one can arrive at tone quality that seeks to enhance the singing of the slave songs.

We tend to lump all spirituals together, but field hollers really don't have religious connotations. I think the term spiritual embraces the largest corpus we know so far—it comes from songs with religious imagery. I believe (because of recordings that take this into account) that the sound of music from the sixteenth and seventeenth centuries is very different from music of the nineteenth century. We need to be conscious and take into consideration what type of vocal timbre and vocal color would reflect the most integrity in the interpretation of the slave song. Much of that understanding comes after listening to professional, well-trained art singers, especially African Americans, who perform the repertoire. This is where you develop a sound ideal.

I am not an ethnomusicologist. I consider my approach a "common sense" approach. Someone may come to me and argue "But Moses Hogan said..."

and I would respectfully reply, "I would imagine that was how Moses responded." Additionally I would also ask, "Do you expect that Bernstein did the same work as von Karajan or Ormandy? No, they were all gifted musicians. I also perform Andre Thomas' pieces, but I don't just take those pieces or Moses' music on face value. I play with "My Soul's Been Anchored in the Lord" because I have other ways of hearing that piece."

This is my personal point of view. The danger of doing a workshop is that I'll say something and people will think I'm "God." The decisions I make are based on some degree of study and trying to put the music into context so the pieces have some integrity about them. This is not a defense—it's just something on which I question Thomas. I feel he is more in the "second school," i.e., takes a hybrid approach. Some of his pieces have the dialect, others don't. He tends to do that. I think that spirituals have more relevance if you put them in the context of performance practice. There is a compelling reason for this.

Many times we have a negative reaction to using any type of dialect, and this was especially true during the period of the Civil Rights Movement. During this time, young African Americans, especially, did not want to be reminded of anything having to do with slavery. During the infancy of the Civil Rights period to the modern day, this has been a point of contention. I believe this argument all goes back to letting these songs have a flavor in their original context to some degree, and language is one way in which that can be done; it should be done. It is integral.

If I were to sing a piece in a foreign language, I would study the piece with the proper pronunciation. It is the same with spirituals. One needs to understand that the people who were brought up in West Africa were some of the most intelligent and best educated people in their countries. They were at the highest level in African society, and the fact they were able to learn a new language through assimilation bears witness to their intelligence. It is the fact that the dialect reflects their appropriation of the English language, coupled with aspects of their own mother tongue and how that was passed down, that supports the use of certain words and dialect. These people weren't ignorant—quite the opposite.

The final point I wish to emphasize is that this music has to be treated with great dignity. The programming of spirituals is integral. We often like to program this music at the end, and there is not a problem with it being at the end of the program as long as one understands that there are many other spots on the program that a spiritual could fill. It is the music of a proud and noble people; it is music that celebrates life and the power of goodness over the power of evil. I think for the people of the twenty-first century it represents an affirmation by a people who faced great adversity but never lost their dignity and that this music is a vehicle to overcome all of the atrocities and injustices of life. This music does and should serve as inspiration for all generations, for young people who understand that one can gain strength, comfort, and inspiration from this music. And for many people, this music leads to healing, to restoration of oneself fully in body, mind, spirit, and voice.

Anton E. Armstrong *is the Tosdal Professor of Music at St. Olaf College in Northfield, Minnesota. He became the fourth conductor of the St. Olaf Choir in 1990 after ten years in Grand Rapids, Michigan, where he served on the faculty of Calvin College and led the Grand Rapids Symphony Chorus and the St. Cecilia Youth Chorale. Active nationally and internationally as a guest conductor and lecturer, he recently conducted the St. Olaf Choir at the Sixth World Symposium on Choral Music, and in June 2003 he conducted performances of Brahms' Ein Deutsches Requiem in Linköping, Sweden. Armstrong is editor of a multicultural choral series for Earthsongs Publications and co-editor of the revised St. Olaf Choral Series for Augsburg Fortress Publishers.*

References

Friends of Negro Spirituals
P.O. Box 71956
Oakland, California 94612
www.dogonvillage.com/negrospirituals/

Sam Edwards
1721 Scott Street
San Francisco, California 94117
415-563-4316
sedwards@stanford.edu

Resources

Armstrong, Anton E. *African American Vocal Music.* (compilation) St. Olaf College. Northfield, Minnesota.

Hogan, Moses, ed. *The Oxford Book of Spirituals.* New York: Oxford University Press. 2002.

Lawrence Burnett Web site, specifically on African American Spirituals. He is repertoire and standards chairman in the ACDA Central Division. www.people.carleton.edu/~lburnett/LawrenceBurnett.

Southern, Eileen. *The Music of Black Americans: A History* (3rd Edition). New York: W. W. Norton. 1997.

Wade in the Water. Bernice Johnson Reagon, Smithsonian curator.

Selected Bibliography

Baker, David N. *The Black Composer Speaks*. Metuchen, New Jersey: Scarecrow Music Press. 1978.

Boyer, Horace Clarence. *How Sweet the Sound: The Golden Age of Gospel*. Washington, D.C.: Elliot & Clark. 1995.

Brooks, Tilford. *America's Black Musical Heritage*. Englewood Cliffs: Prentice Hall. 1984.

Cone, James H. *The Spirituals and the Blues*. Westport, Connecticut: Greenwood Press. 1980.

Courlander, Harold. *Negro Folk Music, U.S.A.* New York: Dover Publications, Inc. 1992.

Curtis, Marvin V. and Lee V. Cloud. "The African-American Spiritual: Traditions and Performance Practices." *Choral Journal* 32, no. 4 (November 1991): 15–22.

DeLarma, Dominque-Rene. *Bibliography of Black Music*, Volume 3. Geographical Studies. Westport: Greenwood. 1982.

DuBois, W.E.B. *The Souls of Black Folk*. New York: Vintage Books/Library of America. 1990.

Epstein, Dena J. *Sinful Tunes and Spirituals: Black Folk Music to the Civil War*. Urbana: University of Illinois Press. 1977.

Floyd, Samuel, Marsha Reisser. *Black Musical Biography: An Annotated Bibliography*. White Plains: Kraus. 1987.

George, Luvenia A. *Teaching the Music of Six Different Cultures* (rev. ed.) Danbury: World Music Press. 1987.

Haskins, James. *Black Music in America*. New York: Crowell. 1987.

Heilbut, Anthony. *The Gospel Sound*. New York: Limelight. 1985.

Hermmitt, Herman (compiler). *Our Afro-American Heritage In Music*. Chicago: Carl Fischer Music Stores. 1987.

Jones, Arthur C. *Wade in the Water: The Wisdom of the Spiritual*. Maryknoll, New York: Orbis Books. 1993.

Lovell, John, Jr. *Black Song: The Forge and the Flame*. New York: Paragon. 1986.

Peters, Erskine, editor. *Lyrics of the Afro-American Spirituals: A Documentary Collection* (The Greenwood Encyclopedia of Black Music). Westport, Connecticut: Greenwood Press. 1993.

The R. Nathaniel Dett Reader: Essays on Black Sacred Music. Durham, North Carolina: Duke University Press. 1991.

Reagon, Bernice Johnson, editor. *We'll Understand It Better By and By.* Washington: Smithsonian Institution Press. 1992.

Roach, Hildred. *Black American Music: Past and Present,* Volume I. Malamar: Krieger. 1992.

Smith, William Farley. "Searching for Didactic Slave Songs in the New Hymnals." *Choristers Guild Letters* 43, no. 6 (January 1992): 145–150.

——. "Searching for Didactic Slave Songs in the New Hymnals, Part II." *Choristers Guild Letters,* 43, no. 7 (February 1992): 185–189.

Southern, Eileen. *Biographical Dictionary of Afro-American and African Musicians.* Westport: Greenwood. 1982.

——. *The Music of Black Americans: A History, Third Edition.* New York: W. W. Norton. 1997.

——. *Readings in Black American Music Second Edition.* New York: W. W. Norton. 1983.

Spencer, Jon Michael. *Black Hymnody: A Hymnological History of the African-American Church.* Knoxville: The University of Tennessee Press. 1972.

——. *Black Hymnody: A Hymnological History of the African-American Church.* Knoxville: The University of Tennessee Press. 1992.

——. *Protest and Praise: Sacred Music of Black Religion.* Minneapolis: Fortress Press. 1990.

——. "Unsung Hymns By Black and Unknown Bards." *Black Sacred Music: A Journal of Theomusicology,* vol. 4, no. 1 (Spring 1990).

Thomas, André J. "Singing Black Gospel Music and Spirituals." *Reformed Worship,* no. 14 (December 1989): 36–37.

Toelken, Barre. *Morning Dew and Roses: Nuance, Metaphor, and Meaning in Folksongs.* Urbana: University of Illinois Press, 1995.

Vanden Wyngaard, Marguerite A. *African-American Choral Music for Secondary Schools.* M.A.T. thesis, Morris, Minnesota: Star of the North Press, University of Minnesota-Morris. 1993.

White, Evelyn Davidson. *Choral Music by Afro-American Composers.* Metachen, New Jersey: The Scarecrow Press. 1981.

DISCOGRAPHY

Chanticleer. *Where the Sun Will Never Go Down.* Chanticleer Records (phone: 415-896-5866 or fax: 415-896-1660).

Hairston, Jester. *The Afro-American Slave Song: Its African Roots and American Development.* Chapel Hill, North Carolina: Hinshaw Music. 1978.

Albert McNeil Jubilee Singers. *They've Got the Whole World in Their Hands,* Volume II.

Plymouth Music Series of Minnesota-Ensemble Singers and Chorus, Philip Brunelle, conductor. *Witness:* Volume I—*Spirituals and Gospels.* Collins Classics 14492. 1995.

The Moses Hogan Chorale Community Ensemble. Moses Hogan, conductor. *TheBattle of Jericho.* MGH Records. 1995. (phone: 504-568-9142 or fax: 504-524-7593.)

The Saint Augustine Choir, Leon C. Roberts, conductor. *Songs of Faith from Lead Me, Guide Me. The African American Catholic Hymnal.* Chicago: GIA Publications, Inc. 1993.

The St. Olaf Choir, Anton Armstrong, conductor. *The Spirituals of William L. Dawson.* St. Olaf Records E-2159. 1997. (phone: 507-646-3048 or fax: 507-646-3779)

The Spirit Chorale of Los Angeles, Byron J. Smith, conductor. *Trust Jesus Christ!* Pro Pianist Entertainment. (fax: 213-756-5334) 1995.

Tuskegee Institute Choir. William L. Dawson, conductor. *Spirituals.* MCA Records #MSD-35340. Reissued 1992.

Wade in the Water. Smithsonian/Folkways Recordings (phone: 202-287-3262 or fax: 303-287-3699) Volume I, *African American Spirituals: The Concert Tradition;* Volume II, *African American Congregational Singing: Nineteenth-Century Roots;* Volume III, *African American Gospel: The Pioneering Composers;* and Volume IV, *African American Community Gospel.*

VIDEO

Hairston, Jester. *The Black Spiritual in America,* Volume 3. The American Choral Directors Association, Lawton, Oklahoma.

HYMNALS

Lead Me, Guide Me (The African American Catholic Hymnal). Chicago: GIA Publications, Inc. 1987.

Lift Every Voice and Sing. New York: The Church Hymnal Corporation. 1981.

Lift Every Voice and Sing II: New York: The Church Hymnal Corporation. 1993.

Songs of Zion. Nashville: Abingdon Press. 1981.

This Far by Faith. Minneapolis: Augsburg Fortress. 1999.

CHAPTER 4

Modern Music

Graeme Morton

Introduction

"You are what you eat"—or so dieticians and health therapists would have us believe. Yet for the choral musician there is great truth in the adaptation of this old adage to "You are what you sing." Choice of repertoire is one of the most significant elements in the development of the choral ensemble and is most significant in the establishment of an ensemble's characteristic sound or range of colors. It is not just one of the media in which we work, as the clay may be for the potter, who can just as well choose another material. Choice of repertoire determines to a large degree what our choir is and what it is to become. It is perhaps the most neglected of the factors that are instrumental, indeed essential, in the development of an outstanding ensemble. Further, modern music (whatever that is) can be a fabulous resource in the journey toward the development of your choir.

Take a minute to consider the great choirs of the world. Draw up a list of ten fabulous ensembles. Chances are the list includes fine ensembles that regularly include contemporary repertoire in their programs. This even applies to children's ensembles—especially children's ensembles! The focus of the world's leading children's choirs on contemporary music attests to its value as a significant tool in the development of an exceptional ensemble.

So why are many of us reluctant to put our musical toes into the modern music water? This chapter looks at modern music, discusses its relevance for the modern choral ensemble, and leads us to immerse ourselves in experiences of contemporary repertoire.

Is "Modern Music" a Dirty Phrase?

Mention "modern music" among any group of choral musicians, and you are inviting division and diversity in the ensuing discussion. Let's face it: modern music is not favored among choral practitioners. Indeed, music must

40

be one of the few other areas in which the term "modern" is treated with such scorn. In other areas, it is the past that is often less favored. There, "modern" is desired. It is seen as better, more effective, more interesting, and progressive. Sadly, in music "modern" has negative connotations, and most musicians instinctively prefer the music of the past.

In music, the masterworks of the past are still here because that is what they are—masterworks. They stand beside the newest offerings from modern composers, defying comparison. And so many of us stay safely away from modern music and live in the musical museum. Of course, this museum is full of beautiful things—wonderful works of ravishing beauty. But it is a museum, nonetheless, and (like a museum) it teaches us, it is relevant to our current lives, and it helps us understand ourselves. However, it is still a museum.

Many musicians do look for something fresh and new, and so they turn to modern music, usually with one of two outcomes. They find music that is too demanding, too complex, and too aesthetically challenging and give up, or they follow the mass of recent easy-to-please, easy-to-practice, and easy-to-perform music that dominates the choral market these days and then wonder why their ensemble fails to grow.

It fails to grow because the "easy" music doesn't stimulate or challenge—because it fails to offer us something new. We are creatures of "newness." While we often appear reluctant to let the past go and are often threatened by change, the truth is that we like things that are fresh and new. Much modern music—the "easy" kind—fails to deliver this. What we often get in a new piece is another version of the last supposed "new" piece. The notes and the words might be different, but the sound is essentially the same. The choir has, in fact, cloned its past experiences rather than created a new one. The piece is not new, and neither are the challenges nor the rewards.

Of course, a discussion like this tends to paint such experiences as black and white. I am not saying that repeating musical styles has no value. There is much to be said for consolidation of musical styles through different works of similar ilk. Also, a new work in a familiar style can give us a wonderful blend of the familiar and the fresh. It mixes elements of our current experience with something that is different. However, my plea is that if you have not yet experienced the unfamiliar in modern music, please go forward in your search for the wonderful riches offered within this genre.

What Is Modern Music?

Here we strike the first dilemma. What exactly is modern music? I have no intention of trying to provide a comprehensive answer to this question within these few paragraphs. However, in the context of this discussion and for those who are not yet in the thick of it all, let me propose a very informal definition. Modern music is music of recent origin that uses techniques of composition with which one is less familiar.

Now, in many ways this is an absurd explanation. It leaves out so much that is a necessary part of our understanding of modern music. It accepts into the definition something of the implication that modern music is strange and not quite normal. It no longer defines modern music only according to the "when" of its origin, but endorses the oft-held view that "modern" in music is unfamiliar, new, and strange. While this definition may have negative connotations, it is actually a positive way to view modern music because it leads us to see new works as always changing. It sees modern music in relation to *me* and where my previous experience has placed me, rather than in relation to itself and its date of origin. As I become familiar with a particular music or style, that which was "modern and strange" becomes less modern and more familiar. Such a view also makes this discussion relevant to us all. All of us have music "out there" that we have yet to experience. Because of the fabulous diversity of music available to us, all of us have new experiences ahead as we journey through modern music.

There is, however, something about modern music itself that slows us down in this journey and impedes us from embracing it with open arms. It concerns the nature of the medium itself and people's response to it. Let me paraphrase Australian composer and journalist Andrew Ford.

> My friend calls me to invite me to a movie. "What is showing?" I ask. "Such and such," my friend replies, mentioning a recent release by name. "Sorry," I say as I decline the invitation, "I've already seen it."
>
> "Well, let's go to a concert," my friend says. "What are they performing?" I ask. "Such and such," my friend replies, mentioning a recent composition by name. "Sorry," I say as I decline the invitation, "I don't know that piece."

This is a classic chicken and egg dilemma. I do not like new music until I experience it, but I do not choose to experience it because I do not like it.

This I partly blame on our failure to understand the proper nature of music. As educators, we often fail to have our students understand what is fundamental to the development of their music-culture framework. By this, I mean that our students, especially those in their formative years, fail to understand that there is not one music, but many "musics," all of which serve different purposes.

Let's look at food again. Ask young singers which is best, an elegant restaurant or their favorite fast-food chain, and they will understand that while both appear to be similar—both have to do with selecting and eating food in exchange for the payment of money—in fact, they serve quite different purposes.

Holding one's school or college graduation celebration at McDonald's is as silly as trying to grab a quick bite on the way to the movies at a silver-service restaurant.

So it is with music. While young musicians may instinctively feel that a choice has to be made between Beethoven and their favorite popular commercial group, no such choice is necessary. While they appear similar (both have to do with listening to pitches, timbres, rhythm, texture, and tonality organized in a logical and meaningful way) in fact, they serve quite different purposes.

Yet we often expect of modern music (meaning here modern art music or "classical" music) to be as easy to listen to as its fast-food equivalent. There is a time and a place for both, and the discovery of modern music (i.e., the art music, classical kind) should be an adventure upon which we all readily embark.

Developing an Appropriate Mindset

To undertake the journey into modern music, it may be useful to consider appropriate mental preparation. If the intellectual and aesthetic framework we have adopted is appropriate to the task of encountering modern music, the journey will be much easier. Consider the following, all of which are inter-related. Ponder how the full adoption of each of these "mindsets" may change the way you would approach the programming and preparation of modern music, and, for that matter, more common repertoire as well.

1. **Be bold!** Most of the choral training textbooks quite rightly exhort us to be fully prepared to rehearse and conduct the ensemble. This involves thorough score preparation in advance of the first rehearsal, a strong sense of the desired musical outcome (which establishes the goal of all rehearsals and performances), and a strong commitment to the aesthetic significance of the chosen repertoire for that ensemble at that particular time. In other words, the end of the journey should be known and understood before the journey commences.

This knowledge has been acquired from a wide variety of sources. These sources may include singing the work in another ensemble, listening to recordings, having taught the same or a similar piece previously, hearing from colleagues that the particular piece works very well, or having studied the piece in college. In fact, for any traditional piece of repertoire, most of our musical experiences contribute to our understanding of the worth of that particular piece and an understanding of how to approach it.

This is not necessarily the case with modern music. In fact, you may be fortunate if you can be sure of the outcome before you commence the journey. Be courageous. Be mentally ready to move forward with your ensemble rather than ahead of them, in a journey of discovery together, without necessarily knowing in advance just what the outcome will be.

2. Enjoy the journey! Many choirs are performance driven. They are focused on results, on "arrivals," and on the public display of achievement. Be careful, because in a school context performance-driven programs are unlikely to be healthy for you or for your singers. It is exceptionally difficult, when performance driven, to resist exploiting the singers for the desired result.

In the area of modern music performance, focused musicians are particularly vulnerable because the audience becomes a significant source of evaluation. I guess the same is true for traditional repertoire, perhaps to a lesser degree. Whether the audience appreciates Palestrina or not, I am more likely to program his music because the choral and artistic community generally affirms it. However, with modern music, no such general acceptance of a particular composer may be forthcoming. Therefore, we may tend to look to the audience (including those in professional authority over us) to understand and value the musical end result. They are less likely to understand modern music because it is often unfamiliar to them, and they seldom have an established framework with which to consider new sounds. The audience may give us less affirmation, and at that point it is possible for conductors to become vulnerable and unsure of our philosophical and musical stance.

Of course, this is easily countered. Be ready to defend the process and to educate the audience. Also be prepared for the fact that the audience may be well ahead of you in this matter. What you may see as modern and "strange" they may see as exciting and wonderful. Why? Simply because we as musicians often let ourselves be daunted by what we *know* about the music. The audience knows less about technique and theory and prefers to evaluate music by what they hear rather than what they know. This can be to their advantage—in fact, it is what we are all supposed to be doing. Music exists as sound in time and needs to be always treated that way, not in the light of how it looks or what we can determine from our academic knowledge about music.

3. Enjoy the company! The *raison d'etre* for the majority of choirs should not be the audience but those involved in the journey. As conductors, our prime responsibility is to the singers—those wonderful people who stand beside us day by day and week by week in pursuit of a common goal. When our prime focus is the singer, not the audience, we are freed of a burden of always "looking over our shoulders" to see how others will judge us.

Our singers do not judge us as the audience does. The singers are fellow travelers. They know us, and they know the struggles and delights of the journey. They understand. They are our affirmation, and together we all work to move forward.

4. Become a risk taker! Move out of your own comfort zone. Try not to limit the choir by your own perceptions or by tentative and cautious decision making. Allow modern music to be an adventure.

Of course, this does not mean becoming reckless, but it may mean becoming more courageous. Remember that your choir members generally will have less of a frame of reference for modern music than you do. They might like to challenge the way you conduct Bach, but modern music tends to put us all on a less-sure footing. In this case, establish a rehearsal environment in which the singers look to you for guidance but not necessarily for answers.

5. Become a true leader! So much of what we do as conductors is concerned with specific issues pertinent to the running of a rehearsal or managing the ensemble that we sometimes forget we also carry responsibility for its leadership and forward growth. Be prepared to become an advocate for modern music, at least amongst your singers. Do not allow yourself to be intimidated by any negativity that may come from them. Understand that its origin is probably personal insecurity or limited experience. Lead and inspire them to move into this new area with bold confidence.

Be passionate. If you are not yet fully passionate about a particular work or style, still be prepared to play the role of passionate advocate. How often do you use modeling in your rehearsals? Chances are this significant learning tool is in constant use as singers adopt the model displayed by you, by other singers, or by their understanding of what a particular style involves.

If this is such a fine tool for singers, then why should it not be for conductors as well? To model the role of advocate for modern music and to model the passionate exponent is to also learn the skills to *be* the advocate and passionate exponent.

6. Play with the music! How often is the word "play" used in relation to music? We play an instrument (I play the flute); we play a composer (I play Bach); and we play a venue (I play Carnegie Hall). But how often does this involve true "play?" When do we as musicians play *with* music?

To me, an important quality of "play" is its apparent lack of purpose. The outcomes are not predetermined, and the direction of the activity may change almost randomly. To those of us schooled in the need to be efficient in rehearsals, to plan the proper use of time, and to establish our desired goals and outcomes, play can be a worrying concept. However, it can be efficient. It does require proper use of time, and it can have established goals and outcomes. Such outcomes might be to discover several ways to perform this aleatoric section of music, to show singers that clusters can be exceptionally beautiful, to free up singers to allow them to explore aspects of their own improvisational skills, and the list goes on. As well as being apparently purposeless, true play is interactive. This leads us to the next aspect of developing an appropriate mental set.

7. Approach rehearsals as workshops! The traditional view of a rehearsal is that knowledge of the music and of the necessary performance skills is passed from conductor to singer. The communication of this acquired knowledge and skill base is then passed back from the singer to the conductor, who in turn responds with further knowledge and techniques. This is a highly structured interplay of ideas and skills.

For the ensemble newly undertaking excursions into modern music, a freer interpretation of the preparation process is often desirable. Outcomes are less clearly defined, ideas are often shared and explored (even when still controlled by the conductor), singers are encouraged to accept "failure" (or even to recognize failure as a means to further progress), new ideas are tried and tested, new techniques are discovered, and special moments of wonderful beauty reveal themselves as if by accident.

Further, don't feel obliged to perform all the repertoire that has been rehearsed or workshopped. Remember that the process is more important than the end result.

8. Break the tyranny of the tune! One of the very significant impediments to an appreciation of modern music is that our singers are fixated on the aspect of melody. This must surely be a drawback that arises from having a melodic instrument within one's own body. From an early age, we learn that we can reproduce melodic ideas that please us. Then instant recall brings back to us the most wonderful musical experiences.

While we can remember a texture or recall that we liked a particular sonority, we cannot recreate them ourselves as we can a remembered melody. This teaches singers, I suspect, that the melodic aspects in choral compositions are the dominant musical aspects. And composers in the past have generally responded to singers' demands for melody. Thus, the cycle continues.

For a singer so conditioned to focus on melody, much modern music may appear particularly strange. Find opportunities to affirm for singers that in this context it is sound itself that is beautiful and that the musical score (even the music itself) is the means by which the revelation of that beautiful sound is justified, legitimized, or made possible. Remind them of the beauty of sound and not necessarily of melody.

9. Avoid repertoire that is modern for modern's sake! The use of a patchwork of modern devices in a composition is not necessarily the sign of a fine modern work. Of course, finding good material is not always easy, since one does not always have the necessary framework or experience with which to evaluate it. If you feel uncertain in your evaluation of modern repertoire, find someone else whose place in the journey enables them to help make these decisions with you. Choose interesting repertoire promoted by people whom you consider to be leaders in the choral field. Purchase recordings, attend concerts, and seek to know *all* repertoire, not merely that relevant to the type of choir you conduct.

Include repertoire that lifts singers above the ordinary. Good texts, poetic imagery, and mature themes are essential in the diet even of young choirs (and their conductors). Children are capable of remarkable things, especially in the medium of choral music.

When you think about it, choral music is perhaps the only area of human endeavor in which the most complete and perfect example of a significant art form is found in the work of children. Children's athletics prepare them for the bigger and better world of adult sports. Children's achievements in academic life are merely preparations for a more significant academic future. Children spend their life in preparation for adulthood.

However, in choral music, the fine children's ensemble is in itself the perfect embodiment of the highest and most mature example of that art form. Adults cannot do it better. Children are the pinnacle of that art. Given the maturity of this form of expression, it stands to reason that children are capable of approaching and understanding music of exceptional maturity, which expresses wonderful and mature themes. Indeed, to involve children in such experiences is to enable them to reach beyond themselves and to model the maturity that, if not yet achieved, will one day be theirs.

10. Develop a diverse palate of colors! So often we train our choirs to believe that one particular choral sound is the most beautiful. This might be a result of our conscious choice, or a subconscious choice, or because there is a particular sound that the choir happens to make well. Teach them that all colors are beautiful, and that although we may have a preference for a particular color, the exclusive use of that color will become tiring for both singers and listeners.

Further, the beauty of a particular color is enhanced, not diminished, if it stands in comparison with other colors. Yellow is most beautiful when it takes its place in contrast to a range of other colors—gray, blue, red, etc.

Setting Out

Having established the appropriate mental set with which to approach modern music, what comes next? Much of the answer to that question depends on your own previous experience and the nature of the choir you conduct. Perhaps many who started reading this discourse have already put the book down. They have established, or clarified, their own framework and are keen to begin without any assistance from me. However, if you are still reading on, perhaps you are seeking just a few clues as to specifics of the musical preparation. How does a rehearsal become a workshop? How do I avoid being performance motivated to the exclusion of the process? What form can musical play take?

While the first step may be to choose some appropriate repertoire for your choir, there is also a good deal of background work that can be achieved during the warm-up phase of the rehearsal. I suggest using this time because singers already consider what happens here as "normal" and will accept new techniques and ideas that may receive more critical attention if encountered in the body of the rehearsal.

While working on technique and also on stimulating the imagination, singers can be introduced to a wide variety of activities that not only develop skills, but also seek to modify attitudes to sound and music itself. For the conductor, the advantage of using the warm-up phase of the rehearsal is that there need be no fear of failure. Some ideas will work, and some doubtless will be far less successful. These less successful ideas may be reintroduced at a later stage or after new strategies for their implementation have been devised. However, by using the warm-up phase of the rehearsal to introduce new and "risky" ideas, you never have to set up special expectations in the minds of your singers that end up being unfulfilled. "Today we are about to do such and such, and it is going to be fantastic" sets up the possibility that the singers will be disappointed if their expectations, or yours, are not met. A warm-up moment carries no such responsibility.

Don't forget to comment on the sound as you proceed. A cluster that the singers may think is simply a means to open their throats can become so highly energized that the conductor stops to enthuse about the fabulous sound. Improvised rainforest sounds that singers think are simply part of the process of engaging the imagination also set the scene for an aleatoric passage in a forthcoming work and are described by the conductor for what they are—beautiful and evocative. Singing fragments canonically at unusual intervals or distances, which singers consider a simple matter of musical independence and concentration, prepares them for interesting linear passages in the future. New vowel sounds, which the singers think are giving them experience in resonance and placement, also allow for the exploration of a new palate of colors appropriate for the work to follow and are again described as interesting and vibrant. Always, the focus is on the wonderful qualities of the sound.

Specifically, what new qualities or techniques appropriate for modern idioms of choral music might be introduced in warm-up activities? Perhaps the most obvious ones are:

1. Clusters. These are, of course, chords comprised of notes that are very close together, using pitches specified by the composer or even selected by each performer. Clusters work well when singers are musically confident and capable of acting independently. The clusters are best when the singers also appreciate the beauty that arises from this compositional device.

These can be explored in a multitude of ways. Here are some suggestions.

- Sing glissandos, inviting singers to pause whenever they wish, sustaining that note until the cut-off.

- Play with the idea of a musical wave. During warm-ups, have singers progressively commence singing from one side of the choir, starting at a pitch higher than the one they hear from those immediately before them. Singers sustain their pitch until all singers have come in. This is, of course, all approximate. There is no need to be precise. It simply encourages singers to act independently, to make musical judgments, and to produce musical sounds that are not necessarily the same as the rest of the group.

- Have singers produce a given tone, and then (upon direction from the conductor) have them sing any note of their choice to form a cluster. Next, have them return to the note a tone above the starting note, then to another cluster, then to another "common" note—a third above the starting note.

- Have the singers sing a familiar melody together, allowing individuals to pause on any note of their choice, which they sustain until the melody is completed by other singers. Make this into a performance moment. Sing a folk song, accompanying the unison melodic line with random clusters formed by singers pausing on pitches derived from the melody.

- Have the singers create a cluster (by singing "any note") while they sing, counting to ten. Make the sound beautiful by exploring different dynamic levels and different articulations. Have the singers respond to changes in your gestures as they sing. Most of all, expect beautiful sounds, and when they happen, acknowledge them publicly to your ensemble. The singers need to see clusters not as "mechanical novelty" but as legitimate harmonic devices that have the potential to be exceptionally beautiful, highly energized, and exciting.

2. Melodic devices. Modern music may, of course, contain unusual melodic leaps or unfamiliar tonal shifts. Do not be daunted by this. The best of the modern composers who write for student voices write well for the voice and build props and cues into the music by which such unusual material can be achievable.

- Make the singing of irregular intervals part of the play of the rehearsal. After assigning numbers to the notes of a scale, have choir members sing their own telephone numbers or other randomly created sequences of pitches (birthdays, dates, note names found in sentences, etc.). This can be done by putting the numbers on a white board and having all singers perform this activity together. After singing the row of numbers, find other patterns to perform—the row in reverse, alternate numbers, etc. Extend the activity into clusters by mixing these options and performing them simultaneously. Alternatively, singers can choose their own number sequence (e.g., their birthday) and perform these simultaneously.

- Practice singing a familiar song (e.g., "My Country 'Tis of Thee"), commencing each new phrase on the note on which the previous phrase ended.

- Practice singing modal patterns or whole-tone scales, or randomly combine scale patterns (upper parts sing a major scale ascending and descending while the lower parts ascend chromatically).

- Sing scales to numbers, omitting various numbers from the sequence. Substitute rests for the missing numbers, or simply delete them from the sequence altogether.

All of these activities develop independence and tonal memory.

3. Rhythm and meter. In modern music, composers often select unusual rhythms and irregular meters, such as 5/8, 7/8, etc., and meters that change frequently.

- One of the best devices is to have members sing the component beats (or sub-beats) to numbers: 1–2–3–4–5, 1–2–3–4–5, 1–2–3–4, 1–2–3–4–5, etc.

- Have singers count beats while the rehearsal pianist plays the material.

- Have singers tap the beats (or conduct them) while they say the words in rhythm.

- Understand the source of the rhythmic ideas. Perhaps a rhythm that appears difficult in notation is simply the natural spoken rhythm of the passage.

- Find works that juxtapose irregular but rhythmically distinctive materials (e.g., "Riawanna" by Stephen Leek). Have singers rehearse for a short time in mixed positions so they gain independence and musical self-reliance.

4. Timbre. Many modern composers look for interesting and new colors to incorporate into their pieces. Often, familiarity with such sounds comes from understanding the composer and the style in exactly the same way that traditional choral color is linked to an understanding of the context from which a work comes.

For example, what sound did Stephen Leek have in mind when writing "Ngana" (see discussion on page 386)? How does one modify the sound of the choir to find such new colors? Some may even want to ask a more fundamental question: Is it desirable for my choir to have to learn a new palate of colors perhaps less typical of traditional repertoire?

Let me address the last question first, and then only in part. As conductors, we often tend to think that composers are there to serve us. They write music for us, and they give our choirs the raw materials with which we create performances. However, in the long journey of music and culture over centuries of time, another model is to consider that we, the conductors, serve the composers. We depend on their wonderful and creative imaginations to provide us with the future of our choral art. They show us the way forward, and they nourish our art in a way that affects us all. In this model, composers are leaders and we, as conductors, seek to follow their leadership. Just as an architect provides a design that the engineer seeks to implement, so the composer sets the goals and we, as conductors, find the means to achieve them. From this frame of reference, we should be excited about exploring the new colors "discovered" by a contemporary composer.

Colors can be explored and developed using some of the following approaches.

- Discover unusual vowel colors for use in warm-ups, and respond enthusiastically to the interesting and vibrant colors produced.

- Select a vowel sound (perhaps "ee") and invite the choir to sing it, modeling different visual colors. Sing it as orange, sing it as deep green, sing it as bright tangerine.

- Select a vowel and link it to emotions—sing it for a sad occasion, sing it for a joyful occasion, make it exciting, make it lazy.

- Select a vowel and link it to exotic places—sing it like a gale of Antarctica, sing the same vowel like the Australian desert, sing it like the Brazilian rainforest.

- Select a vowel, and sing it in the sound of various instruments—sing it like a clarinet, like a ram's horn (whatever that is—it's still a great image), like a *didgeridoo*.

- Teach harmonic overtone singing to your ensemble as a means of opening up a work of new color to the singers. (See references at the end of the chapter for information on teaching harmonic overtone series.)

To understand language is often to understand color as well. Many times the desired color arises out of the sound of the language, especially when the origins of the language are "foreign" or "ethnic" in origin.

Of course, recordings today give us a resource that is invaluable in learning new colors. When possible, find a recording of a choir that has some connection with the composer, since what is recorded will often reflect something specific about the sound the composer had in mind for the piece.

Remember that the music itself is a great teacher, and the colors the choir learns in one piece form the basis of our exploration of color in the next one.

5. Aleatory and graphic notation. In aleatoric music, composers leave many decisions about the performance to the performers themselves. This may include the choice of the actual pitches to be used in a particular place or the speed with which individual singers move through a passage or section.

Graphic notation is where composers represent their ideas using graphic symbols rather than traditional (and specific) notation devices. (Excerpt from "Ngayulyl" (Hawk Dreaming) by Stephen Leek.)

Remind your singers to be confident risk-takers. Having spent all their lives having conductors presume to tell them the composer's specific intentions, it may take them a little time to accept responsibility for such sections of music. However, as they find the excitement or beauty in one or two of these well-written sections, they will approach all new passages with eager confidence.

Now you are ready to begin. However, the most important issue still needs to be stated. It is the repertoire itself that will excite your singers. Once they are interested, excited, and enthused, any challenges that await in the music will be readily solved. They, the singers, will soon discover if a particular piece is worth the effort, and you will soon know if it has captured their imaginations. When it does, the rest is relatively easy. This is not to say that the choir becomes the judge of what is musically good or bad. It *is* to say that success begets success, and enthusiasm begets enthusiasm. One successful modern music experience is a bridge to the next.

And now we have come full circle. Choice of repertoire is one of the most significant elements in the development of the choral ensemble. It is the music itself that teaches our choirs, as our singers respond with imagination to the life experiences available through the wonderful art form of choral music. If we as conductors do no more than act as the catalysts that link our singers with good repertoire, then even that is a significant achievement. We have created an environment in which the singers themselves are able to become engaged in their own learning experience, with music as the real teacher.

So find a composer of modern music whose works appeal to you, and use that as the starting place. For me, one such composer is Stephen Leek, a composer whose music is innovative, creative, imaginative, and always written with the needs of the young singer in mind. Here is a list of some of his works that use techniques discussed in this chapter:

Pieces using flexible voicings:
"Kumbargung"
"Riawanna"
"Black Children"

Pieces for treble choirs:
"Golai-yali"
"Tintinara"

Pieces for mixed voice ensembles:
"Tungaree"
"Ngana"
"Ngayulyul"
"Breakers"
"Kondalilla" (from *Great Southern Spirits*)

This chapter simply encourages you to embark on this journey toward modern music. Once underway, the path forward will reveal itself. Further, you will undertake the journey in good company, and colleagues will readily assist you. Indeed, they already have, since the examples of modern music recommended in this resource provide excellent stepping stones for singers to progress from the familiar to the new. Do not delay, because if you do, this music may well have left you behind. Find it today so that you are then ready for tomorrow's music tomorrow and, beyond that, all the wealth of music as yet unformed.

Harmonic Overtone Singing Information:

Hopkins, Sarah. *Rehearsing and Performing Past Life Melodies: A Resource Guide for Choristers & Choir Directors.* Morton Music: MM 2008.

Sarah Hopkins Rehearses Past Life Melodies, CDMM 3001.

Graeme Morton is Director of Choral Activities at St. Peter's Lutheran College in Brisbane, Australia. One of Australia's more eclectic choral musicians, he conducts the Brisbane Chamber Choir, St. Peter's Chorale, and the choir at Christ Church St. Lucia. During the 2003 season he was Artistic Director and Conductor of the Australian National Youth Choir. He is also passionate about liturgical music and is an accomplished organist. Morton is a champion of Australian composition and is also a composer of note having published with Augsberg Fortress and Morton Music. He regularly tours nationally and internationally, and has received numerous awards for his recordings of new music.

CHAPTER 5

Meeting National Standards for Music Education through Choral Performance

Frank Abrahams

Introduction

During the 1980s, shifting economic priorities caused the demise of many school music programs. Concerned that music learning in public schools would be eliminated completely, a consortium of arts education associations mounted one of the strongest advocacy campaigns in the history of public school music education. Led by the Music Educators National Conference (MENC), now the National Association for Music Education, this consortium produced a document that articulates the content, achievement, and opportunity-to-learn standards for all children in schools.

In 1994 the combined associations published the *National Standards for Arts Education: What Every American Should Know and Be Able to Do in the Arts*.[1] These standards, while voluntary, gave music teachers a framework upon which to develop curricula, assess student achievement, and provide a basis for accountability to their students, administrators, school boards, and communities. The contents of the document also identified benchmarks for all students to meet, providing consistency in music programs nationwide.

This overview of the National Standards for Music Education discusses how choral directors might design their choral curricula, rehearsal strategies, and concert programming to incorporate the National Standards for Music Education. The included sample rehearsal plan provides a model for choral directors who wish to adapt instruction to meet these goals.

History of the Standards

Concern for the ability of American children, not only to compete but to win, was first identified in 1957 when the Soviet Union launched the first space satellite, *Sputnik I*. This concern was further reiterated in 1983 when the federal government published *A Nation at Risk: The Imperative for Educational Reform*. This document stated that the children in American schools were not achieving at a level high enough to "produce an adult population capable of living productive and satisfying lives in the increasingly technological world community."[2] This short document became the manifesto for new initiatives aimed at reforming the system of education in this country, and was aimed at ensuring that American children would be able to outperform children from systems in other countries, principally Japan, France, and Germany.

In their book *World Class Schools: New Standards for Education*[3], Haynes and Chalker discuss their studies of the school systems in Canada, France, Germany, Great Britain, Israel, Japan, New Zealand, and Taiwan. They found that these countries had larger class sizes than in the U.S., assigned more homework, and scheduled a longer school day and academic year; they also found national curricula that identified standards of excellence in academic subject areas.[4] Ravitch added that other countries with world-class standards place more value on education, and teachers receive more respect than they do in this country.[5] Even the federal government agreed that by establishing high standards, everyone in the education system knows where to aim. According to the U. S. Department of Education, "students will learn more when more is expected of them."[6]

The warnings in *A Nation at Risk*, coupled with a sagging national economy, placed music programs in jeopardy. School districts, fighting for funds from state and local coffers, became concerned about raising scores on standardized tests in mathematics and science. In response to this struggle, districts cut back and in some cases eliminated their school music programs. The micro-computer was beginning to find its way into school buildings. School boards, seeing technology as a means to enrich instruction in mathematics and science, began diverting funds from other educational programs, such as music and aligning their financial resources into technology purchases and salaries for a new staff. Audio-visual departments became departments of media services and then departments of technology.

Then, in 1990, President George H. W. Bush appointed a committee of governors and charged them with developing goals that would guide American education into the twenty-first century. Unfortunately, these goals did not include the arts. The national associations of arts educators in music, drama, visual arts, and dance rallied to develop a strategy that would save their disciplines from virtual extinction. Their solution connected to the suggestion of the government that national standards be developed in the "core" subjects. The arts organizations felt that if they had standards, the federal government would recognize their disciplines as "core" subjects also. So, led by the MENC Task Force for the National Standards in the Arts, a consortium of arts associations (including the American Alliance for Theatre & Education, the National Art Education Association, the National Dance Association, and the Music Educators National Conference) was formed to develop national standards that would define what every American child should know and be able to do in the arts.

The National Standards for Music Education were developed by music teachers, university professors, and arts educators at every level. Draft versions of the standards were sent to all members of the participating professional organizations for feedback and suggestions. Forums and symposia were held at national, divisional, and state conferences to provide the opportunity for any-one who wished to give appropriate input to the framers. As a result, the final document did provide the support needed to have the arts included in the Goals 2000: Educate America Act, passed into law by Congress in 1994.

What Are the National Standards for Music Education?

Content Standards

The nine content standards for music education are:

One	Singing, alone and with others, a varied repertoire of music.
Two	Performing on instruments, alone and with others, a varied repertoire of music.
Three	Improvising melodies, variations, and accompaniments.
Four	Composing and arranging music within specified guidelines.
Five	Reading and notating music.
Six	Listening to, analyzing, and describing music.
Seven	Evaluating music and music performances.
Eight	Understanding relationships between music, the other arts, and disciplines outside the arts.
Nine	Understanding music in relation to history and culture.[7]

Achievement Standards

For each content standard there are achievement benchmarks for students in grades K–4, 5–8, and 9–12. For example, the achievement benchmarks for Content Standard Six: listening to, analyzing, and describing music at the high school level, requires that students be able to do the following:

- Analyze aural examples of a varied repertoire of music represent-ing diverse genres and cultures by describing the uses of elements of music and expressive devices.

- Demonstrate extensive knowledge of the technical vocabulary of music.

- Identify and explain compositional devices and techniques used to provide unity, variety, tension, and release in a musical work, plus give examples of other works that make similar use of these devices and techniques.

- Demonstrate the ability to perceive and remember music events by describing significant events (e.g., fugal entrances, chromatic modulations, developmental devices) occurring in a given aural example in detail.

- Compare ways in which musical materials are used in a given example relative to ways in which they are used in other works of the same genre or style.

- Analyze and describe uses of the elements of music in a given work that make it unique, interesting, and expressive.[8]

The Opportunity-to-Learn Standards
Opportunity-to-learn standards set guidelines for curricula, scheduling, staffing, materials, equipment, and facilities. The standards that are relevant to the high school choral program include that:

- Every music course, including performance courses, provide experiences in creating, performing, listening to, and analyzing music in addition to focusing on its specific subject matter. Also included are learning experiences designed to develop the ability to read music, use the notation and terminology of music, describe music, make informed evaluations concerning music, and understand music and music practices in relation to history and culture and to other disciplines in the curriculum.

- The repertoire taught includes music representing diverse genres and styles from various periods and cultures.

- Every music course, including performance courses, meet at least every other day in periods of at least forty-five minutes.

- Choral ensembles and classes be offered during the school day so that all members of each ensemble meet as a unit throughout the year or have equivalent time under an alternative scheduling arrangement. When enrollment justifies, the school offers at least two choruses, differentiated by the experience or age level of their members, or in the case of choruses, by their composition (e.g., treble voices, lower voices, or mixed voices). Other choral ensembles or classes are offered that reflect the musical interests of the community when clearly identifiable.

- At least one performing organization other than band, orchestra, and chorus (e.g., jazz ensemble, madrigal singers, show choir, or gospel choir) be available for each 300 students in the school.

- Every performing group present a series of performances or an open rehearsal each year for parents, peers, and the community. The number of performances is sufficient to demonstrate the nature and extent of the students' learning experiences. However, it should not interfere with the learning process, or reduce the amount of time available to achieve the instructional objectives of the ensemble. The emphasis needs to be on education rather than entertainment.

- Beginning, intermediate, and advanced choral instruction be available.

- A library of music be provided that includes at least seventy-five titles for each type of choral group. At least fifteen new titles for each type of group are added each year so that sufficient repertoire is available for a three-year cycle of instructional materials; new materials should be purchased each year. The library of music for performing groups should be sufficient in size to provide a folder of music for each student in choral groups and be free of materials that violate copyright laws. (The same applies to various types of ensembles. For example, a library of small-ensemble music should be provided that contains at least seventy-five titles with at least fifteen new tittles added each year. The library should likewise be free of materials produced in violation of copyright laws.)

- Every choral rehearsal room contain at least 1,800 square feet of floor space, with the ceiling being at least sixteen-feet high. Every room in which music is taught should have convenient access to a high-quality acoustic or electronic piano. A set of portable choral risers should be conveniently available to every room in which choral music is taught.[9]

More Than "Singing Alone and with Others"
Integrating National Standards
into the Choral Rehearsal

Content Standard One: *Singing, alone and with others, a varied repertoire of music*
Since the very essence of the choral experience involves singing with others, little needs to be said in this regard. Remember to provide your singers with solo opportunities in performance with the choir and also in student solo recitals, which you can schedule once or twice per year. Hopefully many of your singers take voice lessons, and the solo recital is a wonderful opportunity to showcase their progress.

It is the "varied repertoire" that merits discussion. Choosing music for performance is one of your most important responsibilities as a choral director. Find music that both challenges the students musically and is interesting to teach. While music publishers are helpful in providing sample scores and CD recordings of new publications, there are other ways to identify high-quality literature that will be interesting to teach, sing, and perform. This text is a wonderful resource for repertoire, and there are some online resources that are helpful as well. Two good sites are www.choralnet.org/music and www.musicanet.org.

Attend choral conferences and concerts by other colleagues. Save the programs. New York and Texas are two states that publish manuals of choral music that are graded by level of difficulty. Include music from all periods and music from other traditions. The following is a list of publishers of multicultural choral repertoire:

Alliance Music Publications
P.O. Box 131977
Houston, Texas 77219-1977
www.alliancemusic.com

GIA Publications, Inc.
7404 S. Mason Ave.
Chicago, IL 60638
www.giamusic.com
(primarily sacred offerings)

Earthsongs
220 NW 29th Street
Corvallis, Oregon 97330
www.earthsongsmus.com

Plymouth Music
170 NE 33rd Street
P.O. Box 24330
Fort Lauderdale, Florida 33334

World Music Press
P.O. Box 2565
Danbury, Connecticut 06813-2565
www.worldmusicpress.com

Walton Music
P.O. Box 167
Bynum, North Carolina 27228
www.waltonmusic.com

Musica Russica
310 Glenwood Drive
Guilford, Connecticut 06437
www.musicarussica.com

Morton Music
www.mortonmusic.com.au
Distributed in the U.S.A. by Musical Resources
2020 North Holland Sylvania Road
Toledo, Ohio 43615
www.musical-resources.com

Transcontinental Music Publications/New Jewish Music Press
603 Third Avenue, 6th Floor
New York, New York 10017
www.etranscon.com

Find repertoire that has inherent musical value.[10] Choose music that provides a means to teach musical concepts and build musical skills. As you rehearse, use musical vocabulary so that your singers become familiar with the terms. Don't forget to perform music by contemporary choral composers. And don't overlook the opportunity to commission works for your particular groups. Contact the music department at your local college or university to identify composers who could write for your ensembles. (Commissioning is not as expensive as you might think.)

In another book in this series, *Teaching Music through Performance in Band, Volume 2*, Eugene Corporon suggests criteria he uses to select repertoire for his ensembles as a "guide to determining quality, worth, and value." [11] They are appropriate for choral music as well. When adapting them for choral music, these ten principles are:

1. The composition has form—not a form but form—and reflects a proper balance between repetition and contrast.
2. The composition reflects shape and design and creates the impression of conscious choice (of text) and judicious arrangements on the part of the composer.
3. The composition reflects craftsmanship (in voice leading).
4. The composition is sufficiently unpredictable to preclude an immediate grasp of its musical meaning.
5. The route through which the composition travels in initiating its musical tendencies and its probable musical goals is not completely direct and obvious.
6. The composition is consistent in its quality throughout its length and in its various sections.
7. The composition is consistent in its style, reflecting a complete grasp of technical details (including the vocal issues connected to the setting of text), and it avoids lapses into trivial, futile, or unsuitable passages.
8. The composition reflects ingenuity in its development, given the stylistic content in which it exists.
9. The composition is genuine in idiom and not pretentious. (The text is significant and appropriate to the age and level of the ensemble.)
10. The composition reflects a musical validity that transcends factors of historical importance or pedagogical usefulness.

Content Standard Two: *Performing on instruments, alone and with others, a varied repertoire of music*

Although it might seem silly to think that performing on instruments should be part of the choral program, it really is not. While I am certainly not advocating that the singers be accomplished instrumentalists, I am suggesting that it is important to perform music with instruments. Singing with an orchestra, for instance, is a thrilling experience for young singers, and adding the instruments introduces a whole new dimension to your concerts. Further, there are many compositions for choir with percussion, in which members of the ensemble can play the parts. A *Joyous Procession* by Lou Harrision[12] is one such example. The piece is scored for a two-part choir with hand drums, tambourines, and a gong. Members of the ensemble are expected to play while singing.

At Cherry Hill (New Jersey) High School East, a select vocal ensemble sings and accompanies themselves on hand bells. Called "The Belles of East," the group arranges its own repertoire, and members play and sing simultaneously. Other schools include recorders and hand drums as part of their madrigal ensembles. Often the singers double as instrumentalists. They sing some of the songs while they accompany others.

Content Standard Three: *Improvising melodies, variations, and accompaniments*
Many choral directors shy away from improvisation because they associate it with jazz. When you think about it, improvisation gives students an opportunity to share their musical thoughts with you, their peers, and the audience. Since all children have what Howard Gardner calls "musical intelligence,"[13] all have the capacity to express themselves through improvisation. The Orff approach, common to elementary music programs, advocates that children improvise on specially prepared instruments. While this is not always practical in high school or middle school choir rehearsals, it is possible to take time to have students improvise. After all, improvisation develops the ear and the musical mind.

Here is a simple strategy: During the warm-up, choose one part to sing the vocalise normally, and ask the other sections to "harmonize" it. Or take a unison composition, a show tune perhaps, and ask the choir to "invent" their own harmony. During the Christmas season, I often ask a part other than soprano to sing the melody of a particular carol, and then I have the other parts invent their own harmonies. For example, the choir may sing the first verse of "Silent Night" in unison. For the second verse, tenors sing the melody while the sopranos, altos, and basses "invent" harmony parts. This strategy is extremely effective and gives the sopranos something more meaningful to contribute than singing the melody line. It allows another voice part to sing melody. Most importantly, it meets the improvisation mandate of standard three.

Content Standard Four: *Composing and arranging music within specified guidelines*
A variation on the above technique works for students who like to write and arrange their own music. You may not know it, but you probably have students in your choirs who arrange and perform songs they hear on TV or on the car radio. You may also have serious composers in the group. Devote some time on each concert to program music composed and arranged by students. Remember to secure the appropriate permissions before you perform any original arrangements of copyrighted works.

Content Standard Five: *Reading and notating music*
Build reading and writing skills into your warm-up. Choose a solfege system, and use it. While many music teachers use Movable Do, I prefer a system in which the students sing the letter names of the notes. For me, that best reinforces the reading of musical notation. And, if you are programming

contemporary or world music, this modified fixed system can help singers sight-read easily. Chances are you have students in your ensembles who can read music because they play piano or another instrument in orchestra or band. Use those musicians as leaders. Include reading and writing skills as part of your assessments each time you evaluate students for grades. Remember, the only reason your singers cannot sight-read is that you have not taught them or made it a priority in your program.

Content Standard Six: *Listening to, analyzing, and describing music* and
Content Standard Seven: *Evaluating music and music performances*
Technology enables choral directors to meet content standards six and seven. For example, if you are performing a Brahms motet assign students to listen to a movement from one of the symphonies. Assign a listening excerpt from the *Requiem* or the Brahms lieder. You can leave CDs or tapes on reserve in the school library. Then, set up a listserv for the singers in your ensemble and have them send you an "electronic journal entry" reflecting on what they heard. The listserv allows your students to share ideas with you and with their peers. It is a wonderful way to initiate substantial conversation about the music and for you to monitor their responses. Periodically, send some questions to them for thought, and let the students "chat" with you and each other. After each concert, require students to send a reflective evaluation of the performance to the listserv. This will facilitate talking between students outside of class, which will leave more time in class for other activities.

Content Standard Eight: *Understanding relationships between music, the other arts, and disciplines outside the arts*
Howard Gardner writes that learning is authentic when it connects to the world beyond the classroom.[14] Content standard eight addresses this very issue. Additionally, recent research suggests that the study of music, especially at an early age, may contribute to a child's success in spatial development, understanding patterns, and seeing relationships. It also helps students later in life when they reach the more advanced levels of mathematics and science. Most importantly, the study of music teaches children to think creatively. If, as Americans, we are going to be world leaders in science and technology, we need to teach our young people to be creative problem solvers. This happens in music classes, specifically in choral rehearsals. Although choosing to perform Handel's "Hallelujah Chorus" simply because it is a great piece of music might have been sufficient justification in the past, conductors must show how this piece parallels concepts of design, proportion, and balance, which are common problems in the visual arts and mathematics. Study and performance of this great oratorio chorus becomes relevant beyond the rehearsal room.

Content Standard Nine: *Understanding music in relation to history and culture*
Music exists within a social context. Children enter our rehearsal rooms with quite a bit of knowledge in music—some learned in the school music program, but much learned outside of music classrooms and rehearsals. It is a curious phenomenon, but no matter how poor children may be, they have money to buy the latest CD or purchase tickets to a concert by their favorite pop group or singer.

Think about it. Our students have audio collections broader in scope than ours, and they know more about the music of their adolescent culture than we could dream possible. Choral teachers are successful when they are able to tap into that information bank by encouraging students to understand the historical and cultural situations in which the music was produced. What do we know about eighteenth-century Europe as a result of performing a Haydn mass? What do we know about culture and history by singing a Morley madrigal? What do we know about emotion and feeling by singing a Brahms motet? What do we know about our own society when we perform the medley from the latest Broadway show? How will studying these aspects ultimately affect the performance? There are teachers who believe that some music is "our" music and other music is "their" music. Those teachers tend to discourage young people from serious musical study. And just as content standard one suggests that our students sing a varied repertoire of music, we must open ourselves to music from their time as well.

There is a second aspect of choral performance that this content standard addresses. When we perform, and especially when we perform music of other cultures, we must ensure that our performances are as authentic as possible. Mary Goetze, one of America's leading conductors of children's choirs, shocked the profession when she suggested that children sing in chest voice when performing music of African origin.[15] Other colleagues concur. Choral music must be performed in the manner in which its creator conceived it. For classically trained conductors, this means reeducation and a commitment to stretching beyond what was learned in school.

By singing a balanced repertoire, singers gain proficiency in order to:

- Classify unfamiliar music by genre, style, and historical period or culture and explain the reasoning behind their classifications;

- Identify and explain the stylistic features of a given musical work that define its aesthetic tradition and its historical or cultural context;

- Identify and describe musical genres or styles that show the influences of varied cultural traditions, identify the cultural source of each influence, and trace the historical conditions that produced the synthesis of influences.[16]

Planning the Choral Rehearsal to Meet National Standards

Addressing content and opportunity-to-learn standards through choral performances will require that choral directors rethink their rehearsal strategies. While performances are the final goal, the path one travels to the performance will change. The choral rehearsals shift from practicing the music to become a comprehensive musical experience. Jason Iannuzzi, chairman of the performing arts department at Winchester Thurston School in Pittsburgh, Pennsylvania, and former conductor of the Westminster Conservatory Youth Chorale Chamber Singers at Westminster Choir College of Rider University, worked with me to develop the following rehearsal plan.[17] Notice the plan consists of two smaller sections inside four large divisions. Each smaller unit (out of eight in all) has its own objective, activity, and assessment. Musical concepts frame the entire plan.

We develop a plan like this for each piece in the choral folder, and it often takes more than one rehearsal to complete. Because the plan often takes more than one rehearsal to complete, the plans for each piece of music are at various stages of readiness in each rehearsal. While this method of planning may seem confusing or difficult at first, once your thinking shifts toward meeting National Standards, the logic appears clear. In addition to meeting the National Standards for Music Education, the plan also includes strategies to engage singers in higher-order thinking and problem solving. These constructivist techniques are popular in other academic subjects and are applicable to choral rehearsals as well. Further, the plan provides connections to integrate the choral curriculum with the other arts and subjects outside the arts as well as to multiple intelligences.

Finally, the plan incorporates the latest research on music and the brain. Steps 1, 3, 6, and 8 are "right brain" activities because they are holistic and abstract. Steps 2, 4, 5, and 7 are "left brain" activities because they are sequential and concrete. These latter steps often call for singers to verbalize. More information on these ideas and strategies are found in the "Suggestions for Further Reading" at the end of this chapter.

Steps for Formulating a Choral Rehearsal Plan

Author: Frank Abrahams and Jason Iannuzzi
Concept: The choral rehearsal should be a comprehensive musical experience that involves musical thinking, problem solving, and develops choral concepts.
Grade Level: Middle School and High School
(*Note: Remember that singers want to sing in a choral rehearsal, and limit any lecture to a minimum.*)

One	EXPERIENCE
(1) Objective:	To place the piece into a context and facilitate an understanding of its *gestalt*, or relationship to the concept as a whole.
Activity:	Read or play through the piece once, or listen to a recording and have the singers follow along in their scores. Have singers highlight where the main themes occur.
Assessment:	Are the singers following with their scores? Are they engaged during the read-through?
(2) Objective:	For singers to gain knowledge about the nature of the musical issues they will need to solve.
Activity:	Briefly comment on the piece. Why was it selected? Discuss some interesting musical features or ideas, etc. Point out the major issues in rhythm, melody, color, and phrasing. What are the challenges of performance?
Assessment:	Are the singers engaged in the discussion of musical features?
Two	PRESENT
(3) Objective:	For singers to identify the main musical idea(s).
Activity:	Isolate the most important musical statements in the piece, and provide singers with experiences from these parts first. For instance, teach the refrain of a song, or identify the subject/counter-subject of a fugue. Experiences are not limited to singing but may include

	clapping a rhythmic motive, performing hand signs to the main theme, etc.
Assessment:	Do the singers (through singing, moving, discussing, etc.) demonstrate an understanding of the main point of the music?
(4) Objective:	For singers to gain an understanding of the underlying structure of the piece. Whenever possible, music should be learned from the standpoint of how the composer wrote it.
Activity:	• Share with the singers (or lead singers) to discover significant aspects of the structure of the music. For instance, if there is a fugue, isolate the subject and counter-subject and learn those first. If the piece is written in sonata-allegro form, a discussion of the exposition, development, and recapitulation is appropriate. • Singers may listen to other works of the composer or works written in a comparative or contrasting styles. This promotes critique, evaluation, and synthesis. What does the text mean? How is the music connected to the text? Are there images or metaphors? • If preparing a major work, it would be valuable to present a study guide at this point.
Assessment:	Are singers marking their scores? Is the discussion of music and text substantial and of high quality?
Three	**PRACTICE**
(5) Objective:	For singers to polish the fine points of the piece (pitch, rhythm, dynamics, phrasing, diction, etc.).
Activity:	This is the most traditional part of the plan. Teach and rehearse the piece as the composer wrote it, engaging the musical intelligence of the singers whenever possible. Remember, singers must bring something more to rehearsals than their voices. Decide which problems are "self

	correcting" and empower the singers to take responsibility for correct notes, rhythms, and markings.
Assessment:	Does the performance sound secure? Do the singers demonstrate understanding? Are the singers making connections on their own?
(6) Objective:	For singers to build individual musicianship. They will continue to fine-tune the mechanics of the piece using different modalities and find new ways to approach the music being sung.
Activity:	Invent warm-ups for future rehearsals that connect to and address the musical issues in the piece. Be sure that the singers see the connections. Use Kodály hand signs, trace the line of the phrase with the arms, move to the macro beat, and conduct while singing. This engages the kinesthetic modality. Move singers into different formations, such as circles. If members of the group are capable, mix them up so that no two members are standing next to each other. Emphasize listening to other parts.
Assessment:	Are the singers performing with understanding?
Four	EXTEND
(7) Objective:	For the conductor to provide singers with opportunities to make musical decisions and critique their work.
Activity:	During informal cooperative learning, one group listens while another sings and makes suggestions for improvement. If inaccuracies in pitch, rhythm, or diction still occur, give the singers quiet time (a minute or two) to mentally correct their mistakes independently. During the extension part of the process, the conductor continually refines and polishes the work.
Assessment:	Monitor the students' contributions to their cooperative groups. Are the singers taking personal responsibility for the musical issues?

(8) Objective:	For students to synthesize learning.
Activity:	Present a performance of the piece.
Assessment:	Do the singers sing in a way that reflects an understanding of the musical ideas and a mastery of the musical materials?

The Plan in Action

Author: Frank Abrahams and Mellissa Hughes[18]
Theme: Identifying and applying different vocal timbres to world music
Grade Level: High school
Materials: Recording of "Ngana" by Stephen Leek (1996, Morton Music)[19]
Pictures of Australia, didgeridoo, corroboree ritual, and Ayers rock[20]

One	EXPERIENCE
(1) Objective:	To provide a problem, which presents a need to know the answer.
Activity:	Listen to "Ngana" in its entirety. Give the choir an overall sense or *gestalt* of the piece. Ask students to visualize colors that might represent the individual sections.
Assessment:	Student engagement and the quality of their answers.
(2) Objective:	To further motivate students' interest in the music.
Activity:	Discuss the different vocal timbres (i.e., colors) in "Ngana" and compare them with other pieces that the students are currently singing.
Assessment:	Student engagement and the quality of the individual responses.

Two	PRESENT
(3) Objective:	To connect the experience with the theme of the rehearsal.
Activity:	Show posters of Australia. Talk to students about the didgeridoo, the corroboree ritual, and Ayers rock. Ask students to tell you why it is important to sing world music, and why it is important to perform world music as authentically as possible. Show how the colors in the pictures connect to the colors in the music.
Assessment:	The level of student engagement and their ability to make connections.
(4) Objective:	To present the information.
Activity:	Invite students to sing various vocalises as they visualize different colors. Ask the students how this visualization affects their choral sound. Have the students suggest various colors for the individual sections of "Ngana." Explain the technical aspects of producing these vocal colors.
Assessment:	Student engagement in the musical exercises and the quality of their answers demonstrate an understanding of color and timbre.
Three	PRACTICE
(5) Objective:	For singers to polish the fine points of the piece.
Activity:	Rehearse the piece, paying careful attention to contrasting vocal timbres. Correct pitches and rhythms as necessary.
Assessment:	Ability of students to apply new concepts and the demonstration of an understanding of the piece.

(6) Objective:	Singers continue to fine-tune the mechanics of the piece using a kinesthetic modality.	
Activity:	Have treble parts conduct while they sing the canon. Have students pulse eighth notes. Add clapping and stomping in the music where it has been notated.	
Assessment:	The quality of student performance and engagement.	
Four	**EXTEND**	
(7) Objective:	To provide for reflective thinking.	
Activity:	Ask students by section to name three things that they could improve. Give students two minutes to review their parts and to correct their mistakes. Student do this on their own.	
Assessment:	Student engagement, the quality of answers, and their ability to identify and fix problems.	
(8) Objective:	For singers to synthesize learning.	
Activity:	Perform the piece, always attending to contrast of timbre.	
Assessment:	The quality of the final performance. Did the singing reflect an understanding of the contrasting vocal timbres?	

Choose one and complete:

- Listen to the piece "And God Created Great Whales" by Alan Hovhaness. How does the composer use color and texture (and the sounds of real whales) to achieve his musical objectives? Discuss your findings with a friend, your conductor, or with the choir.

- Surf the Web for information on the Aborigines of Australia, and print the sources.

- Interview a "senior" member of your family about the music of your heritage. Tape the session. Learn a song that your relatives might have sung several generations ago.

- Arrange a musical selection from your own cultural heritage for the choir to sing as a companion piece to "Ngana."

How Each Step Correlates to Gardner's Multiple Intelligences

Step 1	Musical, Spatial, Intrapersonal
Step 2	Verbal Linguistic
Step 3	Verbal Linguistic
Step 4	Logical-mathematical
Step 5	Logical-mathematical, Spatial, Musical
Step 6	Bodily-kinesthetic, Logical-mathematical
Step 7	Intrapersonal, Verbal Linguistic
Step 8	Musical, Intrapersonal

Correlation to Thinking Skills
(Higher Order Skills Are in Italics)

Step 1	*Synthesis*
Step 2	Knowledge, Comprehension, Application
Step 3	Knowledge, Comprehension, Application
Step 4	*Analysis, Synthesis, Evaluation*
Step 5	Application
Step 6	Application
Step 7	*Evaluation*
Step 8	Application

Connection to the National Standards for Music Education

Note: *The study and performance of this composition meets National Standard 9: Understanding music in relation to history and culture.*

Step 1	Content Standard 1	Singing, alone and with others, a varied repertoire of music
	Content Standard 5	Reading and notating music
Step 2	Content Standard 6	Listening to, analyzing, and describing music
Step 3	Content Standard 8	Understanding relationships between music, the other arts, and disciplines outside the arts
	Content Standard 9	Understanding music in relation to history and culture

Step 4	Content Standard 1	Singing, alone and with others, a varied repertoire of music
	Content Standard 5	Reading and notating music
	Content Standard 6	Listening to, analyzing, and describing music
	Content Standard 7	Evaluating music and music performances
Step 5	Content Standard 1	Singing, alone and with others, a varied repertoire of music
	Content Standard 5	Reading and notating music
Step 6	Content Standard 1	Singing, alone and with others, a varied repertoire of music
	Content Standard 3	Improvising melodies, variations, and accompaniments
	Content Standard 5	Reading and notating music
Step 7	Content Standard 7	Evaluating music and music performances
Step 8	Content Standard 1	Singing, alone and with others, a varied repertoire of music
	Content Standard 5	Reading and notating music
	Content Standard 9	Understanding music in relation to history and culture

Frank Abrahams is Professor and Chair of Music Education and Arts & Sciences at Westminster Choir College of Rider University in Princeton, New Jersey. He is the founder and conductor of the Westminster Conservatory Chorale and coordinator of Westminster Music Theatre Workshop summer program. He is a consultant for Educational Testing Service and conducts workshops and clinic presentations in learning styles, assessment, and Total Quality Management at national and regional MENC conferences, and for state conferences in Maryland, New York, Massachusetts, Pennsylvania, Texas and New Jersey.

Recommendations for Further Reading

Abrahams, Frank and Paul Head. *Case Studies in Music Education.* Chicago: GIA Publications, Inc. 1998.

Costa, Arthur L. "How World-Class Standards Will Change Us." *Educational Leadership*, February 1993. 50–51.

Daugherty, E. (editor). "National Standards in Music Education" (special issue). *The Quarterly Journal of Music Teaching and Learning* 6, no. 2 (1995).

Lehman, Paul R. "The National Standards for Music Education: Meeting the Challenges." *The Quarterly Journal of Music Teaching and Learning* 6, no. 2 (1995): 5–13.

Mark, Michael L. *Contemporary Music Education* (3rd edition). New York: Schirmer Books. 1996.

McCarthy, Bernice. *The 4MAT System: Teaching to Learning Styles with Right/Left Mode Techniques*. Barrington: EXCEL. 1987.

Music Educators National Conference. *National Standards for Arts Education: What Every American Should Know and Be Able to Do in the Arts.* Reston: Music Educators National Conference. 1994.

Music Educators National Conference. *Opportunity-to-Learn Standards for Music Instruction: Grades Pre K–12.* Reston: Music Educators National Conference, 1994.

Music Educators National Conference. *Aiming for Excellence: The Impact of the Standards Movement on Music Education.* Reston: Music Educators National Conference, 1996.

Notes

1 Music Educators National Conference, *National Standards for Arts Education: What Every American Should Know and Be Able to Do in the Arts* (Reston: Music Educators National Conference, 1994).

2 Michael L. Mark, *Contemporary Music Education*, 3rd ed. (New York: Schirmer Books, 1996), 119–20.

3 Donald M. Chalker and Richard M. Haynes, *World Class Schools: New Standards for Education* (Landham, MD: Scarecrow Press, 1995).

4 Ibid., 23.

5 "A Citizen's Guide to Standards," *American School Board Journal*, February 1995: 35–39.

6 United States Department of Education, *High Standards for All Students* (Washington, D.C.: Government Printing Office, 1994), 2.

7 MENC.

8 Ibid., 61.

9 Adapted from Music Educators National Conference, *Opportunity-to-Learn Standards for Music Education Grades PreK–12* (Reston, VA: Music Educators National Conference, 1994), 17–23.

10 Frank Abrahams and Paul Head, *Case Studies in Music Education* (Chicago: GIA Publications, Inc., 1998), 137.

11 Richard Miles, ed., *Teaching Music through Performance in Band*, vol. 2 (Chicago: GIA Publications, Inc., 1998), 79–80.

12 *A Joyous Procession* by Lou Harrison is published by C. F. Peters, no. 6543.

13 Gardner identifies seven different intelligences. For a complete discussion of multiple intelligences, consult his *Frames of Mind*, published by Basic Books.

14 Gardner suggests five indicators of authentic learning: promotes higher level thinking, emphasizes depth of knowledge, connotes to the world beyond the classroom, encourages substantive conversation, and provides social support for student achievement. He discusses this in an article by Newmann and Whelage called "Five Standards of Authentic Instruction" published in *Educational Leadership*, 1993, volume 50, no 7: 8–12.

15 Mary Goetze is professor of music at Indiana University.

16 MENC, 108.

17 Both rehearsal plans in this chapter are based on the 4MAT System developed by Bernice McCarthy. For more information about the 4MAT System, contact About Learning, Incorporated, 1251 N. Old Rand Road, Wauconda, Illinois 60084, 800-822-4628, 847-487-1800, fax: 847-487-1811, www.aboutlearning.com.

18 Mellissa Hughes is a former conducting intern with the Westminster Conservatory Youth Chorale, Westminster Choir College, Princeton, New Jersey.

19 The composer writes, " 'Ngana' uses as its source an indigenous Australian text which calls to the shark (*ngana*) and the fish (*mangana*) welcoming (*yah*) them to the translucent blue waters (*lina*) around the reef." The vocal placement should be very frontal with much resonance coming from the nose.

20 *Didgeridoo* are ceremonial instruments constructed from hollowed-out logs. They vary in size and are usually painted or decorated in designs according to the taste of the tribes and performers. The technique of circular breathing is integral to the playing of the instrument. Musically, it provides the drone bass for music and can also imitate animal calls or noises (e.g., the laugh of the kookaburra, the howl of a

dingo, etc.) which is necessary in the storytelling of the *corroboree* (pronounced ko-ROB-a-ree), a ceremonial or ritual celebration. The most common image is of aboriginal men dancing around a campfire while older men and the women chant, play instruments (*thora*, clapping sticks, and rattles), and clap. Spears and boomerangs are also used percussively. Typically a corroboree tells a story and is an important part of the oral tradition of historical preservation for the Aboriginal tribe. The chants of "Ngana," while composed by Stephen Leek, are suggestive of the chants that may be sung at a corroboree. Ayers Rock is situated in the Uluru (Ayers Rock-Mount Olga) National Park, Northern Territory, Australia. Consisting of Arkose, a course-grained sandstone rich in the mineral feldspar, Ayers Rock achieves its famous red color and flaky surface from the chemical decay of minerals and mechanical erosion. The characteristic rusty color of the exposed surface of these flakes is caused by the oxidation or rusting of the iron in the *arkose*. The fresh *arkose* is a gray color.

PART II

THE CHORAL CONDUCTOR AS MUSIC TEACHER

Repertoire Resource Guides

Introduction to the Repertoire Resource Guides

Matthew W. Mehaffey

Choosing repertoire for a concert can be a fun, enjoyable task, a sort of scavenger hunt into the annals of choral literature to find pieces that fit perfectly together to form a cohesive whole. Choosing more than one hundred pieces of choral repertoire involves years of second-guessing and worrying if every piece is worthy of inclusion.

For this reason, my co-editor, Heather Buchanan, and I did not choose this repertoire in a vacuum. At the inception of this process, we polled a wide range of highly respected and recognized music educators and choral musicians for repertoire of all genres and styles musically and aesthetically appropriate for high school choral singers. We received hundreds of ideas, all of which were of high quality and could have been included in this initial volume. Through endless revisions and consultations across the profession, we arrived at the list presented to you in this book. It does not include a piece by every great composer for choir; however, you will find that this list includes both familiar titles and new titles, sacred titles and secular titles, *a cappella* and accompanied titles, ancient music and modern music, English language selections and foreign language selections. There is something in this list for everyone, and we guarantee that all of it is of high musical quality.

For each piece in the **Repertoire Resource Guides**, we have provided you with historical, biographical, and analytical information that is helpful in score preparation and useful fodder for teaching. These resource guides are not meant to be complete studies of each piece but offer a place to begin your musical journey. To complete these resource guides, we enlisted the help of graduate students, teachers, and professors from across the country. These authors have graduated from institutions with some of the richest choral traditions in our country. We encourage you to read this book in many different ways: to learn more about old repertoire, to learn about new repertoire, and to refresh your perspective when you feel rehearsals have become stale.

In completing this process, many active clinicians commented that musical rating systems in place for choral music are often confusing and inaccurate. Pieces that should be given a low rating are often rated with a high level of difficulty and vice-versa. During this project we asked several states for their criteria for rating choral music for festivals. Believe it or not, many states have no formal criteria for rating a piece; in fact, the presenting conductor often decides the rating of a new piece.

To this end, we decided this volume should establish a **new rating system** that helps conductors choose repertoire appropriate for their singers. Band pieces are generally rated on a scale from 1–6 with six being the most difficult. Current choral ratings do not provide conductors with enough information to make informed repertoire choices for their ensembles. For instance, the notes of any given piece may be easy to learn for even the most amateur singer, but the range and tessitura might make it far too difficult for a group of beginning singers; a single rating cannot accurately reflect this dichotomy.

We use a five-point scale with Level Five being the most difficult. Each piece has been assigned an **Overall** difficulty rating, which gives the conductor a quick reference point. In an effort to give teachers and conductors more information, we added two additional ratings: **Vocal** and **Tonal/Rhythm**. The vocal rating assesses the vocal difficulty of each piece by considering the range, tessitura, dynamics, and diction issues: the higher the number, the more advanced the required technique. Pieces with a higher number will be more likely to have passages with extreme ranges, long vocal lines, extended vocal techniques, challenging diction, and stylistic issues. The tonal rating assesses how difficult this piece will be to teach/learn from an aural perspective: the higher the number, the more complex the composer's harmonic, melodic, and rhythmic language. Pieces with a higher tonal rating will be more likely to have chromatic and/or modal passages that are outside of the major/minor tonalities, instances of mixed meter, and difficult rhythms. The **Overall** rating is essentially an average of the **Vocal** and **Tonal/Rhythm** ratings; therefore, to have a complete understanding of the difficulty, please consult the additional ratings when choosing repertoire. (N.B.: the number of vocal parts, divisi, length of composition, and intangible "musical" elements were taken into consideration but not as heavily weighted as the aforementioned criteria.) We have calibrated our ratings to the ability of the average high school choir, which should be able to perform, without great difficulty, anything with a rating of three or lower.

The chart below summarizes the criteria typical of the music in each level. However, because the repertoire in this volume is very diverse, not all pieces in each level will contain all of the qualities/criteria listed in the chart, and it should be noted that this list is not exhaustive. Each higher level assumes all the criteria of the previous levels.

LEVEL	VOCAL	TONAL/RHYTHM
1	• Short, simple vocal lines with limited ranges • Conjunct vocal lines prevail • Comfortable vocal range • Manageable tessitura	• Major or minor tonality with little to no chromaticism • No modulations to other keys or tonalities • Straightforward rhythms within simple or compound meter
2	• Phrases of moderately challenging length • Slightly disjunct vocal lines • Brief, yet negotiable forays into extreme ranges • Basic dynamic range • Basic diction challenges in languages commonly encountered in choral music (e.g., English, Latin, German)	• Major or minor tonality with brief, obvious chromaticism • Brief modulations are obvious and move to closely related tonalities • Modal passages • Dissonances are approached and resolved by step • Short passages of challenging rhythm within simple or compound metric structure
3	• Short passages requiring advanced vocal technique • Some passages of challenging tessitura • Long phrases requiring good breath control • Vocal melismas of moderate length requiring *martellato* technique • Wide dynamic range • Extended crescendos and decrescendos • Wide range of languages encountered	• Major/minor/modal tonality • Concrete or implied modulations to different tonalities or modalities • Dissonance approached by leap • Added note harmonies • Imitative and non-imitative counterpoint • Difficult rhythms may occur, but are usually repetitive • Simply constructed mixed meter
4	• Long phrases requiring excellent breath control • Extreme ranges • Vocal lines requiring subtlety of shape, dynamics, and expressivity • Long vocal melismas • Alternative vocal techniques (i.e., non-Western techniques) • Refined diction required as stylistic vehicle	• Extended modal passages • Passages in non-diatonic harmony • Frequent chromaticism • Challenging rhythmic passages may be extended and non-repetitive • Full compositions in mixed meter

Level	Vocal	Tonal/Rhythm
5	• Vocal maturity required • Extreme ranges and tessituras • Repertoire at this level will provide numerous challenges for the experienced choral ensemble	• Atonal passages or passages of extreme dissonance • Unprepared/unresolved dissonant harmonies • Very complex rhythmic/metric structure • Repertoire at this level will provide numerous challenges for the experienced choral ensemble

Following the Resource Guides is the first of the series of **Masterworks** to be reviewed, the Fauré *Requiem*. We selected this piece for inclusion in the first volume because it is ubiquitous; high school choirs, church choirs, college choirs, and professional choirs perform it with great regularity. Bruce Chamberlain, Anthony Reeves, and I compiled this section, which examines the Fauré *Requiem* from all angles. An extended biography of Fauré, historical background behind the work, Herford analyses of each movement and the whole work, rehearsal strategies for choir, orchestra, and organ, and information about French Latin are all included. It is our hope that these writings will shed new light on an old favorite or introduce this work to you for the first time. It is our intention to include a masterwork in every future volume of this series.

We hope you find these resource guides to be helpful in all levels of your music making and inspire you to venture into choral repertoire with renewed dedication to the choral art.

Level One

Repertoire Resource Guide

Be Thou My Vision

arr. Alice Parker
(b. 1925)

Hinshaw Music, Inc.: HMC-135
SATB/Piano or harp
Overall: 1
Vocal: 1
Tonal/Rhythm: 1

Composer

Alice Parker composed her first orchestral work while in high school, and as she approaches her ninth decade, she continues to write, conduct, teach, and lecture. She studied at the Smith College and the Juilliard School.

Parker composes in all choral forms and collaborated with Robert Shaw in choral composition and choir technique. The Melodious Accord, a sixteen-voice professional chorus she founded in 1985, tours, records, and performs widely.

Composition

The hymn "Be Thou My Vision" paired with several sets of words, has been a favorite in many Christian traditions. The lovely tune, SLANÉ, is from the Irish folk tradition and is named for a hill in County Meath upon which St. Patrick is reputed to have defied the pagan King Loigaire. SLANÉ, in turn, comes from the Northern Irish folksong "The Banks of the Bann." It has a relatively wide compass and a four-phrase structure without repetition. The lyrics are from Ireland in the Middle Ages and were translated to prose by

Mary E. Byrne (1905) and versified in the 1912 *Poem Book of the Gael* by Eleanor Hull.

The Parker arrangement begins unison (verse 1) over a flowing keyboard (or harp) arpeggio. Verse 2 features tenors and basses, beginning unison and ending in simple, tuneful harmony. Verse 3 puts an unspecified solo voice over accompanimental sopranos and altos. The last verse, which follows a short instrumental interlude, puts the soloist on a descant above unison choral melody. An alternate voicing mentioned in the score places sopranos and tenors on melody and altos and basses on descant.

Historical Perspective

Audiences perennially love a beautiful melody. Alice Parker sets this one simply enough to let it make the point of the text. You may wish to replace the word "son" in the second verse with "child," although this ruins the rhyme scheme.

Technical Considerations

This is a piece even junior high choirs can perform with élan. Teach the melody, add the words, employ a sensitive pianist, and you have a piece for a concert any time of year.

Stylistic Considerations

The flowing, easy legato throughout should not be allowed to become merely repetitive or boring. Move each phrase toward and away from a point of intensity ("heart," then "save," and so on). Observe the dynamics marked, and work to achieve a beautiful, round sound. The third verse's humming may be done with open mouth, on "oo" or with high palate and closed lips, depending upon the sound you desire.

Form and Structure

The four verses are strophic and in E major.

Text and Translation

Be thou my vision, O Lord of my heart;
Nought be all else to me, save that thou art.
Thou my best thought by day or by night,
Waking or Sleeping, thy presence my light.

Be thou my wisdom, and thou my true word;
I ever with thee and thou with me, Lord.
Thou my great Father, I thy true son,
Thou in me dwelling, and I with thee one.

Riches I heed not, nor man's empty praise;
Thou mine inheritance, now and always.
Thou and thou only, first in my heart,
High King of heaven, my treasure thou art.

High King of heaven, my victory won;
May I reach heav'n's joys, O bright heaven's Sun!
Heart of my own heart, whatever befall,
Still be my vision, O Ruler of all.

Contributed by:

Lani Johnson

Repertoire Resource Guide

Bist du bei mir

Johann Sebastian Bach
(1685–1750)

Unison/keyboard
Gordon Thompson: VG–183–w
Overall: 1
Vocal: 2
Tonal/Rhythm: 1

Composer

Johann Sebastian Bach was born March 21, 1685, in Eisenach, Germany. The extended Bach family were well-known as musicians; J. S.'s father, Johann Ambrosius, was a chamber musician in Eisenach.

J. S. Bach's life is generally divided into six periods, mostly defined by his places of employment: early life (1685–1703); Arnstadt (1703–07); Mühlhausen (1707–08); Weimar (1708–17); Cöthen (1717–23); and Leipzig (1723–50). In these positions, Bach served at various times as organist, teacher, composer, *Konzertmeister* (Weimar), and *Director musices* (Leipzig). He was also appointed *Hofcompositeur* for the Dresden Court in 1736.

J. S. Bach's musical output is overwhelming, including masterworks in almost every musical genre of his era. For example, he wrote cantatas (sacred and secular), large-scale choral works (e.g., St. Matthew Passion and Mass in B Minor), concerti, orchestral suites, organ works, harpsichord works, and pieces for various other instruments and instrumental combinations. Bach died in Leipzig July 28, 1750.

Composition

The aria "Bist du bei mir" (BWV 508) was included in J. S. Bach's second *Notebook* for Anna Magdelena Bach (1725). The work appears as a soprano line above a non-figured bass. Recent scholarship has deducted that this piece was actually composed by Gottfried Heinrich Stölzel (1690–1749), an exact contemporary of Bach's. Stölzel studied in Leipzig from 1707–1710 (thirteen years before Bach's arrival). He then spent time in Italy and Prague and was appointed *Kapellmeister* at the Saxe-Gotha court, where he remained until his death. Stölzel composed operas, chamber music, and sacred and secular vocal music.

Technical Considerations

This short aria contains many challenges for the young singer. It requires frequent change of register, often occurring via leaps.

Because this piece was written without a figured bass line, we cannot be certain of the exact accompaniment Bach intended for this aria. Most editions of this piece contain a keyboard part arranged by the editor. Therefore, it is important that the conductor look at various editions of this aria to find the accompaniment that is most appealing.

Stylistic Considerations

The pronunciation of German is often an enigma to choral conductors but not in the way one might think. German consonants are actually quite predictable once the singer learns the rules; the vowels are what cause singers and conductors great difficulty. American choirs tend to sing vowels far too open for the German language. The only way to learn proper German vowel sounds is to listen to a good German choir or singer. When listening, notice the color of the vowels. Notice how the [u] vowel as sung by Germans is rounder and more closed than the American sound (usually "uh"). The [i] vowel is so much brighter and more closed than the American vowel (usually "ih"). [A] vowels are considerably brighter and more forward than American "ah" vowels. The mixed umlauted vowels are a wonderful combination of two different vowels and supply the music and language with so much color. Choirs that do not learn these sounds cannot perform with a German sound or flavor.

Once the choir has a sound model, instruction is needed. Define for the choir which vowels are formed mainly by the lips (e.g., "oo" as in boot) and which are formed mainly by the tongue (e.g., "ee" as in meek). Umlauted vowels combine the two. It is from these two extremes, lip and tongue vowels, that the choir should begin German pronunciation. It is also helpful to tell the choir that the vowel is "formed on the consonant." This means that their mouths should be in the shape of the vowel when they execute the consonant. These ideas are a solid start to the learning of German diction.

Form and Structure

This aria combines many of the formal aspects of the Baroque era. The first line of the music is repeated, which is similar in form to a typical Lutheran chorale. The B section does not conclude the piece but repeats back to earlier material. In that respect, however, this aria is different from many other Baroque *da capo* arias. The repeat of music in "Bist du bei mir" goes to the second line of music instead of all the way back to the beginning.

Text and Translation

Bist du bei mir, geh ich mit Freuden
zum Sterben und zu meiner Ruh.
Ach, wie vergnügt wär so mein Ende,
es drückten deine lieben [schönen] Hände
mir die getreuen Augen zu!

If you are with me, then I will gladly go
to my death and to my rest.
Ah, how satisfying will my end be,
for your dear, fair hands will shut
my faithful eyes!

Contributed by:

Matthew W. Mehaffey
Anthony Reeves

Repertoire Resource Guide

Gloria ad modum tubae

Guillaume Dufay
(ca. 1400–1474)

SA/2 trombones
GIA Publications, Inc.: G-2150
Overall: 1
Vocal: 1
Tonal/Rhythm: 2

Composer

Guillaume Dufay (pronounced Doo-fah-ee) was born ca. 1400, probably near Cambrai, where he sang as a chorister from 1409 until 1414. His exact movements after 1414 are unclear, but we know he spent much of the time in Italy where he established connections with the powerful Malatesta family. During the 1430s, he was a member of the papal chapel in Rome (and later in Florence and Bologna) and was employed by the court of Savoy. By 1439, Dufay had returned to Cambrai to work at the Cathedral. With the exception of a few trips abroad, Dufay remained in Cambrai for the rest of his life.

Other fifteenth-century musicians regarded Dufay as one of the greatest composers of their era. He wrote complete masses as well as individual mass movements or pairs of movements. Dufay also composed many motets, antiphons, hymns, and various other liturgical compositions, as well as secular *chansons* (almost all three-part with French texts). Dufay died November 27, 1474, in Cambrai.

Composition

"Gloria ad modum tubae" is an independent mass movement; the date of composition is unknown. The Gloria is the second movement of the Mass Ordinary, or the textual portions of the mass that do not change from day to day or season to season (as opposed to the Mass Propers, which do change).

Historical Perspective

Dufay's time was one of transition with regard to musical settings of the mass. By this time, composers were writing complete settings of the Mass Ordinary. (The earliest known setting by one composer is that of Guillaume de Machaut, ca. 1360.) Indeed, Dufay wrote at least seven such mass settings. It was not at all unusual, however, for composers to write settings of single movements of the mass or of pairs of movements (e.g., Kyrie and Gloria, or Sanctus and Agnus Dei). "Gloria ad modum tubae" is such an independent movement.

Technical Considerations

Because the two upper parts are canonic, the entire choir can learn one part and then divide and sing the parts in canon. The conductor may wish to divide the piece into several sections and follow this methodology one section at a time. Dufay supplied no dynamic or articulation markings, so any such directions are editorial and should be followed or not, at the conductor's discretion. A somewhat detached articulation will assist the listener in distinguishing the individual lines and is stylistically appropriate. The original performance space for "Gloria ad modum tubae" would have been quite live acoustically; therefore, a legato articulation would have sounded muddy. The lower parts, whether instrumental or vocal, should utilize similar articulations. Some dynamic contrast would be appropriate, but neither frequent contrasts nor crescendos and diminuendos would be appropriate.

Stylistic Considerations and Musical Elements

"Gloria ad modum tubae" features two voices in canon with two accompanying voices. Dufay labeled the lower "vocal" part *Triplum* and did not label the upper vocal part at all. The two "accompanying" voices were called (top) *Tenor ad modum tubae* and (bottom) *Contratenor ad modum tubae*. Dufay supplied text for the upper two parts but none for the lower. This should not be taken to mean anything concrete, however. In the fifteenth century, it was not unusual for composers to give only partial text underlay (and the extent of Dufay's for this piece varies from one source to another).

It was also not unusual for instruments to double some or all of the parts or for some of the parts to be only instrumental. This clearly opens a world of possibilities for the modern performer, and the conductor is encouraged to experiment with various combinations of voices and instruments. For example, the two upper parts could be SA, TB, or women/men. The piece could also be performed SATB (reading the score from the top down using the notes in the accompaniment) or with tenors and basses singing the canonic parts and soprano and alto singing the accompaniment.

The text for the piece begins "Et in terra pax. . ." This is not the beginning text of the Gloria movement of the Mass, however, so an incipit of "Gloria in excelsis Deo" must be sung before the piece can start; this should be sung by a soloist. Many editions of this piece include an appropriate incipit. If one is not included, or you do not like the one included, you may find other incipits in the *Liber Usualis*. The selected incipit must be transposed to establish the tonality of C major (or whatever key is used).

Form and Structure

The two vocal parts of "Gloria ad modum tubae" are canonic and accompanied by two fanfare-like parts, which function as an ostinato. In fact, this Gloria may be divided into two major sections: mm. 1–32, when the accompanying voices sound only two notes; and mm. 33–55, when the accompanying voices become more adventuresome, even featuring hocket as part of the build-up to the end.

Text and Translation

The text is the Gloria from the Ordinary of the Mass.

Gloria in excelsis Deo.
Et in terra pax hominibus bonae voluntatis.
Laudamus te.
Benedicamus te.
Adoramus te.
Glorificamus te.
Gratias agimus tibi propter magnam gloriam tuam.
Domine Deus, Rex caelestis.
Deus Pater omnipotens.
Domine Fili unigenite,
Jesu Christe.

Domine Deus, Agnus Dei, Filius Patris,
Qui tollis peccata mundi,
miserere nobis.
Qui tollis peccata mundi,
suscipe deprecationem nostram
qui sedes ad dextram Patris,
miserere nobis.

Quoniam tu solus sanctus.
Tu solus Dominus
Tu solus Altissimus,
Jesu Christe.

Cum Sancto Spiritu,
In gloria Dei Patris
Amen.

Glory to God on high.
And on earth peace to men of good will.
We praise thee.
We bless thee.
We adore thee.
We glorify thee.
We give thanks to thee for thy great glory.
O Lord God, heavenly king.
God the Father almighty.
O Lord, the only begotten Son,
Jesus Christ.

Lord God, Lamb of God, Son of the Father,
That takest away the sins of the world,
have mercy on us.
That takest away the sins of the world,
receive our prayer
That sittest at the right hand of the Father,
have mercy on us.

For thou alone art holy.
Thou alone art the Lord
Thou alone art most high,
Jesus Christ.

With the Holy Ghost
In the glory of God the Father
Amen.

Suggested Listening

Dufay: Se la face ay pale. The Early Music Consort of London.
    David Munrow, conductor. (Virgin Veritas VER 5).

Additional Reference and Resources

Fallows, David. *Dufay: The Master Musicians Series.* London: J.M. Dent & Sons, Ltd. 1982.

Contributed by:

Matthew W. Mehaffey
Anthony Reeves

Repertoire Resource Guide

Old Abram Brown

Benjamin Britten
(1913–1976)

SSAA/piano or SATB/piano
Boosey & Hawkes, Inc.: SSAA = OCTB 1787
SATB = OCTB 1786
Overall: 1
Vocal: 1
Tonal/Rhythm: 1

Composer

Benjamin Britten was born in 1913 in Lowestoft, Suffolk, and spent most of his life working as a composer, pianist, and conductor in England. Britten composed a new style of tonal music in an era in which many composers favored esoteric, atonal techniques, which perhaps helped him become one of the most successful English composers in the twentieth century. His output includes operas (most prominently *Peter Grimes*), choral and orchestral works (e.g., *A Hymn to St. Cecelia*, *A Ceremony of Carols*, and *War Requiem*), and music for films, radio, and stage.

Composition

"Old Abram Brown" is the final composition in a set of twelve entitled *Friday Afternoons*. Britten wrote the set for the Clive House School choir in Prestatyn, North Wales, where his brother was headmaster. Originally written for boys choir and piano, it could be performed with any collection of children's voices.

Technical Considerations

The piece contains a single melodic line, sung initially in unison but primarily in canon. Conductors will consequently be able to teach "Old Abram Brown" quickly. The two phrases of this melody move largely by step. The largest leap is an octave (from E to E), a surprising finish to the first phrase. Conductors will need to help singers—especially young ones—prepare for this leap across their vocal breaks to prevent scooping to the pitch. The second phrase has a series of four- to six-note descents down the scale, which have a tendency to sound flat. Asking singers for a different character for each repetition of the motive will help them to avoid stagnation and loss of pitch. Also, rehearse the motive on the syllable "pum," closing quickly to the "m"; the tuning should be more precise and become comfortable in the singers' ears. Finally, practice this line by having singers stop at the two upward leaps of a third to ensure that their pitch remains high.

Conductors will need to attend to the length of consonants. The text has several words with prominent "m" and "n" sounds—"Abram Brown," "gone," "buttoned down"—and in frequent repetition they have a tendency to close and mute. Given their repetition in the canon texture, this would substantially dull the sound. Conductors must teach their singers to recognize and be attentive to this potential problem. Have the choir speak the four-voice canon in rhythm, focusing on the length of their consonants and vowels. In addition, the choir should sing through the commas that divide each of the two lines (after "gone" and "coat") so that the phrases do not feel awkwardly clipped by the final consonants.

The penultimate section, in which the voices split into four and each voice sings the motive twice in a row, must accomplish two dynamic goals. One, the section begins piano with *poco a poco* crescendo to forte: this contrast must happen gradually enough so that the music does not lose momentum by reaching peak volume too early. Two, singers must at the same time leave some sound in reserve so that they can sing fortissimo when the motive stretches to double time. Conductors must build the crescendo concretely into the lines. Tell singers at what dynamic level to sing at each key moment (when it starts, halfway through the text, as it cadences, and again for each in the second repetition of the motive).

Stylistic Considerations

Britten sets the music in the style of a funeral dirge, heard primarily in the trudging piano accompaniment. Its texture changes to signal the changes in the number and character of the canon voices above it; this is most striking during the pounding, dissonant, marcato chords when the melody doubles in time. The accompaniment holds the primary harmonic interest; allow it to play a prominent role in coloring the performance rather than acting only as support.

The tempo called for is *Andante alle Marcia funebre*, so slightly slower than walking will work best. However, conductors must avoid slowing the tempo too much, as this will bog down the presentation of the canon.

Form and Structure

"Old Abram Brown" is a through-composed canon in E minor.

Text

Old Abram Brown is dead and gone, you'll never see him more;
He used to wear a long brown coat, that buttoned down before.

Suggested Listening

A Ceremony of Carols/A Boy Was Born. Copenhagen Boy's Choir. 1953. (Decca Classics 436394).

Contributed by:

Chris Bartley

Repertoire Resource Guide

Simple Gifts (Shaker Song)

Aaron Copland
(1900–1990)

TB/piano, SA/piano, or SATB/piano
Boosey & Hawkes, Inc.: TB = M-051-41903-6,
SA = M-051-41903-6, SATB = M-051-47266-6
arranged by Irving Fine
Overall: 1
Vocal: 1
Tonal/Rhythm: 2

Composer

Aaron Copland was born on November 14, 1900, in Brooklyn, New York. Growing up, he studied piano and music theory, and at age twenty enrolled in the American Conservatory at Fontainebleau, France. There he studied with the renowned teacher Nadia Boulanger for four years. While in Paris, he met many significant musical figures and composers and was exposed to the modern European music of the time. After his return to America, Copland taught at the New School for Social Research and traveled widely, especially to Mexico and Latin America. His music reflects numerous influences, including jazz, American folk music, and Latin American music. He is, arguably, the quintessential American composer. His music includes two operas as well as numerous film scores, songs, symphonies, concertos, ballets, and other significant works. Copland died in Westchester, New York, on December 2, 1990.

Composition

Copland composed "Simple Gifts" for solo voice and piano as a part of his *Old American Songs* in 1950. Copland's friend Irving Fine, a teacher and composer, made the choral adaptation of the song with Copland's permission in 1952. The accompaniment for both arrangements is the same. Such choral adaptations of solo songs are common, and much of Copland's choral music was arranged by Fine. (It should be noted, however, that Copland's output includes several choral pieces, e.g., "In the Beginning" and "Las Agachadas.")

Technical Considerations

The two choral parts are notated soprano (tenor) and alto (bass). While male or female choirs can accomplish effective performances of this music, it could also work well sung by a mixed choir as ST/AB.

The performance direction of "Quietly flowing" and the suggested metronome marking of quarter note = 72 reflect the mood of the piece. The melody, now widely-known, is an early American tune, and Copland's music reflects the simplicity of Americana and the text of the song ("'Tis the gift to be simple..."). The singing should be vocally free and legato. For less experienced choirs, this piece can be a wonderful teaching tool for good resonance and breath support.

The music is in 2/4 and should be conducted that way, with a smooth gesture. The choir should be told to reflect the textual stress in their singing, a matter made much easier by Copland's text setting. The first two notes sung, for example, are anacrustic. The choir should sing them that way, leading to the first strong beat and the first important word. The trick is to point out where the strong beats occur and decide on the most important word in each phrase, which will help the choir artistically accomplish the phrasing much more easily.

Two notated breath marks occur in the piece on pages one and four. This is not meant to imply, of course, that those are the only breathing places, simply that they are mandatory ones. They function as phrase markings and perhaps call for a little extra time. Other breaths may be taken at appropriate places in the music; they make more sense and are easier to accomplish if they occur where punctuation marks exist in the text. The fermatas may be followed by breaths, but if the choir is capable of finishing the phrase without a breath, it can make for a beautiful performance.

Stylistic Considerations

The music bears two notations at the bottom: 1) "To be sung freely, without rigid adherence to strict rhythm" and 2) "Conductors of male choruses may find this arrangement more effective in the key of B-flat." The first note quoted above is the essence of the style of this piece. Rhythmic freedom and reasonable use of rubato is necessary to be Copland's advocate. It is highly doubtful that Shaker housewives kept a strict metrical rhythm as they sang folksongs while sweeping the house!

Form and Structure

This piece consists of two similar musical strophes, or verses, each preceded by a short passage in the piano. A similar piano passage follows the second verse, concluding the piece. The composition is in A-flat major with an unsurprising modulation to E-flat major in the middle.

Additional References and Resources

Copland, Aaron. *What to Listen for in Music*. New York: McGraw-Hill, Inc. 1985.

Contributed by:

Lani Johnson

Level Two

Mixed voices:

Ave verum corpus, Op. 2, No. 1	Elgar, Edward	111
Dadme albricias, hijos d'Eva	Anonymous	115
Die Nachtigall, Op. 59, No. 4	Mendelssohn (Bartholdy), Felix	119
El Grillo	Desprez, Josquin	123
Erev Shel Shoshanim	Dor, Moshe/Hadar, Josef	127
Jasmine Flower	arr. Ling-Tam, Jing	131
Psallite	Praetorius, Michael	134
Silent Devotion and Response	Bloch, Ernest	137

Treble voices:

Fire	Goetze, Mary	140
Gloria tibi	Bernstein, Leonard	143
Savory, Sage, Rosemary and Thyme	Patriquin, Donald	147
The Snow, Op.26, No. 1	Elgar, Edward	151
Three Choral Pieces	Berger, Jean	154

Men's voices:

Der Herr segne euch	Bach, J. S.	157
Let Us Now Praise Famous Men, Op. 35	Finzi, Gerald	160
My Bonnie	arr. Parker, Alice/Shaw, Robert	164
Poor Man Lazrus	arr. Hairston, Jester	167
She Moved Through the Fair	arr. Takach, Timothy	170
Si iniquitates observaveris	Wesley, Samuel	172
Sometimes I Feel Like a Motherless Child	arr. Gilbert, Nina	175

Repertoire Resource Guide

Ave verum corpus, Op. 2, No. 1

Edward Elgar
(1857–1934)

SATB/keyboard
Novello Publications: 032095R
Overall: 2
Vocal: 2
Tonal/Rhythm: 2

Composer

Edward Elgar was one the generation of English composers known as the Neo-romantics. Unlike most of his contemporaries, Elgar was born, raised, and died a Catholic. His father was a piano tuner and church organist, and Elgar learned to play violin at a young age. The young Elgar had no formal training in music beyond instruction in keyboard and violin; he worked in Broadheath (his hometown) as a church organist in the 1880s. In 1890, Elgar moved to London, where the audiences gave his compositions only a lukewarm reception. Consequently, he moved to Worcester in 1891.

Elgar is best known for his *Enigma Variations* (1899), his oratorio *The Dream of Gerontius* (1900), and perhaps best of all for his *Pomp and Circumstance* marches. After his wife's death in 1920, he lost the will to compose. He died in 1934, and was unable to be buried at Westminster Abbey because of his Catholicism.

Composition

This short motet with organ accompaniment can be used liturgically or as a concert piece. It is scored for SATB choir and organ. Motets of this length and ease can prove difficult to find from this era. One can see elements of the English cathedral style in this writing, but it contains far less "pomp" than many of the Anglican anthems.

Historical Perspective

Elgar's Catholicism comes to the forefront with his composition of "Ave verum corpus." This early motet (1887) is in a very simple style, and is similar to his other motets, "Ave Maria" and "Ave maris stella," both of which are believed to date from around the same time as "Ave verum corpus." It is notable that all three motets are settings of ancient devotional texts. "Ave verum" is a Eucharistic hymn, "Ave maris" is a Vesper hymn, and "Ave Maria" is the best known of the Marian prayers. As a devout Roman Catholic, Elgar would have known all three texts from early in his life. His simple yet elegant settings could be imagined to be musical prayers, which would account for the lack of pomp already noted.

Other notable settings of the "Ave verum corpus" text include those by William Byrd (another English Catholic), Mozart, Liszt, and Francis Poulenc. It is interesting that all of these pieces are in contrasting styles and would make for interesting sets when used in concert.

Technical Considerations

This piece contains few difficult vocal problems. The voice parts are in a limited range and usually move diatonically; the chromaticism is almost all stepwise. Breath support and high, forward resonance are important aspects of a successful performance.

Stylistic Considerations

Because Elgar was exposed to the English cathedral tradition, the question of Latin pronunciation becomes important. Because Italians say the word "spaghetti" differently from Americans (the "eh" vowel in particular), it is wrong for Americans to say they understand "Italian Latin" without ever considering how vernacular sounds affect the pronunciation of Latin. In the United States, Bostonians speak differently from people from Alabama. Elgar would have had particular vowel sounds in his ears when he was composing this piece, or any other. To ignore the style of pronunciation, therefore, is to completely ignore style. One must approach the Latin in this piece (or of any piece, for that matter) with the composer's vernacular vowel sounds and voice colors in mind. Adding an "Anglified" pronunciation to the typical Latin vowels will unlock a world of color possibilities to you and your choir. Just think of how Queen Elizabeth speaks!

Musical Elements

The opening soprano line is very melodic and reminiscent of Elgar's songs for solo voice. It should be sung tunefully and with forward motion. It is important to take care to breathe where the Latin text is punctuated and not to breathe when there is no punctuation. For the members of the choir who know the Mozart setting, this may be difficult because they are probably accustomed to breathing after specific words. The two pieces' phrase construction is quite different, however, and using the "Mozart" breath pattern in the Elgar will undermine a successful musical line.

Form and Structure

The piece is in two sections, followed by a short coda. In each major section, the sopranos sing the melody, which is then repeated and accompanied by the choir. The form is AABBC.

Text and Translation

The text is a short Eucharistic hymn believed to have been written in the thirteenth century. It is most commonly sung on the feast of Corpus Christi (Body of Christ). According to arranger and author Ron Jeffers, "The text of 'Ave verum corpus' commemorates Christ's redemptive Sacrifice, and especially focuses on the great symbol of Baptism: the pouring forth of water from his pierced side."

Ave verum corpus, natum (ex) [de] Maria Virgine,
Vere passum, immolatum in cruce pro homine,
Cujus latus perforatum, unda fluxit sanguine,
Esto nobis praegustatum in mortis examine.
(O Clemens), O [Jesu] pie,
O [Jesu] dulcis, [O] Jesu Fili Mariae,
[Miserere mei. Amen.]

Hail, true Body, born of the Virgin Mary,
Who has truly suffered, was sacrificed on the cross for mortals,
Whose side was pierced, whence flowed water and blood:
Be for us a foretaste (of heaven) during our final examining.
O (merciful), O [Jesu] sweet,
O [Jesu] pure, O [Jesu], Son of Mary,
[Have mercy upon me. Amen.]

Words in brackets were omitted by Elgar from the full text. Words in parentheses were added by Elgar.

Suggested Listening

Elgar: Cathedral Music. Worcester Cathedral Choir. Donald Hunt, conductor. (Hyperion Records CDH55147).

Dance, my heart. The Girls and Men of Sheffield Cathedral. Peter Heginbotham, conductor. (Lammas Records LAMM133).

Additional Reference and Resources

Jeffers, Ron. *Translations and Annotations of Choral Repertoire. Volume I: Sacred Latin Texts*. Corvallis, Oregon: Earthsongs. 1988.

Contributed by:

Anthony Reeves

Repertoire Resource Guide

Dadme albricias, hijos d'Eva

Anonymous

SATB
Edited by Noah Greenberg
Associated Music Publishers, Inc.: NYPM 9
Overall: 2
Vocal: 2
Tonal/Rhythm: 2

Composition

"Dadme albricias, hijos d'Eva" is a choral setting of a Spanish *villancico* (see below under Text). This *villancico* is from the *Cancionero de Upsala*, a 1556 manuscript containing fifty-four *villancicos*.

Historical Perspective

The *villancico* in the sixteenth century was a form of Spanish poetry with an *estribillo*, or refrain, alternating with strophes. The lines are usually eight syllables long, but the number of lines is variable. Musically, the *villancico* is a refrain verse form similar to the French *virelai* and the Italian *ballata*. Various forms of *villancicos* exist; "Dadme albricias" is a type called the dialogue, because of the vocal exchange in the text. The *villancico* has a folk-dance and naturalistic rhythmic character and was very popular. Originally quite varied as to subject, the *villancico del Navidad* (Christmas *villancico*) eventually became the dominant type and was the only kind to have survived. Consequently, the word *villancico* is now sometimes used synonymously with Christmas carol.

Technical Considerations

"Dadme albricias, hijos d'Eva" is a brisk, light, dance-like piece and must be sung as such. Spanish is much preferred to the English text. (Be sure to provide a translation for the audience.) Teach the text first on a neutral syllable ("du" would work well), and select a moderate tempo in three. When the notes and rhythms are correct, and they really are not very difficult, gradually pick up the tempo and make the transition into one beat per measure. Then slow the tempo again, and ask the choir to chant the text on a single pitch, which is comfortable for everyone, but using the rhythms of the music. Once the diction has been mastered, gradually increase the tempo again. Finally, when the diction can be chanted at performance tempo, have them add the notes of the music back to the words.

Articulations should be crisp, perhaps close to staccato if you have a "live" performance space. Whatever degree of detachment you choose, however, it is mandatory that the music feel light and dance-like, with much sense of forward motion. This may prove difficult if the choir is unaccustomed to singing in Spanish, but practice (and consistent insistence on the part of the director) will make perfect!

Stylistic Considerations

There is nothing to say this music has to be, or even should be, performed *a cappella*. At the very least, rhythm instruments (e.g., tambourine and drum) would be stylistically appropriate. Other instruments, such as a consort of recorders or strings, or even a broken consort (mixed kinds of instruments) may double the parts in all or any part of the music. Guitar accompaniment works nicely as well. The solo and tutti indications are editorial, not mandatory. They are stylistically appropriate, however, and probably will make the performance more effective, particularly in the first section. An exciting performance could probably be obtained by observing the solo/tutti marks with a drum keeping the beat throughout the piece. (The drum should keep some kind of ostinato, perhaps playing one beat per measure or doubling the rhythm of the melody.) A consort of instruments could play with the tutti sections, and tambourine could join for section B. Be sure to crescendo during the last couple measures of section B each time.

Musical Elements

This music is simple and has dance-like qualities. The rhythms have to dance; be wary, however, of the tendency (especially prevalent in fast triple-meter music) to rush. The tonality is F major throughout, with very few accidentals.

Form and Structure

Villancicos can have various rhyme schemes. The scheme used in "Dadme albricias, hijos d'Eva" is consonant. The musical form of this piece can be simply described as:

Section	Measure
A	1–12
B	13–25
C	26–41
A	42–53
B	54–66

Text and Translation

¡Dadme albricias, hijos d'Eva!
Di, de qué dártelas han?
Qu'es nacido el nuevo Adám.
¡Oh, hí de Dios, y qué nueva!

Dádmelas y haved plazer,
Pues esta noche es nacido
El Mexías prometído,
Dios y hombre, de mujer.

Y su nacer nos releva
del peccado y su afán.
Qu'es nacido el nuevo Adám.
¡Oh, hí de Dios, y qué nueva!

Rejoice, oh Children of Eve!
Tell me, why should they rejoice?
Because the new Adam has been born.
Oh Lord! What news!

Be happy and rejoice,
For this night has been born
Of woman the promised Messiah,
Both God and man.

And his birth relieves us
From sin, and from longing for it.
For the new Adam has been born.
Oh Lord! What news!

Contributed by:

Anthony Reeves

Repertoire Resource Guide

Die Nachtigall, Op. 59, No. 4
Felix Mendelssohn (Bartholdy)
(1809–1847)

SATB/a cappella
Golden Music: G-145
Overall: 2
Vocal: 2
Tonal/Rhythm: 2

Composer

One of the favorite Romantic composers, Felix Mendelssohn (Bartholdy) grew up in Berlin, the child of a German Jewish banker whose establishment survived until the Nazi era. Most of the extended and eminent family converted to one or the other branch of Christianity, and Felix's parents added Bartholdy to the Mendelssohn name when they did so. Both Felix and his older sister, Fanny, showed early musical promise and were given excellent training. Fanny may have been slightly the better pianist, but Felix was no poor pianist himself and also showed talent in score reading, transposing, and drawing. He studied violin and organ and was a "usable," as his conductor commented, choral singer, simultaneously studying counterpoint, drawing, painting, and the Classics.

Mendelssohn's first ambitious work, staged with orchestra to celebrate his twelfth birthday, was written in 1820. So began a prodigious though short career of composition, encompassing dramatic and programmatic works, *Lieder*, sacred choral works, concerti, large symphonic works, arrangements of the old masters, and instrumental solo and chamber pieces—but no grand operas (virtually the only genre in which he did not compose). Mendelssohn served as director of several major German choral societies and spearheaded the movement to study and compile the works of the old masters.

He married in 1837, amid composing and preparing his two completed oratorios, *Paul* and *Elijah*. Only two years after the death of his beloved sister Fanny, he died of a series of strokes at the age of thirty-eight.

Composition

For some reason many conductors in the U.S. believe that the German language is ill-suited to melody because it is "too guttural." This sentiment seems to proliferate among inexperienced musicians, having been passed down from the preceding generation in the company of several other defeatist myths. Of course, the statement flies in the face of multitudinous contrary evidence—the corpus of German-language vocal pieces of all genres—but it presents a perceptible roadblock to the conductor, especially of high school, undergraduate, and newly formed community choirs. This short choral song, composed on a rhymed and metered quatrain, is a good one to introduce singing in German.

Historical Perspective

Mendelssohn and his colleagues spanned the Classical, Romantic, and post-Romantic periods. Beethoven died and Brahms was born in the 1830s, just after the Mendelssohn-energized revival of the Bach St. Matthew Passion. Living at the same time were superb composers, poets, writers of prose, performing virtuosi, visual artists, philosophers, and scientists. Germany was a center of artistic and societal development during the era that led to both the Industrial Revolution and the growth of nationalism.

The folksong-based "Die Nachtigall" fits snugly in the middle class-enlivened artistic culture of the mid-nineteenth century.

Technical Considerations

Despite its date of composition, the language, and plethora of sixteenth notes, "Die Nachtigall" is suitable for inexperienced choirs and should be an audience-pleaser.

The tessitura is not to be feared. The sopranos rise, and the basses sink to A-flats, but only for an instant, twice in each voice. Sopranos who are uncomfortable with the A-flat5 could sing the alto C5 in place of that note. The A-flats will still sound sufficiently. The same is true for young bass-baritones without A-flats; use the tenor C.

The German is the next consideration. Once the conductor is convinced of the pronunciation of the poem, he or she should read it aloud in character. The text is tremendously forgiving because there is only one each of the umlaut, ach-laut, and ich-laut.

The 3/8 meter is not difficult. Conductors could help the chorus by using a macro pattern in one that demonstrates the phrase length and shape.

Look carefully at harmonic structure and density, and avoid difficulties with chromatic inflections in mm. 26–35 by examining what Mendelssohn does there and how each line sounds by itself and in relation to others.

Stylistic Considerations

This is a folksong. There is no need to try to make it heavily meaningful. Apply a sprightly light touch to tempo and color. Ask for clear articulations even before you attach text to the notes, and make sure that from the earliest learning experience on each singer understands and executes appropriate stress to selected downbeat notes—first beat of real measure 1, followed next by the downbeats of measures 3 and 5, for instance. The stress should not be on every downbeat or (worse) on every note because this creates a pedestrian stomp. Follow the contour of the notes; Mendelssohn has provided ample clues.

Throughout the piece, voices temporarily carry the melody. Each section should know when to sing the melody and when to hand it to others and recede from prominence. As is typical of Mendelssohn, the song is strewn with expressive markings. The conductor and singer's challenge is more to observe than deduce the expressions. Luckily, the piece is not weighty, so neither are the markings. Forte is soon followed by pianissimo. The most delicate realization is the crescendo over three measures (starting at m. 33) from *pp* to *p*.

The soprano and bass *sforzando* in the penultimate measure needs some work to sound clearly and only in the two sections.

Form and Structure

The four lines of text are set to two musical phrases comprising a ten-measure period, which is extended by repeating a few words for a nice even twelve measures. Then the voices shift parts and sing it all again twice: AA'A" plus a cute coda. Only the final iteration of the text and music strays from A-flat major, and the excursion is necessarily short—though it interestingly modulates around the circle of fifths—because the end of the piece is imminent.

The entire first statement of the text and music is given to a duet in soprano and alto. They hand the same lines of music to the tenors and basses, which continue, still in duet, to embellish above, first with a phrase in the same rhythm as the two lower voices and then in a canon displaced by one measure with the unison line. All voices come together in measure 10 of this section; only the lower three continue with the codetta. For the final statement, sopranos carry the melody; altos again sing their first line; tenors filigree a middle-voice variant of the soprano A' section; and basses have a rooting line rich in pedal tones. Everyone contributes to the coda, from measure 37 to the end, which progressively fractures the last phrase of the poem, much like a tweeting bird flitting further and further away.

Text and Translation

Die Nachtigall, sie war entfernt, der Frühling lockt sie wieder;
was neues hat sie nicht gelernt, singt alte liebe Lieder.

The nightingale was far away, now spring calls her back.
Nothing new has she learned, she sings the old beloved songs.

Suggested Listening

Felix Mendelssohn Bartholdy: Geistliche und Weltliche Chormusik. Georg Ratzinger, conductor. (Ars musici 1117).

Contributed by:

Lani Johnson

Repertoire Resource Guide

El Grillo

Josquin Desprez
(ca. 1440–1521)

SATB/a cappella
Warner Bros. Publications: LG 51025
Overall: 2
Vocal: 2
Tonal/Rhythm: 2

Composer

Josquin Desprez was one of the most prolific composers of the Renaissance. Scholars believe he was born in Picardy, France, ca. 1440. Very little is known about his early life; the earliest primary evidence is a 1459 notice that lists Josquin as a singer at Milan Cathedral. In 1474, he was a singer in the chapel of Duke Galeazzo Maria Sforza in Milan. Josquin probably went to work for King René of Anjou in 1477 and was sent to the king's duchy of Bar in 1478. Josquin traveled widely and worked in numerous places. He may have worked for King Louis XII from 1501 to 1503, and we know he was *maestro di cappella* at the Court of Ferrara in 1503. By 1508, Josquin was a cleric at Notre Dame Cathedral in Condé-sur-Escaut, Hainaut (France). Apparently, he remained there the rest of his life. He died in Condé August 27, 1521.

Josquin's musical output is impressive, including about twenty masses, more than one hundred motets, and around seventy-five secular works (mostly French *chansons*, but also including Italian-texted pieces and a few instrumental works).

Composition

"El Grillo" is an Italian, madrigalesque composition. The only surviving manuscript of the piece dates from 1505 and lists the composer as Josquin Dascanio. The piece features imitative and homophonic textures and much text-painting.

Historical Perspective

Madrigals were originally a poetic and musical form of fourteenth-century Italy. The popular sixteenth-century madrigal was only distantly related to its ancestor. The earliest printed volume, called *Madrigali*, dates from 1530, but by the 1520s the genre was present in manuscript form. Florentine composers seem to have been the primary crafters of this new genre, which featured poetry set essentially in a homophonic style with graceful imitative passages and sensitivity to textual meaning. That Josquin would have anticipated such a style is unsurprising, given his creativity and wide travel.

Technical and Stylistic Considerations

"El Grillo" is for SATB choir. While a typical SATB configuration can work quite well for this piece, at least a few male altos would lend a particularly authentic and picturesque color. The alto part is low, and if men are not available to double the part throughout, it is highly recommended that some tenors reinforce the altos when they go far below the treble staff (and below the tenors).

A lively tempo is necessary for this piece to work well, but this has to be tempered by what the singers can realistically do with the text. (More experienced singers can probably accomplish a faster tempo than less experienced ones.) The conductor should definitely conduct the piece in two.

Josquin did not indicate dynamics in the music, and sudden extreme changes would be unstylistic. Every effort should be made, however, to support the meaning of the text by gently varying dynamics with articulation and attitudinal changes. The beginning of the piece, for example, is declamatory, featuring longer note values; a well-placed mezzo forte to forte sound would be appropriate. After the first three bars, as the note values decrease and the telling of the story begins, the articulations should be more detached and a slight decrease of dynamic can be effective. In measures 7–9, the sopranos and basses should be cautioned against singing too loudly and the altos and tenors should be encouraged to emphasize their imitation. Measures 11–14 feature antiphonal singing, which can be greatly enhanced by asking singers to emphasize the first (and naturally accented) syllables of each word and deemphasize the second syllables. Measures 15–16 use onomatopoeia, imitating the sounds of crickets. Clarity of consonants and rhythmic security, combined with continued attention to appropriate syllabic emphasis, yield beautiful results. Measures 17–21 repeat the music of measures 1–5, and should be performed similarly.

The next section of the piece (mm. 17–31) is homophonic and calls for attention to balance, syllabic stress, and phrasing. The telling of the story is the important thing in this section.

Measures 32–41, the third main section of the piece, remain essentially homophonic, except for the interesting counterpoint in the concluding three bars. Once again, the singing should be clean and reinforce the meaning of the text. Throughout the piece, longer note values should move musically and not remain static. Encouraging singers to have all accented syllables diminuendo and all unaccented syllables crescendo can assist singers in declaiming the text. This may seem illogical, but it is the diminuendo of an accented syllable that makes an unaccented syllable sound unaccented to the listener's ear; the converse is true as well. It should be noted that in this section we are not speaking of long dramatic crescendos and dimuendos, but of small, tasteful gestures (a beat or two long) that help to clarify the text and phrasing.

Form and Structure

A(aba)BA':

Section	Measure	Event and Scoring
A	1–21	
a	1–10	Declamatory introduction, terminating in imitation leading to cadence; "The cricket is a good singer. . ."
b	11–16	Antiphonal section leads to onomatopoeia; "Sing of good times…"
a	17–21	Opening declamatory section repeated; "The cricket is a good singer. . ."
B	22–31	Homophonic section dedicated to text painting; more introspective part of poem; "But he's not like the other birds. . ."
A'	32–41	Declamatory section, with contrapuntal "coda" leading to final cadence; "When the weather is at its hottest. . ."

Text and Translation

El grillo è buon cantore
Che tiene longo verso.
Dale beve, grillo, canta!
El grillo è buon cantore.
Ma non fa come gli altri uccelli;
Come il han cantato un poco,
Van' de fatto in altro loco:
Sempre el grillo sta pur saldo.
Quando la maggior el clado,
Alhor canta sol per amore.

The cricket is a good singer
Who holds a long verse.
Sing of good times, cricket!
The cricket is a good singer.
But he's not like the other birds;
as soon as they have sung a while,
they are off somewhere else:
the cricket always stays put.
When the weather is at its hottest,
then he just sings for love.

Suggested Listening

Josquin: Motets and Chansons. Hilliard Ensemble. (EMI 749-209-2 CD).

Additional Reference and Resources

Charles, Sydney Robinson. *Josquin des Prez: A Guide to Research*. New York: Garland Publishing, Inc. 1983.

Sherr, R., editor. *The Josquin Companion*. (Oxford, forthcoming).

Contributed by:

Anthony Reeves

Repertoire Resource Guide

Erev Shel Shoshanim

Moshe Dor
(b. 1932)

Josef Hadar

SATB/piano
arranged by Jack Klebanow
World Music Press: WMP 03
Overall: 2
Vocal: 2
Tonal/Rhythm: 2

Composer

Moshe Dor and Josef Hadar wrote this piece, which is now largely considered a "traditional" Israeli song. Although Moshe Dor wrote the melody, he is actually a Bialik Prize-winning poet and has published ten volumes of poetry and multiple children's books, essays, and literary interviews. Born in Tel Aviv in 1932, Dor did his undergraduate work in history and political science. His poetry is marked by a sense of struggle with his Jewish heritage and with his relationship to the state of Israel, although this piece has come to symbolize the connection of the disparate Jewish communities all over the world to Israel. He has recently been the writer-in-residence at American University.

Composition

This piece is a favorite at Jewish weddings and of Jewish folk ensembles. It is often referred to as a folk melody, though it was composed in the 1950s. It became extremely popular in the 1960s, both in Israel and in Jewish communities worldwide, especially through the recordings of Oranim Zabar and Harry Belafonte and Miriam Makeba. The text is reminiscent of the Song of Solomon, but the lyrics are not a direct quote. The piece is also popular throughout the Middle East in a variety of translations, and it is often used as a dance piece, including for belly dancing.

Historical Perspective

Composed in a folk style, this song maintains a clear connection to the long tradition of Jewish folksong. It became popular at the time that the newly created state of Israel was struggling to establish its identity as a Jewish homeland, and it served for many in the far-flung communities as a reminder of their connection to Israel and their Jewish heritage.

Technical Considerations

Rhythms in this piece are simple, comprised of straightforward quarter notes and eighth note pairs. The range throughout is moderate, even in the coda. The moments of modal mixture introduce occasional chromatic motion, though this is usually through half-step ascent or descent and never by leap. The melodic lines in all of the parts, especially the soprano countermelody, are long and sustained, calling for careful support of the extended shapes. The piano accompaniment is not difficult.

Stylistic Considerations

The phrasing and articulation in this piece are straightforward and follow the contours of the song's melody, which is almost always carried in the alto voice. The origin of this work should inform the stylistic decisions made in performance. The intimacy of the text is reflected in the delicate piano part and in the expressive marking, "tenderly." The countermelody of the coda starts out as a whisper, which crescendos to forte after seven measures before quickly falling away, further emphasizing the dramatic component of the original song.

Musical Elements

This piece remains solidly in C minor, but there are instances of modal mixture that hint at other related keys. Chord construction is largely triadic, although added tones abound in inner voices. Non-chord tones typically resolve logically and are often suspensions from previous harmonies. Cadences are strong at the end of each section, and the harmonic progression, while modal, is fairly simple. There are no strongly dissonant sections, and any passing dissonances are amply supported by the piano part.

The voices are largely homophonic. Because the melody is in the alto throughout, the harmonizing soprano voice carries the flavor of the countermelody. The melodic lines in every voice part either move stepwise or leap to chord tones.

Form and Structure

This piece mimics the structure of a song with verses and choruses, and there is an interesting extended coda at the end of the work. After a four-measure piano introduction based on the harmonies of the chorus, the eleven-measure verse and the eight-measure chorus alternate through two cycles. In the eighteen-measure coda, the harmonies of the verse and coda return, but without the originally stated melody. Instead, the chorus sings a counter-melody against the piano, which is derived from melodic material. Not until the final seven measures does the melody return, closing the piece with the second phrase of the chorus.

Text and Translation

Erev shel shoshanim
Neytsena habustan
Mor besamim ulevona
Le raglech miftan...

Evening of roses
Let us go out to the grove
Myrrh, fragrant spices and incense
Are a threshold for your feet...

Contributed by:

Thomas Cunningham

Repertoire Resource Guide

Jasmine Flower

arr. Jing Ling-Tam
(b. 1953)

SATB/piano
Alliance Music Publications: AMP-0183
Overall: 2
Vocal: 2
Tonal/Rhythm: 1

Composer

Jing Ling-Tam is professor of music and director of choral studies at the University of Texas at Arlington. She has conducted all-state choirs and honor choirs throughout the United States and has appeared as conductor and clinician at the American Choral Directors Association's regional and national conventions. A native of Taiwan, she holds advanced degrees in piano performance and vocal performance from the New England Conservatory and the University of North Texas. Ling-Tam is also the Artistic Director of the American Chamber Choir and Associate Conductor with the Fort Worth Opera Association. Alliance Music of Houston, Texas, publishes a choral series in her name.

Composition

"Jasmine Flower" is a setting of a popular Chinese folksong for SATB choir and piano, including an optional percussion part with glockenspiel, antique finger cymbals, and mark tree. The addition of percussion helps evoke the song's Chinese origins.

Although the translation given in the score describes only the beauties of the jasmine flower, the Chinese text uses the jasmine flower as a symbol for a beautiful woman departing for her wedding day. One of the lines makes it clear that the singer yearns for the woman even though she is marrying another. It is a poignant song of loss clothed in a text of simple beauty.

Historical Perspective

Western choral music has long been influenced by the European folk tradition, and it has more recently shown the influences of the folk traditions of the wider world. This piece is part of a growing body of choral music that marries Western compositional practices with the folksong repertoire from non-Western cultures. Simple settings such as this one highlight the role that children play in the dissemination of folksongs across cultural boundaries.

Technical Considerations

The rhythms of this work are extremely simple, featuring simple patterns of eighth notes and quarter notes in 4/4 time. The sopranos, altos, and basses all reach a high G-flat, and the tenors ascend to a high B-flat, presenting possible difficulties in execution. The light, airy style of the setting suggests the performance of the highest notes for the men in *falsetto*.

This "black-key" setting of a pentatonic traditional Chinese melody contains no chromaticism and has no difficult melodic leaps. The piano accompaniment, however, becomes increasingly difficult as the piece progresses, culminating in sixteenth note runs in both hands. The overall mood is one of quiet celebration of the beauties of the jasmine flower.

Musical Elements

The melody of this folksong is pentatonic and set in G-flat major so that every note of the melody falls on a black key on the piano. The first two iterations of the melody are set entirely in unison or in octaves, but the third time through the choir sings three independent melody lines. Although parts of these new vocal lines are newly composed, they still adhere to the pentatonic construction of the traditional melody. The meter is an unchanging 4/4.

Form and Structure

This work is in three parts. The first two parts state the principal melody in unison or in octaves, and the third part creates a three-part polyphonic texture based on that melody. The accompaniment becomes increasingly florid under each of these three iterations of the melody. A short coda closes the work.

Text and Translation

How i duo mei li di mwo li hwa
Fun fang mei li mahn juh yah,
Yoh siang yoh bai jun jun ai
Jahn wuo lai dsiang ni jai sia,
Song gei bie jun dsiah
Mwo li hwa a mwo li hwa.

Oh how lovely jasmine flower!
Gracious beauty blossoms sweet,
Fragrant, chaste, and all adore.
Petals gathered bright and pure,
Share my joy with you.
Jasmine flower, oh, jasmine flower!

Contributed by:

Thomas Cunningham

Repertoire Resource Guide

Psallite

Michael Praetorius
(1571–1621)

SATB/continuo, SAB/continuo, SSA/continuo
Bourne Company: SATB= 106586, SAB=310685; SSA=106588
Overall: 2
Vocal: 2
Tonal/Rhythm: 2

Composer

Michael Praetorius was a German composer and theorist who worked most of his life as an organist to the dukes of Brunswick-Wolfenbüttel. He was one of the most prolific and versatile composers of his generation, known especially for his more than one thousand sacred compositions, many based on Protestant hymns or Lutheran liturgical texts. Particularly important to our study of music of his time is his treatise *Syntagma musicum*, which contains descriptions and illustrations of contemporary instruments.

Composition

This piece is a four-voice Christmas carol with text in both Latin and German. While the text is anonymous, it most likely predates Praetorius' setting of it, although the carol itself is thought to be an original Praetorius composition. The mixing of the two languages may have been an effort to make part of the text understandable to the laity by interjecting lines in the vernacular. The work comes from the sixth volume (of nine) of Praetorius' *Musae Sioniae*, an extensive and widely varying collection of sacred music. This volume was published in 1609.

Historical Perspective

This piece was published in the middle of the most productive creative period of Praetorius' life. As the organist and court Kapellmeister for Duke Heinrich Julius of Brunswick-Wolfenbüttel, he traveled extensively in Europe, where he composed most of his collections of music. At the time this piece was composed, his performing forces were probably six to eight singers and a comparable number of instrumentalists. The Reformation had been introduced by the duke to Wolfenbüttel in 1591, and much of Praetorius' music was based on Protestant hymns and Lutheran texts. Praetorius was held in high regard and was in great demand as a musician.

The first four volumes of *Musae Sioniae* contain principally eight-part works for two choirs based on various hymns. In volume five, Praetorius begins a more systematic setting of the German hymn repertoire in settings for two to seven voices. Volumes six to eight contain primarily simple homophonic settings of various hymns, and volume nine concentrates again on the important Lutheran hymns belonging to the church year in settings for two or three voices. The famous "Es ist ein Ros entsprungen" is from the same volume.

Technical Considerations

This is not a technically challenging piece; the rhythms are all straightforward, the melodies are simple, and the phrases are short. The tempo is brisk, but manageable. The range is extremely limited; if the basses sing their one low G up an octave, the lowest note is the D above that G. Sopranos and tenors don't go higher than D. The only tricky technical aspect of this piece is the return of the opening rhythm on the offbeat. This happens only occasionally, but the strong four-square nature of the rhythm might make it more difficult to sing on a weak beat.

Stylistic Considerations

This is a joyous, rhythmic Christmas carol, and it should be sung with a joyous spirit. The opening rhythm is strongly articulated, and the following eighth note melodies have more horizontal motion. The interior German sections are more tender than the outlying Latin sections, providing a measure of contrast in this short piece.

You may perform this piece *a cappella*, or you may choose a whole consort of instruments to accompany the group *colla voce*. Either option is perfectly acceptable.

Musical Elements

This piece is solidly in G major without a single example of strong dissonance. The texture is largely homophonic with occasional moments of simple polyphony. The opening three-note motive recurs throughout the piece, sometimes on the offbeat and once transposed up a fifth.

Form and Structure

The text of this piece is in Latin and German, which splits the work into three parts: opening section in Latin, central section in German, and closing section in Latin. The Latin text is spoken by the angels described in the German text, allowing for some overlap in between the central section and the final section. The German section is constructed of duets, first between the women's parts and then between the men's parts. This mirrors the structure of the Latin sections, although the duets are shorter in the opening and closing sections. The rhythm of the German section is a bit slower, allowing for a contrast between it and the more rhythmic Latin sections. This distinction reflects the contrasts inherent in the text, allowing the sung words of the angels to be more declamatory and the descriptive German words to be more descriptive.

Text and Translation

Psallite, Unigenito, Christo Dei Filio.
Psallite, Redemptori, Domino
puerulo jacenti in praesepio.

Ein kleines Kindelein liegt in dem Krippelein.
Alle liebe Engelein dienen dem Kindelein,
und singen ihm fein.

Sing to Christ, the only-begotten son of God.
Sing to the Redeemer, our Lord,
the child lying in the manger.

A little baby child lies in the little crib.
All the lovely angels serve the little child,
and sing sweetly to him.

Suggested Listening

Psallite! A Renaissance Christmas. Chanticleer. Louis Botto, conductor.
    (Chanticleer CR 8806).

Contributed by:

Thomas Cunningham

Repertoire Resource Guide

Silent Devotion and Response

Ernest Bloch
(1880–1959)

SATB/optional organ
Broude Brothers Limited: BB 179
Overall: 2
Vocal: 2
Tonal/Rhythm: 2

Composer

Swiss born composer Ernest Bloch began his early studies in violin and composition in his native Geneva, where he studied with Emile Jaques-Dalcroze among others. In the late 1800s and early 1900s, Bloch lived and studied in Brussels, Paris, Frankfurt, and Munich. He ultimately returned home to Geneva to marry and to run his father's bookkeeping and tourism business. During this time, he continued to compose and conduct.

In 1916, Bloch traveled to the United States to work as a conductor for a touring dance company. When the tour failed in 1917, Bloch became one of the first faculty members of the nascent Mannes School of Music in New York City, where he taught theory and composition. In 1920, Bloch became the founding director of the Cleveland Institute of Music. There, he taught a variety of courses, established masterclasses, and proposed radical reforms like the abandonment of textbooks in favor of musical experience and performance of the great composers.

In 1918, he signed a publishing contract with G. Schirmer; the resulting publications, adorned with a six-pointed Star of David with E. B. in the center, established Bloch as a "Jewish composer." Over the next decade, many successful performances of his works, particularly his "Jewish" works, occurred throughout the eastern United States.

In the 1930s Bloch returned to live and Switzerland and maintained an active conducting and composing schedule. (It was during this time that he composed *Sacred Service*.) In 1940, due to rising anti-Semitism and his desire to retain his American citizenship, he accepted a position at University of California at Berkeley where he taught until his retirement in 1952. He died of cancer in 1959 while living in Oregon.

Composition

"Silent Devotion and Response," a musical setting of Psalm 19:14, is a movement from Ernest Bloch's *Sacred Service* or *Avodath hakodesh*, which was written from 1930–33. It is the central movement (No. 7) of this thirteen-movement setting of the standard Friday evening Sabbath service. The piece begins with a keyboard introduction (actually a reduction of the original orchestration) in imitative style. After this sixteen-measure introduction (which could be easily omitted) the chorus enters and sings *a cappella* until the end of the piece. If your choir has trouble with *a cappella* singing, it would be perfectly appropriate for the organ to play *colla voce* with the singers.

Technical Considerations

"Silent Devotion and Response" is very approachable by choirs of all levels. The vocal ranges are limited, and the harmony is rather straightforward with little chromaticism. Have the singers labor to maintain an even legato and pay special attention to singing through tones longer than a quarter note. To achieve legato, have the singers rehearse without consonants on a closed vowel (e.g., [u]). Ask them to use their air consistently and to imagine a musical line with no bumps or breaks. Once they can sing a seamless line, add a consonant to the [u], perhaps a [d], yielding [du]. See if they can still maintain legato without consonantly interrupting the flow of the line. This will be an important concept to have mastered when you teach the Hebrew, as Hebrew's thick consonants can impede legato without proper training. It might also be wise to rehearse this piece at a dynamic louder than *pp* so the singers can become accustomed to the sound. Amateur singers will sing *pp*'s "off the breath"; this yields an airy, unsupported sound that is often out of tune.

It is very important to do this work in its original language, Hebrew, which, like Latin, uses five vowel sounds; you may essentially read all vowels as you would in standard Latin. Consonants are mostly predictable, but there are some sounds that are unique to Hebrew. A variety of Web sites and books are available on this subject, but it is always best to have a "native speaker" teach the diction, so your choir can hear the sounds as they should be produced. Ask your choir members, friends, family, or colleagues who speak Hebrew to coach the diction for this piece. Then be sure to coach the person on how to teach language efficiently. Have them speak slowly so the choir can listen accurately to the new sounds; have the choir repeat. Then speak short phrases in rhythm; have the choir repeat. Then try singing. Allow the choir to make some mistakes and fix them on their own. It will take a few rehearsals for them to feel truly comfortable.

Stylistic Considerations

Jewish folk music is characterized by a wonderful richness and sonorousness. Despite the fact that this piece is largely notated at a soft dynamic, ensure that the sounds being produced are well supported and full bodied; a quiet, "blended sound" would not be stylistically appropriate. Because of the beautiful harmonies, it would be easy to let this work become too "sing-songy" and sound trite. Remember that the title is "Silent Devotion and Response"; work for a sound that remains true to the words. Do not let the tempo skim forward; the slower and more legato you sing this piece, the more beautiful it will be. Be sure the vowels are shaped in a way that yields a sound reflecting the piousness of this text and the depth of its meaning.

Text and Translation

Yihyu lerozon imrei fi,
Vehegyon libi lefonecho,
Adonoy tzuri vegoali.
Amen.

O Lord, may the words of my mouth,
And meditations of my heart be acceptable before thee,
Adanoy, my rock and redeemer.
Amen.

Suggested Listening

New York Philharmonic. Robert Merrill, baritone. Leonard Bernstein, conductor. (Sony Classical SM2K 47533).

London Philharmonic Orchestra. Marko Rothmüller, baritone. Ernest Bloch, conductor. (Jewish Music Heritage Recordings JMHRCD015; Rockport Records 5001).

London Symphony Orchestra. Louis Berkman, baritone. Geoffrey Simon, conductor. (Chandos CHAN 8418).

Contributed by:

Matthew W. Mehaffey

Repertoire Resource Guide

Fire

Mary Goetze
(b. 1943)

SSA/piano
Boosey & Hawkes, Inc.: OCTB6482
Overall: 2
Vocal: 2
Tonal/Rhythm: 2

Composer

Mary Goetze is chairwoman of the Music in General Studies department at the Indiana University School of Music. She conducts the International Vocal Ensemble, a School of Music chorus specializing in the re-creation of music from outside the European and American art traditions. A specialist in children's choirs, she serves as a clinician and guest conductor, and her arrangements and compositions for children's choirs are published in the Mary Goetze Choral Series by Boosey & Hawkes, Inc. A graduate of the Oberlin Conservatory of Music, Indiana University, and the University of Colorado, Goetze has been recognized as an outstanding educator by the Organization of American Kodály Educators and Indiana University.

Composition

This work is a setting for three treble voices and piano of a poem written by thirteen-year-old Patricia Taylor. It was premiered by the Indianapolis Children's Choir at the 1988 MENC national convention.

Historical Perspective

This work is a recent composition for children's choir. The propulsive repetition of the harmonic structure suggests similarities with the idioms of popular music.

Technical Considerations

"Fire" is comprised primarily of simple, extremely repetitive rhythms. The melodic range is limited to the octave between D and D in the treble clef for the two top voices, though the lowest voice descends to B-flat below middle C throughout the central section and once reaches low G. Most of the piece is marked "agitated," but the middle section calls for more legato singing as the tempo relaxes. There is no chromaticism, but the central section is written in modally inflected D minor instead of the predominating modal G minor.

The accompaniment is difficult because of the speed of the piece, so there are alternate passages offered for the most challenging sections.

Stylistic Considerations

The marking "agitated" defines the interpretation of the majority of this piece, calling for a propulsive triple meter and energetic and marked articulations. The straightforward text setting and word painting is highlighted by changes in dynamics and tempo. The setting, especially of the middle, slower section, evokes the "endlessly moving" aspect of fire of which the text speaks using constantly churning eighth notes that crescendo to a climax only to suddenly recede with the dramatic return of the opening section. The overall mood is one of intensity, which is rendered more dramatic by the suddenly shifting dynamics.

Musical Elements

This song is primarily in G minor, but the dominant only appears in minor, giving the impression of modal inflection. This minor dominant reappears as the key area of the central section, which also features a lowered seventh. The melodic phrases are all of simple construction, and the harmonic pattern is repetitive. When not homophonic, the three voices are nearly always imitative. The vocal harmonies are usually uncomplicated, except for the slightly more difficult unaccompanied middle section, which contains a few major sevenths.

Form and Structure

Measure	Event and Scoring
1–4	Piano introduction; G minor
5–21	Theme 1; unison
22–40	Theme 1; varied, three-part
40–44	Piano interlude
45–65	Slower middle section; D minor; largely homophonic
65–68	Piano interlude; G minor transition
69–73	Theme 1; truncated, three-part
73–76	Piano interlude like introduction
77–99	Theme 1; varied, slower; "foe" verse
99–102	Piano interlude like introduction
103–107	Theme 1; truncated, three-part
107–110	Coda; fragments of Theme 1

Contributed by:

Thomas Cunningham

Repertoire Resource Guide

Gloria tibi

Leonard Bernstein
(1918–1990)

SA/piano and percussion (with tenor solo)
Boosey & Hawkes, Inc.: OCTB6344
Overall: 2
Vocal: 2
Tonal/Rhythm: 3

Composer

Leonard Bernstein was one of the central figures in American twentieth-century music. His ability to assimilate all genres of music, from classical and pop to Latin and jazz, is an unparalleled accomplishment. His success was unique; he achieved acclaim at both spectrums of music in New York City: Lincoln Center and the Broadway stage. His best-known work in the Broadway repertoire is *West Side Story*. His more "classical" compositions reflect his assimilation of all things musical, as is seen in his choral works *Chichester Psalms* and *Mass*.

As a conductor, Bernstein delighted audiences with his flair for the dramatic and also educated a whole generation of children with his famous Young People's Concerts. He taught frequently and earned the prestigious Charles Eliot Norton Professorship in Poetry from Harvard University (his alma mater) in 1973. (Incidentally, Igor Stravinsky earned the same honor in 1939.) Through his participation in so many different artistic forums, Bernstein canonized himself in the culture of twentieth-century America.

Composition

"Gloria tibi" is a movement for two part treble choir and tenor solo from Bernstein's composition *Mass: A Theatre Piece for Singers, Players, and Dancers*. This mass is different from the "normal" model in that it not only uses text from the Roman Catholic liturgy but incorporates texts written by the composer and lyricist Stephen Schwartz. "Gloria tibi" is a fragment from the Gloria of the mass.

The original performance of *Mass* was a choreographed, staged affair intended for singers, players, and dancers. The "Gloria tibi" movement may be performed without all of the above, but a full performance of *Mass* would be incomplete without the staging and choreography.

Historical Perspective

Mass was commissioned in 1971 for the opening of the John F. Kennedy Center for the Performing Arts. Jacqueline Kennedy Onassis, President Kennedy's widow, was present at the debut performance and afterward spoke often of her affection for the piece.

Technical Considerations

The entire *Mass* contains passages of rhythmic complexity and the "Gloria tibi" is no exception; this movement is in 5/8. The eighth-note groupings (e.g., 3+2 or 2+3) change throughout the movement, which can be a difficulty for conductor and choir. It is important to know where the 3+2 pattern changes to a 2+3 pattern (e.g., when the singers recite the words "Benedicimus te.") Bernstein changed the pattern of eighth notes to provide proper word accentuation. The conductor should be sure that the singers know where in the music this change occurs and make the necessary alterations to his or her conducting gesture.

The concept of "mixed meter" might be new to many singers. Taking time to explain the math of the rhythm might help many of your singers understand how the music is constructed. Count-singing can be incredibly helpful in teaching singers the rhythm. One can employ two methods when rehearsing with count-singing. The singers could count from 1 to 5 in each measure, or they could divide each measure into two groups: a three group and a two group. For the second method the singers would count (1–2–3–1–2) or (1–2–1–2–3). Both methods are very effective and can be used in alternation if so desired.

Singers will have the tendency to rush through grouping of three eighth notes in each measure; use of a metronome can assist in preventing this problem. It is also helpful to make the "3" portion of the conducting gesture larger because it has to take longer.

The word "Gloria" is very difficult for singers to produce. The "gl" consonant combination can get "stuck" in singers' mouths. If you feel the texture is muddied by the lack of a crisp "gl," try having some of the singers perform "kl." "K" and "g" are executed in exactly the same manner; the only difference is that "g" is a voiced consonant and carries a pitch. The "g" and the "l" can also be performed simultaneously. Have the singers perform the "l" with the tip of their tongues; failure to do so could yield a poorly produced "back" vowel. The second syllable of the word, "ri," can also be problematic. Instruct singers to flip the "r." If singers are unable to flip or roll "r's" have them replace the "r" with a "d"; the "d" will achieve the same effect. All of the vowels should be performed in a closed manner to yield the most tone and pitch. For instance, the vowel in the first syllable, "Glo," should be closer to "oo" as in "boot," than the "awe" sound in "awesome."

Stylistic Considerations

As with all of Bernstein's music, rhythm is a very important consideration. Make every effort to make the rhythm lively and crisp. The dynamic and articulation markings are clear. The performers should take great care to achieve all of these markings, which help make this piece come alive.

Form and Structure

The movement is essentially through-composed and consists of the treble choir answering the tenor solo. The choral answers are sometimes transpositionally related to the solo material but are often an inverted presentation of the soloist's melodic material.

The somewhat lengthy instrumental interlude reviews all of the melodic material presented by the soloist and the choir.

Text and Translation

The text is taken from the Gloria of the mass.

Suggested Listening

Bernstein Mass. Norman Scribner Choir. Leonard Bernstein, conductor.
   (Sony 63089).

Contributed by:

Anthony Reeves

Repertoire Resource Guide

Savory, Sage, Rosemary and Thyme

Donald Partriquin
(b. 1938)

SSAA or SATB/piano and optional percussion
Earthsongs: SSAA=W-07f, SATB=S-54f
Overall: 2
Vocal: 2
Tonal/Rhythm: 2

Composer

From Sherbrooke, Québec, Donald Patriquin studied composition at McGill University and at the University of Toronto, though he also pursued studies in environmental biology. Much of Patriquin's music, both vocal and instrumental, shows a strong affinity for folk melody, and many of his works are based upon collected folksongs and carols of his native Canada. A lecturer for more than thirty years at McGill, Patriquin has recently returned to the Eastern Townships of Québec to focus on composition and conducting.

Composition and Genre

This work is from a collection entitled *Six Songs of Early Canada*, written in 1980 and revised in 1992. The six songs are arranged historically and geographically, and this piece is the last in the series. "Savory, Sage, Rosemary and Thyme" is based on a folksong from British Columbia that originated in England. While it shares part of its title and some of its lyrics with the song recorded by Simon and Garfunkel, this work is from a different folksong.

The work is for SSAA choir with piano and woodblock accompaniment.

Historical Perspective

Modern efforts to revisit folksongs in new contexts continue as part of a long history of folksong influence on choral music. The formal collecting of folksongs has its roots in the nineteenth century and is now an important aspect of ethnomusicological research. Patriquin has taken this folksong from British Columbia and put it into a historical context with the other pieces in the complete *Six Songs of Early Canada*.

Technical Considerations

The vocal lines in this work are comprised almost exclusively of eighth-note passages in quick 6/8 time. The rhythm is rarely complicated, although occasional sixteenth notes do appear in simple patterns, and there is one instance of groups of quarter notes working against the meter. There are also a few measures of 9/8.

Of greater complexity is the harmony, which, while strongly rooted in D major, occasionally ventures into harmonies outside of the key, however briefly. The moments of chromaticism are typically approached by step, simplifying the execution.

The accompaniment to the work is sometimes difficult, featuring frequent sixteenth-note runs in the right hand and widely spaced leaps in the left.

Stylistic Considerations

This folksong is built from several short phrases that do not require extended breath support. The setting is marked "Gaily" at the outset, and this marking applies throughout, reflecting the flirtatious aspects of the lyrics.

Specific dynamic and expressive markings vary from verse to verse, creating a sense of theme and variations as the melody returns six times in different reworkings.

Musical Elements

This work is consistently in D major. While the harmonies tend to feature simple chords and intervals, there are several points where the melody is harmonized by parallel fifths or mild chromaticism. There are also brief moments of dissonance in a repeating figure that ends verses five and six (as labeled in the score).

The texture, though usually homophonic, sometimes features independent vocal lines, at times in imitation of one another. The meter remains in 6/8 through most of the setting with only a few measures of 9/8.

Form and Structure

There are six verses in this folksong setting with only a small interlude that is external to the verse structure. The interlude, though it is not a true verse, is labeled in the score as verse four. Each verse receives its own setting, creating a sense of an initial theme followed by six variations. The work begins with a short piano introduction, and a few bars of piano solo separate the verses. The work closes with a short coda, including six bars marked "presto."

Text

Pray can you buy me an acre or more,
Savory, sage, rosemary, and thyme,
Between the wide ocean and the seashore?
And then you can be a true lover of mine.

Pray can you plow it with one ram's horn,
Savory, sage, rosemary, and thyme,
And sew it all over with one peppercorn?
And then you can be a true lover of mine.

Pray can you reap it with a sickle of leather,
Savory, sage, rosemary, and thyme,
And tie it all up with one peacock's feather?
And then you can be a true lover of mine.

Now you have asked me of these questions three,
And now it is my turn to ask three of thee.

Pray can you make me a fine cambric shirt,
Savory, sage, rosemary and thyme,
Without any seam and all needlework?
And then you can be a true lover of mine.

Pray in yon brook can you wash it and wade,
Savory, sage, rosemary, and thyme,
Where water ne'er flowed since earth it was made?
And then you can be a true lover of mine.

Pray can you dry it on yonder sweet thorn,
Savory, sage, rosemary, and thyme,
Where blossom ne'er bloomed since Adam was born?
Then can you be a true lover of mine.

Recordings

One World Many Voices. earthsongsmus.com. (Earthsongs CD-02).

Contributed by:

Thomas Cunningham

Repertoire Resource Guide

The Snow, Op. 26, No. 1
Edward Elgar
(1857–1934)

SSA or SATB/2 violins and piano
Novello Publications, Inc.: SSA=NOV 160075R;
Hinshaw Music, Inc.: SATB=HMC 1177
Overall: 2
Vocal: 2
Tonal/Rhythm: 2

Composer

Edward Elgar was one the generation of English composers known as the neo-Romantics. Unlike most of his contemporaries, he was born, raised, and died a Catholic. His father was a piano tuner and church organist, and Elgar learned to play violin at a young age. He moved from his hometown of Broadheath to London in 1890; London audiences met his compositions with lukewarm reception. Consequently, he moved to Worcester in 1891.

Elgar is best known for his *Enigma Variations* (1899), his oratorio *The Dream of Gerontius* (1900), and perhaps best of all for his *Pomp and Circumstance* marches. After his wife's death in 1920, he lost the will to compose. He died in 1934 and was unable to be buried at Westminster Abbey because of his Catholicism.

Composition

"The Snow" was composed by Elgar in 1894, with text by his wife, C. Alice Elgar. "The Snow," and its companion piece, "Fly, Singing Bird," were published as Elgar's Op. 26. They were originally scored for SSA choir, piano, and two violins, but an orchestral version was completed in 1903. Elgar arranged a SATB version as well.

Technical Considerations

There are not many technical difficulties inherent in this piece. The pianist and violinist should be of high quality if you want to achieve an artistic performance. The choral parts are not very difficult. Elgar marked a different tempo for each major section of the piece, and it is important that the conductor make the tempos of each section distinguishable form the others.

Stylistic Considerations

This piece requires a great deal of delicate singing. The texture should be pristine, like white snow. Crisp, clear diction can aid in achieving this style. The C section, beginning at measure 35 should be more expansive and out-wardly expressive.

Musical Elements

The music plays with the parallel and relative major keys of the overall tonality, E minor. In each B section of the piece, Elgar uses the parallel key of E major; in the expansive C section, he uses the relative key of G major. These tonal shifts are very easy for the singers to hear and understand.

Form and Structure

ABA'CAB

Text

O snow, which sinks so light,
Brown earth is hid from sight,
O soul, be thou as white as snow.

O snow, which falls so slow,
Dear earth quite warm below;
O heart so keep thy glow,
Beneath the snow.

O snow, in thy soft grave
Sad Flow'rs the winter brave;
O Heart so soothe and save,
As does the snow.

The snow must melt, must go,
Fast as waters flow.
Not thus my soul, O sow,
Thy gifts to fade like snow.

O snow thou'rt white no more,
Thy sparkling too, is o'er;
O soul, be as before,
Was bright the snow.

Then as the snow all pure,
O heart be, but endure;
Through all the years full sure,
Not as the snow.

Recordings

Elgar. London Philharmonic Choir. Vernon Handley, conductor. (EMI Classics 7243-5-65104-2-5).

Echo in My Soul. Northwest Girlchoir and Friends. Rebecca Rottsolk, artistic director. (Arsis CD 121).

Contributed by:

Matthew W. Mehaffey
Anthony Reeves

Repertoire Resource Guide

Three Choral Pieces
Jean Berger
(1909–2002)

SSA/piano
Neil A. Kjos Music Company: 6081
Overall: 2
Vocal: 2
Tonal/Rhythm: 2

Composer

Jean Berger, a twentieth-century choral conductor of international reputation, was born in Hamm, Germany, and subsequently lived in Austria, France, Brazil, and the United States. He taught at Middlebury College, the University of Illinois–Urbana, and the University of Colorado. Berger is best known for his choral compositions, including his *Magnificat* (1960) and his "Cherry Tree Carol" (1975).

Composition

Three Choral Pieces is a lovely set for an amateur treble choir, and the texts are quite comical and lighthearted. This work would fit very well into a program of any kind as a change of pace or for comic relief.

Technical Considerations

Almost all of the music in this collection is very accessible. The ranges are limited, and the alto part stays in the lower register for long periods of time. Because of this, be sure to have the singers mix as much head voice into their singing as possible to avoid "chesty" singing.

The first song in the set provides some tricky "textual" problems. As a conductor, one must decide how to deal with the rests that occur in the middle of words. For instance, four bars from the end of the piece, the syllable "port" of the word "important" appears as a quarter note followed by a rest. The conductor must decide if the "t" in "port" should be placed at the end of the quarter note, or at the beginning of the next measure as the beginning of the "ant" syllable, yielding "tant." Either option is acceptable; however, the choir will have a much easier time if the conductor makes his or her choice clear and consistent from the outset.

The second piece is constructed by stacking each voice part on top of the melody. The voices, therefore, move in parallel motion. This can make some of the chords difficult to tune. During rehearsals, try having the choir sing each chord staccato, and instruct them to hear the next pitch before they sing it. Once they can accurately produce the pitches in staccato, return to legato-style singing. This should help clear up the texture and make each chord sound more clearly. There are also many large leaps in this movement. The staccato method will assist in making these leaps accurate and free of glissandos.

The third song provides some very "close" harmonies. The types of harmonies (e.g., the last five measures) are often challenging for a choir to learn. In this piece, however, they are not so difficult because they result from linear movement of the voices. Rehearse each part individually, so each singer can understand his or her line as a melody, not just notes that sound strange in a chord.

Stylistic Considerations

Because the texts are amusing, it is paramount that the words be comprehensible. Attention to good diction will pay off in concert, as the audience will understand the texts and might even laugh! It might also be effective to instruct the choir to "color" their voices with different attitudes according to the text. For instance, the first piece is a setting of a poem that slanders Lord Heygate. It would be perfectly appropriate for the singers to sound snooty as they tell about this "commonplace peer."

Form and Structure

The three pieces in this set are linked together by key. The first movement is in G minor, the second begins in D minor and ends on a D major chord, and the third is in G major. This key relationship allows all three to be performed without a break (except time for laughter!).

Text

Each of the three songs draws its text from a different author, the first from Hillaire Belloc, the second from F. C. Bentley, and the third from an anonymous author.

Contributed by:

Anthony Reeves

Repertoire Resource Guide

Der Herr segne euch

Johann Sebastian Bach
(1685–1750)

TB/keyboard and continuo instrument
Edition Peters: 6079
Overall: 2
Vocal: 2
Tonal/Rhythm: 3

Composer

Johann Sebastian Bach was born March 21, 1685, in Eisenach, Germany. The extended Bach family were well-known as musicians; J. S.'s father, Johann Ambrosius, was a chamber musician in Eisenach.

J. S. Bach's life is generally divided into six periods, mostly defined by his places of employment: early life (1685–1703); Arnstadt (1703–07); Mühlhausen (1707–08); Weimar (1708–17); Cöthen (1717–23); and Leipzig (1723–50). In these positions, Bach served at various times as organist, teacher, composer, *Konzertmeister* (Weimar), and *Director musices* (Leipzig). He was also appointed *Hofcompositeur* for the Dresden Court in 1736.

J. S. Bach's musical output is overwhelming, including masterworks in almost every musical genre of his era. For example, he wrote cantatas (sacred and secular), large-scale choral works (e.g., St. Matthew Passion and Mass in B Minor), concerti, orchestral suites, organ works, harpsichord works, and pieces for various other instruments and instrumental combinations. Bach died in Leipzig July 28, 1750.

Composition

The piece was originally conceived as a duet for tenor and bass soloist, but it works perfectly well with the tenor and bass sections of the choir. The duet comes from Cantata 196, *Derr Herr denket an uns und segnet uns*. Bach composed this quaint cantata for the wedding of his aunt, Regina Wedemann, to clergyman Johann Lorenz Stauber. The wedding took place June 5, 1708, in the village of Dornheim, just outside of Arnstadt. (Interestingly, this was the site of J. S. Bach's own first wedding). Scholars believe that members of the Bach family were the singers and instrumentalists for the performance of this cantata. This piece would work wonderfully at any wedding, whether sung in German or in English.

Historical Perspective

The compositional style of this early cantata reflects the influence of the North German organ school on Bach, specifically the music of Dietrich Buxtehude. This is not surprising, as it had only been about four years since Bach visited Buxtehude in Lübeck and witnessed examples of his *Abendmusik*. It is amazing to consider that Bach was only twenty-three years old when he composed this cantata!

Technical Considerations

Bach's use of hemiola at cadential points in this duet can cause rhythmic problems for the singers. Rehearse the sections slowly, perhaps with a metronome, using count-singing to overcome this potentially disastrous problem.

It is always a good idea to breathe with the punctuation in German. This is safe rule to follow; that way, you will not (as a non-German speaker) accidentally take a breath in the middle of a poetic thought. If the choir breathes with the punctuation in this duet, all of the phrases are made very clear and are of singable length.

Stylistic Considerations

Frequent ties across the barline provide the singers ample opportunity for *messa di voce*, which requires singers to crescendo and decrescendo on the same pitch, usually when the note value exceeds a quarter note. This sounds very simple, but can actually be quite difficult. Singers should think of the crescendo portion of the technique as an increase in resonance space rather than just as singing louder. If the singers can increase their resonance and follow the increase with a slight closing of the vowel, they will accomplish the technique of *messa di voce* masterfully. The music calls for this technique in almost every measure, particularly on the dotted half notes. A *messa di voce* executed on the dotted half notes will bring the imitative nature of this duet to life.

Form and Structure

The opening of the movement is a neat canon, followed by a more ornate *riternello* version of the canon. The last repetitions of "je mehr und meh" contain further canonical treatment. The second clause (about the children) is set in sixths, contrasting nicely with the imitative sections. At the end of the piece, the strings perform a descending arpeggio for four octaves, as if manna were falling from heaven.

Text and Translation

The text of this movement speaks of God's blessing on the "married couple" and all of their children. It is rather comical that Bach spends only nine of the seventy-two measures talking about the "children." It is as if Bach, the nephew, felt it "scarcely discreet to emphasize the question of offspring when the bride and the groom were no longer young!" (Whittaker 46)

Der Herr segne euch je mehr und mehr;
Euch, und eure Kinder.

May God smile on you;
You, and all your children.

Suggested Listening

Johann Sebastian Bach Complete Cantatas, Volume 1. Amsterdam Baroque Orchestra and Choir. Ton Koopman, conductor. (Erato 4509-98536-2).

Additional References and Resources

Whittaker, W. G. *The Cantatas of J. S. Bach*, 2 Vols. Oxford: UP. 1959.

Contributed by:

Matthew W. Mehaffey

Repertoire Resource Guide

Let Us Now Praise Famous Men, Op. 35

Gerald Finzi
(1901–1956)

TB/keyboard
Boosey & Hawkes, Inc.: M060030352
Overall: 2
Vocal: 2
Tonal/Rhythm: 2

Composer

Gerald Finzi was born in London July 14, 1901; his teachers included Edward Bairstow (at York Minster) and the famous contrapuntalist Reginald O. Morris. Finzi began his career teaching at the Royal Academy of Music in London in 1930. In 1939, having moved to Ashmansworth, he established the Newbury String Players, a chamber orchestra for which he was to compose numerous works. Following service in World War II, Finzi dedicated himself solely to composition and to producing scholarly editions of the works of William Boyce, John Stanley, and other eighteenth-century English composers. He was diagnosed with leukemia in 1951 and died in Oxford September 27, 1956.

Finzi wrote several significant orchestral compositions; his choral works, however, arguably represent his finest work. Some of his better-known pieces in the choral repertoire include *Seven Part Songs* for chorus, Op. 17 (1934–37), *For St. Cecilia* for tenor, chorus, and orchestra, Op. 30 (1947), *Magnificat*, Op. 36 (1952), and *Three Anthems* (including his famous "God Is Gone Up"), Op. 27 (1948–53).

Composition

"Let Us Now Praise Famous Men" is essentially an English cathedral anthem. It is based on a text from Ecclesiastes (part of the Apocrypha). Other well-known settings of this text from Ecclesiastes include those of Ralph Vaughan Williams and Walford Davies. Finzi composed this anthem in 1951, a period during which he wrote other similar pieces.

Historical Perspective

Finzi was a product of two seemingly disparate traditions. Although his parents were Jewish, he was immersed in the English cathedral music tradition from an early age. In addition, Finzi maintained an interest in politics and professed to be an agnostic throughout his life. Although he was a pacifist, he worked in London at the Ministry of War Transport during World War II.

Around the time Finzi composed "Let Us Now Praise Famous Men" (1951), he wrote other similar pieces (e.g., "All This Night," Op. 33 and "Muses and Graces," Op. 34). Other English composers writing music for similar genres at this time included Vaughan Williams, William Walton, and Benjamin Britten. Shorter English choral pieces of the era tended to feature adventuresome (but essentially tonal) harmonic writing, soaring melodies, and a keen awareness of the words and their inherent syllabic stress.

Technical Considerations

Finzi composed "Let Us Now Praise Famous Men" for TB and piano. It could, however, be performed effectively by other voice combinations (such as SA, or even SATB). String parts are available for the music but were added after the original composition.

Finzi was also careful to mark such details as tempo, character (*Tempo di Marcia*), accents, and dynamics. These details, re-created in performing the piece, will lend character and drama, effectively illustrate the text, and make the music educational and interesting for the singers.

It is worth noting that although the tessitura of the choral writing lies within a range comfortable for most singers, Finzi inserted leaps that can be vocally challenging. The first two vocal phrases feature ascending leaps of a sixth (mm. 4 and 9), but the jump from C up to G in measures 12–13 can be extremely difficult, especially for younger or less-experienced singers. Such leaps are components of both parts and should be considered when deciding whether to program this piece. Later (mm. 44–45), the upper part is required to jump from B to G, and then sustain the G for five beats and crescendo from *mf* to *ff*.

The primary conducting difficulty lies in the mixed meters (i.e., 4/4 to 2/4 to 4/4 to 5/4 from m. 23 on). The fact that the quarter note pulse never changes, however, makes these difficulties minimal.

Stylistic Considerations

This is English choral music, and to be most effective it must reflect the "English sound." The conductor, however, should exercise care in how this is accomplished. So-called "straight-tone singing" is really not the road to success. Instead, attention to details of balance (a "thicker" bottom with a "shimmering" top), color (bright and floating, with emphasis on high and forward resonance), and diction will provide satisfying results.

The text is in English, and because Finzi was immersed in the English choral tradition, careful attention to "cathedral" diction is most appropriate. Crisp consonants, attention to tall and closed vowels, and careful consonant-vowel connections are important components of this style. Finzi paid attention to syllabic stress, and care should be taken to reflect that in the performance of the music. For example, the opening phrase features an agogic stress on the word "**now**" as well as metrical stresses on the syllables "**fa**-mous," "**men**," "**fa**-thers," "**that**," and "be-**gat**." Careful attention to stressing these syllables within the overall shape of the line will make the singing much more convincing.

Musical Elements

"Let Us Now Praise Famous Men" begins and ends in C major. In the middle of the piece, Finzi modulates clearly but briefly (ten bars) to E-flat major. Typical of the English choral music of this era, Finzi's music is rarely static harmonically. In this piece, for instance, he wanders through a variety of tonalities after he leaves C major (m. 13) and on his way back to it to conclude the piece. The tonal changes are gentle, however, and feel natural to the ear. They are not as intimidating as they look.

Form and Structure

This piece is cast in one continuous movement and features a "typical" twentieth-century English anthem structure: an instrumental introduction, followed by the various parts singing individually and growing into a tutti climax. An instrumental interlude then leads into the next section, featuring similar construction, and this pattern continues to the end. The anthem concludes as might be expected, with a forte instrumental coda.

Text

The text is from Ecclesiastes 44.

Contributed by:

Matthew W. Mehaffey
Anthony Reeves

Repertoire Resource Guide

My Bonnie

arr. Alice Parker
(b. 1925)
and
Robert Shaw
(1916–1999)

TTBB/a cappella
Warner Bros. Publications: LG 968
Overall: 2
Tonal: 2
Vocal/Rhythm: 2

Composers

Robert Shaw was born in Red Bluff, California, on April 30, 1916. After completing undergraduate studies at Pomona College, he went to work for Fred Waring, who asked him to help organize the Fred Waring Glee Club. In 1941, Shaw established the Collegiate Chorale in New York City and from 1946–48 was director of the choral departments at the Juilliard School of Music and the Berkshire Music Center. From 1948–65, he conducted the internationally renowned Robert Shaw Chorale.

Also an orchestral conductor, Shaw was associate conductor of the Cleveland Orchestra from 1956 until 1967, when he became music director of the Atlanta Symphony Orchestra. In 1988, he was made music director emeritus and conductor laureate of the Atlanta Symphony. Shaw's impact on choral singing throughout the world cannot be overstated, and as a professional conductor and teacher, he promoted choral singing throughout his life. Shaw died in New Haven, Connecticut, on January 25, 1999.

Alice Parker was born in Boston on December 16, 1925. After graduating from Smith College and the Juilliard School of Music, she worked as an arranger for the Robert Shaw Chorale, taught at Westminster Choir College, and founded Melodious Accord, Inc. She has written more than 400 compositions and is arguably best-known for her collaborations with Shaw on folksongs, hymns, and spirituals.

Composition

"My Bonnie" is a four-part *a cappella* men's choir arrangement of the popular folksong. Like so many of the Parker-Shaw collaborations, it was originally recorded by the men of the Robert Shaw Chorale.

Technical Considerations

This arrangement is for TTBB choir and features reasonable ranges and comfortable tessituras. Parker and Shaw call for a tempo of "Very fast (one to the bar)." The conductor will want to ensure the tempo remains under control, however, so it is probably best to begin rehearsing the piece in three, and then speed up to one.

The music becomes more complex as the variations develop, and the singers need the ability to function independently. The parts are all lyrical, however, and mostly diatonic.

Stylistic Considerations

Because "My Bonnie" is a folksong arrangement, it is important to keep the original melody clear. The conductor is obliged to ascertain that every singer knows where the melody is at all times and that it comes through. The boisterous nature of this tune and arrangement will make it quite tempting for the singers to bellow. While this tune is exhilarating, however, it is not raucous and should not be sung that way. Despite the "one to the bar" marking, the inherent lilting quality of a triple meter should still prevail.

The music falls into very neat four-measure packages. The conductor can aid the singers in achieving line and structure by conducting in a macro pattern of 4/1.

This arrangement works well with legato, well-supported singing. It is important for the men to keep the resonance high and forward and to strive for some gentleness of tone, which can become more fervent as the piece crescendos and accelerandos toward its conclusion.

Musical Elements

This arrangement is in C major with a short, transitory modulation to G major. Parker and Shaw use basic theme-and-variation technique. Measures 1 to 32 are a straightforward, homophonic statement of the basic tune (tenor 1) and musical material. Successive stanzas move the melody to different voices and surround it with different styles of choral accompaniment. The conclusion of the piece, especially from measure 140 onward, is a frenzied march to the inevitable conclusion.

Form and Structure

"My Bonnie" is a set of choral variations on a strophic folksong featuring four strophes (or stanzas) and concluding with an extended coda. It is interesting that in the common version of this folksong, each strophe is followed by a refrain. Parker and Shaw, however, include the refrain within each stanza; it never appears the same way twice.

Contributed by:

Matthew W. Mehaffey
Anthony Reeves

Repertoire Resource Guide

Poor Man Lazrus

arr. Jester Hairston
(1901–2000)

TTBB, SATB, or SSA/a cappella
Bourne Company: TTBB = 103937, SSA = 103938, SATB = 103936
Overall: 2
Vocal: 2
Tonal/Rhythm: 2

Composer

Jester Hairston was born in Belews Creek, North Carolina, July 9, 1901. A graduate of Tufts University and the Juilliard School of Music, Hairston is perhaps best known as an actor. He was also a musician, and in that realm is well known as an arranger of African American spiritual tunes. He worked as music director for several Broadway musicals and composed background music for movies, worked as a choral conductor and clinician, and toured extensively in the United States and abroad (under the auspices of the state department). Hairston died in Los Angeles on January 18, 2000.

Composition and Genre

"Poor Man Lazrus" is an arrangement of an African American spiritual. Spirituals are classified in three groups: the call and response; the slow, sustained, long-phrased melody; and the syncopated, segmented melody. This is an example of the call-and-response type, which usually call for a fast tempo and fiery spirit.

167

Technical Considerations

"Poor Man Lazrus" is arranged for a four-part *a cappella* men's choir. The ranges and tessituras are accessible (low G in the bass to the G above middle C in the first tenor). The notes and rhythms of this arrangement are not difficult as long as adequate singers are available to cover all the parts.

The conductor should work for a dark and open tone quality. This is not shy music, and Hairston supplies many dynamic markings. (In fact, dynamic variations are one of the most interesting aspects of this arrangement.) The singers will need to be able to sing from *ff* to *pp*; many times controlled crescendos and diminuendos are prescribed. It is the conductor's responsibility to assure that the singers maintain good breath support regardless of the dynamic and that the breath remains connected to the resonance. Good breath support and high, forward resonance enable the color and personality of this piece to shine through; any attempts (which are especially likely from the basses) at producing dark tone quality should be strongly discouraged.

The most efficient way to teach this piece is to use the following plan:
1. Divide the piece into sections for teaching purposes.
2. Have the choir speak the rhythms on [tu] at a moderate tempo and *mp* dynamic.
3. Teach the notes, in rhythm, on the syllable [du] at a moderate tempo and *mp* dynamic.
4. Ask the choir to add the dynamics to their singing.
5. Have the choir speak the words in rhythm with the dynamics intact.
6. Have the choir sing the words in rhythm with dynamics.
7. Gradually increase the tempo—but do not rush; keep a steady pulse!

Stylistic Considerations

The call-and-response pattern comes from the time of slavery when men would work in the fields; a leader sang a line, and the group sang a response. The call-and-response style was carried over into the worship of the slave churches. This should be reflected in performances of this music by a change in attitude and tone between the "lead" lines and the response sections. Fortunately, Hairston helped by marking dynamic changes at all such places. Because of the many repeats, it might be interesting to experiment with one singer on a part singing the leads.

"Poor Man Lazrus" is a style piece. The choir must sing with attitude and a commitment to the style. In this music, that is easy to accomplish, as most singers will be enchanted by the music and its lively rhythms. The conductor must ensure that the pulse remains steady and that the dynamics will be followed scrupulously. After all, if the entire piece rushes, the music will sound frantic instead of impressive.

Musical Elements

This arrangement reflects standard harmonic practices. It is in G major almost throughout, and many stretches of the piece feature extended I–IV–V–I progressions. The only deviation from G comes late in the piece as part of his march to the conclusion, when Hairston suddenly modulates to B-flat major and then to C major, where the piece concludes.

Form and Structure

AAA'B

Additional References and Resources

Work, John. *American Negro Songs and Spirituals*. New York: Crown
   Publishers. 1940.

Contributed by:

Anthony Reeves
Matthew W. Mehaffey

Repertoire Resource Guide

She Moved Through the Fair

arr. Timothy Takach
(b. 1978)

TBB/a cappella
Neil A. Kjos Music Company: 5578
Overall: 2
Vocal: 3
Tonal/Rhythm: 2

Composer

A native of Lake Zurich, Illinois, Timothy Takach started singing and playing piano at an early age. Involvement in high school choral music in Eden Prairie, Minnesota, led to his matriculation at St. Olaf College, where he was a member of the St. Olaf Choir. During his time at St. Olaf, he joined the nascent men's ensemble, Cantus, which is now a professional male choir that appears throughout the United States and abroad to sold out audiences. Takach sings bass in the group and serves as its promotional manager.

Composition

"She Moved Through the Fair," for unaccompanied TBB voices, is a ballad with text by the Irish poet Padraic Colum (1881–1972), a contemporary and close friend of James Joyce. The melody, based on an old Gaelic tune, is by Belfast born Herbert Hughes (1882–1937), folksong collector and arranger, editor of *Irish Folk Music* magazine, music critic of the *Daily Telegraph*, and father of "Spike" Hughes, a well-known writer on jazz and opera.

Technical Considerations

Takach's haunting arrangement begins with all parts singing in unison. It can be tricky for young male voices to get this piece started, as it starts low and on a relatively quick triplet and immediately ascends a fifth. Make sure your singers breathe with enough space for the higher pitches; this will allow the voices to sound spacious and in-tune. The tone should always have as much head tone mixed in to the voice as possible.

The melody, in mixolydian mode, appears to be simple, but there can be many pitfalls. Counting the tied notes can be problematic for inexperienced singers. Be sure they always are aware of the pulse. That being said, a metronomic reading of the piece would be quite boring; learn the music exactly in tempo, then experiment with rubato and shaping of phrases.

The third verse has a seemingly tricky rhythmic figure in measure 29. To make this section correct, have the singers count-sing in 6/4 meter. They should pulse the eighth note subdivision (e.g., one-and, two-and). Each of the notes in the tenor and bass parts should get one and a half beats of duration. The baritone part will simply change pitch on the fifth beat. Once they can count and change pitch with success, remove the counting and sing the text.

There are two endings for this piece. One requires seven parts, the other three. Choose the one that works best for your ensemble.

Stylistic Considerations

For the most part, attention to the text and phrasing will aid in achieving style for this piece. Work hard to make all words intelligible. The strophic nature of the text and music does not mean all verses should sound the same. Each has a very different mood. Strive to get the singers to change vocal color with each phrase and with each verse. Phrases should have a fair amount or rubato to make the delivery of the text sound like the telling of a story.

The vocal style should be light and spacious with special care to ensure in-tune singing. The second verse, with its organum style of harmony, must be perfectly in tune.

Form and Structure

"She Moved Through the Fair" is a strophic song in three verses. The first verse is unison, and the second verse begins unison and expands to three parts. The third verse is in three pats throughout.

Contributed by:

Matthew W. Mehaffey

Repertoire Resource Guide

Si iniquitates observaveris

Samuel Wesley
(1766–1837)

TBB/a cappella
Oxford University Press: 0-19-385757-X
Overall: 2
Vocal: 3
Tonal/Rhythm: 2

Composer

Samuel Wesley was one of the most brilliant English organists of his day. A child prodigy, Wesley wrote an oratorio at the age of six, although he didn't learn how to write it down until the age of eight. Exposed early on to the "ancient" music of Handel and Corelli, Wesley eventually became an ardent supporter of the music of J. S. Bach, combining the sensibility of the older style with more modern compositional trends in his own works.

A great fan of Roman Catholic music, Wesley wrote a great deal of it, and even converted briefly. Unfortunately, scandal in his personal life (he did not marry his first wife until she was pregnant, and he eventually left her for a sixteen-year-old girl whom he also refused to marry) and frequent bouts of depression kept him from achieving any sense of professional stability. By the time he died in 1837 after a short illness, he had already been in physical and mental decline.

Composition

"Si iniquitates observaveris" is part of a setting of the *De profundis clamavi* for men's voices and is the third verse of Psalm 130. *De profundis clamavi* is part of a group of compositions Wesley wrote after a period of withdrawal and depression which ended in the late 1790s. Also from this time is Wesley's magnum opus, *Confitebor tibi, Domine*.

The work is a polyphonic psalm setting, following a long line of similar settings for the Catholic church.

Historical Perspective

Wesley, although strongly influenced by the "modern" music of J. C. Bach, was also well-versed in older styles. This simple setting has strong connections to Renaissance compositional practice, with long, stepwise melodic lines and careful handling of suspension and dissonance. It is a conservative setting, perhaps motivated by a desire for acceptance within the Catholic service.

Technical Considerations

This work is composed almost entirely of eighth notes and quarter notes and uses very straightforward rhythms. The tenor part reaches a high A at the climax, and the bass descends to a low F-sharp, but only for one measure. There is almost no chromaticism. The vocal lines are long and sustained, moving largely by step. The work presents no specific difficulties.

Stylistic Considerations

The extended phrases in this piece lend themselves to a sustained delivery, especially as each phrase comes to a close and becomes more melismatic. The piece is conservative, both melodically and harmonically, suggesting a contemplative, pious mood.

Musical Elements

The work is solidly in G major with a brief shift to D major. Chords are largely constructed as triads with frequent passing motion and suspensions. Cadences are standard patterns, and suspensions are logically resolved. The work is mostly homophonic, although there are a few moments of polyphony. The meter remains in 4/4 throughout.

Form and Structure

The piece is in four parts.

MEASURE	EVENT AND SCORING
1–12	Ends in a half cadence (G to D)
13–25	Movement from G major to D major
26–31	Restatement of opening in B minor, ending with climactic D^7
32–38	Restatement of opening gesture, cadencing in G major

Text and Translation

Psalm 130: 3
Si iniquitates observaveris, Domine, quis sustinebit?

If thou shouldest mark iniquities, O Lord, who shall stand?

Contributed by:

Thomas Cunningham

Repertoire Resource Guide

Sometimes I Feel Like a Motherless Child

arr. Nina Gilbert
(b. 1956)

TTBB or SSAA/a cappella
Mark Foster: TTBB = MF1024, SSAA = MF0927
Overall: 2
Vocal: 2
Tonal/Rhythm: 2

Composer

Nina Gilbert is the director of choral activities at Lafayette College. Her career has ranged from translating a Schubert mass into Swahili while a Peace Corps volunteer in Kenya to serving as the associate conductor of the New York Choral Society. Gilbert holds degrees from Stanford University, Indiana University, and Princeton University.

Composition

This work is a setting of a traditional spiritual for four-voice male choir. This particular setting is a slow, meditative interpretation of the familiar song.

Historical Perspective

The spiritual developed in the United States out of nineteenth-century African American songs. Spirituals were originally associated both with work and with religious meetings and became concert pieces through the work of such pioneers as the Fisk Jubilee Singers and William Dawson of the Tuskegee

Institute, who performed them with a trained choir in sophisticated arrangements. In some cases, spirituals have been used as thematic material for large scale symphonic works, such as Dawson's *Negro Symphony*, though they are more commonly seen today in settings for choir of varying complexity.

Technical Considerations

The rhythms in this piece are simple, but sometimes syncopated. The range is moderate, with a high G expected from the tenor 1 voice. The expressive marking that begins the piece is "chant-like," describing the slow, sustained melody lines. There is no chromaticism. The work is largely homophonic, although the most difficult section is six measures of four independent vocal lines.

Stylistic Considerations

This work is marked "meditative, chant-like" and carries further instructions, such as "smoothly" and "gently." Even the accents are marked "non troppo." It is a thoughtful setting of the spiritual with gentle dynamics that slowly build to a climax and then die away.

Musical Elements

The work has a solid tonal center of E and uses only the notes of the E natural minor scale. The chords are inflected triads and sevenths, and the gentle dissonances are gracefully resolved. The work is entirely homophonic except for six measures and is comprised of a harmonized melody; the melody moves from voice to voice.

Form and Structure

This work is in three verses. Verses one and three are almost identical homophonic settings, and verse two features polyphonic imitation. There is a short coda at the end of verse three.

Text

Sometimes I feel like a motherless child,
a long way from home.

Sometimes I feel like an eagle in the air,
a long way from home.

Sometimes I feel like I'm almost gone,
a long way from home.

Contributed by:

Lani Johnson

Level Three

Mixed voices:

Alleluia	Larsen, Libby	181
Ave verum corpus, K. 618	Mozart, Wolfgang Amadeus	184
Bogoróditse Djévo	Pärt, Arvo	189
Cantique de Jean Racine, Op. 11	Fauré, Gabriel Urban	193
Circus Band	Ives, Charles	199
Dirait-on	Lauridsen, Morten	204
A Gaelic Blessing	Rutter, John	208
Gloria	Haydn, (Franz) Joseph	211
Hallelujah, Amen	Handel, George Frideric	215
Haneirot Halalu	Hoffman, Stanley M.	218
He, Watching Over Israel	Mendelssohn (Bartholdy), Felix	222
Innoria (Huron Dance Song)	Patriquin, Donald	225
Johnny Has Gone for a Soldier	arr. Parker, Alice/Shaw, Robert	228
Jubilate Deo in C	Britten, Benjamin	231
The Last Words of David	Thompson, Randall	234
Let Their Celestial Concerts All Unite	Handel, George Frideric	237
Muié Rendêra	arr. Pinto Fonseca, Carlos A.	242
Musicks Empire	Pfautsch, Lloyd	246
Notre Père, Op. 14	Duruflé, Maurice	250
Salmo 150	Aguiar, Ernani	254
Set Me as a Seal	Clausen, René	258
Shenandoah	arr. Erb, James	261
Sicut cervus	Palestrina, Giovanni Piermigi da	264
Sure on This Shining Night	Barber, Samuel	268
Time and Concord	Britten, Benjamin	272
Vamuvamba	arr. Mganga, Boniface	276
Wade in the Water	arr. Hogan, Moses	280
When David Heard	Weelkes, Thomas	283
With Drooping Wings	Purcell, Henry	287
Zigeunerleben, Op. 29, No. 3	Schumann, Robert	291

Treble voices:

God's Bottles	Thompson, Randall	297
He's Gone Away	arr. Nelson, Ron	301
Ihr Heilgen, lobsinget dem Herren, SWV 288	Schütz, Heinrich	304
Nigra sum	Casals, Pablo	308
Our Father (Otche Nash)	Kastal'sky Alexandr	312
Stabat Mater	Pergolesi, Giovanni Battista	316

Men's voices:

Repertoire Resource Guide

Alleluia

Libby Larsen
(b. 1950)

SATB/a cappella
E.C. Schirmer Music Co.: 4829
Overall: 3
Vocal: 3
Tonal/Rhythm: 3

Composer

An American composer, Libby Larsen was born in Delaware and has studied and worked in Minnesota. She co-founded the Minnesota Composers Forum (since 1996, the American Composers Forum), which aims to define a role for composers outside academics. Larsen is publicly active in other music and music education issues. Her oeuvre includes work for the stage, orchestra, concert band, chamber and solo instruments, solo voice, and chorus.

Composition

Larsen's SATB a cappella choral piece "Alleluia" might be called semi-secular; although its sole word is ubiquitous in sacred literature, it also is celebratory in secular usage. "Alleluia" is peppy (quarter note = 120), full of changing meters and seventh (and ninth) chords, but is neither terribly difficult nor esoteric. This is a fun piece for the chorus and an audience pleaser, too.

As she often does, Larsen establishes a set of concise, understandable elemental motives and then mixes, matches, slightly alters, and transposes them. Motives are tossed back and forth across the sections, giving a share of the limelight and everyone a bit of "oo-ah" accompaniment.

There are two active motives: four staccato eighth notes and a swinging three eighth notes followed by a quarter tied to a dotted-quarter. Other motives may be derived from these as lyrical, accompanimental, barline-obscuring, or augmented permutations. The primary tonal center shifts as often as the meter does, while remaining tonal.

Anyone who knows Larsen's work will notice the clever text-rhythm setting, although in the absence of her more usual excellent lyrics, this facet may not be obvious to a first-timer.

Technical Considerations

Needless to say, the text presents no problem. Whether the shifting meters defeat, discourage, or energize the choral ensemble depends upon the conductor. It will be worth one's while to introduce the piece by selecting repeating rhythmic, melodic, and harmonic sections, and cannily presenting them. Some might even be excerpted as choral warm-up exercises.

Certainly, it would pay to speak areas of rhythm without pitches attached and to point out how small motives and more sizeable four-voiced sections reappear in identical or only slightly different guises. The first three measures, for instance, are repeated with some pitch alterations, and thereafter herald the beginning of each new section. Once the basic motives are well in hand, combining them goes fairly easily.

The same is true of the harmony. A cross relation (e.g., mm. 1–2, D in the alto against D-flat in the bass) may look daunting, but it is not hard to manage in context if the conductor presents a single instance carefully and subsequently expands the technique.

Voice sections often speak as three against two. As long as each section knows its current rhythm, this should not be difficult because all voices converge frequently on the same rhythm or held note.

The editor provides a piano reduction, which further eases beginning rehearsal steps.

Stylistic Considerations

Peppy and light overall, the intermittent lyrical sections (e.g., mm. 20–28, soprano and tenor duet) provide welcome contrast but should be rendered without vocal weight (although with round vowels and tone to preserve pitch altitude). Both tempo changes and expressive markings are plentiful and unambiguous, easing the conductor's preparation.

Because the motives and their altered forms are so plainly discernable, this piece offers the chance to characterize each motive differently— "bouncy," "sad," "awestruck," "each note separated," "ultra-smooth," "dry"— empowering the ensemble to create a constantly shifting mosaic of color.

Form and Structure

The composition takes an overall *ritornello* form, with the introductory material punctuating each new idea.

Contributed by:

Lani Johnson

Repertoire Resource Guide

Ave verum corpus, K. 618

Wolfgang Amadeus Mozart
(1756–1791)

SATB/keyboard or strings and continuo
Hinshaw Music, Inc.: HMC490
Overall: 3
Vocal: 3
Tonal/Rhythm: 3

Composer

Wolfgang Amadeus Mozart was born in Salzburg, Austria, January 27, 1756. Wolfgang's father, Leopold, a violinist and composer at the court of the prince-bishop of Salzburg, instructed the young Mozart in music from a very early age. Wolfgang was a prodigy; his earliest known compositions date from 1761, also the year of his first public performance.

Beginning in 1762, Leopold took Wolfgang and his sister Maria Anna on a series of concert tours around Europe during which they played for several of the European monarchs. The Bishop of Salzburg appointed Wolfgang *Konzertmeister* in 1769, the first of many honors he was to receive. Despite his prestigious position, Mozart wanted to leave Salzburg. In 1777, he unsuccessfully sought a job at the Mannheim court. The Archbishop of Salzburg granted him wide latitude, but finally released Mozart from his service in 1781.

In 1782, Mozart moved to Vienna, married Constanza Weber, composed a great deal, and enjoyed favor with Emperor Joseph II. Leopold died in 1787; in 1789, Mozart embarked on an extensive trip around Europe with Prince Karl Lichnowsky. Emperor Joseph died in 1790, and Mozart fell ill soon after going to Frankfurt for the coronation of Joseph's successor. He died in Vienna on December 5, 1791.

Mozart's output was extraordinarily extensive, considering his short life. His compositions include masses, motets, operas, symphonies, concertos, chamber music, and various other genres.

Composition

"Ave verum corpus," K. 618 is an accompanied motet. Mozart composed the piece in June 1791 in Baden, Austria, for the feast of Corpus Christi. Accompanied motets are not as common as unaccompanied ones in the history of music but became an established part of the literature starting in the Baroque era onward.

Historical Perspective

The feast of Corpus Christi was of special importance in Austria. Its observance included a community procession that stopped in front of four stations, and the feast was intended to unite Mother Church with Mother Earth. H. C. Robbins Landon believes that although Mozart composed "Ave verum corpus" for the feast, he actually intended the motet to help establish (along with his *Requiem*) a "new style of church music . . . unadorned, devotional and easily understood."

"Ave verum corpus" was first performed in the Baden parish church on Corpus Christi, 1791. Mozart's autograph manuscript is dated June 17, 1791.

Technical Considerations

The choral writing in this motet is simple. It is mostly homophonic, featuring several places where the lower three voices continue singing under a soprano held note (m. 15), one place where the lower two voices enter in imitation of the upper voices at a distance of one measure (mm. 30–31), and some light contrapuntal writing within the homophonic texture (m. 40).

In his manuscript, Mozart marks the instruments and voices *sotto voce* at the beginning and provides no dynamics. While soft singing is a definite requirement of this motet, the conductor is encouraged to ascertain that singers are using sufficient breath and that it is well-connected to the resonating chambers at all times. It is perhaps more advisable to think of the dynamics in this piece falling between mezzo piano and mezzo forte than to think of greater extremes, especially with less experienced singers. The melody resides in the soprano throughout; therefore, it is important for the sopranos to sing with a light but clear, forward, and spinning tone. The lower voices should be cautioned to listen not only to the sopranos but to one another; the sopranos should be cautioned to listen to the rest of the choir because their melody should not overwhelm the accompaniment.

Breathing is a challenge in this motet. Mozart's marking is *Adagio* in cut time. An overly slow tempo will impede a feeling of forward motion and make it impossible to sing the phrases comfortably and beautifully. On the other hand, however, an overly fast tempo will destroy the simple, peaceful beauty of the motet. Experimentation is encouraged; it will likely be necessary for the conductor to alternate between beating two and four. It is quite effective to breathe with the punctuation; for example, a short lift after the initial "Ave" before it is repeated helps to punctuate the text.

The notes are mostly simple to sing, and even the accidentals sound quite harmonic. It is important to pay careful attention at times, however, to the intonation. For example, at measure 24, the choir must sing a real C major-minor seventh chord to set up the resolution to F major. The notes in measure 27 can be difficult to achieve, and it helps for the choir members to understand the progression: a fully diminished seventh chord, followed by two major triads in first inversion accomplished by chromatic movement (except for the tenors, who have to sing a diminished fifth to a dominant seventh chord, etc.). The parts may be rehearsed individually to achieve security, but the singers must understand where they fit into the harmony. Measure 39 can seem challenging until the tenor and sopranos realize their interval is actually a minor third; the basses should be cautioned to sing small descending half steps in measures 39–41.

Stylistic Considerations

Simplicity is the key word for this motet. Extremes do not result in good performances. The conductor should avoid extreme dynamic contrasts and should be very judicious in his or her use of rubato. Its judicious use can be effective (m. 42), but realize that a little goes a very long way! What feels expressive in isolation can actually destroy the effectiveness of the music, which needs simple forward momentum throughout.

The conductor is also encouraged to experiment with using Austro-German Latin pronunciation as opposed to standard-liturgical Latin. The Austro-German version would have been what Mozart knew and used and would have affected the sounds he had in his ear. Beautiful color can be achieved with attention to this matter; Austro-German pronunciation is usually fairly simple for choirs to learn. (See Jeffers, referenced below.)

Musical Elements

"Ave verum corpus" is written for SATB choir and a small orchestra (strings and basso continuo). The choral writing is essentially homophonic. The orchestral parts sometimes double the choral writing (or *colla parte*), but are also independent. Organ or piano alone would be acceptable alternatives if the entire instrumental complement is unavailable.

Form and Structure

ABC

SECTION	MEASURE	EVENT AND SCORING
A	1–21	D major to A major.
B	22–29	A major, modulating to F major, ending on a dominant seventh of D major
C	30–46	D major

Text and Translation

Ave, verum corpus
natum de Maria Virgine,
Vere passum immolatum
in Cruce pro homine,
Cujus latus perforatum
unda fluxit et sanguine,
Esto nobis praegustatum
in mortis examine.

Hail, true body
born of the Virgin Mary,
Who truly suffered sacrifice
on the Cross for man,
From whose pierced side
blood streamed and flowed,
Be for us a foretaste
Of the test of death.

Suggested Listening

O Magnum Mysterium. The Westminster Choir. Joseph Flummerfelt, conductor. (Chesky Records CD083).

Choral Masterpieces. Atlanta Symphony Chorus. Robert Shaw, conductor. (Telarc 80119).

Additional Reference and Resources

For information on Austro-German Latin pronunciation:
Jeffers, Ron. *Translations and Annotations of Choral Repertoire. Volume I: Sacred Latin Texts*. Corvallis, Oregon. Earthsongs. 1988.

For the Urtext of Mozart's score:
Mozart, W. A. *Neue Ausgabe sämtlicher Werke: Serie I, Geistliche Gesangwerke.*
    Bärenreiter-Verlag Kassel. 1963. 261–62.

For general information:
Robbins Landon. *Mozart's Last Year.* Thames and Hudson. 1988.

Contributed by:

Matthew W. Mehaffey
Anthony Reeves

Repertoire Resource Guide

Bogoróditse Djévo

Arvo Pärt
(b. 1935)

SATB divisi/a cappella
Universal Edition: UE 30414
Level: 3
Vocal: 3
Tonal/Rhythm: 4

Composer

Arvo Pärt is one of the best-known Estonian composers outside of Estonia. After graduating from Tallinn Conservatory in 1963, Pärt made a living as a recording engineer and a composer of film and theater music. His early serious compositions were officially criticized by the Soviet authorities for their serialist leanings. A growing fascination with the music of J. S. Bach lead him to compose works in imitation of Baroque style, even basing tone rows on the notes B-A-C-H. (In German notation, "H" stands for B natural and "B" stands for B flat.) His *Credo* is a combination of the famous C major prelude from Bach's *Well-Tempered Clavier* and serial techniques. This work earned censure not only for its serial compositional content but also for its Christian subject matter.

Pärt composed very little between 1968 and 1976. He spent his time studying early music, especially Gregorian chant, and creating a new style of composition that would become the hallmark of his later works. Called *tintinnabuli*, the name of the style makes reference to the sounds of bells, which Pärt feels his technique evokes. Most of Pärt's works since the evolution of this new style have been choral, including the St. John Passion from 1982, which makes rigorous use of the *tintinnabuli* style.

Composition

"Bogoróditse Djévo" was commissioned by Stephen Cleobury and the King's College Choir for a Christmas Eve Festival of Lessons and Carols. The mixed meters typical of Pärt are infrequent in this work. A rhythmic pattern (two sixteenths, then a succession of eighth notes) characterizes the outer sections, and a prevailing quarter-note, organ-like tactus characterizes the middle section. Although it is easy at the beginning to identify a *tintinnabuli* voice on the repeated "E," it seems the treatment is not pervasive. Probably *tintinnabuli* is at work in the first and last sections, but it is overlaid by the tertian harmony throughout—mostly I–V in the first and last sections and I–IV spiced with vi and ii in the middle. This is a good introduction to Pärt for choirs that have not yet experienced his works, and audiences also like it. The text is from the Gospel of Luke.

Historical Perspective

In the twentieth century, a number of composers, including Arvo Pärt, strove to incorporate the history, culture, and philosophy of their nations into their music. Lacking a worldwide canon for musical technique, this led to a multiplicity of styles, subjects, media, and sound that choral conductors and their ensembles can benefit from discovering.

Technical Considerations

Probably the most valuable thing a conductor can do is prepare this piece before facing the choir. It falls into quarter-note and dotted quarter-note tacti. Measures 22 and 25 may—and most likely should—be subdivided (m. 22: duple, duple, triple, triple; eighth-note tactus and m. 25: duple, two triples; quarter-note tactus), or the choir and even the conductor may get lost in the syllables and miss appropriate word stresses. Both the conductor's and the singers' scores should be marked with the tactus of each measure grouping's conducting pattern. Deciding the subtleties of accelerando, decelerando, crescendo, and decrescendo, and which voice predominates will complete preparation.

The piece must continue from beginning to end without a break, except for the eighth rest in measure 27. A good approach is to designate sectional breaths—never two sections at the same time—when a principal idea moves from one voice part to the next. For instance, tenors may snatch a quick and quiet breath at the end of measure 15 to come in fresh in 16. Should the conductor decide to allow other unified breaths, instead, a second strategy is to clip the note (see m. 21, which would become dotted half, quarter rest), but be sure the impetus of motion does not cease when sound, temporarily, does.

Very clean entries and cutoffs are necessary to keep the moving idea unbroken. Use the syllable "bim" once in awhile in rehearsals to reinforce accurate rhythm, onset, and cutoff. Also practice smooth, silent onset of phonation.

Pärt and Universal Edition provide a helpful pronunciation guide, which the non-Russian-speaking conductor must know very well before presenting the text.

Stylistic Considerations

The dynamic range of "Bogoróditse Djévo" is great: *p* to *ff*. Pärt intends all levels to be performed. Furthermore, the static *tintinnabuli* should be audible whenever present, the better to appreciate the melodic and harmonic voices moving around it. The return of the A section as four-voiced static chords can sound boring if not energized. A bouncy presentation of measures 27–38 will provide excitement and contrast with the first fifteen measures, which set some of the same text. A bouncing conducting gesture will elicit a lightly bouncing choral response.

The repeated rhythmic figure helps identify the beginning of phrases. A further help to interpreting the piece is Pärt's barring: a noticeable but not overly heavy downbeat marks the beginning of each measure and explains the shifting meters.

Notice in measures 16–19 that Pärt has made no attempt to set parallel text statements ("blessed…and blessed") in parallel musical structures. In fact, his first divergence from the rhythmic figure is at the second "blessed." With the appearance of successive quarter notes (measure 17, beat 3), the chorus should round and enrich their sound toward one characteristic with Slavic choral music. The tenors and basses should make this vocal color transition earlier, at measure 16. Alternating between that rich sound and a more declamatory one (declamatory: mm. 22–23, back to rich: mm. 24–26) will enliven the performance.

Do not allow anyone to let down when the notes and rhythms settle down at measure 27. It may be easy to sing from here on, but it is very difficult to sing *well*. The piece should end with awe and intensity at the piano dynamic.

Form and Structure

ABA or ABC, A major

Text and Translation

Bogoróditse Djévo, rádujssja,
Blagodátnaja Maríje, Gosspód ssTobóju;
blagosslovjéna Ty v zhenákh I blagosslovjén plod chrjéva Tvojégó,
Jáko Sspássa rodilá jeessí dush náshikh.

—transliterated from Cyrillic script

Rejoice, O virgin Mary, full of grace, the Lord is with thee:
Blessed art thou among women,
and blessed is the fruit of thy womb,
For thou has borne the Savior of our souls.

—translation as printed in the score

Suggested Listening

Arvo Pärt: I Am the True Vine. Pro Arte Singers. Paul Hillier. (Harmonia Mundi HMU 907242).

Contributed by:

Lani Johnson

Repertoire Resource Guide

Cantique de Jean Racine, Op. 11

Gabriel Urbain Fauré
(1845–1924)

SATB/keyboard
Hinshaw Music, Inc.: HMC933
Overall: 3
Vocal: 3
Tonal/Rhythm: 3

Composer

Born in the French town of Pamiers and youngest of six siblings in the schoolteacher's family, Gabriel Fauré was an excellent pianist from childhood. He moved to Paris and entered the École Niedermeyer at the age of nine, where he studied under Camille Saint-Saëns. He left the school at twenty, taking with him awards for excellence in several areas. He found his first professional position a rural bore and so returned to Paris, helped once again by lifelong friend Saint-Saëns. For the next several decades, he worked at the Madeleine church, supplementing his salary by giving lessons in piano and harmony. When the Franco-Prussian War began in 1870, Fauré joined the army as a messenger, a singularly dangerous job at the time.

Through his middle age, Fauré served as organist at various Paris churches, including the Madeleine, but did not join the Paris Conservatory teaching staff until 1897. In 1905, in the aftermath of a scandal over Ravel's refusal to accept the Prix de Rome, Fauré accepted directorship of the Conservatory, undertaking major reforms to its agenda.

Fauré was unlucky in marriage. He took Marguerite Hasselmans, 30 years his junior, as his mistress later in life and continued seeing her until his death.

The composer retired in 1920, focusing for the next four years on composition.

Fauré's oeuvre includes piano, chamber, and vocal music; sacred and secular choral works; and orchestral and stage works. His style is typically divided into four periods:

YEAR	STYLE	TYPIFYING COMPOSITION
1860–70	Classical	*Elégie*
1880s	Parnassian poets	*Clair de lune*
1890s	mature, expressive	great piano works
1900–24	economy of expression, bold harmony, infusion of polyphony	Nocturne No. 11

Composition

The sacred choral cantata *Cantique de Jean Racine*, Op. 11 (1865, 1876) for mixed chorus and organ was twice revised: in 1866 for mixed chorus, harmonium, and string quartet and in 1906 for orchestra (two flutes, two oboes, two clarinets, two bassoons, two horns, harp, violin 1 and 2, viola, cello, and bass). It is essentially homophonic and sometimes contrapuntally enlivened, with occasional imitative passages.

Technical Considerations

For a French composition, *Cantique* is not pitched particularly low; in fact, the tessitura can be an asset in inexperienced, young, or aging choirs. Fauré works with very few pitches overall to achieve this moving work.

TESSITURA	LOW PITCH	HIGH PITCH	TYPICAL
S	E4	G5	A4–D5
A	C4	C-flat5	F4–B-flat4
T	E3	G4	B-flat3–E-flat4
B	F2	B-flat3	C3–F3

The harmonic rhythm is quick throughout—seldom does a chord last a full measure—but it is tonal. The most adventurous excursions are to VII and III, with a few augmented or diminished chords, all carefully prepared and executed. More typical are two harmonic progressions: I–V^7–I with a walking bass passing through vi, iii^6, and IV$^{6/4}$ to I^6; and I–IV–V^7/V–V^7–I. The B section, developmental in nature, modulates, to be sure, but logically and mostly stepwise.

The choir generally sings in quarter note and half note values, which can add up to eighty-eight boring measures with the *Andante* tempo marked quarter note = 80 unless the conductor pays attention to Fauré's composed-in help. The long phrases are written to contour, and the occasional eighth note passages beg for a bouncier articulation than the prevailing descending quarter note theme. The choir will appreciate a carefully prepared score with prudent breaths specified. In addition, the conductor should take care that the theme emerges from the texture, whichever voice it temporarily resides in.

The French text presents a challenge to many American ensembles. English translations are not really adequate, as may be seen from my mostly literal translation and from Harold Heiburg's poetic one, printed on the Broude Brothers choral score. In several places, the text phrases differ among the voices, with one voice beginning or finishing what another has carried along. If the text is to be heard—one recording I heard delivers beautiful music but no recognizable text—it must be coached separately from notes and rhythms and by someone who understands how to pronounce both spoken French and its sung counterpart.

The melody and accompaniment admirably express a clam longing for salvation, and the textual reference to God is generic except in measure 60. For those with sectarian constraints, it might be possible to creatively edit this one word.

Stylistic Considerations

The choice of accompanimental ensemble will likely limit, but not eliminate, the conductor's first decision: which edition to choose. Several publishers offer choral scores; fewer have full scores; and fewer still publish sets of instrumental parts. Given the sublime arpeggiated accompanimental pattern that pervades, the least tempting option is to perform *Cantique de Jean Racine* with a piano playing the orchestral reduction. Much better to hire a harpist, if only one accompanimental instrument is possible. If, however, exigency dictates piano, coach the pianist for an expressive, flowing, expertly pedaled style.

The accompaniment's overriding pattern is monodic, with the melody carried either in the treble or the bass. An anticipatory statement of each melodic phrase precedes the choral entry at the beginning of each section.

If the rehearsal pianist delivers the accompaniment in a legato style that emphasizes the melody with phrasing the conductor has coached, the choir will soon follow suit.

Form and Structure

The overall form is Introduction–A–B–A–Coda.

SECTION	MEASURE	EVENT AND SCORING
Introduction	1–13	Instruments; 7+6 phrase; melody, call and response

SECTION	MEASURE	EVENT AND SCORING
A	14–31	Chorus enters; 7+6+6 phrase; developmental and unsettled, melody travels among voices
	31–39	Instruments; 6+2 phrase
B	39–47	Chorus and instruments; voices share melody; 6+3 phrase
	47–51	Paired entries of SA/TB, most adventurous harmony
	51–59	4+4 phrase; fugal, adventurous harmony
A	59–79	Chorus and instruments; mm. 60–71, same as mm. 2–11, 15–23; mm. 70–75, same as mm. 28–31; mm. 76–79, sequence 70–75
Coda	79–88	Chorus and instruments; 4+5 phrase; instruments/voice conversation

Imitation, paired entries, homophony (with the main melody migrating through the voice parts) and restrained polyphony express rather than illustrate the text. The work dies virtually to *niente*.

Text and Translation

Verbe égal au Très-Haut, notre unique espérance,
Jour éternel de la terre et des nuit,
De la paisible nuit, nous rompons le silence.
Divin Sauveur, jette sur nous les yeux!

Répands sur nous le feu de ta grâce puissante,
Que tout l'enfer fuie au son de ta voix,
Disipe le sommeil d'une âme languissante,
Qui la conduit à l'oubli de tes lois!

Ô Christ, sois favorable à ce peuple
Fidèle pour te bénir maintenant rassemblé,
Reçois les chants qu'il offre à ta gloire immortelle
Et de tes dons qu'il retourne comblé!

Word of the Most High, our sole hope,
Eternal day of the earth and skies,
In this peaceful moment, we break the silence.
Divine Savior, let your eyes fall upon us!

Send upon us the fire of your powerful grace,
Which all realize who flee at the sound of your voice.
Disperse the sleep of the [our] languishing soul[s],
That lead[s] [us] to abandon your laws!

O Christ, look favorably on your faithful people,
Who, kneeling, pray to you.
Accept the songs we offer to your immortal glory
and these, your gifts, which we return abundantly to you!

—translation by Lani Johnson

Suggested Listening

Fauré: Sacred Music. The Cambridge Singers. John Rutter, conductor. (Collegium records CD COLCD 109).

Panis Angelicus. The Choir of Westminster Cathedral. James O'Donnell, conductor. (Hyperion Records CDA66669).

Contributed by:

Lani Johnson

Repertoire Resource Guide

Circus Band

Charles Ives
(1874–1954)

SATB divisi/piano four-hands
Peermusic Classical: 60187-1360
Overall: 3
Vocal: 3
Tonal/Rhythm: 3

Composer

Danbury, Connecticut owes part of its identity to the Ives family. Charles Ives' great-grandfather moved there in 1785 after graduating from Yale, wed his way into two founding families and into the hat-manufacturing industry (through which nineteenth-century Danbury flourished). Ives lived in and around the town for much of his adult life and retreated to a home in nearby West Redding when he retired from public view.

The son of a bandmaster, Ives was an organist, insurance magnate, seminal financial planner, an unwilling pupil of Horatio Parker, a political activist, and a writer of sales and philosophical monographs. He never made a living by composing, but earned several fortunes in insurance and is one of the founders of the American flavor of both that industry and of estate planning. Ives' music was generally disdained until late in his life, when it (and he) received an impressive array of national and international awards. His reputation as a composer began to grow after his death and continues to do so to the present.

Ives incorporated pre-existing tunes into his music, especially hymns. He also drew from ragtime, blues, and other contemporaneous musical developments that used clusters, bitonality, and other "twentieth-century" techniques. Ives loved sonority for its own sake and vital rhythmic effects; he had a clear understanding of orchestral timbres, a large world view, and a ready wit. (Notice how he placed the final "not" of "Circus Band" one beat late.) He transcended or ignored—it depends upon one's point of view—the musical mores of the time. In a different way from Copland, Ives demonstrates an idiomatically authentic American music. Much of his output languished, unperformed for decades after completion.

Composition

It is difficult to place "Circus Band" chronologically and probably unnecessary to do so because this piece was as frequently revised as many of the composer's works. In a scant 96 measures, it illustrates many of Ives's trademarks. It is melodically cogent, organized into regular sections of a predictable number of measures. "Circus Band" contains clusters of notes (e.g., E–F-sharp–G–A-flat–B-flat chord in m. 41), circus rhythms, boyish exclamations, ragtime and barbershop licks, a couple of pre-existing tunes, syncopation, and a "misplaced" note, as if the basses got off track and had to finish late.

The instrumental introduction (mm. 1–8) moves from F-sharp minor to A major using secondary-dominant modulations that characterize the whole piece. The A section begins the story (mm. 9–24) in A major, ending on the tonic, which is the dominant of D major, in which the B section (mm. 25–40) is written. In turn, it ends on its tonic, but the harmonic connection to the C section is less straightforward.

A sprightly instrumental cluster of notes interrupts the orderly motion of the piece (mm. 41–44), which gets back on track with an F-sharp diminished seventh to C major chord progression, the second chord establishing the F major of the key signature in measures 45 to 49. At measure 49, voices reenter. By now the original cut time has become 6/8, perhaps to evoke the rolling gait of circus elephants bearing the performers whose appearance constitutes the storyteller's nostalgic queries. Each query is punctuated by an instrumental section that employs wonderful extended sonorities (yes, plural): blues, ragtime, dissonance for its own sake, and octave displacement. The C section stays pretty much in F major. The second query (mm. 81–96) is reiterated, overlaid by a reflective commentary, presumably by the circus performers, and ends with a delightful "not" after all voices but one are finished.

Historical Perspective

Probably aptly, Jan Swafford classifies this twentieth-century American composer "important" rather than "great." His lifetime spanned the turn of the twentieth century, two World Wars, the Roaring Twenties and the Great

Depression, and the eclipse of Romantic, tonal music by structured, mannered (some might say ill-mannered) compositional techniques. Ives' New England, Yankee moral sensibilities kept him in the limelight while his personality was savaged by the disapproval his philosophies engendered. Although tremendously emotional and often celebratory, Ives' music tends to elude the grasp of many, perhaps exactly because it incorporates so many stylistic and technical features into works that are frequently celebratory, investigative, and rambunctious.

It's possible to provide historical perspective for this piece alone, thanks again to Jan Swafford, whom I both paraphrase and quote: The original version may be lost—the catalogue of Ives's works is unclear (see *New Groves* article on Charles Ives to learn why)—but may have been from about 1894 and for band. The piano version probably dates from 1899. At some point, Ives added the delightful words for the song version, published in *114 Songs*. In the 1930s, his copyist, George Roberts, probably arranged it for chamber orchestra with optional chorus. What is pretty certain is that it was originally a regular band march (or a piano version of it) to which words were added.

The text comes from a time that cannot be recaptured. It illustrates the excitement that accompanies the arrival of a circus in a small, summertime New England community when even a child's memory could be measured in years instead of thirty-second increments.

Technical Considerations

The underlying tempo "in quickstep time" calls to mind the thirteen-year-old Ives' first composition to be performed in public, a march for band. Metronome markings are given throughout, making it easier for those of us unfamiliar with quickstep. The accompaniment constitutes a full voice, not simply a background; it would be wise to coach the pianists to deliver their parts with humor, as the accompaniment sets up the various choral entries; playing with personality will help the choir achieve a more parade-like enthusiasm.

Because most of the piece is in unison it is accessible to choirs of many levels. This is an opportunity to bring Ives's music to students and audiences—without undue anxiety.

A major consideration in teaching "Circus Band" is that it is typically Ivesian: rhythms are not predictable. The rhythms should be under the singer's control before pitches are introduced. Speaking words in rhythm, with desired articulations and cutoffs, will save later frustration. Recordings are available, and some conductors may find it useful to play one from time to time throughout the learning process.

The most difficult section is from measure 81 to the end: the polyphonic section. Designate a group of three to five of the more mature voices to present the semi-chorus line during the repeat of the third section. This line is, after all, an adult's comment. First sopranos and first tenors sing together, as do second sopranos and second tenors. Altos are paired at the octave with first basses. Otherwise, there are three melodies in these fifteen SSATTBB measures: semi-chorus, soprano 1 and tenor 1, and bass 2 lines. The other voices fill in. All three melodies should be discernible, and the supporting parts should do just that. During this rollicking collage of sound, the accompaniment doubles the voices.

That having been said, it would be a good idea to woodshed the notes (after rhythms are well learned). A small group from all voices in the choir (semi-chorus) could be sent off to become experts in the notes and expressions of their parts. Soprano 1 and tenor 1, soprano 2 and tenor 2, alto and bass 1, and bass 2 each should learn parts separately. Then, in tutti rehearsal, before launching into full tutti, combine soprano 1 and tenor 1 with, soprano 2 and tenor 2 with alto and bass 1, and the semi-chorus with bass 2 and alto and bass 1.

"Circus Band" is accessible, although middle-aged and senior singers' notion of melody may not be as free as that of younger singers. The tessitura is moderate. This is a fun piece!

Stylistic Considerations

The ad lib sections may be repeated as notated or a predesignated number of times. This decision will depend upon how one programs "Circus Band" in a concert. One fun way to use this piece in a choir of sufficient size would be to move from one choral configuration to another with singing. Part of the choir could walk without singing while the rest repeats the A or B section.

This text tells a story; the musical setting does likewise. Elicit a light, conversational style. Phrasing is dictated by the text and supported by the composition, and so are dynamic and tempo changes as well as articulations.

Form and Structure

Overall, the form is Introduction–A (repeated)–B (repeated)–C (repeated), following what is apparently Ives' own text. The keys change frequently but understandably, and there are touches of extended chromatic chords.

Suggested Listening

Ives: An American Journey. Michael Tilson Thomas, conductor. (RCA 63703).

Westminster Choir at Spoleto Festival U.S.A. Joseph Flummerfelt, conductor. (Gothic Records 49078).

Additional References and Resources

Swafford, Jan. *Charles Ives: A Life with Music*, W.W. Norton, 1996.

Contributed by:

Lani Johnson

Repertoire Resource Guide

Dirait-on

Morten Lauridsen
(b. 1943)

SATB/piano, SSA/piano, or TTBB/piano
Peermusic Classical: SATB=61846-122, SSA=61922-106,
TTBB=61880-120
Overall: 3
Vocal: 4
Tonal/Rhythm: 3

Composer

The music of Morten Lauridsen has come to the forefront of American music culture. His music, full of added note chords, captures the serenity of the texts that he sets. Born in Washington State, Lauridsen studied at Whitman College and the University of Southern California. He studied composition with Ingolf Dahl, Halsey Stevens, Robert Linn, and Harold Owen. He is currently professor of music at the University of Southern California. Lauridsen's works are enjoying unprecedented popularity. His works for choir include "O Magnum Mysterium" and the song cycles *Lux Aeterna*, *Madrigali: Six "Firesongs" on Italian Renaissance Poems*, and *Mid-Winter Songs*.

Composition

"Dirait-on" is the fifth song of choral cycle entitled *Les Chanson des Roses*. The entire set features five French poems by Rainer Maria Rilke. In the preface to this composition Lauridsen says, "His [Rilke's] poems on roses struck me as especially charming, filled with gorgeous lyricism, deftly crafted and elegant in their imagery. These exquisite poems are primarily light, joyous, and playful, and the musical settings are designed to enhance these characteristics and capture their delicate beauty and sensuousness."

"Dirait-on" is the only piece from the set of five that has accompaniment. If you perform the whole set, the adventuresome choir director can choose to segue the fourth piece, "La Rose Complete," directly into "Dirait-on." If the choir is not perfectly in tune, however, it will be very apparent, as the piano plays on the downbeat. Lauridsen gives an optional ending of "La Rose Complete" for the weak of heart!

Historical Perspective

Les Chansons des Roses was composed for the professional chamber chorus Choral Cross-Ties, conducted by Bruce Browne. The premiere occurred on April 23, 1993.

Technical Considerations

French is difficult for any choir to sing. The conductor should carefully prepare to coach the pronunciation or recruit someone qualified to do so. It is important to realize, however, that the diction rules for sung French are different in some ways from spoken French. The conductor is strongly encouraged to separate the text from the music at the beginning of the learning process. Learn the notes and rhythms via count-singing and neutral syllables. Then, take the notes away from the words. Speak the text in rhythm, being extremely careful that the choir observes all articulations and breath marks. When this is mastered, the words, notes, and rhythms can be reunited.

The piano part is not very difficult. It should, however, be played with great expression with particular sensitivity to the vocal texture.

Stylistic Considerations

Lauridsen is very particular with his compositions. He takes great time to mark in slight changes of dynamic or tempo. The conductor should ensure that the choir performs all of these markings. Careful score study is necessary with Lauridsen's music, as there are so many subtle changes of which the conductor needs to be aware.

Musical Elements

Lauridsen's music is easily recognized by his use of first inversion chords. The constant use of first inversion provides a delicate, sometimes ethereal sound to the music. It is important to realize that voice leading, particularly for the basses, will be much different from what they are used to singing. They need to realize that in Lauridsen's music they do not sing the root of the chord very often. This has implications on the intonation. If the basses sing the "third" of the chord (the bass note of a first inversion chord) in the same way they would the root of the chord, the choir will never sing in tune. The third (or Mi) always needs to be slightly higher in intonation. Awareness of this fact will help the singers understand how to sing in tune.

Form and Structure

The form of "Dirait-on" is built on a verse/refrain format. The women begin with the first strophe of the text; they continue with refrain, which comes from the last two words of the first strophe ("dirait-on"). The men present the second strophe of poetry, which is followed by a unison refrain. Lauridsen then presents the refrain in a quasi-canonic fashion; the men follow the women at a distance of one beat. The sopranos return to the first strophe, and the altos then present the second strophe. The basses sing in canon with the sopranos and the altos during this time; the tenors sing a beautiful accompanimental vocal line. The tenors will tend to sing too loudly during this section; remind them that their part is the least important. A slow transition leads back to a final refrain and coda.

Text and Translation

Abandon entouré d'abandon,
tendresse touchant aux tendresses. . .
C'est ton intérieur qui sans cesse
se caresse, dirait-on...

Abandon surrounding abandon,
tenderness touching tenderness. . .
Your oneness endlessly
caresses itself, so they say. . .

—translation by Barbara and Erica Muhl

Suggested Listening

Echo in My Soul. Northwest Girlchoir and Friends. Rebecca Rottsolk, conductor. (SSA version, Arsis CD 121).

Lux Aeterna. Los Angeles Master Chorale. Paul Salamunovich, conductor. (RCM 19705).

Contributed by:

Matthew W. Mehaffey
Anthony Reeves

Repertoire Resource Guide

A Gaelic Blessing

John Rutter
(b. 1945)

SATB/keyboard or SSA/keyboard
Hinshaw Music, Inc.: SATB=RCSM 501, SSA=RCSM 521
Overall: 3
Vocal: 3
Tonal/Rhythm: 4

Composer

Born in London in 1945, English composer John Rutter has become one of the most performed choral composers of the late twentieth and early twenty-first century. Following his education at Clare College–Cambridge, Rutter went on to teach at the University of Southampton and Clare College. He left Clare in 1979 to pursue composition and ultimately established the Cambridge Singers, a professional choral ensemble, in 1981.

His compositional career has yielded small works, including anthems and carol arrangements, and large works, like *Gloria*, *Requiem*, and *Magnificat*. He has also written children's operas and music for television. He has coedited many choral anthologies, including four volumes of *Carols for Choirs*. His music, inspired by his English predecessors, including Vaughan Williams, Howells, and Britten, is always tuneful and employs a colorful harmonic language.

Composition

"A Gaelic Blessing" is an anthem setting of an old Gaelic rune for SATB choir and organ. The text and musical style of the piece make it a wonderful benediction for a church service or a final encore of a concert. The work was commissioned by First United Methodist Church in Omaha, Nebraska; it was published in 1978 and was one of Rutter's early successful compositions.

Technical Considerations

A recording of "A Gaelic Blessing" makes the work seem to be a simple, beautiful anthem setting. Be advised: it would be unwise to underestimate the difficulty of this piece. It sounds very simple because of Rutter's well-crafted voice leading and sense of melody. There are many accidentals, subtle rhythmic changes, and suspensions that make an easy read of this piece for an amateur choir a rarity. It might be wise to have your choir listen to a good recording of this work a few times before starting the reading process. (The number of times may vary depending in the skill of your choir.) This will allow the singers to assimilate Rutter's harmonic language and will get them excited about working hard to achieve this beautiful piece. After they have listened to the piece a few times, work to get the lower three voices confident about their parts, as they essentially serve as accompaniment to the soprano melody. Do not underestimate the difficulty of the rhythm in this piece, particularly when you put all parts together. It is important that each part is completely accurate rhythmically so all of the voice leading is clear and the new harmonies always sound on time. To achieve this, count singing could be very helpful.

Stylistic Considerations

As this piece is composed in the English choral style, all vowels should be formed in a tall, narrow shape, and all consonants should be light and crisp. Vowels should all be more closed and placed more forward in the resonance than the vowels in American English. The musical line should be continuous from the beginning of the piece until the end. It would be easy for this piece to sound trite if the tempo gets too fast and if there is no musical line (legato) throughout the piece.

Musical Elements

The piece begins and ends in E major but takes a harmonic trip through many tonalities. As mentioned above, the voice leading is well executed, but it can be difficult for amateur singers to anticipate the sudden changes of tonality. Take time to work transitions between tonalities in isolation (e.g., sing just the two chords in question several times in a row).

Hemiolas occur frequently in the soprano part and occasionally in the lower parts. This type of rhythmic pattern can cause train wrecks without much warning. Make singers aware of these places and instruct them to count carefully and not to rush through the middle note of the hemiola.

Form and Structure

"A Gaelic Blessing" is a through-composed setting of an old Gaelic rune (from German *runa*, meaning secret). The four part choral writing is in melody and accompaniment style.

Text

Deep peace of the of the running wave to you,
Deep peace of the flowing air to you,
Deep peace of the quiet earth to you,
Deep peace of the shining stars to you,
Deep peace of the gentle night to you,
Moon and stars pour their healing light on you,
Deep peace of Christ the light of the world to you,
Deep peace of Christ to you.

Suggested Listening

Gloria: The sacred music of John Rutter. The Cambridge Singers. John Rutter, conductor. (Collegium Records CD COLCD 100).

Contributed by:

Matthew W. Mehaffey

Repertoire Resource Guide

Gloria

(Franz) Joseph Haydn
(1732–1809)

SATB/keyboard
Warner Bros. Publications: OCTB 02575
Overall:3
Vocal: 3
Tonal/Rhythm: 3

Composer

Joseph Haydn was the most celebrated composer of his time by the 1780s and is commonly considered the father of both the modern symphony and the string quartet. After a youth spent as a boy chorister in Vienna, Haydn found employment as a freelance musician and then as a music director for a local count. After the orchestra was disbanded, Haydn was employed by Prince Esterházy, enjoying decades of royal patronage.

The music-loving prince and his successor, Prince Nikolaus, made great demands on the composer, resulting in the production of an enormous amount of music for their orchestras, their theaters, their chapel, and for their own use in small chamber ensembles. Upon the death of Prince Nicholas, Haydn was free to travel and made two celebrated trips to England where several of his now best-known symphonies were performed to great acclaim. Upon his return to Vienna, Haydn composed the bulk of his large-scale works, including six grand masses and two oratorios (inspired by concerts of Handel's music witnessed in England).

Composition

Haydn's first and last completed compositions were mass settings, and vocal music comprises half of his output. This movement is taken from the *Mariazellermesse HXXII.8*, which is part of the first group of masses Haydn composed. The work was commissioned by Anton Liebe von Kreutzner, a retired military man living in Vienna who wished to have a mass composed for the pilgrimage church at Mariazell. The work is scored for oboe, bassoon, trumpet (or horn), timpani, strings, continuo, SATB chorus, and soloists, but it can also be performed with piano accompaniment. This movement is actually only a part of the Gloria from the Roman Catholic mass, comprising only the first four lines of text. As was typical for a large mass at the time, the *Mariazellermesse* is broken up into many movements each of which carries only a few lines of text and varies in scoring from one movement to the next.

Historical Perspective

The *Mariazellermesse* was composed shortly before the effects of Emperor Joseph II's reforms, commonly called Josephinism. These reforms lessened the importance of music in the churches of Austria by banning instrumental music except on Sundays and holidays, removing financial support for church musicians and choirs, and by closing many of the monasteries. These withdrawals of official support for church music led to a general decrease in the output of sacred music during the time of their enforcement. Haydn's composition of sacred music was also affected by these reforms, dividing his sacred works into two groups: those composed before the reforms and those composed after. This particular mass (1782) comes from the first group of masses and was one of the last works composed before the reforms took effect.

The musical language of this work fits squarely in the classical conception of melody and harmony that Haydn did so much to establish.

Technical Consideratirons

This work is a dramatic setting of the Gloria text, requiring both forceful declamation and lyrical singing at a piano dynamic. The rhythms are largely quarter notes and eighth notes in regular patterns, although a pattern of dotted eighth notes and sixteenth notes predominates in the opening section. The rhythms are further simplified by the homophonic texture, and there is one small section with imitation in the alto part which complicates the rhythm slightly. The vocal range is not extreme, requiring two high G quarter notes of from the sopranos and nothing lower than B-flat from the basses. The sixteenth notes in the opening section require some attention to articulation, but the rest of the piece is more concerned with extended, sustained melodic lines. There is some chromatic inflection throughout, largely in the context of applied dominant chords and nothing too far from the home key of B-flat major. The accompaniment, if performed on a keyboard instrument, is not difficult.

Stylistic Considerations

There are sections of declamation in this work that require crisply articulated singing, and there are sections of lyrical melody better suited to sustained singing. The section beginning "Et in terra pax," for example, starts with descending half notes in octaves for all the vocal parts, contrasting sharply with the sixteenth note dominated opening. Still, the overall impression is one of strong rhythmic punctuation, and the sense of rhythmic motion and clarity must be present even in the softer and more lyrical sections. As is consistent with the period, this Mass setting is a public setting intended not for personal but for communal worship. The setting is never sentimental or overtly personal, but ceremonial. Though dynamics are absent from the piece, variations were certainly expected and can be sought out from a particular edition (if not determined solely by the conductor). When there is a shift of dynamic, it is almost always accompanied by a shift of texture and a change in the meaning of the text.

Musical Elements

The tonality of the work is strongly rooted in B-flat major. Cadences are strong and marked, bringing clear closure to a section. The harmonic progression moves logically, without any sudden surprises, except for a shift to begin a harmonic sequence at measure 33. Here, however, the accompaniment carries the new harmonic material for a full quarter note before the choir enters, simplifying the shift for the singers. There is also a short section of more distant harmonic material at measure 25, although each voice part approaches the new harmonies by step, and the tensions are resolved logically and by step. The texture is predominantly homophonic, featuring only one moment of imitation in the alto part in measures 34–42. Each section of the piece has its own melodic motive, and the opening melody returns slightly transformed in the closing section. The meter is an extremely regular 4/4.

Form and Structure

This work breaks into very clear sections based upon its text, with each section punctuated by a strong cadence.

MEASURE	EVENT AND SCORING
1–2	Instrumental opening; B-flat major
3–14	"Gloria in excelsis Deo"; B-flat major
15–28	"Et in terra pax"; cadence in F major

MEASURE	EVENT AND SCORING
28–32	"Laudamus te"; F dominant seventh chord
33–37	"Adoramus te"; modulatory
37–49	"Glorificamus te"; B-flat major
49–51	Instrumental coda; B-flat major

Text and Translation

Gloria in excelsis Deo,
Et in terra pax hominibus bonae voluntatis.
Laudamus te, Benedicimus te.
Adoramus te, Glorificamus te.

Glory to God in the highest,
And on earth peace to all those of good will.
We praise thee, we bless thee.
We worship thee, we glorify thee.

Contributed by:

Matthew W. Mehaffey
Anthony Reeves

Repertoire Resource Guide

Hallelujah, Amen

George Frideric Handel
(1685–1759)

SATB/keyboard
Novello Publications, Inc.: 34.0062.10
Overall: 3
Vocal: 3
Tonal/Rhythm: 3

Composer

Handel was born in 1685 in Halle, Germany (the same year as J. S. Bach). By the age of nineteen, he had moved to Hamburg to play violin and harpsichord for the Hamburg Opera, which also gave him the opportunity to write and perform his first operas. In 1706 he moved to Italy and established himself firmly as composer.

Though he lived for a time in Germany, he spent most of his life in England. His output was vast, including solo songs in five different languages, as well as sacred and secular choral works. His grandest achievements lie in his dramatic operas (*Esther, Ariodante,* and *Alcina* among others) and oratorios (*Judas Maccabeus, Jephthe*); he is best known for the popular oratorio *Messiah*.

Composition

"Hallelujah, Amen" is the final chorus from the oratorio *Judas Maccabeus*, composed in 1746. It is polyphonic with some melismatic activity. The full score is for SATB choir, two trumpets, two oboes, timpani, two violins and viola that sometimes play *colla parte*, and basso continuo. In addition, some scores contain an additional melody for children's choir.

Technical Considerations

The primary motive appears initially in the bass and repeats in all voices throughout the chorus. This is an advantage in teaching the piece. Conductors should teach the whole choir this phrase simultaneously so that they learn to recognize its appearance. In this phrase, the word "Hallelujah" is first set with a fast, ascending melodic line. The tendency for singers will be to punch the final syllable (Hal-le-lu-JAH!). Teach them to sing this line to sound more like speech, with proper emphasis on "LU" and with little weight on the final syllable "jah." Further, this motive (and its harmonic pair—the motive most often appears with another voice singing harmony with the same rhythm) should jump out of the texture whenever it appears. Have the choir sing out whenever they have the motive and sing less when another voice has it. To help the singers recognize this, rehearse them by having them raise their hands when they sing this phrase. They will hear it more easily and will be more aware when other voices have it.

All cutoffs must be rhythmic, particularly when the chorus finishes a phrase together. The "s" sound of "rejoice," for example, will bleed into the texture if the chorus does not keep it short and rhythmic. And the choir will fall behind the orchestra if they are not prepared to breathe quickly. Practice ends of phrases fastidiously, first speaking the text and then on pitch.

Further, even when smaller phrases end, they are often immediately connected to another short phrase. (See the settings of the words "Rejoice O Judah in songs divine" in particular.) Even in the presence of these rests, the overall line continues. Place active consonant cutoffs at the end of these phrases to help propel the singers to the correct placement of the next phrase. If singers struggle with this—falling behind and loss of sound will be the most prominent symptoms—have them snap their fingers in unison on the eighth note rests. This creates an aural connection from phrase to phrase and is an activity they can remember to become more aware of the larger phrase in which the smaller units are embedded.

Some phrases need to have the lengths of the final notes adjusted for rhythmic clarity. For example, in the first section where the chorus repeats the words "Hallelujah, Amen," the altos and basses finish their first long phrase simultaneously with the sopranos, but the sopranos immediately begin again. All three parts must shorten their final note to an eighth note and insert an eighth rest. In addition, have the altos and basses breathe with the sopranos so that they all finish together.

Stylistic Considerations

"Hallelujah, Amen" requires crisp, Baroque articulations. As Handel asks, the tempo must be fast (*Allegro, a tempo giusto*). Eighth and sixteenth note passages need to be detached, light, and clean, with strong diaphragmatic support. In addition, some simple ornamentation of the phrases at their cadences is not only appropriate but necessary. Plan for these ornaments so that singers can be taught them accurately and rhythmically.

This chorus connects directly with the final bass aria "Rejoice, O Judah!" It is awkward to perform "Hallelujah, Amen" without "Rejoice." Not only are the choral motives and text introduced in the aria, but the chorus makes more sense as a joyous response to the solo music. In the absence of the aria and short orchestral interlude, the chorus is stripped of context and consequently feels as though it starts cold and lasts for too short a time for such a rousing piece. Try to include the aria in your performance.

Form and Structure

"Hallelujah, Amen" is a through-composed chorus in D major that punctuates the *Judas Maccabeus* oratorio.

Text

Hallelujah, Amen!
Rejoice, oh Judah!
And, in songs divine, with cherubim and seraphim harmonious join!

Suggested Listening

Judas Maccabaeus. Philharmonia Baroque Orchestra. Nicholas McGegan, conductor. (Harmonia Mundi 907077).

Contributed by:

Chris Bartley

Repertoire Resource Guide

Haneirot Halalu

Stanley M. Hoffman
(b. 1959)

SATB and tenor solo/a cappella
E.C. Schirmer Music Co.: ECS 5492
Overall: 3
Vocal: 3
Tonal/Rhythm: 4

Composer

Composer, conductor, singer, and Cleveland native Stanley Hoffman studied at the Boston Conservatory, the New England Conservatory of Music, and Brandeis University. He lives in Boston where he works for E.C. Schirmer Music Co. as an editor. Most of his works draw from his Jewish faith, and his music is often rhythm and contains colorful harmonic language.

Composition and Genre

"Haneirot Halalu" is an original setting of the traditional Chanukah prayer. It is symmetrical and balanced: the ever-changing meters of the first and last sections give way to a slow, chant-influenced middle section in 4/4 time.

Set for *a cappella* SATB choir and tenor solo, the piece begins with a fast eight-measure theme that the tenors and basses intone in unison. The meter changes every measure, but is easily mastered because the music has repeated themes. The tenor soloist enters in measure 19 after a fermata, repeating the phrase "that you performed for our ancestors" in a cantorial chant-like pattern. The first section closes with a choral repetition of the phrase.

The middle section begins with the soloist singing *cantabile* over choral harmonic support to convey instructional text. The choir reenters on the words "so that we may offer thanks" and finishes the section.

Except for an altered solo line in measure 59 to 61, a corresponding adjustment of the choral accompaniment and a slight change to craft a final cadence, the beginning section is repeated.

Historical Perspective

When the army under the five Maccabee brothers reclaimed Israel from the Syrians, the Hebrew people were eager to purify and rededicate the Temple in Jerusalem. They lit the eternal light, the *N'er Tamid*, but had only one day's worth of oil. It took eight days to fetch additional oil and during that entire week, miraculously, a single day's supply kept the *N'er Tamid* alight. The festival of Chanukah ("rededication") lasts a week, from sunset on 25 Kislev to 2 Tevet (Hebrew months) and is celebrated with prayer, rejoicing, and gift giving. Each night, an additional candle on the menorah is lit. Family singing, crafts, and games, including spinning the dreidel, are among traditional activities.

Technical Considerations

The first consideration of this piece is definitely the rhythm in the first sixteen bars. The meter changes every measure, but it is really not difficult to learn. Many of the measures contain mixed meter. Be sure you have figured out the macrostructure of each bar before the first rehearsal; this will aid in determining your conducting patterns. (Conducting this section takes practice!) For instance, the first 9/8 bar divides into a 2+3+2+2 eighth note pattern. It will be easy to conduct if you just organize this bar into a four pattern; the second beat will have a duration of three eighth notes instead of two. Every measure will be easy to determine as long as you follow the natural text stress of the Hebrew. Once you have figured out the patterns, share this information with the choir, so they understand the music's construction. For rehearsing, it will be good to count-sing each phrase. An example from measure 1 would be: "**one**-two/**one**-two-three/**one**-two/**one**-two." This is preferable over counting to nine, as the iteration of "one" demonstrates to the singer the occurrence of a macrobeat; continue in this fashion for all measures in the mixed meter section.

Many American musicians are afraid of languages other than French, Spanish, Italian, and German. This fear is not well founded. Hebrew is an easy language to pronounce as it uses the five Latin vowels, and its consonants behave very predictably. When teaching diction to a choir, it is always a good idea to have a native speaker introduce the text. In the case of Hebrew, depending on your location, it is not difficult to find a community member, or even a member of your chorus who has a mastery of the rules and pronunciation. Using a native speaker allows singers to hear authentic sounds and colors of the language; this is necessary for the choir's diction to sound natural.

Stylistic Considerations

Although this piece is an original composition, it draws in many ways on the Jewish vocal tradition. The sound should be full bodied, rich, and round. The soloist should be a man with a strong voice evoking the sounds of a Temple cantor. Remember that although this is a song of celebration, it is also a song of thanksgiving. Work for a color change as the text changes in affect.

Form and Structure

The form is ABA, in keeping with the text, fast-slow-fast. The key is D minor with shifting meters. The harmony is simple with some dissonance.

Text and Translation

Haneirot halalu anachnu madlikin
al hanisim,
v'al haniflaot v'al hat'shuot
v'al hamilchamot
sheasita la-avoteinu
bayamim haheim baz'man hazeh...

   —traditional Hebrew prayer, transliterated by Stanley M. Hoffman

We kindle these lights
because of the miracles,
the liberations
and the wonders
that you performed for our ancestors
in those days and in this season...

   —translated by Stanley M. Hoffman

Additional References and Resources

Stanley M. Hoffman's Web site: www.members.aol.com/smhoff/index.htm.

Contributed by:

Lani Johnson

Repertoire Resource Guide

He, Watching Over Israel

Felix Mendelssohn (Bartholdy)
(1809–1847)

SATB/keyboard
E.C. Schirmer Music Co.: 2786
Overall: 3
Vocal: 4
Tonal/Rhythm: 3

Composer

Felix Mendelssohn was born in Hamburg, the second of four children, to Jewish banker, Abraham Mendelssohn. In 1811, the Mendelssohn family moved to Berlin, where Felix was surrounded by wealth and culture. In 1816, his father converted all of the children to Christianity and added the name Bartholdy as a surname.

Mendelssohn began to compose when he was eleven and proved to be very prodigious in his output. When he was twenty, he traveled throughout Europe; this trip exposed him to many of the great musicians of the time. He finally settled in Leipzig in 1835, where he built the Gewandhaus Orchestra into a major performing ensemble. During his time in Leipzig he cultivated a love for the music of J. S. Bach and also familiarized himself with the genre of English oratorio. His beloved sister, composer and pianist Fanny Mendelssohn, died suddenly in 1847. In poor health himself (he suffered from migraines and minor strokes), Mendelssohn lived through the summer, but died in November that same year.

Composition

"He, Watching Over Israel" is a choral movement from the oratorio *Elijah* (1846). The dramatic story of Elijah is an adaptation of 1 Kings 17–19. The oratorio relates the story of Elijah's life: the curse of the Lord, the seven-year drought, the revival of the widow's son, his confrontation with the Baal worshipers, his confrontation with Ahab and Jezebel, his flight to the wilderness and encounter with the Lord, and his journey to Mt. Horeb and ascension to heaven in a flaming chariot. "He, watching over Israel" is a chorus from the second part of the oratorio; its text comes from the psalms.

Historical Perspective

This piece was composed in the tradition of the great Handelian oratorios. The text was originally written in German by Schubring. It was translated for the premiere (August 26, 1846) by W. Bartholomew. The work was revised in 1847 and published in the same year.

Technical Considerations

The accompaniment is in triplets, but the choir must sing in even eighth notes above the pattern. The choir will want to sing the eighth notes to match the accompaniment figures of the orchestra.

Although the words "slumbers" and "sleeps" end with an "s," they are not formed in the same way. "Slumbers," must end with a "z" sound; "sleeps" should end with an "s" sound. Also, the conductor must decide whether the singers should form consonant combinations or separate consonants of words. This is always an important decision but is especially crucial in this piece, as the words can change based on this decision. For instance, "Slumbers not, nor sleeps," sung using consonant combinations might sound "Slumber snot, nor sleeps!" This approach, while it may be more rhythmically accurate, might get some chuckles from the audience, which is not a desirable reaction to this work!

Stylistic Considerations

Attention to dynamics and phrase shape are very important. In the imitative sections, each time a new voice enters, the other voices should fade into the background, allowing the imitative nature to become audible. The choir should be told when they have "melodic material" and when they have "episodic material"; the former should be in the forefront of the texture. Teach each motive to the choir as whole. Spend time getting the shape you desire, and then insist that each entrance of the motive be shaped by each section. This will yield an interesting contrapuntal texture.

Form and Structure

The form of this piece is generated by an imitative treatment of two short melodic themes. Mendelssohn shows his mastery of harmony and counterpoint as he weaves the two melodies together for a serene, gentle texture.

Text

He, watching over Israel, slumbers not, nor sleeps.
Shouldst thou, walking in grief, languish, He will quicken thee.

Suggested Listening

Elijah. Atlanta Symphony Chorus and Orchestra. Robert Shaw, conductor. (Telarc CD 80389).

Choral Masterpieces. Atlanta Symphony Chorus. Robert Shaw, conductor. (Telarc 80119).

Contributed by:

Anthony Reeves

Repertoire Resource Guide

Innoria (Huron Dance Song)

Donald Patriquin
(b. 1938)

SATB, SAB, or SSA/piano and optional percussion
Earthsongs: SATB = S-54a, SAB S-74b, SSA=W-07a
Overall: 3
Vocal: 3
Tonal/Rhythm: 3

Composer

From Sherbrooke, Québec, Donald Patriquin studied composition at McGill University and at the University of Toronto, though he also pursued studies in environmental biology. Much of Patriquin's music, vocal and instrumental, shows a strong affinity for folk melody, and many of his works are based upon collected folksongs and carols of his native Canada. A lecturer for more than thirty years at McGill, Patriquin has recently returned to the eastern townships of Québec to focus on composition and conducting.

Composition

This work is from a collection entitled *Six Songs of Early Canada*, written in 1980 and revised in 1992. The six songs are arranged historically and geographically, this piece being the first in the series. "Innoria" is a dance song, which was collected in 1911 in the Huron village of Lorette. The words are nonsense syllables that would have been sung in connection with a tribal ceremony.

Historical Perspective

Modern efforts to revisit folksongs in new contexts continue as part of a long history of folksong influence on choral music. The formal collecting of folksongs has its roots in the nineteenth century and is now an important aspect of ethnomusicological research. The music of "Innoria" was borrowed by Patriquin from a collection of seven dance songs notated by Marius Barbeau in 1911. Patriquin has taken the general shape of this Native American dance and brought it into a modern context in this piece, which is part of the complete *Six Songs of Early Canada*.

Technical Considerations

This dance piece is most unusual in its sharp, almost shouted texture and its sudden and dramatic rhythms. The heavily accented short-long rhythmic pattern defines the persistent pulse. The melodic material is extremely limited and uses a small range and a modal melody without chromaticism. The overall effect is largely a dramatic, rhythmic one rather than a harmonic-melodic one.

Stylistic Considerations

The style of this piece is taken from Huron dance music and can be accompanied by an appropriate drum beat. The uncomplicated melodies are in characteristically pentatonic shapes. The simple structure is built around a careful control of dynamics, which are marked with precision in the score. The performance of this piece requires a strong commitment on the part of the choir and director to evoke the high energy and drama of these short, rhythmic lines, which build very quickly to a roaring climax.

Musical Elements

The work is comprised entirely of short, pentatonic melodies with sharp, angular rhythms. There are prolonged major seconds, though the harmony is otherwise simple. The texture is almost exclusively homophonic or imitative, with a steady 3/8 pulse throughout. The piano part consists of a pulsing left-hand rhythm and prolonged chords in the right hand.

Form and Structure

The form of this short piece is clear and straightforward:

MEASURE	EVENT AND SCORING
1–16	Two initial intonations
17–38	A slow build-up, climax, and sudden fade
39–43	Forte coda

Text and Translation

The text is from Huron, but uses nonsense words:

Innoria, kwenotane, hahe.

Contributed by:

Thomas Cunningham

Repertoire Resource Guide

Johnny Has Gone for a Soldier

arr. Alice Parker
(b. 1925)
and
Robert Shaw
(1916–1999)

SATB/a cappella with soprano solo
Warner Bros. Publications: LG51452
Overall: 3
Vocal: 3
Tonal/Rhythm: 3

Composers

Alice Parker was born in Boston, December 16, 1925. After graduating from Smith College and the Juilliard School of Music, she worked as an arranger for the Robert Shaw Chorale, taught at Westminster Choir College, and founded Melodious Accord, Inc. She has more than 400 compositions to her name, and is arguably best-known for her collaborations with Shaw on folksongs, hymns, and spirituals.

Robert Shaw was born in Red Bluff, California, on April 30, 1916. After completing undergraduate studies at Pomona College, he went to work for Fred Waring, who asked him to help organize the Fred Waring Glee Club. In 1941, Shaw established the Collegiate Chorale in New York City, and from 1946–48 was director of the choral departments at the Juilliard School of Music and the Berkshire Music Center. From 1948 to 1965, he conducted the internationally renowned Robert Shaw Chorale.

Also an orchestral conductor, Shaw was associate conductor of the Cleveland Orchestra from 1956 to 1967, when he became music director of the Atlanta Symphony Orchestra. In 1988, he was made music director emeritus and conductor laureate of the Atlanta Symphony. Shaw's impact on choral singing throughout the world cannot be overstated, and he promoted choral singing throughout his life as a professional conductor and teacher. Shaw died in New Haven, Connecticut, on January 25, 1999.

Composition

"Johnny Has Gone for a Soldier" is an *a cappella* setting of a Revolutionary War lament; the tune is an American adaptation of the Irish tune SHULE AROON, which dates back to the seventeenth century. In this edition, the soprano solo is supported by an SATB chorus.

Historical Perspective

Military families during times of war live in daily awareness that their sons, daughters, husbands, or fathers are in danger. They understand they cannot prevent pain or fear and will not know for some time what has happened. They must accept that every leave-taking may be the last. War has been this way since its inception, and "Johnny Has Gone for a Soldier" carries a universal message, even though it was born during the struggle for American independence.

What separates this text from the reality of modern soldiering is that in times past a fighter who volunteered left his family's livelihood to relatives, usually his wife and children. A soldier's pay was poor and irregular, not to mention difficult to send home. In addition, each soldier was responsible for equipping—and often feeding—himself: this is highlighted in the third verse. In this verse, the wife sells her spinning wheel and the raw materials for making yarn to provide her husband with a decent weapon. Or, in an alternative explanation, she turns from spinning for the family's use to commercial production. In either case, one pillar of family provision goes to war, leaving those at home impoverished.

Technical Considerartions

The notes and rhythms of this piece are very simple, as the choir functions mainly as an accompaniment throughout the work. The vocal ranges are all well within the limits of an amateur choir. However, just because the basic elements are simple does not mean this piece should be taken lightly: a truly effective performance will have beautifully shaped phrases, color changes with each strophe, and careful attention to articulation and text delivery, even though the choir is merely an accompaniment. (See below.)

It is important that the soloist have a strong voice; she should not only manage the notes of the piece but provide a dramatic performance tied to the words of the song. The choir should work to create a smooth, rich sound because this will allow the soloist to feel supported and free to sing with full resonance. Phrases are not long but must be sung "on the breath" by all parties as a sound that is too "blended" will sound weak and pallid.

The several changes of meter are easy to negotiate but important to highlight to the singers, as the changes of meter coincide with a slight change in the strophic setting of the poem.

Stylistic Considerations

Because the melody in the solo voice is the vehicle for the text in this piece, accompanimental voices should remain in the background. These choral parts should not, however, be monochromatic: they echo (mm. 10–12), sound a dirge drum (tenors and basses, mm. 18–23), duet in canon with the soloist (altos, mm. 20–25), and carry the melody (sopranos, mm. 25–30). From measure 25 on, the sopranos have the melody as the soloist sings a descant.

Otherwise, the choral sound should be round with unified vowels to form a plane of sound from which the soloist can emerge. Niceties of dynamic expression and mood are noted in the score and should be followed exactly.

Form and Structure

There are three sections in keeping with the three strophes of text and tune. The piece is in the key of C minor throughout, with several changes of meter.

Text

Here I sit on Buttermilk Hill, who could blame me, cry my fill,
And every tear would turn a mill: Johnny has gone for a soldier.

Me, oh my, I loved him so, broke my heart to see him go,
And only time will heal my woe! Johnny has gone for a soldier.

Oh I will sell my flax, I'll sell my wheel, buy my love a sword of steel.
So it in battle he may wield: Johnny has gone for a soldier.

Contributed by:

Lani Johnson

Repertoire Resource Guide

Jubilate Deo in C
Benjamin Britten
(1913–1976)

SATB/organ or piano
Oxford University Press: 42.848
Overall: 3
Vocal: 3
Tonal/Rhythm: 3

Composer

Benjamin Britten was born in 1913 in Lowestoft, Suffolk, and spent most of his life working as a composer, pianist, and conductor in England. Britten composed a new style of tonal music in an era in which many composers favored esoteric, atonal techniques, which perhaps helped him become one of the most successful English composers in the twentieth century. He steadfastly employed his trademark but tonal language in works that span dramatic, choral, chamber, film, and symphonic genres.

His youth on the Suffolk coast of England was typical for a dentist's son, encompassing sports as well as superior achievement in piano and an interest in drama. By the age of 14, he catalogued a hundred opus numbers and began studying composition with Frank Bridge. In due course, he moved to London, entered the Royal College of Music, and won several composition prizes.

Britten was an avowed pacifist, a philosophy borne out in many of his works, including the massive *War Requiem*. He wrote many vocal pieces specifically for tenor Peter Peers and maintained friendships with William Walton, Sergey Koussevitzky, W. H. Auden, and other outstanding figures.

From early adulthood, Britten nurtured an interest in the music of the East. He eventually indulged his interest by incorporating the sounds of the Balinese gamelan into several pieces, including the controversial *The Turn of the Screw*. His output includes operas (most prominently *Peter Grimes*), choral and orchestral works (e.g., *A Hymn to St. Cecilia*, *Ceremony of Carols*, and *War Requiem*), and music for films, radio, and stage.

Composition

"Jubilate Deo in C," written in 1961 for St. George's Chapel, Windsor, at the request of the duke of Edinburgh, serves as a companion piece for Britten's "Te Deum" of 1934. An anthem setting of Psalm 100 that concludes with a *Gloria Patri*, "Jubilate Deo" is a prime example of Britten's skill in text setting. The meter changes frequently to ensure proper word stress (prosody), but the resultant music flows from phrase to phrase with predictability. The piece, written for choir and organ, may be performed with equal success with piano accompaniment. This piece is an excellent concert opener.

Technical Considerations

Composed in the style of Stanford and Ireland, "Jubilate Deo" begins with a rhythmic organ introduction that provides the spark for the rest of the piece. In the first choral section, the sopranos and tenors pair together, as do the altos and basses. Note that the men's parts move in a very simple stepwise manner; the women's parts are really just slight ornamentations of the men's part. Begin by having all choristers sing the men's part on a neutral syllable (slowly). After this is mastered, have the women sing their parts alone, then with the men. This works very well except for the two brief portions of four-part singing (mm. 21–25 and 35–38).

At measure 39, the music modulates into the key of E major. The choral parts should now be sung legato and at a piano dynamic. Notice, however, that Britten does not indicate that the tempo should slow here! The choir will slow when they sing softly.

Short interjections from the organ remind us of the previous section and foreshadow what will come shortly. At measure 49, the choral parts are written in half note triplets; conduct the bars the choir sings in three (your beat must be faster as the length of the measure must stay the same) and the bars where just the organ plays in two. It will be very hard for the choir to sing the triplets evenly and smoothly with the conductor beating two.

At measure 59, music reminiscent of the beginning evokes the enduring of truth promised to all generations as the voice parts enter in succession to complete the final verse of the psalm. Next, the text of the *Gloria Patri* (a verse placed at the end of Psalms to "Christianize" them) repeats musical fragments from the beginning, this time in a four-part texture. A final quiet section brings the piece to a halt on a contemplative "Amen" before Britten ends the work with a jubilant "Amen" using material from the very beginning of the work.

Stylistic Considerations

As with all British cathedral music, it is important to work for a choral sound that is spacious, high, bright, and forward. Consonants should be light and crisp, and, in the case of this piece, should help propel the rhythm forward. Vowels should be formed in a tall, narrow shape to best emulate the sounds of English cathedral choirs. Don't be afraid to use vowels that are more closed than those used in American English.

Observe all of Britten's printed dynamics to ensure the piece changes character and color where appropriate. The color of the sections B and B' (see chart below) should be more subdued and rounded than the boisterous beginning and the third section.

Be sure the choir performs the dotted eighth-sixteenth note rhythm that dominates the fast sections in a crisp, almost militaristic style. Don't let the choir get lazy and turn the figure into a quasi-triplet; the innate rhythmic energy will be lost.

Form and Structure

The work contains five distinct sections in two styles. Sections 1, 3, and 5 all use similar melodic and rhythmic material and can thus be labeled as A, A', and A''. Sections 2 and 4 (B and B') are quiet interludes that interrupt the constant flow of sixteenth notes in the organ part and add a measure of serene beauty to this otherwise bubbly gem of a piece.

SECTION	MEASURE	EVENT AND SCORING
A	1–38	Psalms 100: 1–3
B	39–58	Psalms 100: 3–4
A'	59–91	Psalms 100: 4 and *Gloria Patri*
B'	92–108	*Gloria Patri*
A''	109–119	Amen

Text

Psalm 100 sung in English with the *Gloria Patri* (Doxology)

Suggested Listening

Britten Choral Edition, Volume 2. The Finzi Singers. Paul Spicer, conductor. (Chandos Records CD 9598).

Contributed by:

Matthew W. Mehaffey

Repertoire Resource Guide

The Last Words of David

Randall Thompson
(1899–1984)

SATB/keyboard or TTBB/keyboard
E.C. Schirmer Music Co.: SATB= 2294, TTBB= 2154
Overall: 3
Vocal: 3
Tonal/Rhythm: 3

Composer

Randall Thompson was one of the most significant American choral composers of the twentieth century. He studied at Harvard University, where Archibald Davison was one of his teachers. He received the prestigious Prix de Rome in 1922, which enabled him to study in Rome for three years (1922–25). After he returned to the United States, he received critical acclaim for his Second Symphony (1931). His favorite genre of music, however, was choral music. Generations of Americans have enjoyed his vastly popular collections (e.g., *Frostiana*, *The Testament of Freedom*, and the *Peaceable Kingdom*), as well as his shorter works, such as "Alleluia" and "The Last Words of David."

Thompson was an influential teacher; he served on the faculties of Wellesley College, the University of California–Berkeley, the Curtis Institute, the University of Virginia, Princeton University, and Harvard University. Many academics dismiss Thompson's music as amateurish, but his music has always spoken to many people with its gentle harmonies, wonderful texts, directness, and simplicity.

Composition and Genre

"The Last Words of David" is an anthem; it can used very effectively in both liturgical and concert settings.

Historical Perspective

In the summer of 1949, Sergey Koussevitsky (conductor of the Boston Symphony and a champion of new music) asked Thompson to write a choral work in honor of his twenty-fifth anniversary with the Boston Symphony; the piece was to be composed for the chorus of the Berkshire Music Center and the Boston Symphony. Under enormous time constraints, Thompson found words from 2 Samuel. Interestingly, he came upon this text in a hotel room Gideon Bible during one of his many cross-country trips while writing *College Music*. Thompson began to associate the words of David with Maestro Koussevitsky. With this in mind, maybe all conductors should keep the first line of this anthem in their minds at all points while conducting: "He that ruleth over men must be just!"

Technical Considerations

The technique of *sforzando* can be quite difficult for a choir to perform. Thompson calls for this technique in measure six. It can be helpful to ask the choir to sing the attack of that measure **ff**, take a very quick breath, then start singing (on the same pitch) at a level of **p** and follow that with a crescendo. The listener's ear will hear Thompson's desired effect, and the choir will have a much easier time achieving it.

Thompson went to great effort to make his intentions clear. All of the markings on the score of "The Last Words of David" are the composer's. Therefore, to be the composer's advocate, one should follow all of them. For example, note all the different markings that appear between measures 8–13, particularly regarding tempo.

Stylistic Considerations

Thompson goes to great lengths to paint the words with appropriate music, so textual clarity is, therefore, a paramount consideration. A good example of this occurs on the word "springing." The choir should take full advantage of the onomatopoeia on "spr" in "springing."

Musical Elements

The piece is scored for orchestra and choir. Piano and organ are acceptable alternatives to the full orchestral compliment. The choir parts are in accessible ranges. Thompson frequently ties long notes to eighth notes. For clarity's sake, it would be much better if the choir cut off "on the beat" instead of adding the eighth note value to the longer note. This practice will make it considerably easier to attain crisp and aligned consonants.

Form and Structure

This piece is essentially in three parts. The first, a fanfare-like opening, proclaims the first verse of the biblical passage. In the second part, Thompson's creative harmonic language depicts the rising of the sun. The third section, in imitative style, is the "Alleluia" section. The three parts are all very different and require the choir to change attitude and color for this piece to be effective.

Text

The text of this work is 2 Samuel 23:3–4.

He that ruleth over men must be just, ruling in the fear of God. And he shall be as the light of the morning, when the sun riseth, even a morning without clouds; as the tender grass springing out of the earth by clear shining after rain. Alleluia.

Suggested Listening

An American Voice: Music of Randall Thompson. Roberts Wesleyan Chorale. Robert Shewan, conductor. (Albany Records Troy 362).

Favorite Hymns and Anthems. The Westminster Choir. Joseph Flummerfelt, conductor. (Gothic Records 49044).

Additional Reference and Resources

Benser, C. C. and D. F. Urrows. *Randall Thompson: A Bio-Bibliography*. New York: Greenwood Press. 1991.

Forbes, E., et al. "The Choral Music of Randall Thompson." *American Choral Review*. xxii/2. 1980.

Contributed by:

Matthew W. Mehaffey
Anthony Reeves

Repertoire Resource Guide

Let Their Celestial Concerts All Unite

George Frideric Handel
(1685–1759)

SATB/keyboard or TTBB/Keyboard
SATB=Alfred Publishing Co.: 16310
TTBB=E.C. Schirmer Music Co.: 39
edited by Patrick M. Liebergen, with two optional trumpets
Overall: 3
Vocal: 3
Tonal/Rhythm: 3

Composer

Handel was born in Halle, Germany, in 1685 (the same year as J. S. Bach). During a long and successful career, this entrepreneurial musician produced music in every genre of his time: orchestral symphonies, suites, concertos, overtures; operas, oratorios, and other stage music; vocal music in Latin, English, Italian, and German; solo and ensemble cantatas; songs and hymns in English, Italian, French, German, and Spanish; instrumental sonatas and solo works; masses; keyboard music; chamber music; and even didactic pieces.

Handel's father, a barber-surgeon in the service of the duke of Saxe-Weissenfels, saw no future in music for Handel. It is said the boy practiced harpsichord secretly in the attic until the duke persuaded his father to allow him musical tuition. Sadly, his father died when Handel was eleven, making the boy responsible for his family's living. By the age of eighteen, Handel had given up all thought of studying law and moved to Halle, one of Europe's opera centers, where his first opera was staged in 1705. He also traveled to Italy, where he found patrons for sacred music and solo cantatas. He returned to Germany, successfully attracting patrons and audiences for chamber and theatrical works, including Italian-style opera. Handel eventually relocated to England, writing Italian operas, symphonic, and chamber works, and, as the popularity of opera faded in Britain, the relatively new genre, oratorio. He is credited with developing the oratorio form of the eighteenth and much of the nineteenth centuries.

He generally produced his own events, which were a major source of his living. England's royalty, nobility, and common people loved Handel and his music. The first Handelian revivals began in 1784, shortly after his death.

Contemporaries remember a rough but genial portly man whose wit was more frequent than his smile and whose broken English could turn impatient outbursts into humor.

Composition

Immediately following the completion of *Messiah*, Handel composed the oratorio *Samson* in 1741–42, using Newburgh Hamilton's libretto setting of Milton's *Samson Agonistes*. The oratorio premiered at Covent Garden Theatre during Lent 1743. It was initially more acceptable to the clerical segment of London's theater-going public than was *Messiah*, probably because the libretto, while spiritual and moralistic, did not quote scripture "on the stage."

Historical Perspective

As the 1730s waned, it became obvious to the self-employed composer and impresario that Italian opera was falling from favor in London. The dramatic and musical forces that had made it possible to stage operas, however, remained and Handel put the virtuosi singers, including castrati and females, to good use in the opera-drama-cantata-historia hybrid form he developed. Other composers were willing to capitalize on his success, and the oratorio became a popular genre and maintained its popularity through the nineteenth and into the twentieth century.

Technical Considerations

"Let Their Celestial Concerts All Unite" has a limited amount of tonal and rhythmic content, is structurally predictable, and sounds "just like a Handel chorus." The tessitura lies in a comfortable range for all voice parts through-out the composition.

You will quickly find that making all words intelligible will be a major challenge. To make this a reality, begin by teaching notes and rhythms on a neutral syllable with a closed vowel and an articulate consonant (e.g., "du"). Once the music is learned, have the choir speak the words of the each phrase in rhythm without pitch. Ask the choir to use a heightened speaking voice with musical expression during this exercise. Listen carefully to the group's articulations. If they cannot achieve the desired effect while speaking, they will certainly not be articulate enough while singing. Once the choir can speak flawlessly, combine words and rhythms with the pitches; continually monitor the intelligibility of the group's diction.

Before you enter the rehearsal for the first time, be sure you understand the construction of this piece. "Let Their Celestial Concerts All Unite" is the development of a few musical motives. To save time in rehearsal, teach each motive in isolation to the entire choir. It may even be effective to label them (A, B, C, etc.); this will assist in creating a hierarchy in the midst of the fugatos. Teaching each motive in isolation is efficient because each section of the choir has each of these motives at some point in the piece; the notes might not be transposed exactly, but the choir will at least have learned the contour of the music and the appropriate articulations. As this piece is very tonal, adjusting to the correct notes for each reiteration of a motive will not be difficult for singers of even modest experience.

Stylistic Considerations

Much of the piece is at a fortissimo dynamic, which, given the enthusiasm of many choral ensembles, especially during concerts, could yield an unsupported, throaty sound. The dynamic contrast is not extreme but should be observed. It would not hurt to take the entire dynamic down one level; this would allow the choir to maintain the light, buoyant sound required in Baroque music.

Imitative part writing always benefits from phrase contouring. Each motive should be introduced with its own expressive shading and dynamic contour and should always be sung in that manner. Be sure to have a clear understanding of each line before you have your first rehearsal. The fastest way to teach articulation is to model for the choir. Even if you are not the best singer, do not be afraid to sing these lines for the choir. Every time you perform for them, be sure your articulation is exact and exaggerated (this takes practice). Your example will not only make your intentions clear to them but will communicate your enthusiasm for making this music. Identify areas like measures 28–38 in which several motives appear either simultaneously or consecutively. When two appear simultaneously, decide which should emerge from the blend and instruct that voice to sing assertively and all other voices to back off. Consecutive motives can be faded in and out of the texture.

Note durations of dotted quarter and larger (i.e., "all" of the first theme) should swell and diminish (*messa di voce*). Similarly, use the sequences to make an expressive statement. In the soprano voice (e.g., mm. 11–12) bounce the first three notes; smooth the next five, but cut off the fifth; renew and smooth the next five, again cutting off the fifth one; swell the next three and diminish the last three, all in a small but cohesive phrase, clipping the final note (using a sixteenth and a sixteenth rest or simply gentle staccato plus a quick breath) to enable a reliable, breath-renewed attack on "Let."

Musical Elements

The Alfred edition is from *George Friedrich Händels Werke*, vol. 10, published by Breitkopf & Härtel (1861) transposed down a step. With the exception of the additional staff for trumpets and the trumpet part on the back of the octavo, this appears to be the same edition as the Schirmer. Measures are approximately two instead of three to a line, so the two editions line up on every other page. The Schirmer edition has rehearsal notes instead of measure numbers. Otherwise, the topography is same. Liebergen's trumpet part is faithful to the style and within most high school instrumentalists' ability.

Form and Structure

Rondo or *ritornello* form seems most descriptive for this chorus. Handel states the first theme (mm. 1–4), goes on to a fugato with two motives (mm. 5–12), and returns to the first theme, as he does after every excursion during the rest of the chorus. The second "excursion" incorporates one of the fugato motives in inversion in the bass, harmonized by other motives that reappear. Measures 17–19 in the alto reappear as 43–44 in the tenor, for instance. This excursion modulates to the subdominant key briefly before returning to tonic. It is here, measures 28–30, where the composer first combines the descending motive and the first theme, setting up another "excursion," this one a true episode, which tosses pre-existing motives into various contexts, sometimes literally stated and sometimes altered (inverse is frequent). Measure 39 reprises the first theme followed by another episode, leading (at measure 49), to the climactic section and beginning of the end. Theme one returns in measure 55, at the end of the climax, with an instrumental fanfare completing the climax and leading to the repetition of measures 49–58, then the real end.

The original piece is in D major, and these octavos are in C major with short modulations to nearby keys.

Text

Let their celestial concerts all unite,
Ever to sound His praise in endless morn of light.

Suggested Listening

Handel: Samson. Arnold Schoenberg Chor. Nikolaus Harnoncourt. (Elektra/Asylum 74871).

Georg Frideric Handel: Samson. Maulbronn Monastery Edition. Michael Chance. (The Orchard 5745).

Samson. Sixteen Christophers. (Coro).

Contributed by:

Lani Johnson

Repertoire Resource Guide

Muié Rendêra

arr. Carlos A. Pinto Fonseca
(b. 1933)

SATB or SSAA with optional percussion
Earthsongs: SATB= S-76, SSAA=S-210
Overall: 3
Vocal: 3
Tonal/Rhythm: 3

Composer

Well-known conductor C. A. Pinto Fonseca was born in Belo Horizonte, Brazil, in 1933. He won conducting competitions in Brazil, Argentina, and Italy and was the founder of Madrigal Ars Nova, a choir that gained worldwide fame and esteem through their international tours. Pinto Fonseca is best known for his arrangements of folk music, and his most popular composition is probably the *Missa Afro-Brasileira* (1976).

Composition

"Muié Rendêra" is a composite folksong arrangement of two of Brazil's most popular folksongs, "Olê, Muié Rendêra" and "É Lampa, é Lampa, é Lampeão."

Historical Perspective

Folk tunes are usually memorable and often catchy, probably because of the oral tradition by which most of them have survived. Pedro Alvares Cabral claimed Brazil for Portugal in 1500. The country won its independence in 1822 and today is one of the world's largest countries. The cultural combination of the indigenous population, the Portuguese, and the Africans

(Brazil did not abolish slavery until 1888) has enabled a fascinating musical heritage to evolve. Music seems to be ubiquitous in Brazil, drawing from an amazing array of musical forms and traditions; the melodic, expressive, and vibrant qualities of Brazilian music are contagious. *Samba* and *bossa* are two of the better-known Brazilian contributions to world music, largely due to their association with jazz. Airto Moreira and Flora Purim are two Brazilian artists who made large contributions to the development of the sub-genre called jazz fusion.

"Muié Rendêra" also draws from the true story of Virgulino (nicknamed Lampeão). Reminiscent of the American outlaw duo Bonnie and Clyde, Virgulino and his female accomplice, Maria Bonita, tried to be careful to rob only the wealthy. Sadly, Virgulino and Maria Bonita met a tragic end similar to that of their American counterparts.

Technical Considerations

The two most important considerations in preparing this piece are rhythm and clarity. The notes are not difficult to learn and often consist of repeated patterns. The rhythms themselves, also often repeated patterns, are mostly simple. The complications arise when one seeks precision in the written rhythms and of the various, changing accentuations marked by Pinto Fonseca. The tempo, unspecified in the score, should be on the fast side. Brazilian friends of mine who know the folksongs and the *baião* form can perform segments of this piece incredibly fast. A wise conductor will teach the rhythms slowly at first, not allowing any sloppiness, and gradually increase the tempo.

Further complicating the matter is the Portuguese text. While not difficult to pronounce, the language itself is unfamiliar to most English-speaking choirs. Fortunately, a pronunciation guide is available from the publisher. Teach the music and the text separately, and then have the choir speak the words using the rhythms. Then, start again at a slow tempo and gradually increase it.

Stylistic Considerations

The setting is in the tradition of the Brazilian *baião*—a popular genre generally requiring at least three performers: one who sings and plays the accordion, one who plays bass drum, and one who plays triangle. The musical depiction of the *baião* should be easy to hear. The quick, uniquely accented sixteenth note patterns depict the triangle, rhythmic ostinato in the bass and tenor represent the bass drum, and the predominant melodies are obviously vocal lines.

Musical Elements

The music is in E major and duple meter (4/4 and 2/4) throughout. The harmonies are mostly simple but sometimes a bit unpredictable. It is important to pay great attention to the melodies and assure they are always audible. The rhythmic complexities will assure that neither the choir nor the audience will be bored!

Form and Structure

SECTION	MEASURE	EVENT AND SCORING
Introduction	1–9	
A	10–41(42)	"Olê, Muié Rendêra"
B	43–65	"É Lampa, é Lampa, é Lampeão"
Transition	66–70	
A'	71–96	"Olê, Muié Rendêra"
Transition	97–99	
Coda	99–100	

Text and Translation

Olê, muié rendêra,
olê, muié renda,
tu me ensina a faze rendá,
que eu te ensino a namorá.

Virgulino, é Lampeão.
É Lampa, é Lampa, é Lampa,
é Lampeão.
O seu nome é Virgulino,
o apelido é Lampeão.

Hey, lacemaker woman,
hey, lacemaker woman,
if you teach me how to weave,
I'll teach you how to court.

Virgulino is Lampeão.
He is Lampa, Lampa, Lampa,
he is Lampeão.
His name is Virgulino,
his nickname is Lampeão.

Suggested Listening

Musica de Latinoamerica. Various artists. (Earthsongs CD-01).

Contributed by:

Anthony Reeves

Repertoire Resource Guide

Musicks Empire

Lloyd Pfautsch
(1921–2003)

SATB/a cappella
Warner Bros. Publications: LG 51418
Overall: 3
Vocal: 3
Tonal/Rhythm: 3

Composer

Lloyd Pfautsch, a Missouri native, taught at Southern Methodist University in Dallas, Texas, from 1958 until 1992. Under his leadership, the Southern Methodist choral program flourished; the University Choir toured extensively and was widely regarded as one of the nation's leading choral ensembles. Pfautsch founded the Dallas Civic Chorus, which performed and recorded on its own as well as with the Dallas Symphony Orchestra. Pfautsch was also a widely published composer and author, with hundreds of published choral pieces to his credit. His music, mostly vocal, spans many styles and sets a wide variety of texts. It was important to Pfautsch to have the music reflect the meaning of the words as clearly as possible, as is evident in "Musicks Empire."

Composition

"Musicks Empire" is a modern sectionalized motet.

Historical Perspective

Lloyd Pfautsch composed "Musicks Empire" in 1969, at a time when considerable experimentation existed in choral music. Much music from the middle

246

twentieth century used aleatoric procedures, and composers of serious choral music often avoided traditional tonal practices. Pfautsch, who wrote his own share of such compositions, used very traditional procedures and harmonic practices in this piece, which is logical when one realizes he sought to trace the history of music as the piece progresses.

Technical Considerations

The piece is highly sectionalized, and each section presents its own challenges to the singers. The first section, for example, requires a beautiful unison sound with subtle forward motion and attention to syllabic stress. The second section requires careful listening as the tenors sustain a single pitch over the melody. All singers must be cognizant of unisons and dissonances and be careful that perfect intervals are perfect.

Phrasing and articulation are important in the third and fourth sections. In section three, the men and women must be very secure in their phrasing and breathing places, and section four, with its faster tempo, requires a careful mixture of detached and legato articulations. Diction is tremendously important throughout, and I remember that Pfautsch worked carefully for precisely coordinated and audible final consonants, clear differentiation between voiced and unvoiced consonants, and pure, unified vowel sounds. Dynamic markings should be taken quite literally with little adjustment from the conductor. (One detail I remember Pfautsch's working on, however, which is not indicated in the music, involves a slight crescendo through the word "Wind" in measure 32; this effect gives a marvelously onomatopoeic character to the word.)

Stylistic Considerations

As a conductor, Lloyd Pfautsch worked for a bright, energetic, well-supported, intelligent sound. It is no coincidence that such a sound works best for his music. It is important not to let the men focus their sound too far back in an effort to generate richness; they will be tempted to do so, especially in the first two sections. Men and women should sing with high, forward resonance, concentrating on tall, well-shaped vowels and crisp, well-articulated consonants. If the singers understand this piece—the meaning of the poetry and how Pfautsch reflected that in music, as well as the appropriate sound for each section (i.e., its related stylistic period in music history)—the music will be engaging and beautiful.

Musical Elements

Pfautsch's aforementioned desire to have his music reflect as clearly as possible the meaning of the text is quite evident in "Musicks Empire," a setting of a lyric poem by the English metaphysical poet Andrew Marvell

(1621–1678). Marvell's poem speaks eloquently of music as an integral component of creation, and Pfautsch reflects this in the musical setting, with each of the poem's six stanzas set in a style reminiscent of an era of Western music history: stanza 1, Gregorian chant; stanzas 2 and 3, organum; stanza 4, polyphony; stanza 5, Romantic music; and stanza 6, twentieth century.

Due to the regularity of Marvell's meter, Pfautsch's phrasing is regular throughout the piece, often falling in predictable four-measure units. Departures from this are generally due to cadential rhythmic augmentations.

The melody utilized in the first three sections is in dorian mode. Singing warm-ups in the mode and simply singing the mode itself (Re to Re) will help imbed the modality in the singers' ears. Section four begins to feel more tonal, although careful examination shows it is still in D dorian. The beginning of section five, sung by three part women, features the first significant major chord of the piece; the section is easy for most singers to assimilate, as it is in D major. Section six maintains a major-minor tonality, but with strong elements of Dorian modality still present.

Form and Structure

"Musicks Empire" consists of seven sections, derived from the six stanzas of Marvell's poem plus a musical coda.

MEASURE	EVENT AND SCORING
1–9	Two phrases; 4+5
10–18	Two phrases; 4+5
19–27	Two phrases; 4+5
28–37	Two phrases; 4+6
38–48	Two phrases; 5+5
48–59	Two phrases; 5+5+2; measure of repetitive tag
60–68	Coda; two phrases; 4.5+4.5

Text

First was the World as one great Cymbal made,
Where Jarring Windes to infant Nature played.
All Musick was a solitary sound,
To hollow rocks and murm'ring Fountains bound.

Jubal first made the wilder Notes agree;
And Jubal tuned Musicks Jubilee:
He call'd the Echoes from their sullen Cell,
And built the Organ's City where they dwell.

Each sought a consort in that lovely place;
And Virgin Trebles wed the manly Bass.
From whence the Progeny of numbers new
Into harmonious Colonies withdrew.

Some to the Lute, some to the Viol went,
And others chose the Cornet eloquent,
These practising the Wind, and those the Wire,
To sing men's triumphs, or in Heaven's choir.

Then Musick, the Mosaique of the Air,
Did of all these a Solemn noise prepare;
With which she gain'd the Empire of the Ear,
Including all between the Earth and Sphere.

Victorious Sounds! yet here your Homage do
Unto a gentler Conqueror than you;
Who though He flies the Musick of his praise,
Would with you Heaven's Hallelujahs raise.

Contributed by:

Anthony Reeves

Repertoire Resource Guide

Notre Père, Op. 14

Maurice Duruflé
(1902–1986)

SATB/a cappella
Éditions Durand: 14075
Overall: 3
Vocal: 4
Tonal/Rhythm: 3

Composer

Maurice Duruflé was born in 1902. Educated in Rouen from 1912–18, he attended the Paris Conservatory in 1920, where he obtained first prizes in organ and composition and studied with such luminaries as Paul Dukas and Louis Vierne. He held dual positions throughout much of his musical career as organist at St. Étienne-du-Mont (from 1930 until his death) and as professor of harmony at the Paris Conservatory (1943–70). In many of his works, Duruflé shows an abiding interest in Gregorian plainchant and modal harmony, although he was also capable of composing in the Impressionistic harmonic idiom of Debussy and his teacher Dukas. His introspective, self-critical, and religious nature had a profound impact on his compositional style.

Composition

"Notre Père" is a setting of the Lord's Prayer in French intended for the Catholic worship service. It is for SATB *a cappella* chorus, written in a strictly syllabic, homophonic style.

Technical Considerations

This simple but elegant setting of the Lord's Prayer can be an excellent introduction to singing in French. There are, however, some issues with which the conductor and his or her ensemble must contend. One of the greatest challenges in a homophonic composition such as this one is to maintain complete rhythmic precision within the ensemble. Consonants not exactly on the beat mar the effect of the beatific calm that is required. It is suggested that the conductor rehearse for rhythmic precision at the same time the notes are learned through the initial use of a voiced consonant combination such as "bim" rather than a more liquid vowel/consonant combination such as "loo." This way, the singers will know immediately when they are off with each other. The conductor should listen carefully to make sure that the singers move from pitch to pitch with complete accuracy and stop them whenever they do not.

Once the rhythmic precision of the ensemble has been established, the conductor should focus on ensemble tuning and blend. The homophonic texture of the piece demands that the singers unify every vowel as well as every rhythm. This awareness can be inculcated by having the choir sing the pitches on an "oo" vowel combined with a consonant. It is suggested that the conductor initially use a more percussive consonant, such as "t" or "d," in combination with the vowel, then introduce a liquid consonant such as "l" for legato phrasing. Because of the primacy of ensemble considerations in this work and the relative ease of the pitch content, conductors should always rehearse all voice parts of the choir together whenever possible instead of isolating individual parts.

The shifting meters in this work may seem daunting to the singers at first, but the changes are very natural in accordance with the shift of text emphasis. Once the ensemble sings through the piece once or twice, its members will probably find this not to be particularly problematic. If the ensemble continues to have difficulties with the metric changes, the conductor should have the ensemble count-sing so that they understand where the meters shift.

The harmonies in the work are not especially difficult, but there are a few moments in the piece that can give the choir some trouble. It is incumbent on the director to analyze the piece and determine where the modal harmonies and the seventh and ninth chords lie so that he or she can direct the attention of the ensemble to those occurrences in the piece.

The indicated dynamic level can also be problematic for the singers. The conductor should be aware that the dynamic is marked piano from the beginning of the piece up to measure 23, at which point there is a solitary mezzo forte marking, followed two measures later by a diminuendo to piano. The choir should sing the piano dynamic with a gentle but well-supported tone. The director may need to aid the development of an energized piano dynamic by asking the singers to use the same breath support, if not more, as when the choir sings a comfortable forte.

The greatest difficulty in performing this piece with American choirs is the French text. The conductor should prepare the text carefully in order to aid the singers in correct pronunciation. Sources, such as Pierre Bernac's *The Interpretation of French Song* and Thomas Grubb's *Singing in French*, should be consulted even if the conductor has had some experience with spoken French as the rules of spoken and sung French differ. Particular attention must be paid to the mixed and nasal vowels because these sounds are foreign to native English speakers. Also, the director should take great care to mark (in the music) where consonants and vowels are to be elided. It is strongly suggested that the director isolate the text from the music until both are absolutely secure.

Stylistic Considerations

Overall, French vocal music seems to be governed by a set of aesthetic principles, namely elegance, textural clarity, an avoidance of emotional outburst, and, most importantly, the concept of *le bon goût*, or good taste. "Notre Père," in its charming simplicity, embodies all of these characteristics. It is important for the choir to understand that a light vocal quality and a restrained use of vibrato are key to effecting these qualities in the music.

Scrupulous attention to tempo is an extremely important and often neglected aspect of the French aesthetic. As a general rule, rubato and other alterations of tempo are to be avoided in French vocal music unless the composer indicates these changes specifically in the score. This is particularly crucial at the ends of phrases in which it might be tempting to slow down a little to be "expressive." Adherence to the given tempo (quarter note = 66) in this piece is important so that the one notated fluctuation in tempo, the *molto rallentando* indicated by the composer in the last four measures of the work, has real musical impact.

Another stylistic decision concerns the two sets of *ossia* measures in this piece (measures 5–6 and 26–27). The *ossia* measures contain repetitions of text, which are used when the piece is to be performed in the context of Catholic worship. It is suggested that the conductor omit the *ossia* measures in concert performances.

Form and Structure

The work is through-composed when the *ossia* measures are omitted. The key is F major.

Text and Translation

Notre Père qui es aux cieux,
Que ton nom soit sanctifié,
Que ton règne vienne,
Que ta volonté soit faite
sur la terre comme au ciel.
Donne nous aujourd'hui
notre pain de ce jour,
Pardonne nous nos offenses
Comme nous pardonnons aussi à ceux
Qui nous ont offensés,
Et ne nous soumets pas à la tentacion,
Mais delivre nous du mal.

Our Father, who art in heaven,
Hallowed be thy name,
Thy kingdom come,
Thy will be done
On earth as in heaven.
Give us this day
Our daily bread,
Forgive us our offenses
As we also forgive those
Who commit offenses against us.
And do not let us fall into temptation,
But deliver us from evil.

Suggested Listening

Duruflé Requiem. The Choir of Westminster Cathedral. James O'Donnell,
    conductor. (Hyperion Records. CDA66757).

Like as the Hart: Psalms and Spiritual Songs. Westminster Choir. Joseph,
    Flummerfelt, conductor. (Chesky Records CD138).

Contributed by:

Christopher Jackson

Repertoire Resource Guide

Salmo 150

Ernani Aguiar
(b. 1949)

SATB/a cappella, TTBB/a cappella, or SSAA/a cappella
Earthsongs: SATB=S-40; TTBB=S-240, SSAA=W-40
Level: 3
Vocal: 3
Tonal/Rhythm: 3

Composer

Brazilian composer Ernani Aguiar has garnered impressive success in Brazil and abroad with performances, recordings, and broadcasts of his works. He is professor of music at Federal University of Rio De Janeiro (UFRJ). He has also worked with musicologist Francisco Curt Lange on revising and editing works by composers of the Minas Gerais School of the eighteenth century. Significant examples of his wide-ranging production are works for *a cappella* choir, such as "Salmo 150" (which has been performed by hundreds of choirs across the U.S.), the *Christmas Cantata*, *Missa Brevis IV*, the *Sinfonietta Prima*, and the opera *O menino maluquinho*. Aguiar's *Four Moments* No. 3 for symphony orchestra rates as one of the most often played pieces by a Brazilian composer. His numerous prizes include the Sharp, APCA, and Acorianos awards.

Composition

"Salmo 150" is a rhythmic motet setting of Psalm 150. It is characterized by playful rhythms, relentless energy, and a quickly presented text. This piece is sure to please any audience.

Technical Considerations

Maintaining a quick tempo and crisp articulation will be among the challenges in performing "Salmo 150." The opening rhythmic figure in the alto and tenor voices pervades the entire work; this motive must start with energy and continue to drive the piece forward throughout. This is easier said than done. The syllable [la] can actually be difficult to produce. Be sure to instruct the singers to use just the tip of the tongue when singing [la]. Otherwise, a thick American [l] will yield a sound that is not articulated, weight will be added to the sound, the pitch with not be as clear, and the piece will slow down.

Your singers will not a have a problem learning the notes to this piece; they are very straightforward. The difficulty of this piece lies in the declamation of the text. Aguiar sets the text syllabically at a fast tempo; the words can become real tongue-twisters. Try to avoid teaching the piece with text; in fact, it would be wise to teach the work on a syllable like [tu], as the [t] will help with articulation and the closed vowel [u] will help focus the pitch. You can even instruct the singers that the formation of the [l] conso-nant in [la] should feel similar to the production of the [t] in the neutral syllable [tu]. Once the notes and rhythms are in place, slowly add the text. It would be wise to speak the tricky portions of the text slowly and in rhythm (e.g., tenor part in measure 9, bass and alto parts in measure 18). Once you put it all together, make sure all consonants are produced in a light, quick manner so they remain energized and contribute to the aggressive articulation of the work.

Stylistic Considerations

This work comes from Latin America, and it must be performed with great flare. The beginning rhythmic figure must stay energized throughout the entire work. Put a slight accent on the first note of each grouping, as if it were a downward strum on the guitar. The meter marking of 12/8 means that this piece is in compound time. Amateur singers will naturally want to divide every macrobeat into two parts, not into three, as compound time requires. Compound time must have a feeling that is more "round" than that of simple time.

It is crucial that the singers feel a kinesthetic difference between simple and compound time. It is the roundness (some may call it swing) of the mac-robeat (in this case, the dotted-quarter note) that makes this piece sound exciting and alive. Lack of this "swing" will cause the piece to slow down and sound labored. Failure to "feel" compound time will wreak havoc with the rhythm and tempo in the choir. It is possible to teach this feeling through movement. Have singers walk to the big beat (the dotted quarter note) while lightly clapping the microbeat (the eighth note). Instead of accenting in a downward manner on each beat, ask them to feel an upward spring from each beat, as if they were being tossed in the air by a trampoline. It can also be useful to clap the macrobeat in a circular shape and contrast this by clapping with an angular movement (more indicative of simple time).

Musical Elements

As mentioned above, the harmony of this piece is rather straightforward. The tonality is clearly in A natural minor. Measures 16 to 17 abruptly leap into B-flat and E-flat minor, but A minor quickly returns in measure 18. It would be wise to rehearse the transition from measures 15 to 16 several times, to make sure that the B-flat in the altos and tenors is high enough; it is easy for the piece to go flat at this point.

It is effective to start measure 20 piano and crescendo each statement of "jubilationis" until the choir reaches forte. A quick cutoff of the final "nis" is crucial because the sopranos and tenors immediately present the opening rhythmic motive in measure 21. In measure 25, the meter and natural prose of the text do not match up. Your singers will want to accent the "num" of "Dominum" because it lies "on the beat." Ask them to accent "Lau" of "Laudate" instead of "num"; this will give the piece a feeling of drive to the end and make it even more exciting.

Form and Structure

"Salmo 150" is based on a rhythmic accompanimental motive and a simple, one-bar melody. Each voice part sings the melody and the accompaniment figure many times during the course of the piece. It can also be seen as a modified AABA' form.

Text and Translation

Laudate Dominum in sanctis eius laudate eum in firmamento virtutis eius
Laudate eum in virtutibus eius laudate eum secundum multitudinem
    magnitudinis eius.
Laudate eum in sono tubae: laudate eum in psalterio et cithara.
Laudate eum in tympano et choro: laudate eum in cordis et organo.
Laudate eum in cymbalis bene sonantibus laudate eum in cymbalis
    iubilationis:
Omnis spiritus laudet Dominum.

Praise ye the Lord in his holy places: praise ye him in the firmament of his
    power.
Praise ye him for his mighty acts: praise ye him according to the multitude
    of his greatness.
Praise him with sound of trumpet: praise him with psaltery and harp.

Praise him with timbrel and choir: praise him with strings and organs.
Praise him on high sounding cymbals: praise him on cymbals of joy:
Let every spirit praise the Lord.

Suggested Listening

Musica de Latinoamerica. Maria Guinland and Alberto Grau, conductors.
    (Earthsongs CD-01).

Contributed by:

Matthew W. Mehaffey

Repertoire Resource Guide

Set Me as a Seal

René Clausen
(b. 1953)

SATB, SSAA, TTBB/a cappella
Mark Foster Music Company: SATB=MA2047,
SSAA=MA0925, TTBB=MF1027
Overall: 3
Vocal: 4
Tonal/Rhythm: 3

Composer

René Clausen is the conductor of the Concordia Choir of Concordia College in Moorhead, Minnesota, as well as the artistic director of the Concordia Christmas Concerts, which are featured by PBS stations throughout the country. In 1998, he established the René Clausen Choral School, a week-long program for choral conductors that meets each summer at Concordia College. Also an active composer, Clausen has written more than forty-five commissioned works, including the "Canticle of Praise" for the Mormon Tabernacle Choir and the King's Singers. In 1990, he conducted the Dale Warland Singers in a recording of *A New Creation*, from which "Set Me as a Seal" is taken.

Composition

This hymn is part of *A New Creation*, Clausen's first major work, and, though Christian, it is not composed for a particular denomination. It fits well within a modern sacred aesthetic, serving as a subject for quiet meditation during a church service or for a concert. In *A New Creation*, Clausen strives to address various aspects of the relationship between God and humanity. "Set Me as a Seal" deals with the unshakable trust of the faithful in their God.

Historical Perspective

This is a very recent composition and is one of Clausen's most frequently performed works. It is a short setting of a sacred text, linking it to hymns and motets of the recent and distant past, but the gently inflected harmonies are part of a modern vocabulary. The melody lines, which are mostly stepwise, reinforce a connection to music of the past with similarities to chant, although the resemblance is in reference only, not in derivation.

Technical Considerations

This is not a technically challenging piece. The rhythms are largely straight-forward, aside from a moment of quarter note triplets against eighth notes. Most of the work is homophonic, though the central nine measures are poly-phonic and imitative. The ranges for the voice parts are low, though not extreme, calling for a low G from the altos and a low D from the basses. The principal technical difficulty is the sustained nature of the melodic lines, which often extend for several *sostenuto* measures in a gentle arch without break. Though there are occasional chromatic pitches, they are approached stepwise and resolved logically.

Stylistic Considerations

This is a modern, sacred piece set in a restrained church style. The overall style is one of gentle consonance and affirmation in the statement of unbreakable faith. There is more motion and more strain heard in the middle section, although the tension that builds through the rhythmic variation and the increased dynamics bleeds away through each statement of the imitation, leading to a return of the earlier mood.

Musical Elements

The tonality is strongly D major, asserted through slowly flowing quarter note motion. The harmonies are often colored by added tones and suspensions, but non-chord tones are resolved logically. The texture is almost exclusively homophonic, although the middle section sets the women against the men rhythmically. In one measure, the basses have quarter note triplets where the tenors have eighth notes, and as the repeated imitation closes, the section each voice part has a rhythmically independent statement of the motive. The melodic design is typically constructed of large arches, which are approached and resolved stepwise.

Form and Structure

The structure of the work is ABA; the first statement of the A section contains two complete statements of the opening melody with the second reharmonized and revoiced. The closing A section is an almost literal repeat of the second harmonization from the opening A section. The musical structure is matched by the textual structure in which the words from the opening section are repeated in the closing section.

Text

Set me as a seal upon your heart,
as a seal upon your arm,
for love is strong as death.
Many waters cannot quench love;
neither can the floods drown it.

Suggested Listening

The Choral Music of René Clausen. Concordia College Choir.
    (CRN2134CD).

Contributed by:

Thomas Cunningham

Repertoire Resource Guide

Shenandoah

arr. James Erb
(b. 1926)

SATB divisi/a cappella
Warner Bros. Publications: LG51846
Overall: 3
Vocal: 4
Tonal/Rhythm: 3

Composer

James Erb is professor emeritus of music at the University of Richmond, where he conducted the university choral ensembles. In addition to his work as a music editor and arranger, he has achieved scholarly distinction through his research and modern editions of works of Orlando di Lasso. Erb is currently director of the Richmond Symphony Chorus.

Composition

Erb's arrangement of the American folksong "Shenandoah" was composed in 1971 for the University of Richmond Choir's European tour and remains one of the most beloved American choral works to date. In fact, for those working and singing in the world of choral music, it is difficult to separate the notion of the original folk tune from Erb's popular arrangement.

Technical Considerations

"Shenandoah" is arranged for unaccompanied SSAATTBB choir. Although gratifying to sing, the work requires a substantial amount of stamina from singers to sustain the many long phrases, especially at the arranger's tempo indication of quarter note = 58–60. With this in mind, Shenandoah works well with larger choirs because of the greater ability to mask the necessary breaths needed by younger and amateur singers during the extended phrases. (Interestingly, Erb provides no breath marks in the opening ten measures of the piece, in which the sopranos and altos sing the melody in unison, whereas the remainder of the work is littered with precise breath marks in all parts. Whether this means the first occurrence of the melody should be sung entirely without audible breaths is up to the director to decide.)

Aside from the sostenuto issue, "Shenandoah" provides few real challenges for the conductor or singer. As is typical for most folksongs, the vocal range of the melody is limited to an octave, with the exception of the opening anacrusis on the fifth below the tonic. The tessitura of most parts is easy and suitable for adult singers of any age group. It does, however, require true second basses with the ability to sustain many low tones, but always at a low dynamic marking. Erb indicates that the piece may be sung a half-step higher, presumably to ameliorate the low bass notes.

For the conductor, one of the most challenging aspects will be to coordinate the many breaths indicated by the arranger as well as encouraging the singers to maintain the smooth, tender mood of the piece by carefully following the dynamics indicated in the score (which rarely fall above mezzo forte).

The piece ends with all singers on a unison E above middle C on the final syllable of the word "Shenandoah." Erb indicates that the basses are to sing in *falsetto*, and the tenors should be "barely audible." This might take some focused coaching during the rehearsal process to convey the appropriate vocal technique needed to produce this effect.

A repeat of the first verse is used in the second half of the piece as a three-part canon for divisi sopranos and altos. The director could certainly choose to divide the soprano and alto sections into an equal three-part split to even out the number of voices for this particular section.

Form and Structure

The text is English, and the three verses of the folksong are through-composed in a seamless fashion. The duration is approximately four minutes.

Text

O Shenando', I long to see you,
And hear your rolling river,
O Shenando', I long to see you,
'Way, we're bound away,
Across the wide Missouri.

I long to see your smiling valley,
And hear your rolling river,
I long to see your smiling valley,
'Way, we're bound away,
Across the wide Missouri.

'Tis sev'n long years since last I see you,
And hear your rolling river,
'Tis sev'n long years since last I see you,
'Way, we're bound away,
Across the wide Missouri.

Suggested Listening

Folk Songs. The Westminster Choir. Joseph Flummerfelt, conductor.
(Gothic Records. 38130).

Musica. Pacific Chorale. John Alexander, conductor. (Gothic Records
38130, www.pacificchorale.org).

Contributed by:

Wayne Glass

Repertoire Resource Guide

Sicut cervus

Giovanni Pierluigi da Palestrina
(1525–1594)

SATB/a cappella
GIA Publications, Inc.: G–2141.
edited by Maynard Klein
Overall: 3
Vocal: 3
Tonal/Rhythm: 3

Composer

Giovanni Pierluigi is known by the place where he is thought to have been born: Palestrina, in the Sabine Hills near Rome. The composer may have actually been born in Rome, where he also had his training. His career was entirely based in Rome and started with successive positions as chorister at Santa Maria Maggiore, San Giovanni Laterano, and San Pietro churches. Palestrina probably studied with Robin Mallapert in 1538–39, a certain "Robert" in 1540, and Firmin Lebel from the end of 1540 at Santa Maria Maggiore. His first leadership position was as organist at San Agapito in Palestrina in 1544.

Palestrina married Lucrezia Gori in 1547 and had three children. He remained a provincial musician until 1551, and his compositional output was not documented at all until his first publication in 1554; however, he probably began to develop and refine his knowledge of and technical skills in counterpoint during the early years of his education. In 1551, Palestrina was appointed to succeed Mallapert as *magister cantorum* of the Cappella Giulia, which was the training institution for native Italian musicians. He became *magister cappellae* in 1553, but his position carried no responsibility for composition.

In 1555, Palestrina was admitted to the Cappella Sistina, the pope's official musical chapel in spite of the fact that he was married. However, when Paul IV became the new pontiff, the rules of the chapel were again strictly enforced, and Palestrina was dismissed. He was then appointed to *maestro di cappella* of San Giovanni Laterano in 1555. Palestrina left San Giovanni Laterano in 1560 because of a conflict about funding for the chapel musicians.

In 1561 Palestrina gained employment at the basilica of Santa Maria Maggiore, where he had been trained. He became the *maestro* at the newly erected Seminario Romano in 1566. Cardinal Ippolito II d'Este offered him a position in 1567 and Palestrina held both positions until 1571. At that point, he returned to the post of choirmaster of the Cappella Giulia at San Pietro where he remained until his death. Palestrina was a tremendously prolific composer of liturgical music, but he was also a skilled composer of secular music.

Composition

This is one of the most representative motets in Palestrina's opus. The transparent *stile antico* structure built on clear points of imitation creates a continuous flow uninterrupted by cadences. The notation in Palestrina's time was usually double the note values that appear in this edition; thus, the whole note was the tactus, the half note was the division, and the quarter note was the subdivision. Palestrina adhered to strict rules when setting text contrapuntally: melismas appeared only on the stressed syllable of a word, and the shortest note value that would receive a syllable was the half note. (In this edition, the quarter note is the shortest note to get a syllable.)

Motet texts are usually divided into two parts called *prima pars* and *secunda pars*. "Sicut cervus" is the *prima pars* of such a pair. The parts function well as musical pieces in their own right; thus, the *secunda pars*, "Sitivit anima mea," is rarely performed. Liturgically, the two function as a unit because the text must appear in its entirety. The foremost importance of text in the liturgy influenced the composers who set those texts for use in the Catholic Church.

Historical Perspective

Palestrina wrote "Sicut cervus" in 1584, which makes it one of his mature works. He had lost his wife four years earlier, but he married a well-to-do widow from Rome in 1581. This marriage freed him from the financial shackles imposed on him by the Roman Catholic Church. However, he was a devout Catholic and continued to serve the Church faithfully by supplying liturgical music.

Technical Considerations

Each voice part is completely independent, making specific demands on the singers. The singers have to be secure in their parts while actively listening to all the other parts for tuning and balance. The parts are imitative but depart after the initial point of imitation to varying degrees.

The ranges of the individual voice parts are not challenging. Originally, the piece was in F major; however, the key of A-flat major may be an accurate estimate of the pitch standard for Rome during Palestrina's time.

The challenging issue is rhythmically precise execution of the individual parts. It quickly becomes obvious if the choir has an understanding of the rhythmic language of this piece. Only a choir in complete command of the rhythm can exhibit a clean performance of this work.

Stylistic Considerations

Measure lines are in the score only to aid the modern performer. It is difficult to ignore them; however, it is imperative to disregard the beat structure of the modern measure. The first beat of the measure is not necessarily a strong beat—the text governs the stress structure of the phrase. The points of imitation should be performed with identical emphasis. The performers in Palestrina's time did not have scores; they had part books. Because the singers only saw their own parts, they articulated as they would a solo while listening to the other voices for balance and tuning.

Performers should minimize vibrato to make tuning easier. Singers should not have to sing completely void of vibrato, but vibratos may have to be matched closely among the singers to facilitate tuning.

There is no need for a ritardando at the end unless the director deems it necessary. Palestrina has written the ending to have a slowing effect harmonically and rhythmically. If a ritardando is needed for effect, a slight slowing should be sufficient.

Phrases in Palestrina's works usually exhibit an arch construction. This arch dictates the shape of the phrase with a build-up, a climax, and a tapering off.

The composers of this time period and of this style of music handle dissonances in a very controlled manner. The dissonances have to be prepared as a consonance, remain stationary when other voices move to make a dissonance, and finally resolve properly according to the strict rules of counterpoint. The dissonances should not receive excess emphasis, but they should be treated as organic parts of the phrases. Dissonances are harmonic occurrences that result from the movements of the individual parts, which do not include any melodic dissonances.

Musical Elements

The harmony stays with in the mode consistently. The only chromatic alterations in this style are controlled by strict modal harmonic rules. Phrase lengths vary with the melismatic content; however, the phrases are usually six to eight measures long. They adhere to a basic arch form that has a climax and a resolution to the last note, which is a whole note or a half note in this edition.

Form and Structure

The form is through-composed. The two lines of text are separated by a Renaissance cadence, a major sixth between the soprano and tenor expanding to an octave in measures 22 to 23; however, this cadence is overlapped by the alto voice, which has not yet finished the line of text, and by the bass, which begins the new line of text in measure 23. That same major sixth progressing to the octave cadence appears often in the music, but the pattern is most often weakened by overlapping voices or different text. The only authentic cadence in the piece is in measures 54 to 55 between the soprano and tenor. It is true that the bass overlaps the cadence, but the soprano has already finished the text and stays on the *finalis*. The three lower voices sing a portion of the last line of text in what is called an extension.

Text and Translation

Sicut cervus desiderat ad fontes aquarum,
ita desiderat anima mea ad te Deus.

As the dear longs for the water
so longs my soul for you, God.

Suggested Listening

Beyond Chant: Mysteries of the Renaissance. Voices of Ascension. Dennis Keene, conductor. (Delos Records CD 3165).

Exultate Deo—Masterpieces of Sacred Polyphony. The Choir of Westminster Cathedral. James O'Donnell, conductor. (Hyperion CDA66850).

European Choral Music 1525–1751. Christ Church Cathedral Choir Oxford. Stephen Darlington, conductor. (Nimbus Records MVP1758).

Contributed by:

G. Mikael Lindström

Repertoire Resource Guide

Sure on This Shining Night
Samuel Osborne Barber
(1910–1981)

SATB, SA, or SAB/piano
G. Schirmer, Inc.: SATB=HL 50308930, SAB=HL 50480265,
SA=HL 50485025
Overall: 3
Vocal: 3
Tonal/Rhythm: 3

Composer

Samuel Osborne Barber is considered one of the most successful American composers of the twentieth century. He was born on March 9, 1910, in West Chester, Pennsylvania. His father was a prominent doctor, and his mother was an amateur pianist. But it was Barber's musical aunt and uncle, Louise and Sidney Homer, who heavily influenced his musical upbringing. Young Samuel began his piano study at age six and began composing at age seven. He became the organist at a local church and also led a high school orchestra while still in his teens.

In 1924, Barber entered the newly founded Curtis Institute where he studied composition with Rosario Scalero, piano with George Boyle and Isabelle Vengerova, conducting with Fritz Reiner, and voice with Emilio de Gogorza. He developed an attractive baritone voice and even considered a career as a professional singer. In the early 1930s, Barber was given charge of the choir at the Curtis Institute and composed many pieces for this ensemble.

He graduated from Curtis in 1934 and traveled to Europe numerous times to study composition. On one such trip, he and his good friend Giancarlo

Mennoti befriended Arturo Toscanini. Barber returned to the Curtis Institute in 1939 to work as a professor but quickly left again 1942 to serve in the U.S. Air Force during World War II. He continued to compose throughout the war. When he returned, every major orchestra in the country was programming his works.

Barber befriended many prominent musicians of the day, including Ormandy, Szell, Walter, Koussevitzky, Horowitz, Leinsdorf, and Mehta. His success continued throughout the rest of his life. Barber composed music for almost every genre, which garnered him several prominent awards, including the Prix de Rome and two Pulitzer Prizes.

Composition and Genre

"Sure on This Shining night" was originally set as the third song in Barber's Op. 13, a collection of songs for voice and piano (1938). This opus also includes Barber's familiar "Heaven-Haven." Barber arranged both of these pieces for choir and piano in 1961. The text of "Sure on This Shining Night" is excerpted from the poem "Permit Me Voyage" by the American poet James Agee. "Sure on This Shining Night" has become one of Barber's most well known and often performed choral works. This SATB setting combines the homophonic texture of the piano accompaniment with polyphonic and imitative voice parts.

Technical Considerations

"Sure on This Shining Night" is a beautiful piece that is accessible to choirs of all ability levels. The choral parts are highly polyphonic and filled with imitation. Barber is able to maintain the beauty and elegance of the original solo setting of Op. 13 by scoring each of the choral parts in a soloistic fashion. The combination of Barber's lyrical melodic writing and lush, romantic harmonic language invites the singers to use a rich, well supported tone.

Barber contrasts the vocal polyphony with the original homophonic piano accompaniment from the Op. 13 setting. This contrasting accompaniment provides harmonic support for the voices, yet does not double their parts. Hence, the choir must be able to hold their individual melodic lines, or the conductor can expect to rehearse each voice part line by line. To avoid this, the conductor should have the choir speak the text in rhythm until the singers have a firm understanding of how their individual rhythms fit into the greater whole of the texture. After the rhythm is secure, notes can be added, but the fear of the independent rhythms will be alleviated.

The tessitura of each voice part is comfortable for both younger and more experienced choirs. The ranges are: soprano C4–G5, alto G3–C5, tenor F3–F4, and bass G2–D4. If the piece is being performed by younger singers, the conductor would be wise to have a few tenors double the alto G3 in measure

8. This exposed note may cause some young altos to oversing in chest voice and sacrifice the lyrical vocal production required of this piece.

The slow *Andante* creates long, sustained lines for the singers to maintain. This provides an excellent lesson on breath management and energy skills. One obvious, yet helpful, technique is to have the choir sing the piece on a neutral syllable (such as "doo") while subdividing each beat so that the ensemble sings every eighth note. This will encourage the choir to sing through the long notes instead of "sit" on them. This also shows singers how much air is required of them between the allocated breath marks. It will be easy for the singers to fall into bad breathing habits while learning the piece, so the conductor would be well advised to determine breath markings ahead of time and insist that the singers follow them, even while they are learning the notes.

The singers should also be made aware of the voice pairing and imitation that occurs throughout the piece. Locating and isolating these sections will help the choir learn the piece easily and quickly and will also help them understand how the piece is formally constructed. For example, isolating the soprano and tenor parts, and then the bass and alto parts in measures 2–9, will help the singers realize whether their function is melodic or harmonic in nature. It will also help them discover if their part imitates another voice part. This idea can then be translated throughout the rest of the piece, and the learning process will be significantly shortened.

Stylistic Considerations

Barber's music is filled with inherent lyricism and romantic expressiveness. He is often criticized as being conservative, a romanticist in expression and a classicist in his use of form. In many ways, Barber's music recalls the harmonic language of Brahms, whom he studied in great detail. Barber's genius lies in his ability to gracefully fuse romanticized melodies, polyphony, and complex musical textures into a coherent and unified piece of proportionate music, a feat that few others have accomplished. As a result, Barber's music is often well received by choirs and audiences alike.

There are, however, moments when Barber veers away from his romanticized harmony and instead uses poignant, dissonant harmonies to provide bits of word painting. The conductor should take the time to isolate these dissonances and explain how they function harmonically in the texture. By doing this, the ensemble will achieve appropriately balanced chords that enhance instead of interrupt the overall lush harmonic structure. Barber also composes many unexpected harmonic shifts. Luckily, he often guides these shifts with the piano accompaniment. Even with the help of the piano, the choir will have to listen closely to each other to achieve the subtle musical blend and phrasing required by the music.

Form and Structure

"Sure on this Shining Night" can loosely be described as ABA'. The piece is in B-flat major and very tonal.

Text

Sure on this shining night
Of star-made shadows round,
Kindness must watch for me
This side the ground...

Suggested Listening

Samuel Barber Choral and Organ Works. Cambridge University Choir. Tim Brown, conductor. (Gild Music GMCD 7145).

Inscription of Hope. Northwest Girls Choir. Rebecca Rottsolk, conductor. (Treble version, Arsis CD 109).

Additional References and Resources

Hennessee, Don A. *Samuel Barber: A Bio-Bibliography*. Westport, Connecticut.: Greenwood Press. 1985.

Heyman, Barbara B. *Samuel Barber: The Composer and His Music*. New York: Oxford University Press. 1992.

Contributed by:

Lee D. Nelson

Repertoire Resource Guide

Time and Concord

Benjamin Britten
(1913–1976)

SATB/a cappella
Boosey & Hawkes, Inc.: "Choral Dances from Gloriana"=17411,
single octavo=M051450152
Overall: 3
Vocal: 3
Tonal/Rhythm: 4

Composer

Benjamin Britten was born in 1913 in Lowestoft, Suffolk, and spent most of his life working as a composer, pianist, and conductor in England. Britten composed a new style of tonal music in an era in which many composers favored esoteric, atonal techniques, which perhaps helped him become one of the most successful English composers in the twentieth century. He steadfastly employed his trademark but tonal language in works that span dramatic, choral, chamber, film, and symphonic genres.

His youth on the Suffolk coast of England was typical for a dentist's son, encompassing sports as well as superior achievement in piano and an interest in drama. By the age of 14, he catalogued 100 opus numbers and began studying composition with Frank Bridge. In due course, he moved to London, entered the Royal College of Music, and won several composition prizes.

Britten was an avowed pacifist, a philosophy borne out in many of his works, including the massive *War Requiem*. He wrote many vocal pieces specifically for tenor Peter Peers and maintained friendships with William Walton, Sergey Koussevitzky, W. H. Auden, and other outstanding figures.

From early adulthood, Britten nurtured an interest in the music of the East. He eventually indulged his interest by incorporating the sounds of the Balinese gamelan into several pieces, including the controversial *The Turn of the Screw*. His output includes operas (most prominently *Peter Grimes*), choral and orchestral works (e.g., *A Hymn to St. Cecelia*, *Ceremony of Carols*, and *War Requiem*), and music for films, radio, and stage.

Composition

"Time and Concord" is third movement in a cycle of six choral dances from the opera *Gloriana*, which portrays a woman's struggle with the traditionally male role of the English monarch. The movements include: "Time," "Concord," "Time and Concord," "Country Girls," "Rustics and Fishermen," and "Final Dance of Hermitage."

The text is by William Plomer, and each movement builds from the previous one. In *Time*, Plomer asserts, "Time is at his apogee, lusty and blithe." Concord "endue[s our land] with plenty, peace and happiness…Concord and Time each needeth each." Then, in a "gracefully swaying" tempo, "Time and Concord" (text below) points to an enumeration in "Country Girls" of all sorts of fertile flowers, in "Rustics and Fishermen" of plenteous fruits of land and sea, and, finally, all this bounty is offered to the princess soon to be crowned queen. One is reminded of the anthology *The Triumphs of Oriana* by Morley also in honor of an English queen, in this case, Queen Elizabeth.

Historical Perspective

Britten was commissioned to compose the opera *Gloriana* for the coronation of Elizabeth II. In *Gloriana*, Britten explores matters of sexuality, gender roles, and the relationship of Queen Elizabeth I and the Earl of Suffolk. It was first presented in Covent Garden during Coronation Week in 1953. The content of the opera is said to have disturbed the new monarch and was poorly received by the British public. It was Britten's first failure in the genre of opera.

That being said, the *Gloriana* dances are wonderfully interesting pieces for a good amateur choir. Their secular texts and diverse movements make them ideal additions to any concert.

Technical Considerations

Upon first examination of "Time and Concord," it seems that the rhythm, melody, and harmony will be difficult for singers to learn; however, further score study reveals that not to be the case. There is actually very little musical content in the chorus; Britten was a master of efficiency. Examine the soprano and alto parts from measures 1 to 8. Next look at the tenor and bass parts for the same measures. You will notice that they are identical.

Britten creates a wonderful tonal world in which time sounds suspended by setting the men's parts in canon with the women's parts. In measures 9 to 16, the men and women reverse roles in the canonic structure. A canonic *stretto* of sorts occurs in measures 17 to 24 as the men and women switch canonic roles after four measures instead of eight. Six measures before the end, at the tempo marking "Broadly," the men and women sing in homophony for the first and only time during the piece. As you can see, what looks and even sounds confusing upon first inspection is really very simple. To teach this efficiently, begin by having the sopranos and tenors sing the soprano and the basses and altos sing the alto part for the first eight measures. Once this is secure, try having each section sing its written part for measures 1 to 8 and then measures 9 to 16. Repeat for each section.

"Time and Concord" is marked "Gracefully Swaying." The text and musical motives are so short and repetitive that the conductor should be vigilant, or the performance could easily sound choppy. Most of the song is set to a long-short-short-long rhythmic pattern within a compound meter. To allow a graceful sway, be sure the choir has compound time kinesthetically organized. Amateur singers will perform in simple time as a default because most do not understand compound time. It is important that the conductor assure proficiency in compound time, or this piece will never sound correct. As an exercise to initiate this, one might ask the choir to feel each beat as being a round shape as opposed to square; the roundness of the beat will aid in division of the beat into three equal parts. You could also ask the singers to shift their weight from one foot to the other at the beginning of each short motive, *swaying* back and forth with the phrases.

Britten's setting does not accommodate natural word stresses. The conductor will have to confront, for example, the word "bounty" set to an eighth note followed by a quarter note instead of using the more natural opposite allocation. The rise in pitch at the end of many motives will present a continual temptation to land heavily on the wrong syllable. Be insistent that this not occur; sculpt these short phrases dutifully and incessantly. One final textual danger is that the familiar melodic line later begins on an offbeat after the choir has become used to it beginning on the beat. Two possibilities for confusion then arise: waiting for a comfortable downbeat and ignoring text stress already trained in.

Stylistic Considerations

This is not a heavy song; keep the energy flowing. Vertical (harmonic) considerations are less important than horizontal ones. Make it clear that each part of the canonic duet (SA and TB) understand it has a phrase contour to effect: the dynamic rises to the middle of the text phrase and falls to the fermata that marks the phrase's end. At measure 28, phrases become shorter, but Britten has marked them as clearly as he has their predecessors. Stressed notes are marked both accented and marcato.

The dynamic rises to forte only once, at the introduction of Gloriana's name near the end. Otherwise, dynamic contrast is subtle. The first two verses begin and end *pp*; the next, *mf*, has two arches instead of one. The last verse begins *pp*, rises to *f,* and ends *ppp*. Only in this last section does the meter change to a single 9/8 bar from the lyrical 6/8.

Bringing out the punchline of the piece (from measure 28 onward) will be, in Pomel's word, the ensemble's "pleasance." As the dynamic drops, intensity should rise so that the repeated "all our love" phrase drills into the audience instead of being lost to it.

Form and Structure

Canonic treatment of simple rhythmic motive

Suggested Listening

Britten: Gloriana. Sir Charles Mackerras, conductor. (Polygram Records).

Britten: Choral Edition, Volume I. Finzi Singers. Julie Cooper, conductor. (Chandos 9511).

Contributed by:

Lani Johnson

Repertoire Resource Guide

Vamuvamba

arr. Boniface Mganga
(b. 1954)

SATB/percussion
Earthsongs: S-61
Overall: 3
Vocal: 3
Tonal/Rhythm: 3

Composer

Boniface Mganga graduated from the University of Nairobi in 1979 and studied choral conducting in the United Kingdom. He founded the Muungano National Choir in 1979 and still directs the group. The choir has toured extensively around the world and was featured at the 1999 World Choral Symposium at Rotterdam. They are in a sister partnership with the renowned St. Louis African Chorus.

Mganga, a popular conductor and clinician, is a member of the Board of the International Federation for Choral Music (IFCM) and is deputy secretary at the Ministry of Education in Kenya as well as chairman of the Kenya Music and Cultural Festival.

Composition

"Vamuvamba" is Boniface Mganga's adaptation and arrangement of a traditional Tiriki melody. It was included on a recording with the *Missa Luba* in 1991, published in the United States by Earthsongs in 1996. Strophic in nature, "Vamuvamba" has all the qualities one expects of a folksong; it is simple, lyrical, and repetitive. Its Christian text and joyous nature clearly place it as a religious praise song.

Historical Perspective

Tiriki is one of the living historical languages of Kenya and is found in the Kakamega District of the Western Province. While we do not know the origins of this melody, the text is religious. Although the Kenyan culture is ancient, today approximately 70 percent of the population is Christian. Missionary activity began in earnest in the nineteenth century with the building of the railroads, and Christian churches have tended to be homogenous, ethnically. Many groups reflect Anglican and Roman Catholic practices, but many others are independent groups. Some have sought to incorporate indigenous beliefs into Christian practice.

In any case, Kenyan Christians are in harmony with most of their African neighbors, tending toward more evangelistic, fundamentalist practices and beliefs. The uplifting, repetitive nature of this piece reflects such practices and is not so different from the kind of music used in evangelical religious practice throughout the world.

Technical Considerations

The piece is incessantly rhythmic, with long notes coming only at cadences. The many dotted rhythms can lead to a kind of "rhythmic fatigue," resulting in a choir's tendency to turn the dotted eighth-sixteenth note rhythms into triplet-like figures. The music bears no indication that this is desirable, and the music retains a much more exciting sense of forward motion when the choir maintains the integrity of the written rhythms.

One often repeated rhythmic figure presents a special challenge: a dotted eighth note followed by a sixteenth note, which is tied to a longer note following it. The director is encouraged to incorporate such rhythms into warm-up drills and to be insistent on their accuracy from the beginning. Only one other rhythmic problem seems to confront most groups, which is beginning phrases on offbeats following brief rests on the strong beats. Again, incorporating this challenge into warm-ups and maintaining a consistent expectation of correct performance of such places tends to be quite successful.

The text presents a significant challenge to most groups. Few singers have sung in Tiriki, and it takes some time to become comfortable with the sounds. Initial teaching using neutral syllables will help over come the rhythmic problems described above and allow the singers to feel comfortable with the music. When this is accomplished, add the text in short segments, allowing the singers to master one section before proceeding to the next. A pronunciation guide is included with the music, and conductors should not underestimate the time required to master the text.

Stylistic Considerations

"Vamuvamba" is *a cappella* except for a notated conga part. For most American choirs, the music will feel like a cross between a spiritual and a gospel song. An important goal in preparing performances of this piece is to attempt to allow it to sound easy and natural. If one exercises care in teaching the rhythms and text as described in the preceding section, the energy of the music will create enthusiasm in the choir. Allowing the music to dance and project the happy message of the text (we were saved through the betrayal and crucifixion of Jesus) while maintaining the musical integrity of the piece will result in a performance enjoyed by performers and listeners alike. One should be careful to recruit the correct number of conga players for the size of the choir and resonance of the hall, and, if they are good players, encourage them to improvise somewhat instead of maintaining the strict ostinato rhythms notated. Soloists should be carefully rehearsed.

Musical Elements

The music is in G major and common time throughout. The chord progressions may feel simplistic to more advanced choirs, but the fairly complex rhythmic demands will prevent them from being bored.

Form and Structure

MEASURE	EVENT AND SCORING
1–16	Stanza 1; SATB choir
17–24	Refrain 1; SATB choir
25–36	Stanza 2; refrain integrated
25–28	Tenor section melody
29–36	SATB choir refrain with tenor interjections
37–44	Stanza 3; SA choral duet ending with tenor tag
45–52	SATB choir refrain with tenor interjection
53–60	Stanza 4; SATB choir with tenor tag
61–68	SATB choir refrain
69–81	Stanza 5; soprano soloists over SATB choral interjections and repetitions
82–89	SATB choir refrain

Text and Translation

Ni litsulitsa lio mwami weru Yesu lwa yavambwa,
Lwa Yuda yatsama Yesu vamuvamba.
Na vutswa khandi khwasoma ivanjeli ka handikhwa,
Ubwoni bweru bwachira vamuvamba.
Vali Vayuda vamuvamba,
mwami wanje Yesu vamuvamba, ha!
Lwa ndali muheyi ndamuvamba,
Mwami wanje Yesu ndamuvamba.
Mu masahi gege Yesu, khwasameha bwoni bweru.
Mu masahi gege Yesu, khwahonyiywa myoyo gyeru.
Mu livambwa lyelye Yesu, kwaverelwa tsimbavasi.
Lwa ndali muloji, lwa ndali muyenji,
Iwa ndali muheyi ndamuvamba.
Yesu khwamuvamba, Yesu vamuvamba.

In remembrance of our Lord Jesus
when he was crucified:
When Judas betrayed Jesus,
they crucified him.
Again we read in the Bible,
our sins crucified him.
When I sinned,
I crucified him.
In his blood we were forgiven,
in his blood our hearts were saved.

Suggested Listening

One Word, Many Voices. (Earthsongs CD-02)

Contributed by:

Anthony Reeves

Repertoire Resource Guide

Wade in the Water

arr. Moses Hogan
(1957–2003)

SATB and solo/a cappella
Hal Leonard Corporation: HL 8741180
Overall: 3
Vocal: 3
Tonal/Rhythm: 3

Composer

Moses Hogan was born in New Orleans in 1957. He studied at the New Orleans Center for Creative Arts, Oberlin Conservatory of Music, the Juilliard School of Music, and Louisiana State University in Baton Rouge. Hogan performed as a concert pianist, receiving a number of awards. He founded the Moses Hogan Singers, which recorded many of the composer's works. Hogan edited the *New Oxford Book of Spirituals* and may be best known for his settings of spirituals, including "Wade in the Water."

Composition

The traditional spiritual predates gospel music and has its roots in the experience of enslaved Africans in America. Spirituals fuse the sounds of traditional African music and instruments, the ideas of African ancestral religions and Christianity, and the occasional coded messages that were used during life in slavery. George White, treasurer of Fisk University in Nashville, Tennessee, organized the first touring choir with repertoire devoted to spirituals, the Fisk Jubilee Singers, as a vehicle for raising funds for the university. Composers, including John Work II (1873–1925), John Work III (1901–1968), William

Dawson (1899–1990), and Undine Smith Moore (1904–1989), soon began notating and arranging this repertoire for wider use.

"Wade in the Water" begins with a statement of the last phrase of the refrain, leading into the refrain. Before each recurrence of the refrain, the basses walk a downward pattern. The syncopated rhythm established in the title phrase's first iteration continues throughout and serves as accompaniment to the solo line. The soloist adds a written cadenza at the end.

Historical Perspective

"Wade in the Water" is an arrangement of a folk spiritual in the call-and-response style. The whole congregation probably sang the refrain, leaving verses to a soloist or soloists. The repeating phrase admonishes escaping slaves to "wade in the water" to elude tracking dogs. "God's gonna trouble the water" probably refers to the parting of the Red Sea in biblical times, expressing the belief that God will aid escaping slaves as he did the Israelites.

Technical Considerations

If the ensemble is not accustomed to this style of music, it will take a little time to establish effortless syncopation. The "wade in the water" phrase must be very solid because it is the rhythmic foundation of the entire piece.

There are several interesting and typical "licks" that allow one voice part or another to emerge for an instant. The descending bass pattern already mentioned in measure 14 ("Oh children") and the sopranos' descending pattern in the same measure are two examples.

In this piece, work for a balance of exact articulation (appropriate at "wa-din-the-wa-ter") and affectation ("wah-tuh"). The first example propels the repeating phrase; the second sounds inauthentic. See the composer's note at the bottom of the first page on voicing the "t" in "water."

Choose a singer with a warm, confident voice who can maintain integrity over the choral accompaniment and interact easily with the ensemble for the solo. It would be good to coach syncopated rhythms with words spoken in time before adding pitches.

The fermatas in the closing can and should be dramatic but will need rehearsing. Nothing ruins a dramatic fermata like one early voice.

Stylistic Considerations

Hogan has written expressive and dynamic instructions throughout, but there is room for individual interpretation. The worst transgression in preparing this piece would be to square it off or to de-emotionalize it. An explanation of the depth of despair, suffering, and hope expressed in these lyrics may aim the choir toward an inspired performance.

Form and Structure

Refrain and two verses, strophic, E-flat major.

Text and Translation

Wade in the water.
Wade in the water, children,
Wade in the water.
God's gonna trouble the water

See that host all dressed in white.
God's gonna trouble the water.
The leader looks like an Israelite.
God's gonna trouble the water.

See that band all dressed in red.
God's gonna trouble the water.
Well it looks like the band that Moses led.
God's gonna trouble the water.

—traditional African American spiritual

Suggested Listening

Choral Series 2002. Moses Hogan Chorale. Moses Hogan, conductor. (DJ Records 6706C). Two CDs.

Contributed by:

Lani Johnson

Repertoire Resource Guide

When David Heard

Thomas Weelkes
(ca. 1575–1623)

SSAATB/a cappella
E.C. Schirmer Music Co.: 3.0672
Overall: 3
Vocal: 3
Tonal/Rhythm: 4

Composer

Thomas Weelkes was an English organist and composer born in Sussex ca. 1575. He published his first volume of madrigals in 1597 and became organist at Winchester College in 1598. In that year and again in 1600, he published two additional volumes of madrigals. Around 1602, he was appointed organist and *informator choristarum* at Chichester Cathedral; he received a music degree from New College, Oxford the same year.

Weelkes published his fourth and final volume of madrigals in 1608. In January 1617, following years of inappropriate behavior, Weelkes was dismissed from his position at Chichester because of drunkenness. Weelkes's wife died in 1622, by which time he was again employed as an organist. He died in London November 30, 1623.

Composition

"When David Heard" may be described as a sacred madrigal; the music highlights the depth of sorrow felt by King David on the death of his son, Absalom. It is written for six vocal parts (SSATB) and is rather contrapuntal in nature. As is typical of the madrigal genre, the text is quite dramatic and picturesque;

Weelkes makes significant use of text-painting in his composition. The style of the vocal writing is important in telling the story and expressing the emotions inherent in the text.

Historical Perspective

The date of composition of "When David Heard" is unknown. Almost all of Weelkes's musical output was vocal and may be divided into the following categories: Anglican services, sacred anthems, madrigals, and sacred madrigals.

Other composers active during this era included William Byrd, John Bull, Thomas Morley, and Thomas Tomkins. This was a period in English history when the emphasis was on music of varying styles to be used in Anglican worship; drama often had a high place in the music, achieved primarily through text painting.

Technical Considerations

The original six-part voicing indicated by Weelkes uses vocal ranges quite consistent with what is today a SSAATB texture. It is important to realize, however, that this is not writing for "first and second" sopranos and altos in the sense that the "first" parts are higher in tessitura or range than the "second" parts. Because the voice parts are of equal importance, as one would expect in contrapuntal writing, it might work best to ensure that each part is covered by singers capable of singing the full range of the parts.

Stylistic Considerations

It is important to bear in mind the madrigalian nature of this piece. Each part should strive to achieve independence within the overall framework of the piece. It is important that the choir do this, however, with careful consideration of the text and its syllabic stress. Breaths, also, should be taken at appropriate places to punctuate the text (e.g., each part lifts at commas, so the lifts are consistent from part to part but occur at different times in the music.)

Also important is that the choir understand the phrase structure, especially with regard to the occurrence of cadences. Within this English madrigal style, it is most appropriate for each line to "fade" into its cadential resolution.

In the relatively few occurrences of homophonic texture, the choir should be especially careful with regard to balance and awareness of phrase structure and cadential "fading."

Musical Elements/Form and Structure

The music is essentially tonal within a modal perspective. Accidentals tend to be present either to serve these modal inheritances or to assist with text painting. One of the "hallmarks" of Weelkes's writing is the entrance of one vocal part immediately followed by entrances of the others below it (often in a somewhat homophonic manner). A clear example of this occurs at the beginning of the piece. The underlying, or supportive, parts almost always have an anacrustic function; the phrase structure will be strengthened if this is emphasized.

The phrases within the music are all text-based; the most exciting performances proceed from careful consideration of textual accentuation and its relationship with Weelkes's melodic and harmonic writing. One of the most interesting aspects of this piece is that the harmony, while essentially resulting from the counterpoint, is nonetheless interesting and seems to show signs of some overall planning.

Text

The text of this piece is 2 Samuel 18:33.

Suggested Listening

Cathedral Music by Thomas Weelkes. Winchester Cathedral Choir. David
    Hill, conductor. (Hyperion Records CDA66447).

Additional Reference and Resources

Brown, David. "The Anthems of Thomas Weelkes," *PRMA.* xci. 1964–65.
    61–72.

Brown, David. *Thomas Weelkes: A Biographical and Critical Study.* New York:
    Frederick A. Praeger. 1969.

Collins, Walter. "Recent Discoveries concerning the Biography of Thomas
    Weelkes." *ML*, xliv. 1963. 123–31.

Le Huray, Peter. *Music and the Reformation in England, 1549–1660.* London:
    Herbert Jenkins. 1967.

Contributed by:

Matthew W. Mehaffey
Anthony Reeves

Repertoire Resource Guide

With Drooping Wings

Henry Purcell
(ca. 1659–1695)

SATB/continuo
Bourne Company: 148416
Overall: 3
Vocal: 3
Tonal/Rhythm: 4

Composer

Henry Purcell was one of the greatest of all English composers and one of the most important composers of the seventeenth century. A chorister at Westminster Abbey in his youth, by 1679 he was the organist there. While at Westminster, he composed various anthems, services, and other sacred works. Appointed to the Chapel Royal in 1682, he served under Charles II and James II as composer, organist, and instrument keeper. His output turned largely to the needs of the court, resulting in various odes, symphony anthems, and songs. The coronation of William and Mary in 1689 ended his career as a composer at the court, and his subsequent compositions are mostly for the theater. *Dido and Aeneas* probably was composed in 1689, which is the date of the first documented performance, although there is new evidence that it may have been composed earlier. This first performance was at Josias Priest's boarding school for girls. Purcell died suddenly of an unidentified sickness in 1695.

Composition

Dido and Aeneas, from which this lament is taken, was unusual in Purcell's output in that it was all sung. Most of Purcell's compositions for the theater were for spoken plays, as all-sung opera was not popular with the English public. This work has a prominent chorus part and the singers in the chorus are expected to dance during the performance. As one of the earliest examples of English opera, *Dido and Aeneas* is one of Purcell's most famous works, and this lament is one of the most famous numbers from the opera. The piece depicts the lamentation of the chorus over the body of Dido, Queen of Carthage, who has killed herself because of the departure of Aeneas.

Historical Perspective

Purcell's all-sung opera is one of the earliest of its kind, though it is patterned strongly after its predecessor, John Blow's *Venus and Adonis*. Purcell is celebrated for his attention to the rhythms of English speech and his setting of music appropriate to the cadences of the language. While the imitative entrances of "With Drooping Wings" recalls Renaissance practice, the strong connection of the music to the text suggests the overt word painting of the early Baroque. The bass part, although it participates in the imitation, frequently functions as a harmonic bass against a soprano melody, especially at the end. This role of the bass line also forms a connection to the practices of the Baroque period.

Technical Considerations

This slow, somber piece is composed primarily of long, slow, descending melodic lines in close imitation in every voice. The rhythm is almost exclusively quarter notes and pairs of eighth notes with an occasional dotted eighth and sixteenth note pair. The vocal ranges are moderate, with some high G's in both the soprano and the tenor part, though the alto part is quite low, reaching low G and F-sharp in two passages. The chromatic inflections are those typical to G minor, but the alternation between E-natural and E-flat and between F-sharp and F-natural may confuse some singers. There is some voice crossing, but it is not prolonged.

Stylistic Considerations

Each phrase of text is set to its own melodic fragment, which is then treated imitatively by each vocal part. The delicate interdependence of the vocal lines is the principal stylistic difficulty in this piece because it calls for a careful attention to detail in every voice part. Phrase shapes are determined as much at the level of the individual line as they are by the overall melodic and harmonic motion. Voice parts typically come together at cadences, simplifying the texture somewhat, but the entrance of each voice establishes both its independence as a melody and its role in the overarching musical goals.

The quality of the vocal sound is also a consideration in the performance of a piece from this time period. The commonly accepted style of singing early Baroque music calls for much less vibrato and a purer tone than modern singing practice. The historical pronunciation of the English language, both spoken and sung, may be of importance to the director when preparing this piece as well, especially as it affects the choice of prolonged vowels.

Musical Elements

This piece is primarily in a modally-inflected G minor with strong implications of D minor in the central section and several hints of B-flat major. The major and minor seventh and the major and minor sixth are all prevalent throughout the work, requiring careful attention by the singer to the inflections of these scale degrees. Each section ends with a clear cadence, and dissonances are resolved logically. Melodic lines are largely constructed of long, sustained phrases of almost exclusively stepwise motion, although there are sections at the end of short phrases filled with rhetorical pauses.

Form and Structure

The work is a striking marriage of text and music, each evoking the heartache and poignancy of the other. Purcell sets each line of text to its own melodic fragment, which is then imitated by each voice in turn. The first section depicts the "drooping wings" of the mournful Cupids in a long, slow descent through the G minor scale repeated despairingly by each voice part several times. The second section, "And scatter roses at her tomb," is set to rising and falling eighth notes with a hint of B-flat major. The gentle two-note sighing motive of the third section moves toward D minor on the words, "Soft, soft," and the work closes with a section of short phrases broken by dramatic pauses. In this final section, as the Cupids are implored to keep watch over the tomb, there are again hints of B-flat major, implying a touch of solace, though the halting texture returns in the end to a quiet cadence in G minor.

Text

With drooping wings, ye Cupids come
And scatter roses on her tomb,
Soft, soft and gentle as her heart.
Keep here your watch and never, never part.

Suggested Listening

Dido and Aeneas. English Chamber Orchestra. Raymond Leppard. (Phillips 416299).

Purcell: Dido and Aeneas. Scholars Baroque Ensemble. (Naxos 8.553108).

Contributed by:

Thomas Cunningham

Repertoire Resource Guide

Zigeunerleben, Op. 29, No. 3
Robert Schumann
(1810–1856)

SATB/piano
Warner Bros. Publications: LG 51413
Overall: 3
Vocal: 3
Tonal/Rhythm: 3

Composer

Robert Schumann was an equally gifted composer, pianist, and journalist. Unfortunately, he was born into a family with inherent mental and physical problems, which he inherited later in life. (These problems ultimately led to his death.) He showed great ability as a pianist and composer in his childhood. His father, a bookseller, encouraged the young Schumann to pursue literary studies, and this became one of Schumann's lifelong passions.

In 1821, Schumann traveled to Leipzig to study law, but instead spent his time in musical, social and literary circles. After convincing his family that he should give up law in favor of a musical career, Schumann went to live and study with Friedrich Wieck. This is where Schumann met Wieck's gifted nine-year-old daughter, Clara. Soon after the studies began, Wieck and Schumann's relationship diminished, and Schumann began studies with other notable composers of the time. He also began utilize his journalism skills by writing for the noted *Allgemeine Musikalische Zeitung*. In 1834, Schumann founded a new music journal, the *Neue Zeitschrift für Musik*. He was the editor and leading writer of this journal for ten years.

By 1835, Schumann had fallen in love with Clara Wieck, but her father did his best to separate them. Despite Wieck's adamant disapproval, Clara and Robert pledged their love to each other in 1837 and were married in 1840. This was an important year in Schumann's life. Not only was he newly married, but he also began a systematic, year by year process of composing and mastering established musical genres: 1840–*Lied*, 1841–orchestral music, 1842–chamber music, 1843–oratorio, 1845–canon and fugue, 1846–47–*a cappella* choral music, and 1847–49–dramatic and stage music. By the end of this process, Schumann was able to masterfully write in all genres.

Sadly, his physical and mental health was quickly deteriorating. By 1854, his intense hallucinations reappeared and never left. Schumann was soon placed in a sanatorium where he returned to the interest of his youth, piano music. He died in July 1856.

Composition

"Zigeunerleben," Op. 29, No. 3 (1840) is from a set for mixed voices entitled *Drei Gedichte* (Three Poems). It is unusually scored for SATB, piano, and optional triangle and tambourine (ad lib). The texts are by Emanuel Geibel, a well-known writer of "gypsy poems." "Zigeunerleben" was written shortly after his marriage to Clara in 1840. It was a creative time in his life when Schumann turned from composing piano music to composing for voice. This resulted in approximately 150 of his finest songs.

Technical Considerations

"Zigeunerleben" is a fun, secular piece accessible to choirs of all ages. The piece is mostly homophonic but has a four-measure polyphonic interpolation (mm. 20–23). This section is mostly imitative, but it may catch the singers off guard during the initial reading of the piece. The conductor would be well advised to address these measures at the beginning of the learning process so the choir can read the entire piece with more success.

One of the greatest challenges of this piece is the rapid declamation of the extensive German text. One of the first decisions a conductor has to make is whether to perform the piece in the original German or to sing a poetic English translation. Many younger choirs have chosen to perform the piece in English with great success. There are several editions of this piece, all with different poetic English translations. The conductor would be wise to compare these editions and choose the one they feel most comfortable performing. Editions also vary greatly in the ad lib triangle and tambourine parts. Some editions include a realized triangle and tambourine part in the octavo while others do not. Again, it is up to the conductor to choose the edition that would most benefit the performance situation.

"Zigeunerleben" is basically divided into three sections. The opening and closing sections are soft and mysterious, set in E minor. The closing section recalls the opening music with only minute changes. The middle section is boisterous and set in C major with an augmentation of the contagious "long–short–short" rhythm that unifies the piece. This section also introduces the gypsies at play, represented by short, playful solo passages for all voice parts. This provides a wonderful opportunity to feature members from each section of the choir. There are even two short duet passages, one for two sopranos and another for two tenors. These solos are especially nice for inexperienced soloists because they are short, and the piano supports the soloist melodically and harmonically.

Schumann also illuminates the extensive text with dramatic dynamic shifts and subtle tempo changes. The conductor should take great care in making sure the text is cleanly and accurately articulated. If the choir performs the piece in German, the conductor should carefully prepare to coach the pronunciation or recruit a professional to do so. The conductor would also be well advised to separate the text from the music at the beginning of the learning process. The choir should learn the notes on a neutral sound that reflects the character of the piece. For example, having the choir sing the opening section on "bmm" will result in a light and rhythmic sound that appropriately reflects the gypsies as they mysteriously enter. Once the notes are secure, the choir should "chant" the text with the appropriate diction and at the appropriate dynamic levels. Once this is mastered, the choir will be able to successfully reunite the text and music.

The range and tessitura are quite comfortable for the basses and the altos, but inexperienced tenors and sopranos may find their parts to be a bit uncomfortable in some passages. These sections, however, are not extensive and are comfortably spaced apart. The conductor should encourage the singers to use a light, buoyant, and articulate sound throughout the piece. The ranges for each section are: sopranos, E4–G5; altos A3–E4; tenors D3–G4; and basses G2–E4. The piece is strictly in four parts until the last five measures where the basses divide and the baritones have a crucial chromatic descent from D4–B3. This exposed line can be difficult for inexperienced baritones to keep in tune, so the conductor should encourage them to use a light production with much breath energy.

Stylistic Considerations

Schumann had a unique understanding of poetry. He believed in making the music a "resonant echo" of the text. Hence, the conductor should take the time to explain how the elements of the music (i.e. melody, harmony, rhythm, etc.) combine with the text to create this resonant echo. For example, at the beginning, the sopranos and altos move in parallel thirds, representing two gypsy violins dialoguing with the rest of the gypsy band (the piano, triangle, and tambourine). Their timbre, dynamic, and articulation should all combine to enhance the text and reflect the mystical entrance of the gypsies.

"Zigeunerleben" also requires a sensitive and experienced accompanist. Schumann, an accomplished pianist, gives the piano an equal role with the voices. The piano represents the exotic character of the gypsy life with sharp accents, exaggerated dynamic contrasts, and jagged, dance-like rhythms based on the modal harmony of the "gypsy scale" (a minor scale with a raised fourth degree.) These gypsy-like characteristics are exaggerated further through the use of the ad lib triangle and tambourine parts. This, combined with Schumann's understanding of the poetry, creates a mysterious and magical atmosphere, which will excite the singers and audiences alike.

Form and Structure

The form of "Zigeunerleben" closely follows the text. The opening and closing sections are set in E minor and use the same music to depict the gypsies as they quietly enter and mysteriously disappear. The contrasting middle section is set in major keys and describes the gypsies' activities around the campfire: dancing, singing, playing instruments, telling tales, eating, drinking, and sleeping.

Text and Translation

Im Schatten des Waldes, im Buchengezweig
da regt's sich und raschelt und flüstert zugleich.
Es flackern die Flammen, es gaukelt der Schein
um bunte Gestalten, um Laub und Gestein.

Das ist der Zigeuner bewegliche Schaar
mit blitzendem Aug' und wallendem Haar,
gesäugt an des Niles geheiligter Flut,
gebräunt von Hispaniens südlicher Glut.

Um's lodernde Feuer in schwellendem Grün
da lagern die Männer verwildert und kühn,
da kauern die Weiber und rüsten das Mahl
und füllen geschäftig den alten Pokal.

Und Sagen und Lieder ertönen im Rund,
wie Spaniens Gärten so blühend und bunt,
und magische Sprüche für Not und Gefahr
verkündet die Alte der horchenden Schaar.

Schwarzäugige Mädchen beginnen den Tanz,
Da sprühen die Fackeln in rötlichem Glanz,
Es lockt die Gitarre, die Cymbel klingt,
Wie wild und wilder der Reigen sich schwingt!

Dann ruh'n sie ermüdet vom nächtlichen Reih'n;
es rauschen die Buchen in Schlummer sie ein.
Und die aus der glücklichen Heimat verbannt,
sie schauen im Träume das glückliche Land.

Doch wie nun im Osten der Morgen erwacht,
verlöschen die schönen Gebilde der Nacht;
Es scharret das Maultier bei Tagesbeginn,
fort zieh'n die Gestalten, wer sagt dir, wohin?

In the shadows of the forest, among the beech trees,
something moves and rustles and whispers all at once.
Flames are flickering, their glow dances
Around colorful figures, around leaves and rocks:

It is the roaming band of gypsies
With flashing eyes and waving hair,
weaned on the holy waters of the Nile,
tanned by Spain's scorching sun.

Around the fire in the swelling green forest
Wild and bold men are resting,
women squat to prepare the meal,
and busily fill ancient goblets.

And tales and songs resound all around,
telling how the gardens in Spain are so full
of bloom, so full of color;
and words of magic to ward off need and danger
the wise old woman recites for the listening crowd.

Dark-eyed girls begin their dance
While torches flicker in reddish glow;
The guitar casts its lure and the cymbal sounds;
The dance grows wild and wilder.

Then they rest, weary from the night of dance,
and the beeches rustle them to sleep.
And, banned as they are from their blissful homeland,
they see it in their dreams, that happy land.

But now, when the morning awakes in the east,
so vanish the beautiful visions of the night
at daybreak the mules paw the ground,
the figures move away, who knows where?

Suggested Listening

Schumann: Werke für Chor. Rundfunkchor Leipzig. Horst Neumann, conductor. (Berlin Classics 0091912BC).

Additional References and Resources

Todd, R. Larry, editor. *Schumann and His World*. Princeton, New Jersey. Princeton University Press. 1994.

Walker, Alan. *Robert Schumann: The Man and His Music*, second edition. London: Barrie and Jenkins. 1976.

Contributed by:

Lee D. Nelson

Repertoire Resource Guide

God's Bottles

Randall Thompson
(1899–1984)

SSAA/piano
E.C. Schirmer Music Co.: 2549
Overall: 3
Vocal: 3
Tonal/Rhythm: 4

Composer

Randall Thompson was one of the most significant American choral composers of the twentieth century. He studied at Harvard University, where Archibald Davison was one of his teachers. He received the prestigious Prix de Rome in 1922, which awarded him three years of study in Rome (1922–25). After he returned to the United States, he received critical acclaim for his Second Symphony (1931). His favorite genre of music, however, was choral music. Generations of Americans have enjoyed his vastly popular collections (e.g., *Frostiana*, *The Testament of Freedom*, and the *Peaceable Kingdom*), as well as his shorter works, such as "Alleluia" and "The Last Words of David."

Thompson was an influential teacher; he served on the faculties of Wellesley College, the University of California–Berkeley, the Curtis Institute, the University of Virginia, Princeton University, and Harvard University. Many academics dismiss Thompson's music as amateurish, but his music has always spoken to many people with its gentle harmonies, wonderful texts, directness, and simplicity.

Composition

"God's Bottles" is the third movement of *Americana,* a five-movement cantata written by Thompson in 1932. The whole work was commissioned by the League of Composers. It was originally written with piano accompaniment, but the composer completed an orchestral version in 1940.

Historical Perspective

The texts for the movements are taken from *American Mercury,* an editorial magazine edited by H. L. Mencken from 1924–34. The magazine's mission was to "attempt a realistic presentation of the whole gaudy, gorgeous American scene." A regular column of the magazine was entitled "Americana." This section consisted of quotes from the American news media, each preceded by a satirical comment. Thompson chose five of the quotes for his work *Americana.* "God's Bottles" is about the temperance movement in 1920s America.

In the preface to the score, Thompson writes, "'God's Bottles,' suitably enough, is set for women's voices. Dare one hope that this music will do for prohibition what *Uncle Tom's Cabin* did for slavery?" Prohibition ended in 1933, one year after Thompson's piece was composed!

Technical Considerations

The four-part women's chorus is always tricky to put together, specifically because of the limited range of the total complement. The soprano part of this piece never gets very high, but the tessitura of the alto rides rather low. Many close harmonies approached by leap or by cross voicing appear in this piece. Take time to make sure each voice part can sing their part in isolation. This will make the cross voicing seem less intimidating.

Because there is so much text and the composer asks for so many different articulations, it would be wise to teach the notes and rhythms devoid of text. This will allow the singers to master the elements of the piece without having to worry about spitting out all of the words. Once the choir masters the music, add the words; this technique may seem time-expensive, but will ultimately prove to be more efficient.

Every voice part is required to sing octave leaps. Do not let the singers change register, especially when they jump down an octave. The women should sing in head voice all of the time. Use of the chest register adds more sound to the lower alto parts but should be used judiciously.

Stylistic Considerations

Because this piece has the ability to be comical, it is important that the words be comprehensible. To help the words project, pay careful attention to diction, particularly crisp consonants. The authors of this text, a group of zealots, took its content very seriously. Therefore, the singers must be very serious in their conviction about the text, even though in the present day it seems somewhat ridiculous. The more fervent the text delivery in this piece, the more the audience will understand the satirical nature of Thompson's music.

Musical Elements

Because the text for this piece is extracted from a magazine article, it is not poetic. It does not have a meter, or a rhyme scheme. Thompson reflects this lack of structure in his music. The meter of the piece changes frequently to accommodate for appropriate word stress, and the measures in 3/8 should have more lilt or swing to them. The measures in duple time should feel more square. Experiment with adding movement into your rehearsal technique to enable singers to kinesthetically feel the difference between duple and triple.

Form and Structure

The form is based on the two paragraphs from the original magazine article. The music, as the text, is through-composed.

Text

The text for "God's Bottles" was published in a leaflet issued by the National Women's Christian Temperance Union.

APPLES ARE GOD'S BOTTLES: The sweet juice of the apple God has placed in His own bottles. What a beautiful rosy-red bottle it is! These red bottles hang on the limbs of a tree until they are all ready for us to use. Do you want to open God's bottle? Bite the apple with your teeth, and you will taste the sweet juice God has put in His bottle for you.

GRAPES ARE GOD'S BOTTLES: These purple and green bottles you will find hanging on a pretty vine. See! So many little bottles are on a single stem! Put a grape in your mouth and open God's bottle. How nice the juice tastes! Some men take the juice of apples and grapes and make drinks that will harm our bodies. They put drinks in glass bottles, but we will not drink from such bottles. We will DRINK FROM GOD'S BOTTLES.

Suggested Listening

Americana: Choral Works by Randall Thompson. Elliott Carter and Seymour Shifrin. The University of Michigan Chamber Choir. Thomas Hilbish, conductor. (New World Records 80219).

Contributed by:

Matthew W. Mehaffey

Anthony Reeves

Repertoire Resource Guide

He's Gone Away

arr. Ron Nelson
(b. 1929)

SSA/piano or SATB/piano
Theodore Presser: SSA: 362-03075, SATB: 362-03379
Overall: 3
Vocal: 3
Tonal/Rhythm: 3

Composer

Ron Nelson is a native of Joliet, Illinois. A product of the Eastman School of Music, he studied at the Paris Conservatory under a Fulbright Grant in 1955. The following year, he joined the faculty at Brown University and taught there until his retirement in 1993. He has won numerous composition prizes, including the National Band Association Prize, the American Bandmasters Association Ostwald Prize, and the Sudler International Prize. All three of these awards went to the same piece in 1993, his *Passacaglia (Homage on B-A-C-H)*. He currently resides in Scottsdale, Arizona.

Composition

This work is a setting of a traditional Appalachian folk song for piano and treble voices. The soprano voice often breaks into two parts, making this a setting largely for three voices. This piece is from a collection called *Three Mountain Ballads*, which includes settings of "Will He Remember?" and "Barbara Allen."

Historical Perspective

This is a modern setting, published in 1959. The melody is a traditional one, and the setting respects the folk source of the melody with a simple and direct arrangement. The piano accompaniment and the melancholic wandering of the harmonic structure give this piece a more modern feeling and produce a sense of contemporary reflection on an old idea. The wistfulness of the text is supported by the accompaniment, especially in its enigmatic close, creating a new connection to a traditional song.

Technical Considerations

This piece is not technically difficult. The rhythms are simple quarter note and eighth note combinations with occasional syncopation. The meter shifts, but mostly between duple choral sections and triple instrumental interludes. The range is moderate, extending from a high F-sharp in the soprano part to a low G in the alto part.

The melodic lines are extended legato phrases and require solid vocal support. While there is some chromaticism, it recurs in the same place in each verse and each chorus, so it can be reinforced through repetition. The most striking element of this delicate arrangement is the piano accompaniment, which, while not difficult, utilizes a rich harmonic language over which the comparatively simple choral parts sound. This additional harmonic element may make the choral parts more difficult to sing in the context of the accompaniment.

Stylistic Considerations

This work is a setting of a traditional Appalachian folksong and maintains a connection to the simplicity of its origins. The melody is always set in a straightforward manner, simply harmonized in the voices. The uncertainty of the text is reflected in the melancholic accompaniment, which shifts unsettlingly between G major and E minor. The composer indicates that the pianist should subtly break the block chords of the accompaniment in an effort to simulate a harp, perhaps the native harp of the Appalachian region. This harp effect underscores the delicacy of the arrangement.

Musical Elements

This piece begins and ends ambiguously, starting with an E minor sound that quickly leads to a tentative G major and ends with a weak resolution to G major, which trails away with the suggestion of the major seventh. While never overtly dissonant, the shifting bass line forces reinterpretations of the simple melody line, denying strong cadences and statements of firmly directed harmonic motion. The choral parts are almost always homophonic although the moving eighths beneath the folk melody sometimes give a sense of melodic independence. All of the vocal lines share a sense of simplicity with the folk melody. The meter shifts occasionally, but the quarter note is constant, and, aside from a single measure of 5/4 in each verse and a single measure of 2/4 between each chorus and verse, the metrical changes occur in the instrumental interludes.

The choral parts almost always move in simple intervals, such as thirds and sixths, though there are many passing tones, suspensions, and appoggiaturas that complicate the lines.

Form and Structure

The structure of this piece is straightforward, adhering closely to traditional song form. The piece begins with a three-measure piano introduction, and the six-measure chorus and the first ten-measures of the verse follow. After a four-measure piano interlude, the chorus returns in the same harmonization, followed by a slightly reharmonized verse with new vocal parts. The piece concludes with a three-measure instrumental fade.

Text

He's gone away
for to stay a little while
But he's comin' back
if he goes ten thousand miles.

Oh who will tie my shoes?
And who will glove my hand?
And who will kiss my ruby lips
when he is gone?

Oh he's gone
look away over yandro.

Oh it's pappy'll tie my shoes
And mammy'll glove my hands.
And you will kiss my ruby lips
when you come back.

Look away,
look away over yandro.

Contributed by:

Thomas Cunningham

Repertoire Resource Guide

Ihr Heiligen, lobsinget dem Herren, SWV 288

Heinrich Schütz
(1585–1672)

SA/keyboard and continuo
Hanssler-Verlag: HE 20.288
Overall: 3
Vocal: 3
Tonal/Rhythm: 3

Composer

Heinrich Schütz was arguably the greatest German composer before Bach. Schütz's first musical training was from local Kantor Georg Weber in Weissenfels, but he received the bulk of his early training at the Collegium Mauritianum at Kassel. He matriculated at the University of Marburg in 1608, then went to Venice to study with Giovanni Gabrieli. His first significant compositions constituted a book of five-voice Italian madrigals (1611) written under Gabrieli's tutelage and dedicated to Schütz's benefactor, Landgrave Moritz. Schütz returned to Germany in 1613 and worked as organist in Moritz's court. He traveled extensively throughout his life.

Schütz's employment circumstances were complicated by the Thirty Years' War (1618–48). The base of his operations was Dresden, where he was appointed *Kappellmeister* at the Saxon court in 1619, but he traveled throughout Germany, returned to Venice in 1628 to study with Monteverdi, and spent time at the Danish court in Copenhagen. His compositional output was extensive. Among Schütz's most notable contributions are: *Psalmen Davids sampt etlichen Moteten und Concerten* (1619); three collections of

Symphoniae sacrae (1629, 1648, and 1650), and two volumes of *Kleine geistliche Konzerte* (1636 and 1639).

Composition

Schütz called this piece a "small sacred concerto." It is scored for two sopranos accompanied by basso continuo. While it may have been performed by only two singers and the continuo players, it is perfectly appropriate to be sung as a two-part choral piece.

Historical Perspective

Published in the middle of the Thirty Years' War, the two volumes of *Kleine geistliche Konzerte* (Small Sacred Concerti) reflected the diminished resources and personnel of the era. (Male singers were especially scarce as so many were at war.) Schütz published Volume I, from which this piece comes, in 1636; it was his first publication in seven years and was dedicated to Heinrich von Friesen, head of the appellate court in Dresden.

Technical and Stylistic Considerations

Two players are required to realize the continuo part of this concerto: an organist and someone (e.g., a cellist) to double the bass part. This kind of piece requires light, almost detached, singing to allow textural and rhythmic clarity. It probably goes best conducted in two, not too fast, but lively. The conductor should strive to accomplish a feeling of dialogue between the two parts.

Stylistically, a few tricks can make a huge difference in this music: 1) use the lightly detached articulation already discussed; 2) delete the dots after dotted notes and replace them with a rest of the same value; 3) use a small crescendo during any notes tied across a barline; and 4) use *messa di voce* (a smooth crescendo/decrescendo performed on the same note) for any notes longer than a half note.

Musical Elements

This piece is centered around D and has many characteristics of mixolydian. As is typical of Schütz's music, however, it displays many modal alterations.

Form and Structure

Section	Measure	Event and Scoring
A	1–22	Dialogue between the two parts
B	22–34	Imitative polyphony
C	35–81	Dialogue

Text and Translation

The text is Psalm 30:4–5

Ihr Heiligen, lobsinget dem Herren
danket und preiset seine Herrlichkeit.
denn sein Zorn währet einen Augenblick;
und er hat Lust zum Leben:
den Abend lang währet das Weinen,
aber des Morgens die Freude.

Sing praise unto the Lord, O ye saints of his,
And give thanks to his holy name.
For his anger is but for a moment;
in his favor is life:
weeping may tarry for the night,
but joy cometh in the morning.

Suggested Listening

Kleine geistliche Konzerte. Concerto Vocale. René Jacobs, conductor. (Harmonia Mundi HMC 901097).

Additional Reference and Resources

Köhler, Siegfried. *Heinrich Schütz: Anmerkungen zu Leben und Werk*. Leipzig: VEB Deutscher Verlag für Musik. 1985.

Moser, Hans Joachim. Translation by Carl Pfatteicher. *Heinrich Schütz: His Life and Work*. Saint Louis: Concordia Publishing House. 1959.

Contributed by:

Matthew W. Mehaffey
Anthony Reeves

Repertoire Resource Guide

Nigra sum

Pablo Casals
(1876–1973)

SA divisi/piano
Tetra: TC120
Overall: 3
Vocal: 4
Tonal/Rhythm: 3

Composer

Pablo Casals was a cellist, conductor, and composer from the Catalan region of Spain. His early chance encounter with the Suites for Unaccompanied Cello by J. S. Bach proved to be formative, inspiring him to master the cello as his chosen instrument. After studying at the Madrid Conservatory and the Brussels Conservatory on scholarship, Casals returned to Barcelona to teach between international tours. His international reputation reached its peak in 1914 when his performances were renowned for their beauty of tone and intellectual integrity.

Casals believed that the artist's chief responsibility was to the tireless search for truth and beauty. He also had a passion for bringing music to the working man and organized concerts for workers with his own orchestra. Faced with execution after the Spanish Civil War, Casals moved to Prades, France, just over the border. He refused to play publicly in any country that recognized the Franco regime and began a period of self-isolation. This inactivity was relieved by his celebration of the Bach bicentenary in 1950, shortly following which he moved to Puerto Rico and began a series of festivals there in his name. Casals won the United Nations Peace Prize for his efforts to bring worldwide peace in the shape of international performances of his oratorio *El pessebre*.

Composition

This work is a sacred motet with piano or organ accompaniment for women's voices. The text is a biblical text, although the words come from the Song of Solomon, a love poem with many possible interpretations. It was composed in 1942, but not published. Many of the composer's works were not published during his lifetime, though the monks of Montserrat made much use of his sacred works, published and unpublished.

Historical Perspective

This piece was composed in 1942, only six years after Casals left Spain and settled in France, though he was still in the Catalan region. He initially intended his stay in Prades to be temporary, but as the situation in Spain remained the same, he made Prades a more permanent home.

The style of the work is conservative with modally inflected harmonies comfortably contained in an overall Romantic harmonic framework. The harmonies are strongly triadic and do not reflect the more tumultuous experimentation occurring in the world of musical composition at the time of this work's creation. Casals was known to have had little patience with modern trends in composition and spoke disparagingly of what he called "experimental" music, drawing the ire of some of his contemporaries. This work's gentle style has modernist elements but fits well within a late-Romantic harmonic conception. The melody is so overwhelmingly comprised of stepwise motion or of small leaps that the contours of chant are brought to mind, further rooting this work in music of the past.

Technical Considerations

The rhythmic language of this piece is straightforward, comprised principally of flowing eighth notes and gently moving quarter notes. The lines are rarely rhythmically independent, even when the voicing expands from two parts to four. The range is moderate for women's voices, from low A to high G, and the melodic motion is largely stepwise throughout. The phrases are occasionally long and sustained, though opportunities for short breaths come frequently, even in the long phrases. The only difficult technical aspect of this piece is a propensity to shift suddenly into a distant, chromatic tonal area, although the piano accompaniment supports these changes in a logical way.

Stylistic Considerations

This piece is predominantly composed of gentle phrases in the voices supported by flowing piano or organ accompaniment. The dynamics are largely soft, with markings such as *dolce* and *molto espressivo*. The vocal parts and the accompaniment often move in thirds and sixths, contributing to the tender mood of the piece. The timbre of Casals' instrument, the cello, emerges in the sweeping bass lines of the accompaniment and the expressive nature of the melodic lines. Overall, the work is one of intimacy and delicacy, reflecting the tenderness of the text.

Musical Elements

"Nigra Sum" is largely in the key of E, beginning with a modally inflected sense of E minor, passing through sections in G major and C major, and ending in an affirming E major. The voices often move in thirds and sixths, and momentary dissonances resolve logically. Sections are marked by cadences, but eighth notes in the accompaniment typically roll through the cadence. The piece begins with a three-note motive comprised of parallel thirds, which becomes a recurring structural gesture. The accompaniment especially adopts this idea when it move into its most chromatic tonal areas.

Form and Structure

The structure is largely determined by the text. The work opens with the young woman's description of herself and her encounter with the king; it is set in E minor with a brief move to G major at the mention of the king. This first section is repeated verbatim.

After a short piano interlude dominated by the opening gesture in parallel thirds, the voices introduce the words of the king on a unison B. The new section begins in G major as the king implores his love to rise up and come away with him. A two measure instrumental interlude, again featuring the opening gesture, introduces the third section in E minor, which describes the passing winter and rain. The tonality moves through G major to C major, slipping gently into E major as the last section begins. This final section describes the emerging flowers and coming time of renewal, ending with a tender, E major "Alleluia."

Text and Translation

Nigra sum, sed formósa
Filiae Jerúsalem:
Ideo dilexit me Rex,
Et introdúxit me in cubiculum suum.

Et dixit mihi:
Surge et veni amica mea,
Jam hiems transit,
Imber abiit et recessit,

Flores apparu erunt in terrat nostra,
Tempus putationis ad venit.
Alleluia.

I am very dark, but comely,
O daughters of Jerusalem:
Therefore the King loved me,
And brought me into his chamber.

And he said to me:
Arise, my love, and come,
For now the winter is past,
The rain is over and gone.

The flowers have appeared in our land,
The time of pruning is come.
Alleluia.

Suggested Listening

Classic Elektra. Elektra Women's Choir. Diane Loomer and Morna
    Edmundson, conductors. (Skylark 9402).

Inscription of Hope. Northwest Girls Choir. Rebecca Rottsolk, conductor.
    (Arsis CD 109).

Contributed by:

Thomas Cunningham

Repertoire Resource Guide

Our Father (Otche Nash)

Alexandr Kastal'sky
(1856–1926)

SSAA/a cappella
Musica Russica: KS 134
Overall: 3
Vocal: 3
Tonal/Rhythm: 3

Composer

Alexandr Kastal'sky was a Russian composer and a collector of Russian folk-songs. He studied at the Moscow Conservatory, and upon the recommendation of his teacher, Tchaikovsky, he joined the Moscow Synodal Academy as a piano teacher. Kastal'sky was active as a choral conductor and by 1903 was the precentor of the Synodal Choir. His first works date from his early years at the school and were written for the Synodal Choir, clearly showing the influence of his studies of indigenous folksongs and Russian music of the Middle Ages. By 1917, he had written more than 130 works for choir, establishing him as the foremost composer of Russian liturgical music. His position at the Synodal School (director of the school, 1910–18) expanded his impact on Russian composers, including Rachmaninoff. After 1917, Kastal'sky primarily arranged Russian folksongs.

Composition

This work is a motet for four-part women's choir. The text is the Our Father from the Russian Orthodox liturgy and is in Church Slavonic. This type of modal homophonic motet is common in the Russian Orthodox church and has a strong affinity to the motets of Rachmaninoff's *All-Night Vigil*.

Historical Perspective

Kastal'sky lived during a time of great awareness of the European influence on Russian classical composition and of renewed interest in native Russian sources of compositional inspiration. His predecessor at the Synodal School, Stepan Smolensky, encouraged composers to look to native Russian materials as a source for modern compositions. Kastal'sky himself was a student of folksongs and ancient Russian music, and the influence of both traditional sacred and secular music in his work is strong; the melodic lines of this motet bear the mark of Russian chant.

Technical Considerations

The rhythms of this work are not difficult, predominantly quarter notes and eighth notes, and the range is not extreme, extending from low G in the alto voice to high E in the soprano voice. The melodic structure is composed of extended, sustained vocal lines. There is very little chromaticism, although the work uses a modal E minor scale with a lowered sixth and seventh scale degrees.

Stylistic Considerations

This work poses certain challenges due to the flowing, elastic nature of the phrases, which often end in softly repeated chords. The dynamics shift often, usually suddenly, though not jarringly. The overall mood of the work is one of somber piety.

Musical Elements

The piece uses a modal E minor scale with a lowered sixth and seventh with almost no chromaticism. Chords are of standard construction (triads and seventh chords), but there are no strong cadences, partially due to the lack of dominant seventh chords. The last cadence, for example, is ii$^{6/5\varnothing}$–I. There is no strong dissonance in the work, and the texture is almost exclusively homophonic. The melody moves in stepwise motion through a constant 2/4 meter.

Form and Structure

MEASURE	EVENT AND SCORING
1–5	Opening phrase; closes with E minor chords
5–11	Second phrase; closes with G major chords
11–17	Similar to opening
18–29	Central section with hints of dominant; closes with B minor chords
30–34	Similar to opening; closes with E minor chords
35–41	Strong closing phrase; closes with E minor chords

Text and Translation

Otche nash, Izhe yesi na nebeseh,
da sviatitsia imia Tvoye,
da priidet Tsarstviye Tvoye,
da budet volia Tvoya,
yako na nebesi i na zemli.
Hleb nash nasushchniy dazhd nam dnes,
i ostavi nam dolgi nasha,
yakozhe i mi ostavliayem dolzhnikom nashim;
I ne vvedi nas vo iskusheniye,
no izbavi nas ot lukavago.

Our Father, Who art in heaven,
hallowed by Thy name.
Thy Kingdom come,
Thy will be done
on earth as it is in heaven.
Give us this day our daily bread,
and forgive us our debts,
as we forgive our debtors;
and lead us not into temptation,
but deliver us from the Evil One.

Contributed by:

Thomas Cunningham

Repertoire Resource Guide

Stabat Mater

Giovanni Battista Pergolesi
(1710–1736)

SA/keyboard and continuo
Excerpts, Hinshaw Music, Inc.: HMB 209,
Full score, Kalmus K 06375
Overall: 3
Vocal: 4
Tonal/Rhythm: 3

Composer

Giovanni Battista Pergolesi was a true prodigy despite his illness-plagued childhood. He studied violin from a very early age and soon was playing professionally around Naples, Italy. Best known for his contributions to the genre of opera (Naples was one of the thriving opera centers in Europe during the early 1700s), Pergolesi is one of many composers whose work became more renowned after his death. A 1752 Parisian performance of his intermezzo *La serva padrona* sparked heated and prolonged discussion about musical style; this controversy is known as the *Guerre de la Buffons*, or "War of the Buffoons."

In addition to his dramatic output, Pergolesi composed many sacred pieces, including masses and various other liturgical pieces. Pergolesi's prodigious output was cut short by his untimely death of tuberculosis at the age of twenty-six.

Composition

Stabat Mater for soprano, alto, strings, and basso continuo is one of Pergolesi's best-known liturgical compositions. Originally intended for two solo singers, the piece works quite well as a two-part choral selection. Pergolesi composed the work in 1736 at Pozzuoli, just before his death.

The *Stabat Mater* text is one of the five great sequences. It did not survive the Council of Trent; however, the Roman Catholic Church restored it to the liturgy in 1727. The rhymed text depicts the darkest hour of Christ's passion and is based on texts from the biblical books of John, Luke, Zacharias, 2 Corinthians, and Galatians. The text is appropriate for two days of the liturgical year, the Friday after Passion (Palm) Sunday and on September 15, Holy Cross Day.

Historical Perspective

Stabat Mater demonstrates Pergolesi's mastery of two disparite styles, *stile antico* counterpoint and Neapolitan opera style. The mixture of the old and new musical styles provides wonderful dissonance and suspensions that make the meaning of the text even more poignant.

Although Pergolesi composed the piece in Italy in 1736, it was not published until 1749 in London. The composer/critic Jean-Jacques Rousseau said the first movement was "the most perfect and touching duet to come from the pen of any composer." The final movement, the "Amen," can be heard at the end of the movie *Amadeus*. Mozart was a great admirer of Pergolesi's music.

Technical Considerations

Pergolesi's frequent use of dissonance can be highlighted by the use of *messa di voce*. Mastery of this technique is important in realizing accurate performances of pre-1800 music. *Messa di voce* requires singers to crescendo and decrescendo on the same pitch; usually when the note value exceeds a quarter note. This sounds very simple, but it can actually be quite difficult. Singers should think of the crescendo portion of the technique as an increase in resonant space rather than just singing louder. If the singers can increase their resonance and follow the increase with a slight closing of the vowel, they will accomplish the technique of *messa di voce* masterfully. The music calls for this technique in almost every measure, particularly when notes are tied across the barline. When this is the case, instruct the singers to sing into the barline (this will usually be the place where Pergolesi places a dissonance). The crescendo into the barline, followed by an immediate tapering, will bring the dissonance of the music to the forefront.

Stylistic Considerations

Diction! Diction! Diction! All of the *messa di voces* in the world will not conquer bad diction. If the vowels are too open, the beauty of the dissonance will be lost because the pitches of the voices will be obfuscated. Many handbooks on Latin pronunciation talk about the open sound of the language; while this is true in Italian Latin, this is not so for other forms of Latin (i.e. Austro-German Latin and French Latin). Pergolesi was Italian; therefore, Italian Latin (also known as standard-liturgical Latin) is the most appropriate choice. However, remember to approach the rules of Italian Latin not as an English speaker, but as an Italian speaker. Imagine a native Italian speaker saying the word "spaghetti." The "eh" sound is much different from the open and wide "eh" sounds most American-English speakers produce. Singing Italian Latin with American vowels is like performing Shakespeare with a southern drawl; it is incongruous. Listen to Italian singers and model the colors of their vowels for the choir. They will quickly hear that diction can augment the authenticity of a performance; the zealous members of the group will enjoy experimenting with the different pronunciations.

Musical Elements

Pergolesi scored this piece for strings and organ. The violins often play the same notes as the two voice parts (*colla parte*). Many editions contain suggested ornamentation. However, they do not always provide the same ornamentation in the string parts. It is incumbent upon the conductor to reconcile any differences between the voice parts and the string parts. Failure to do so will result in rhythmic and tonal conundrums.

Form and Structure

The entire work is divided into twelve movements; movements 2,4,6,7, and 10 are for one voice part. Even if you are performing this piece with a choir, any or all of these movements may be performed as solos by members of the choir. Many editions of this piece have extracted movements to form a smaller piece. This "extraction" technique works well for concert use but would be inappropriate for liturgical use.

Text and Translation

Stabat Mater dolorosa
iuxta crucem lacrimosa,
dum pendebat Filius.

Cuius animam gementem
contristatam et dolentem
pertransivit gladius.

O quam tristis et afflicta
fuit illa benedicta
mater Unigeniti!

Quae moerebat et dolebat
pia mater cum videbat
nati poenas incliti.

Quis est homo qui non fleret,
matrem Christi si videret
in tanto supplicio?

Quis non posset contristari,
piam matrem contemplari
dolentum cum Filio?

Pro peccatis suae gentis
vidit Iesum in tormentis
et flagellis subditum.

Vidit suum dulcem Natum
morientem, desolatum,
cum emisit spiritum.

Christe, cum sit hinc exire,
da per matrem me venire
ad palmam victoriae. Amen.

The grieving Mother stood
beside the cross weeping
where her Son was hanging.

Through her weeping soul,
compassionate and grieving,
a sword passed.

O how sad and afflicted
was that blessed
Mother of the Only-begotten!

Who mourned and grieved,
the pious Mother, with seeing
the torment of her glorious Son.

Who is the man who would not weep
if seeing the Mother of Christ
in such agony?

Who would not be have compassion
on beholding the devout mother
suffering with her Son?

For the sins of his people
she saw Jesus in torment
and subjected to the scourge.

She saw her sweet Son
dying, forsaken,
while he gave up his spirit.

Christ, when it is henceforth in need to pass away,
grant that through your Mother I may come
to the palm of victory. Amen.

Suggested Listening

Pergolesi: Stabat Mater. Barbara Bonney and Andreas Scholl. Christophe
Rousset, conductor. (Decca 466 134-2).

Pergolesi Stabat Mater. Gillian Fisher and Michael Chance. Robert King,
conductor. (Hyperion CDA66294).

Contributed by:

Matthew W. Mehaffey
Anthony Reeves

Repertoire Resource Guide

Wir eilen mit schwachen, doch emsigen Schritten

Johann Sebastian Bach
(1685–1750)

SA/keyboard
E.C. Schirmer Music Co.: EC 2506
Overall: 3
Vocal: 4
Tonal/Rhythm: 3

Composer

Johann Sebastian Bach was born March 21, 1685, in Eisenach, Germany. The extended Bach family were well known as musicians; J. S.'s father, Johann Ambrosius, was a chamber musician in Eisenach.

J. S. Bach's life is generally divided into six periods, mostly defined by his places of employment: early life (1685–1703); Arnstadt (1703–07); Mühlhausen (1707–08); Weimar (1708–17); Cöthen (1717–23); and Leipzig (1723–50). In these positions, Bach served at various times as organist, teacher, composer, *Konzertmeister* (Weimar), and *Director musices* (Leipzig). He was also appointed *Hofcompositeur* for the Dresden Court in 1736.

J. S. Bach's musical output is overwhelming, including masterworks in almost every musical genre of his era. For example, he wrote cantatas (sacred and secular), large-scale choral works (e.g., St. Matthew Passion and Mass in B Minor), concerti, orchestral suites, organ works, harpsichord works, and pieces for various other instruments and instrumental combinations. Bach died in Leipzig July 28, 1750.

Composition

The duet "Wir eilen mit schwachen, doch emsigen Schritten" is an excerpt from Cantata 78, *Jesu der du meine Seele*. This piece would have been sung by soloists in Bach's time, however, it is completely appropriate to use this piece with a treble or women's choir.

Historical Perspective

The first performance of the work was at the *Thomaskirche* in Leipzig, Germany, on September 10, 1724, just one year after Bach moved to Leipzig. He in was in the midst of composing his cycles of church cantatas and was essentially composing one cantata each week, a remarkable feat.

Technical Considerations

The singing of this duet requires the complicated singing technique of *martellato*, a clear, non-legato (but non-staccato) musical line. It is called for in singing the melismas found in Baroque music. Singers need to be sure to sing each note with precision, not just slide through a series of fast notes. The best description of *martellato* is in the book *Group Vocal Technique* by James Jordan and Frauke Haasemann, published by Hinshaw Publications. This text offers many useful exercises for teaching the technique of *martellato*.

Stylistic Considerations

Many editions of Bach's music contain editorial markings. Remember, Bach did not provide many written instructions in his music. Long, drawn out crescendos and frequent use of *rubato* are not stylistically appropriate for the music of J. S. Bach, or other Baroque composers for that matter.

The piano was available in Bach's lifetime. This piece would be very rewarding if you could play the keyboard part on an organ, even a small positiv organ, and have a cello play the bass line. This would yield an accurate presentation of the way Bach would have heard this music.

Musical Elements

The original scoring for this duet was for continuo instrument and violone. Realize that Bach wrote only a bass part with numbers under it (figured bass). The keyboardist would have known to improvise an accompaniment from these numbers. The violone part can be found in the NBA collected works edition in volume 21. The addition of the violone would be a nice timbral addition. The original parts in the NBA version are in the key of B-flat. Some editions print this duet in the key of A-flat.

Form and Structure

This duet is in *da capo* form: ABA.

Text and Translation

Wir eilen mit schwachen, doch emsigen Schritten,
O Jesu, O meister, zu helfen zu dir.
Du suchest die Kranken und Irrenden treulich.
Ach höre, wie wir
Die Stimmen erheben, um Hülfe zu bitten!
Es sei uns dein gnädiges Antlitz erfreulich!

We hasten with weak, yet eager steps,
O Jesus, O master, for help to thee.
Thou seekest the sick and erring faithfully.
Ah hear, how we
Our voice raise, for help do entreat thee!
May thy gracious countenance smile upon us!

Suggested Listening

Die Bach Kantate – Vol. 10. Bach-Collegium Stuttgart. Helmuth Rilling, conductor. (Hanssler 98.861).

Cantatas BWV 78 and 198. La Chapelle Royale. Philippe Herreweghw, conductor. (Harmonia Mundi HMC 901270).

Additional References and Resources:

Haasemann, Franke and James Jordan. *Group Vocal Technique*. Chapel Hill, NC: Hinshaw Music. 1991.

Contributed by:

Anthony Reeves

Repertoire Resource Guide

Confirma hoc, Deus

Jacob Handl
(1550–1591)

TTBB/a cappella
Alliance Music Publications: AMP 0396
edited by James Rodde
Overall: 3
Vocal: 3
Tonal/Rhythm: 3

Composer

Slovenian composer Jacob Handl is often thought to be a composer of lesser importance, yet he was a masterful contrapuntist, which is especially apparent in his numerous motets. His works exhibit many Franco-Netherlandish traits, and he was clearly influenced by Palestrina and Lassus. Some trademarks of his compositional style are rhythmic intricacy, leanings toward major/minor tonality, and textural complexity, including polychordal writing, for which he was criticized by many of his contemporaries.

Handl was likely born in Ribnica, but left there in 1566 to live in Austria and, later, Bohemia. He was a devout Catholic and was associated with a number of monasteries throughout his life. He sang under Phillip de Monte at the imperial court of Maximillian II and held other posts including choirmaster at Olomouc as well as St. Jan na Brzehu in Prague. He composed mostly liturgical works, including the *Opus musicum* (which is discussed at greater length below) as well as settings of the mass. He wrote a small number of secular works, the most well-know being the *Moralia*. Handl is also know by the Latin name Jacobus Gallus.

Composition

"Confirma hoc, Deus" is a freely-composed, imitative motet for four equal voices (TTBB). It is based on Psalm 68:28–29, although the text, set in syllabic style, is very loosely paraphrased. It is found in Volume 3 of the *Opus Musicum*, a four-volume collection of motets arranged in the order of the liturgical year for the Proper of the Time (Volumes 1–3) and the Proper of the Saints and Common of the Saints (Volume 4). The motet is listed under the subtitle "De Spiritu Sancto," and is intended for the offertory on the day of Pentecost. It ends with an Alleluia, which is very common in psalm settings of this type. The editor includes implied *musica ficta* (at cadences, for example) as part of the score.

In addition to "Confirma hoc, Deus," Volume 3 of the *Opus Musicum* includes settings from the Lamentations of the Prophet Jeremiah and texts relating to the resurrection and ascension of Christ. Under each subtitle, the motets are categorized by number of voices, ranging from four to twelve, with many instances of polychoral writing. For example, there is a setting of "Cantate Domino" for three choirs, each containing four voices.

The *Opus Musicum* is considered one of the monuments of Renaissance polyphony. It can be found in its entirety in the collection *Denkmäler der Tonkunst in Österreich*, Jahrg. XV/1. Band 30.

Historical Perspective

The composer was closely associated with the Catholic church during the Counter-reformation, so, generally speaking, much of his work is reflective of the reforms in liturgical music during that time. It is clear from his contact with the monasteries in Austria and Bohemia that he was committed to those reforms.

Technical Considerations

The motet is written for four equal voices (*ad aequales*), and although there are certainly vertical harmonic considerations, each part is inherently horizontal and independent of the others. Great care must be taken to develop the melodic lines so that each phrase has linear shape. The key to generating the line is developing a constant sense of pulse through rhythmic subdivisions. Once the pitches are secure, it may be helpful to pulse eighth note subdivisions on pitch, using a neutral syllable such as "noo." (Count-singing the rhythm, however, is not recommended for this style.) Once the chorus understands the underlying pulse, the lines will have energy and direction, and the long notes will maintain vitality throughout their duration. Then, the chorus will be ready to sing without the subdivisions while continuing to feel the pulse.

Tonally, the chorus may find the *musica ficta* difficult from the standpoint of intonation. For example, in measures 11–17, there is a continual shift between D-natural and D-flat in the upper two parts. Because these two notes often define the harmonic context (i.e., they determine the quality of the triads), it is important that the chorus tune these pitches in relation to that context. Although having each section learn their respective part separately from the others will help with style and melodic continuity, the intonation will be best served in group rehearsals.

Because of the equal-voice texture, careful balancing of the ensemble is crucial for this style of singing. Although tenor 1 and 2 are not extremely high, these voices are required to sing in the "medium-high" range quite often. For example, in the first section of the piece, the first tenor sings E-flat4 for nearly one third of the time, which may be vocally challenging, especially if the singers are young. The tessitura in this case may warrant a softer dynamic.

Stylistic Considerations

The tone quality for performance should be moderately bright with very little vibrato. Adding *messa di voce* on long notes will help propel the long lines forward and bring richness to the overall sound and direction of the piece.

The tempo will depend on the acoustics. In a cathedral setting, a slower tempo may be necessary, so that the text is not lost in the delay caused by reverberation. Consonants will invariably need overemphasis to maintain the clarity of the text. However, in less reverberant acoustics, a faster tempo may help the lines stay energized. In this case, since the length of time that the vowel sounds are carried in the space is much less, consonants should be executed quickly and lightly so they do not interrupt the legato of the vowels.

Musical Elements

This edition of "Confirma hoc, Deus," is essentially in A-flat major (to use a "modern" term) with a lowered seventh near the end. The voices enter imitatively, but each develops independently of the others after a few measures. Although the work was composed prior to the tonal system, the use of triadic harmony is apparent throughout.

Form and Structure

In its original form, the motet is through-composed. It can be divided into three sections, according to the text: A–"Confirma hoc, Deus," B–"quod est in," and C–"Alleluia."

In the Alliance edition, there is a repeat of the B and C sections, which the editor added.

Text and Translation

Psalm 68:28–29, paraphrased

Confirma hoc, Deus, quod operatus es in nobis a templo sanctuo,
quod est in Jerusalem. Alleluia.

Confirm, God, what you have brought about in us from your temple in Jerusualem. Alleluia.

Additional References and Resources

Bezecny, Emil and Josef Mantuani. Introduction to *Denkmäler der Tonkunst in Österreich*, Jahrg. XV/1. Band 30. Vienna: Akademische Druck U. Verlangsanstalt. 1908. Reprinted, Graz: Akademische Druck U. Verlagsanstalt. 1959.

Egbert, Louard Edward. "The Opus musicum of Jacobus Gallus, and performance problems of selected motets." Dissertation. University of Kentucky. 1976.

Kmetz, John. "Jacobus Gallus, *Opus Musicum*." *Notes*. March 1996. 1018–1020.

Pokorn, Danilo and Allen B. Skei. "Handl [Gallus, Händl, Handelius], Jacobus [Jacob, Jakob]. *The New Grove Dictionary of Music and Musicians*.

Contributed by:

Russell Nelson

Repertoire Resource Guide

Down Among the Dead Men

Ralph Vaughan Williams
(1872–1953)

TTBB/a cappella
E.C. Schirmer Music Co.: 1.5025
Overall: 3
Vocal: 4
Tonal: 3

Composer

Ralph Vaughan Williams was born October 12, 1872, in Down Ampney, Gloucester, to a moderately wealthy family. Although he originally desired to play the viola, his family persuaded him that the organ would be much more respectable. The fact that his father had been a clergyman gave Vaughan Williams a strong connection to the church and great respect for the musical traditions thereof. He took part in selecting tunes for the *English Hymnal*, including some he himself composed. Despite his religious background, however, Vaughan Williams declared himself agnostic.

He studied during two different periods at the Royal College of Music, where, later in life, he became a faculty member. There, he studied composition under Parry, Wood, and Stanford. He also studied at Trinity College, Cambridge in between his stints at the RCM. His compositional style is one that is considered highly individual and national, epitomized by his regard for the indigenous music of the English folksong tradition.

His works include a wide variety of genres, from large-scale orchestral works to very intimate partsongs and other vocal compositions, as well as works for the stage and even incidental music for theater and film. Although he declined the honor of knighthood, he received numerous accolades, including the Order of Merit and several honorary doctorates, and was firmly established as one of the most respected proponents of the English school by the time of his death.

Vaughan Williams' musical style and compositional skills were a long time in the making, and it was not until his later years that his work came to full maturity. Long-time friend Gustav Holst played a major role in Vaughan Williams' development, and the two spent a great deal of time together comparing their compositions and making suggestions to each other. Vaughan Williams benefited greatly from these "field days," as they often referred to them.

The fact that the composer was nationalistic does not mean he had no respect for continental European music. He felt that much could be learned from that scene and that anyone desiring to glean from those traditions should do so. This is apparent in that he himself studied briefly in Europe, first in Berlin with Bruch (1897) and later in Paris with Ravel (1908). However, he felt that whatever was taken from continental Europe should be applied at home in a way that was applicable to the local community. This is best summed up in his own words:

> I am told that when grape vines were first cultivated in California the vineyard masters used to try the experiment of importing plants from France or Italy and setting them in their own soil. The result was that the grapes acquired a particular individual flavor, so strong was the influence of the soil in which they were planted. I need hardly draw the moral of this, namely, that if the roots of your art are firmly planted in your own soil and that soil has anything individual to give you, you may still gain the whole world and not lose your own souls. (Vaughan Williams 11)

Ralph Vaughan Williams died August 26, 1958, and his ashes are buried at Westminster Abbey.

Composition

"Down Among the Dead Men" is a partsong for male voices (TTBB) based on an English folk melody. Although the piece is mostly homophonic, there are four measures at the beginning of the refrain that are imitative (baritone imitates tenor 1 and bass imitates tenor 2). The tune is present in tenor 1 in every stanza.

Historical Perspective

During Vaughan Williams' lifetime, there emerged a renewed interest in music that was inherently English, and his work contributed to a renewal of nationalism in musical composition. Music in England had long become the business of foreigners, with the influence of Germany being very prevalent, even in the works of composers such as Edward Elgar. England was considered by many to be a land without music, and it was this mentality that Vaughan Williams decried. Important to the nationalistic style, the composer viewed the English folksong idiom to be of paramount importance to musicians.

Technical Considerations

While the harmony is easy to grasp, the melodic nature of each part is somewhat disjunct, and leaps wider than a third are very common. This, combined with a fast tempo (*allegro*) and a quick harmonic rhythm will make it very difficult to sing the pitches accurately while aligning them rhythmically with the other parts. It is vital that the pitches be learned on a neutral syllable ("dee" or "doo" are suggested) at the very beginning because the text can initially inhibit the clarity of the pitch. The first readings should be done without concern for the articulation markings, which can be added later. Once the pitches are secure, it may be helpful thereafter to sing the notes staccato. This will ensure that the choir members are immediately sure of each pitch both because they will be unable to slide and that they know whether they are placing notes too early, too late, or on time.

The next step in the process is to instill rhythmic energy, as there is an element of "drive" to the pulse, which will aid the style. The most effective tool is count-singing, in which the rhythm is counted on pitch in accordance with the written notes. For example, "Here's a health to the King," would become "four-and-one-two-and-tee." (It should be noted that "three" is replaced with "tee," as the "thr" sound is cumbersome and may interrupt the energy of the counting.) The chorus must be encouraged not to count-sing through the rests, which will prove a most helpful discipline once the text is added.

The wide leaps in each voice part may also create vocal problems. Executing leaps with the voice can be very taxing, especially during the early stages of the learning process. It is extremely important that the singers learn the piece at a slow tempo and at a moderate dynamic. This is even more crucial for sections in which the vocal range is high, as singers are often tempted to sing loudly and off the breath as they ascend in pitch, which produces an undesirable tone quality and is vocally unhealthy.

Stylistic Considerations

There is nothing sophisticated or proper about this partsong. Because it is a setting of a drinking song, it is meant to be fun and even raucous. The tone quality should be rich and full-bodied with full use of vibrato, producing a sound that comes across as very natural and robust.

The work is very repetitive, as each stanza is harmonized identically. This presents quite a challenge in keeping the listener's interest. The most obvious option for variety comes from the dynamic markings, which often change suddenly from one phrase to the next. In addition, the conductor should pay close attention to the markings at the beginning of the first and last stanzas. The first is marked *risoluto* (resolute), while the last is marked *leggiero* (light). These indicate two different styles of singing. The first may be interpreted to mean non-legato, perhaps even marcato, while the last may also suggest non-legato, but in this case staccato (which is affirmed by the articulation markings). Although the second and third stanzas have no directions in this regard, it is suggested that these be sung quasi-legato to reflect the nature of the text, which will add further interest to the performance.

Musical Elements

"Down Among the Dead Men" is in E minor (harmonic form) with a hint of the relative major as each stanza moves into the refrain.

Form and Structure

The work is in strophic form with four stanzas, each followed by a refrain. Following the fourth stanza, the refrain is slightly altered to create a more dramatic ending.

Text

Here's a health to the King, and a lasting peace,
To faction an end, to wealth increase;
Come, let us drink it while we have breath,
For there's no drinking after death,
And he who will this health deny,
Down among the dead men let him lie.

Let charming beauty's health go round,
In whom celestial joys are found,
And may confusion still pursue
The senseless woman-hating crew;
And they that woman's health deny,
Down among the dead men let him lie.

In smiling Bacchus' joys I'll roll,
Deny no pleasure to my soul;
Let Bacchus' health round briskly move,
For Bacchus is a friend to love;
And he that will his health deny,
Down among the dead men let him lie.

May love and wine their rites maintain,
And their united pleasures reign,
While Bacchus' treasure crowns the board,
We'll sing the joys that both afford,
And he that won't with us comply,
Down among the dead men let him lie.

Suggested Listening

Vaughan-Williams: Over hill, over dale. Holst Singers. Stephen Layton,
    conductor. (Hyperion 66777).

Additional References and Resources

Heffer, Simon. *Vaughan Williams*. London: Weidenfeld and Nicholson. 2000.
    Reprinted, Boston: Northeastern University Press. 2001.

Kennedy, Michael. *The Works of Ralph Vaughan Williams*. Second edition.
    London: Oxford University Press. 1980.

Ottaway, Hugh. "Vaughan Williams, Ralph." *The New Grove Dictionary of
    Music and Musicians*.

Vaughan Williams, Ralph. *National Music and Other Essays*. Second edition.
    New York: Oxford University Press. 1987.

Contributed by:

Russell Nelson

Repertoire Resource Guide

Noel!

Steven Sametz
(b. 1954)

TTBB/a cappella
Alliance Music Publications: #0089
Overall: 3
Vocal: 3
Tonal/Rhythm: 4

Composer

Steven Sametz is the Ronald J. Ulrich professor of music and director of choral activities at Lehigh University. He has both received commissions from Chanticleer and conducted the group in the Monteverdi *Vespers of 1610* in New York and San Francisco. In addition to Chanticleer, he has been commissioned by the National Endowment for the Arts, the Dale Warland Singers, Philadelphia Singers, and the king of Thailand. Sametz conducts several choirs at Lehigh and also directs the Princeton Singers, an *a cappella* choir in Princeton, New Jersey.

Composition

This work is an adaptation of the text of a medieval carol for four-voice men's choir. While it is modal and has the flavor of a medieval piece, the complexity of the rhythm suggests a modern perspective. It is not a traditional carol, but the combination of four independent melodies into a single dense, rhythmic texture.

Historical Perspective

This is a modern work with ties to ancient music through its text and scale choice. As a setting of an ancient text, it has connections to many modern works that look to the past for literary inspiration, including Orff's *Carmina Burana* and Britten's *Sacred and Profane*.

Technical Considerations

The rhythms in this work are challenging with frequent syncopations in 6/8 meter. The range is moderate, stretching from an A2 for bass 1 and bass 2 to a single A4 per verse for tenor 1. The work features rapid articulations and extremely rhythmic phrases without chromaticism.

Stylistic Considerations

The work is modern but has a playful style full of rhythmic drive. Every vocal line is either accented and marked or broadly sustained in contrast. The dynamics are clearly marked to produce a crescendo over the fourth and fifth verses, which continues the crescendo created by the simple accretion of voices over the first three verses. The tempo is brisk.

Musical Elements

This piece has a solid tonal center of D, utilizing a modal scale with a lowered third and seventh. Dissonance only arises from the simultaneous sounding of four distinct melodies. Each voice gets its own melodic material, which it repeats through five verses; the entire work is polyphonic until the closing gesture. These four melodies are filled with runs and leaps, and all four have rhythmically complex phrases. Throughout, the meter is steady.

Form and Structure

The work is constructed of five verses and a coda. The voices enter one at a time, with bass 2 alone on the first verse, tenor 2 entering on the second verse, bass 1 joining on the third verse, and tenor 1 completing the texture on the fourth verse. The fifth verse uses all four voices and crescendos to a climactic homophonic coda.

Text

Noel! Sing we Noel!
Sing we both all and some, Noel!

Out of your sleep awake
for God mankind now hath he take
all of a maiden without any make.

Contributed by:

Thomas Cunningham

Repertoire Resource Guide

Song of Peace

Vincent Persichetti
(1915–1987)

TTBB or SATB/piano
Theodore Presser Company: TTBB=362-00130,
SATB=362-03336
Overall: 3
Vocal: 3
Tonal/Rhythm: 4

Composer

Vincent Persichetti was one of the preeminent American composers of the twentieth century. He studied many instruments (piano, organ, and double bass) from the time he was young. As he matured, he studied composition with Roy Harris (in Colorado) and conducting with Fritz Reiner (at the Curtis Institute).

In 1947 he joined the faculty of the Juilliard School, where he taught until his death. His book *Twentieth Century Harmony* is one of the best guides to his music and is still used as a theory book around the world. Most of his compositions, while complex, are very accessible to amateur singers and instrumentalists.

The second edition of the New Grove Dictionary of Music and Musicians says "Persichetti himself identified two main currents within his creative disposition: one 'graceful' and the other 'gritty.' Beyond this, his music is characterized by lucid texture, sparse gestures, epigrammatic forms, a fondness for pandiatonic and polytonal harmony, a playful rhythmic vitality, and a pervasive geniality of spirit."

Composition

The Colgate University Chapel Choir commissioned "Song of Peace" in 1959. It is a setting of an anonymous text for TTBB choir and piano. (There is also an SATB version available from the publisher.) This short piece consists mostly of sung "Alleluias."

Historical Perspective

This piece was written at the end of the 1950s, the decade in which Persichetti was most active as a composer. His most often performed pieces come from this decade. During this period, he developed his own system of form in which a small musical unit saturates a large composition; "Song of Peace" falls right into that category.

Technical Considerations

Persichetti alternates the texture of unison singing with fuller two- or four-part textures throughout. It is important that the singers realize where these changes occur. When the texture returns to unison, the singers must listen in a different way; they must all agree on the same pitch. Unison singing is one of the most difficult effects to accomplish in choral music and is arguably much more difficult than singing in multiple parts because the intonation is so exposed.

The word "Alleluia" is a nightmare for singers because it is full of diction pitfalls. The vowels have a tendency to fall "back" into the singers' throats; remember, high-forward resonance is desired all the time! The vowels will fall "back" if singers do not produce the "l's" correctly. Instruct the singers to sing the "l's" very quickly and with the tip of their tongues. Singers love to grind through "l's"; this is not a desired effect.

Stylistic Considerations

Very clean intonation is necessary for this piece to be effective; lack of good intonation will obfuscate the wonderful "modal" dissonances Persichetti sought. The composer placed all of the expression markings in the music; it is important to follow them.

Musical Elements

Persichetti constructed this piece around a short lydian motive that appears in the first measure of the piano part. This motive is everywhere throughout the piece—in the piano part and each voice part—in augmentation, transposition, and in retrograde. It would be wise to introduce the choir to the lydian motive before reading the piece for the first time. Show the choir all of the places the motive occurs to allow them to assimilate Persichetti's challenging harmonic language more quickly.

Form and Structure

The form is essentially through-composed, however, the motive discussed above is the germ around which the form revolves. Essentially, Persichetti was experimenting with different ways he could present the small motive.

Additional Reference and Resources

Persichetti, Vincent. *Twentieth Century Harmony*. New York: W.W. Norton and Co. 1961.

Contributed by:

Thomas Cunningham

Repertoire Resource Guide

Soon Ah Will Be Done

arr. William L. Dawson
(1899–1990)

TTBB or SATB/a cappella
Neil A. Kjos Music Company: TTBB=T 101-A, SATB=T102-A
Overall: 3
Vocal: 3
Tonal/Rhythm: 3

Composer

William L. Dawson, composer, conductor, and college professor, was born September 23, 1899, in Anniston, Alabama. He was first educated at the Tuskegee Institute and thereafter completed degrees at the Horner Institute of Fine Arts (Kansas City) and the American Conservatory of Music (Chicago). In the 1930s, he returned to the Tuskegee Institute as a member of the faculty and began his long tenure as conductor of the Tuskegee Choir, for which he is most noted. This chorus, often 100 voices strong, gained notoriety under his direction, including a feature performance for the opening of Radio City Music Hall, New York; appearances before two presidents; and wide acclaim both in America and in Europe. He retired from Tuskegee in 1955 and died February 5, 1990.

Although Dawson composed in many genres, he is perhaps most widely known for his arrangements of African American spirituals. His numerous arrangements are available in the Tuskegee Choir Series published by Neil A. Kjos Music Company.

Composition

"Soon Ah Will Be Done" is a choral arrangement of an African American spiritual for male voices (TTBB, *a capella*). It is homophonic, with a slow harmonic rhythm. There are also brief elements of call and response, for example, in the second stanza when the low bass voice sings "No more weepin' an' a wailin'" while the upper three voices repeat the words "No more," and "wailin'."

Although the work is intended for concert hall performance, the religious nature of the text makes it equally appropriate for the sacred venue. A version for mixed chorus (SATB, *a capella*) is also available.

Technical Considerations

One of the most challenging elements of the piece is that it is riddled with expression markings (*fz*, *ffz*), as well as many accents. This can be problematic from a vocal standpoint because choirs are prone to either come off the breath or "press" on the sound with a throaty tone quality. Further, choristers may be tempted to focus solely on the accents or other markings while forgetting that they must at the same time be accurate in pitch. This can contribute to a sound that resembles shouting or yelling instead of pitched singing. It is important for the conductor to practice without the expression markings first to ensure proper vocal production and accuracy of pitch. Once these have been established, the choir can then perform the markings with greater success.

The piece requires a very visceral, somewhat dark quality of sound. The tone is covered, with vowels relatively closed and rounded. Vowels that are too open will produce a sound that is much too thin and bright. The pulse must also be very grounded, so it is suggested that the conductor keep his or her gesture low with a marcato style, being careful not to "skim" off the beats. He or she may find it helpful to teach the piece starting with the text from the very beginning (instead of on a neutral syllable for the first few readings) because the style of the piece, the rhythmic content, and the overall emotional expression are largely communicated through and encapsulated within the declamation of the text. Although the piece is very rhythmic in nature, the rhythmic elements are repetitive and overall very accessible. The prevailing figure is the dotted eighth-sixteenth combination, which must be clearly articulated and unified between each section of the choir.

At first glance, the text looks very simple; however, there are a few details that are often misunderstood. Below are several examples of common mistakes:

WORD/PHONEME	INCORRECT	CORRECT
ah	"ah"	"uh"
a–	"ah"	"uh"
de	"dee"	"duh"
t'	"too"/"tah"	"tuh"
final t	exploded	stopped

Many conductors choose to change some of the words so that they are in keeping with modern English, devoid of any colloquialism. That issue is addressed below.

Stylistic Considerations

African American spirituals tend to express a feeling of melancholy and a fixation on the afterlife, in the sense that the world to come brings with it relief from the plight of slavery. There are also elements of hope and urgency, as many spirituals are believed to contain code language for the Underground Railroad, as well as metaphorical references to lands of freedom, such as the Northern states, for example. Also inherent to the style is a strong, grounded sense of rhythm because many slave songs were used to accompany work.

It must be clearly understood that modern arrangements of African American spirituals are *interpretations* of music transferred orally for hundreds of years. Such pieces are meant to mimic the style of the slave song as best understood by the arranger. In "Soon Ah Will Be Done," the element of melancholy and longing for the next life (and/or freedom in the present life) is overtly apparent and should be emphasized through the elements of tone described in the above section, as well as through the pedantic and grounded nature of the rhythm. It is suggested that the tempo be slow to moderate. Otherwise, the meaning of the text may become trivialized.

The style of text, which imitates slave dialect, is an important and sometimes controversial issue to consider. There has been some disagreement over whether pronouncing the text in the colloquial style is demeaning to the heritage of the African American community. For example, some conductors choose to "correct" the text by changing "de" to "the" and "wid" to "with." Others feel that because there were generally no sounds for "th" in the African dialects, it is more accurate to pronounce it as Dawson has indicated. Certainly, there are no absolutes, and this is a decision that must be made according to the cultural prescriptions of the community in which it is performed. However, it is my opinion that the colloquial pronunciation is stylistically correct. James Weldon Johnson addresses more fully the issue of "Negro dialect" in his preface to *The Books of American Negro Spirituals* with some helpful examples of common pronunciation.

Musical Elements

The work is in G minor, usually in the harmonic form, ending abruptly in the major key on the final chord. With the exception of several tonicizations of the dominant, there are no significant harmonic shifts. Seventh chords are used sparingly and for the purpose of text emphasis or elaboration ("no more wailin'," for example).

Form and Structure

"Soon Ah Will Be Done" is in strophic form, beginning with the refrain. The first stanza is the most straightforward, with an exact repeat. The second and third stanzas also repeat but include a second ending that in each case is more elaborate than the first. The work concludes with the third stanza without a repeat of the refrain.

Text

Soon ah will be don' a-wid de troubles ob de worl',
Goin' home t'live wid God.

I wan' t' meet my mother
I'm goin' t' live wid God.

No more weepin' an' a wailin',
I'm goin' t' live wid God.

I wan' to meet my Jesus, I'm goin' t' live wid God.

Suggested Listening

Deep River. (Cantus Recordings CTS-1203).

The Spirituals of Williams L. Dawson. St. Olaf Choir. Anton Armstrong, conductor. SATB version. (St. Olaf Records #2159).

Additional References and Resources:

Hogan, Moses. Introduction to *The Oxford Book of Spirituals*, ed. Hogan. New York: Oxford University Press. 2002.

Johnson, James Weldon. Preface to *The Books of American Negro Spirituals*. J. Rosamond Johnson, James Weldon Johnson, and eds. New York: Viking Press. 1925 and 1926. Reprinted, New York: Da Capo Press. 2002.

Southern, Eileen. "Dawson, William L." *The New Grove Dictionary of Music and Musicians*.

Contributed by:

Russell Nelson

Repertoire Resource Guide

Widerspruch, D. 865

Franz Schubert
(1797–1828)

TTBB/piano
Warner Bros. Publications: LG 00513
Overall: 3
Vocal: 4
Tonal/Rhythm: 3

Composer

Franz Schubert was born January 31, 1797, to Franz Theodor Florian and Maria Elisabet Katherian Vietz. His earliest musical training was by his father, who taught him the violin, and soon thereafter he began his studies with Michael Holzer, a local organist and church musician. In 1808, he became a choirboy at the imperial court chapel, which afforded him the opportunity to study at the Imperial and Royal City College. There, he composed under the tutelage of Antonio Salieri.

Schubert spent most of his life in Vienna, with a few brief absences, including a stint in Hungary with the Esterházy family. His musical life revolved around the cultivated middle class, through which many of his compositions were heard and revered. He maintained a close circle of friends and acquaintances, many of whom were musicians, artists, and poets (Mayhofer and Seidl among them). These artistic friends and acquaintances were Schubert's most devoted audience, and many of his compositions were heard and enjoyed at their gatherings, which were referred to as *Schubertiads*.

Schubert composed in a number of genres, including dances and sonatas for piano, symphonies, chamber pieces, theatrical works, and sacred compositions. He is perhaps most noted for his *Lieder*, in which he shows a strong sensibility for melodic writing, as well as innovative harmonic creativity brought to life through expressive accompaniments. He was also a prolific composer of partsongs, usually deriving textual material from contemporary poets such as Schiller, Goethe, Mayhofer, Seidl, Schober, and others, as well as a few texts he wrote himself. His partsongs for male voices are by far the most numerous, although he composed settings for mixed and female voices as well. The composer gained posthumous fame for his larger works, but it is the smaller, more intimate genres for which he was most noted during his lifetime.

In 1828, Schubert became gravely ill and died an untimely death November 19 of that year.

Composition

"Widerspruch" is a partsong for male voices (TTBB) accompanied by piano. It was probably composed around 1826 and published in 1828. It is homophonic with the melody in the first tenor. The text, set in syllabic style, is by Austrian poet Johann Seidl. There is also a version for solo voice with an identical piano part.

Technical Considerations

Although the tessitura overall is not very high, there are moments when the higher ranges of the voices are employed, and these must be treated very carefully. For example, in the B section the chorus sings in unison for more than twenty measures, and portions of this melody exploit the upper range for the basses, the highest note being D above middle C. Because this section is marked piano, it may be helpful to have the basses tacet in measures 55–76, depending, of course, on the skill of the singers at hand. In addition, the first tenors are expected to sing above the staff in measures 36–42 and 115–121, and, in both cases, the dynamic level is fortissimo. It is likely the first tenors will need to sing forte (and, in some cases, mezzo forte) to balance their part with the rest of the chorus. By nature of the tessitura in those measures, the tune will certainly be heard!

Conversely, there is one passage (mm. 83–88) in which the first tenor descends below the second tenor and baritone, taking the melody into the lower range while the other two parts remain relatively high. It is crucial that the chords are balanced so the melody can be clearly heard. In this case, since the dynamic is pianissimo, the first tenors will probably need to change the dynamic to piano to maintain the audibility of the melody within the texture. Further, because there is a diminuendo at measure 85, another strategy is to allow the lower three parts to diminuendo while the first tenor maintains a constant dynamic.

The unison measures in the B section present further challenges. Although at first glance, the passage seems straightforward, it is a difficult one to sing in tune. At measure 69, the harmony begins to shift via chromatic alterations, finally landing on a C-sharp, which becomes a common tone for the modulation to F-sharp major in measure 79. To make matters worse, the piano plays the same pitches in octaves, so there is no chordal undergirding to which the singers can aurally relate, making their sound very exposed. The best time to address this problem is during the warm-up. For the portion of the rehearsal process devoted to note-teaching, the conductor can check the singers' ability to tune in unison through specific exercises and thereby reinforce their listening skills. He or she may even find it helpful to excerpt portions of the piece and practice them on a neutral syllable (e.g., "noo") as part of the group intonation regimen. In any case, unison singing is the most telltale sign of how well an ensemble can sing in tune, and it requires tremendous aural discipline on the part of the singer and the conductor.

The tempo is marked *Ziemlich geswind* (fairly quick), which presents perhaps the greatest challenge of the piece. Although the work is somewhat repetitive rhythmically, the text is quite intricate, and, at a fast tempo, it is very difficult to annunciate accurately and clearly. The chorus should learn the text by chanting it slowly in rhythm on a sung pitch or static chord, carefully matching the vowels to the rhythm while placing initial consonants before each vowel and quickly placing final consonants before each successive word. A slight space before words beginning with a vowel should also be expected for the sake of clarity. Once the choristers are comfortable with the pronunciation, they can gradually increase the tempo and finally transfer the text to the actual written notes. Proper demonstration and instruction are vital to the outcome of this piece in that the articulation and style are largely driven by the phrasing and syntax of the language. The pitch and rhythm should first be taught separately on a neutral syllable.

Stylistic Considerations

"Widerspruch" is music for the pleasure of singer and listener. Unlike Beethoven and Mozart, Schubert was not admired by royalty but by the middle class social circles to which he belonged. In these circles were many music admirers, as well as many capable amateurs, and it is likely that a great number of his partsongs were composed at the request of friends. It is with this understanding that the work should be performed. A brief description of poetic style among Schubert's contemporaries may also help the chorus grasp the context in which the partsongs were composed.

With regard to the text, this edition includes an optional English setting by Alice Parker. Although the translation is not exact, considering the need for poetry and rhyme, it is very adequate and clearly communicates the spirit of the German text.

Musical Elements

"Widerspruch" is in D major with a direct shift to the minor mode in the B section. Schubert maintains harmonic interest via brief key changes (B-flat major and F-sharp major), which appear very abruptly in most cases.

Form and Structure

The work is in ABA form with a piano introduction and coda.

Text and Translation

Wenn ich durch Busch un Zweig brech auf beschränktem Steig,
wird mir so weit, so frei, will mir das Herz entzwei.

Rings dann im Waldeshaus rücken die Wänd' hinaus,
wölbt sich das Laubgemach hoch mir zum Schwindeldach,
webt sich der Blätter schier jades zur Schwinge mir,
dass sich mein Herz so weit, sehnt nach Unendlichkeit...

When through bush and branch I strike out on the narrow path,
it becomes for me so open, so free, my heart almost bursts with joy.

All 'round this forest-house the walls recede,
Above, the leafy chamber forms for me a roof of dizzying height,
nearly every leaf waves itself into a wing for me,
so that my heart yearns for an infinity so vast...

—translation by Jeffrey W. Baxter

Suggested Listening

Schubert: Complete Part Songs for Male Voices, Vol. 1. (CPO Records 999397).

The Hyperion Schubert Edition 26—An 1826 Schubertiad. The London Schubert Chorale. Stephen Layton and Christine Schäfer, conductors. (Hyperion 33026).

Schubert Songs for Male Chorus. Robert Shaw Chamber Singers. Robert Shaw, conductor. (Telarc CD-80340).

Additional References and Resources

Brown, Maurice. "Schubert, Franz." *The New Grove Dictionary of Music and Musicians*.

Gibbs, Christopher. *The Life of Schubert*. Cambridge: University Press. 2000.

Jones, Nick. Liner notes for *Schubert Songs for Male Chorus*. Robert Shaw Chamber Singers. Robert Shaw, conductor. Telarc, CD-80340. 1994.

Youens, Susan. *Schubert's Late Lieder: Beyond the Song-Cycles*. Cambridge: University Press. 2002.

Contributed by:

Russell Nelson

Level Four

Mixed voices:

Treble voices:

Men's voices:

Repertoire Resource Guide

Ave verum corpus

William Byrd
(1543–1623)

SATB/a cappella
Oxford University Press: TCM3
Overall: 4
Vocal: 3
Tonal/Rhythm: 4

Composer

London-born William Byrd belonged to a class of minor gentlemen and received a good education, probably in the Chapel Royal, but certainly under Thomas Tallis, who remained a close friend. Byrd began composing in his teens. His first paying post was a responsible and well-paying one at Lincoln Cathedral, which he took in his early twenties.

Byrd married in 1568 and became the father of five children. *The New Grove Encyclopedia of Music and Musicians* characterizes Byrd's Roman Catholicism as "stubborn" and "a defining feature of Byrd's life and works." Happily, he was able to use courtly influence and personal circumspection to continue working and composing, even in an inimical religious climate.

Byrd handily composed in a multiplicity of genres. He developed English virginal music to its height, expanding technique and form as well as writing advanced consort songs (instrumental ensemble pieces). On the vocal side of his oeuvre are songs, sonnets, psalms, madrigals, verse anthems, and polyphonic music for both Anglican and Roman Catholic liturgies.

Composition

"Ave verum corpus" is a Latin motet that was considered stylistically avant-garde at the time it was written. It was published in the 1605 collection *Gradualia*, which was revised and republished ten years later. There is some cause to believe that this motet, as with many others composed late in Byrd's life, was intended in two veins: to be acceptable in Anglican usage and for use in underground celebrations of the Catholic Mass. It was in this way that Byrd "got away with" much music that might otherwise have been suppressed.

The *a cappella* motet is freely composed on the pre-existing prayer text which, although it twice mentions Mary, is not Marian. The rhymed and metrical text is often used for Communion during a Roman Catholic Mass, but it also works as a concert piece (as it may have been used in some Elizabethan underground Catholic's parlor).

Historical Perspective

The death of Queen Mary in 1558 brought anti-papal sentiment to the fore in English politics. Persecution that had led to atrocities against Protestants during her reign were now initiated against Roman Catholic clerics and civilians. During Byrd's life, one patron, the Earl of Northumberland, was executed, and another, Lord Paget, fled England. However, Queen Elizabeth I was a Byrd benefactor, granting him and Thomas Tallis joint exclusive rights to publish part-music and staff paper. The Latin motet, having died in England, came to new prominence through his contemporaries' skills and devotion to the genre.

Technical Considerations

"Ave verum corpus" moves from minor to the relative major key and back for the "Amen" section, charmingly, a plagal cadence. At times, the expected V–i cadence instead resolves V–I. Chromatic inflections are frequent but reinforce the harmonic scheme. Because the piece was conceived horizontally as well as vertically, the harmonic rhythm is fast, often changing several times in a single measure.

Each voice must sound if the motet is to make aural sense. Therefore, teaching each section its line in one or two sectional rehearsals may ease the learning process for those singers less accustomed to Renaissance polyphony. This is not to say that the motet should be rehearsed exclusively in individual sectional rehearsal: measures 1 to 8, 15 to 18, and 23 to 28 are mostly homophonic, and voices throughout frequently pair (e.g., alto and bass, mm. 1–4) or trio (alto, tenor, and bass, mm. 29–31). These will only make sense with all voices present.

Some cadences are elided, some entries are anticipatory or delayed, and there are minor instances of imitation among voices.

The rhythms primarily owe their makeup to the text, and Byrd does not ignore text stresses. However, some rhythms are tricky enough that it would help to speak the words or note values in rhythm before attaching notes to them. Chief among these is the tenor line (mm. 20–22), which may elude even the best rhythm readers without up-front assistance, both alone as a section and with the other sections speaking the same rhythms. Be sure the singers understand how their rhythm relates to the tactus (i.e., which notes are "on the beat" and which are syncopated).

Latin presents no abnormal challenges to veteran choral singers, but there are a few lesser-known words to pronounce and translate, as well as the familiar quest to achieve pure vowels unified over the entire choir. It will be the conductor's choice to elicit an informed color. As with all British cathedral music, it is important to work for a choral sound that is spacious, high, bright, and forward. Consonants should be light and crisp and enhance the flow of the legato line. Vowels should be formed in a tall, narrow shape to best emulate the sounds of the English cathedral choirs. Don't be afraid to use vowels that are more closed than standard-liturgical Latin.

Stylistic Considerations

This is an emotional prayer, and the color of the sound should reflect the text. The sound at the beginning should have an awe-full quality. At "O dulcis," it would be appropriate to change color considerably; the composer changes style completely, at last indulging in the sort of imitation one expects. It would be best to make the first statement very different from the second because the final few measures, a sort of coda, follow the main text's V–I cadence with a plagal "Amen."

The first expressive arch climaxes at "pro homine," the second at the repeated "sanguine," and the third arguably at the word "mortis." Thereafter, very short phrases ("O dulcis," "O pie," "O Jesu") each contain an expressive hairpin (crescendo-decrescendo), but pile upon one another to build intensity through "Maria," after which the kernel of the supplication, "miserere," cascades through the choir to the cadence. All this being said, there seems little reason ever to rise much above *mf*, given the nature of the prayer.

Form and Structure

Byrd's contrapuntally enlivened, not particularly imitative two-minute work repeats the "miserere" section, a hallmark of the composer. As we might expect, the supplicatory text beginning with "O pie" is set evocatively in "sigh" motives.

The overall form is ABB, and the key varies from edition to edition, but it is harmonically cogent.

Text and Translation

Ave verum corpus, natum de Maria Virgine.
Vere passum immolatum in cruce pro homine:
Cuius latum perforatum aqua fluxit et sanguine.
Esto nobis praegustatum in mortis examine.
O Jesu dulcis! O Jesu pie! O Jesu Fili Mariae, miserere mei. Amen.

Hail, true body, born of the Virgin Mary.
Truly suffering, was sacrificed on the cross for mankind,
From whose pierced side flowed blood,
Be for us a foretaste in the final judgment.
O sweet, O merciful, O Jesus, Son of Mary, have mercy on me. Amen.

Suggested Listening

Treasures of English Church Music, John Rutter, conductor. (Collegium 302).

Masters of English Church Music: Byrd, Stanford, Howells. (Collegium 301).

O Magnum Mysterium. The Westminster Choir. Joseph Flummerfelt, conductor. (Chesky Records CD083).

Contributed by:

Lani Johnson

Repertoire Resource Guide

I Love My Love
Gustav Holst
(1874–1934)

SATB divisi/a cappella
G. Schirmer, Inc.: 50299220
Overall: 4
Vocal: 4
Tonal/Rhythm: 4

Composer

British composer Gustav Holst was born into a musical family in Cheltenham, England. He began to study music at a young age. After a brief spell at Oxford to study counterpoint in 1892, he moved to London to study with the composer C. V. Stanford. In 1893, he enrolled in the Royal College of Music. Two years later, in 1895, he met fellow student and eventual lifelong friend, Ralph Vaughan Williams.

Holst held many teaching jobs and also performed as a professional trombonist. He was excused from World War I because of his health. Despite his avoidance of combat, he went to Turkey and Greece in 1918 to organize concerts for the troops. After a nervous breakdown in 1923, he resigned most of his teaching duties and dedicated all of his time to composing. His orchestral suite *The Planets* remains one of the canonized pieces of orchestral literature.

Composition

Holst and his friend Vaughan Williams traveled throughout the British countryside for many years, collecting folksongs of the native people. Many of these songs have been arranged for choir by them and countless others. "I Love My Love," is a Cornish folksong. Oddly enough, it was not collected by Holst or Vaughan Williams, but by G. B. Gardiner. One of six songs from Holst's Op. 36b, *Six Choral Folksongs*, it was arranged for SATB in 1916–17. Other songs in the set include: "I Sowed the Seeds of Love," "There Was a Tree," "Matthew, Mark, Luke, and John," "The Song of the Blacksmith," and "Swansea Town."

Technical Considerations

Any piece that features variations on a tune has the potential to get boring. Holst used many expressive markings in the score; if the choir can achieve all of his markings, this piece will come alive and be very interesting to the listener.

This piece is a story. The choir should take on the persona of a storyteller in the first and last strophe but should assume the personality of the two characters (when applicable) in the other strophes. It would be wise to work for a tone color change with the change of each new strophe. This will make each verse have its own character and help the audience follow along.

This piece would be best performed by a larger choir because the long vocal lines might prohibit a smaller ensemble from maintaining the necessary *sostenuto* texture. The lines of the melody and the inner voices should flow and roll like the hills of the English countryside. A whole phrase should be the smallest unit of consideration; in other words, don't let the choir get stuck on individual notes; be sure they are always moving the sound forward.

Stylistic Considerations

This piece should be sung using British English, not American English. The different vowel and consonant sounds of the British English will lend this piece the tenderness and pastoral quality it requires. All of the consonants, therefore, should be light and quick; vowels should be tall, bright, and narrow.

Musical Elements

This piece is in dorian mode, and this tonality could cause problems for singers. Be sure to include modal melodies in your warm-up exercises to familiarize your singers with different tonalities.

Form and Structure

"I Love My Love," is a strophic setting of a six-stanza poem. Holst uses different compositional techniques with each strophe of the text, although the same tune occurs on every strophe. The first and second strophes have rather homophonic settings, and the tune is in the soprano part. For the third strophe, Holst places the melody in the tenor and has the women sing an accompanimental figure. The bass rests during this verse. The beginning of the fourth strophe overlaps the end of the third, when the basses enter with the melody. The climax of the piece occurs in this strophe when the text speaks of the return of the subject's love from the sea.

The fifth strophe features a conversation between the man and the woman. The marking of *parlante* above the soprano indicates the necessity of speechlike recitation of the text. The sixth strophe features the return of the melody to the tenor part with the women's accompaniment figure. This strophe also tells the moral of the story; maids should be patient when their love is away at sea. The piece fades away to nothing, and at the end the tenors sing the last note alone.

Suggested Listening

This Have I Done for My True Love. The Holst Singers. Stephen Layton, conductor. (Hyperion CDH55171).

Additional Reference and Resources

Holst, Imogen. *Holst.* London: Faber and Faber. 1981.

Holst, Imogen. *The Music of Gustav Holst.* Oxford: Oxford University Press. 1985.

Contributed by:

Matthew W. Mehaffey
Anthony Reeves

Repertoire Resource Guide

Il est bel et bon

Pierre Passereau
(b. 1953)

SATB/a cappella or SSAA/a cappella
Bourne Company: SATB= 053856, SSAA= 053858
Overall: 4
Vocal: 4
Tonal/Rhythm: 3

Composer

Pierre Passereau was a French composer who wrote chansons almost exclusively. All that has come down to us representing his sacred output is a single motet. Most of his pieces are descriptive or narrative works (as is "Il est bel et bon"), and they are almost always merry or cheerful. His writing is characterized by graceful melodies, syllabic text setting, and freely imitative polyphony, occasionally alternating with chordal passages. Spirited rhythm and repeated notes are also notable features of his compositional style. The texts he set tend to be unsophisticated—utilizing frank language and unsubtle puns. This was not unusual for many of the *chanson rustique* of the time.

Composition

"Il est bel et bon," published by Attaingnant in 1534, is an *a cappella* chanson written for SATB choir and is Passereau's best-known piece. The texture is highly imitative and syllabic, with almost all of its short phrases concluding with a clear-cut cadence. Typical of the narrative chanson, the text declamation is rapid-fire throughout. Note also the passage intended to humorously represent the clucking of hens, another stylistic trait of chanson from the early sixteenth century–particularly those of Janequin.

Technical Considerations

TESSITURA: The tenor and soprano lines ride fairly high throughout, while the bass and alto lines only descant to a D. For this reason, the conductor may want to consider lowering the key by one or two half-steps.

PHRASING: Because there is so much imitation in the piece, the conductor can easily point out musical and textual high points in each phrase for the singers to aim for (e.g., "Commère c'est pour RIre.") Because each voice part arrives at the high point at a different time, the subtle interweaving of the polyphony is made clear this way.

TEXT: If the conductor is not entirely comfortable with French diction, it would be advisable to call on someone who could successfully coach the singers (possibly a member of the choir or a teacher at school). Focus on learning the pitches and rhythms first by having the choir sing on a neutral syllable, and then introduce the text by speaking it in rhythm before finally combining all the elements.

Stylistic Considerations

The basic tempo of the piece is fast but fluid. The conductor should encourage the ensemble to sing lightly, following the correct accentuation of the spoken French. Some conductors feel that in a chanson as short as this there should be one uniform tempo throughout. I offer the suggestion that, in a refrain-verse form such as this, a subtle difference in tempo between the verses and the repeating refrains may give the work a nice shape. But whatever the conductor's opinion concerning tempo, I'm sure most would agree that a change of *character* between the refrain and the narrative sections (the verses) is essential. The singers must "tell the story"; they must find *musical* ways to realize (or "act out") the drama with changes in articulations, dynamics, and expressions. There is wonderful potential in the phrase toward the end containing the onomatopoetic imitation of the clucking of hens for a choir willing to risk straying momentarily from a traditional approach to vocal color!

The conductor may wish to have the choir listen to a fine recording of the piece (such as that by the King's Singers) for them to grasp more readily the concepts of style, and to learn the degrees to which it is possible to go in terms of expression of the text.

Form and Structure

The form is: Refrain–Verse 1–Refrain–Verse 2–Verse 3–Verse 4–Extension (hens)– Refrain–Refrain (with augmentation). The refrain is heard mainly at the beginning and the end, with the majority of the narrative taking place in the center of the piece.

Text and Translation

Il est bel et bon commère, mon mari.

Il estoit deux femmes toutes d'un pays.
Disans l'une à l'autre: avez bon mari?

Il est bel et bon commére, mon mari.

Il ne me courousse, ne me bat aussi.
Il fait le ménage, Il donne aux poulailles,
Et je prends mes plaisirs,
Commère, c'est pour rire,
Quand les poulailles crient:
Petite coquette (cocococo dac), qu'est-ce ci?

Il est bel et bon, commère, mon mari.

"He is handsome and good, neighbor, my husband."

(There were two women from the same region
Saying to each other, "Do you have a good husband?")

"He is handsome and good, neighbor, my husband."

He doesn't annoy me or beat me,
He does the housework and feeds the chickens
While I enjoy myself.
I tell you, neighbor, it's a laugh,
When the chickens cry:
"Little coquette (cock-a-doodle-do), what is this?"

He is handsome and good, neighbor, my husband."

Suggested Listening

Madrigal History Tour. King's Singers. (EMI 69837).

Contributed by:

J. Aaron McDermid

Repertoire Resource Guide

Jauchzet dem Herrn alle Welt, SWV 36

Heinrich Schütz
(1585–1672)

SATB double choir/basso continuo
Barenreiter: BA480
Overall: 4
Vocal: 4
Tonal/Rhythm: 4

Composer

Heinrich Schütz was arguably the greatest German composer of the seventeenth century, and he was also the first German composer to attain international stature. Schütz's father provided his children with a thorough religious and liberal education. He presumably received musical instruction from the local *Kantor*, Georg Weber, as well as from the organist Heinrich Colander, who taught him to sing well at an early age.

In 1598, Landgrave Moritz von Hessen-Kassel stayed at one of the inns owned by Schütz's father. Moritz was an amateur composer, and he was impressed with Schütz's voice, so he asked permission to take the boy with him and teach him music at his court. Schütz's father, Christoph, resisted until 1599 when he brought his son to the court at Kassel. Schütz excelled in all subjects, and after his voice changed he was offered the opportunity to study with Giovanni Gabrieli. The teacher-to-student relationship was close, and Schütz never acknowledged anyone else as his teacher. He returned to Moritz's court in 1613 and was nearly convinced by his family to leave music in favor of a secure profession. However, in 1614 the Elector Johann Georg I of Saxony made moves to acquire Schütz as his *Kapellmeister*. After some travel back and forth between the two courts, Schütz finally left for Dresden in 1615 where he would remain until his death.

Schütz was prolific in his output of primarily sacred music at the Electoral court. He traveled to Denmark quite often to serve the royal court in Copenhagen, and in 1634 he received the title of *Kapellmeister* to King Christian IV of Denmark. Schütz wanted to retire in 1645 and spend most of his time away from the court in Dresden; however, the Elector only gave him permission to spend some time away, not to retire. Retirement became a reality when the Elector died in 1657, and the heir combined his own chapel with that of his father. Schütz was still connected to the court but spent most of his time writing music and working on the Becker Psalter. He spent his last years in an apartment near the court. For more than 250 years after his death, he influenced the traditions of high craftsmanship and intellectual depth that marked the best of German music and musical thought.

Composition

Psalm 100, SWV 36 is one of the polychoral *Psalmen Davids*, Op. 2 with basso continuo that Schütz wrote in a style inspired by his teacher, Giovanni Gabrieli. Schütz intended the *Psalmen Davids* for liturgical use, and liturgy demanded that psalms end with the lesser doxology or the Gloria Patri; all of the psalm settings in Op. 2 end with the lesser doxology.

Historical Perspective

Psalmen Davids were published in 1619, the year that Schütz was married and the beginning of an extremely productive period in his life. This was the first collection of sacred music he published. Schütz dedicated the collection to his employer, Johann Georg I, the elector of Saxony. With the appearance of the psalms he fulfilled his aspiration to "distinguish [himself] properly by bringing forth a worthy piece of work."

Technical Considerations

The conductor's main concern is deciding where to place the two choruses so that everybody can see the conductor. If the basso continuo is used, the instrumentation and players must be decided as well as whether there should be a continuo group for each choir. It is possible to sing this work unaccompanied, depending on the acoustical circumstances and how far apart the choirs are.

This edition uses original note values, which initially can be intimidating; however, it is important for students to experience original notation in their training so that they are not surprised later in their professional careers. Some modern transcriptions of early music use note values that are half or even a quarter of what the original publication uses because it is easier for modern performers to read.

The parts are not difficult as long as the singers are aware of the meter changes. There are some chromatic alterations due to change of tonal center that usually involve entire phrases or groups of phrases.

Stylistic Considerations

Success in Baroque music performance depends on the "strong–weak" principle; that is, if there is a pair of a rhythmical value (phrase, measure, beat, division, or subdivision) the first entity of the pair should receive a greater emphasis than the second.

Schütz did not put any dynamics in the score. The editor derived the dynamic distinction between Chorus I and Chorus II from the echo designation. This does not mean that the piece should be void of dynamic contrast within the phrases. Schütz usually indicates musical emphasis on the important words in phrases by agogic stress, high-point stress, or melismatic stress.

Melismas, or runs of eighth notes, should receive as clear articulation as possible without compromising the tempo using diaphragmatic articulation can be strenuous and could slow the tempo; therefore, aspirated consonants could prove effective as an alternate method of articulation. Original Baroque treatises on singing suggest this kind of articulation as accurate performance practice. Use extreme care when teaching this kind of articulation. Younger singers could damage their voices by adding tension when using this articulation.

Musical Elements

G major is the predominant key, but Schütz uses mostly direct modulation between phrases within the boundaries of the closely related keys.

Form and Structure

The piece is basically through-composed; however, harmonic, melodic, and rhythmic patterns recur because of the limited vocabulary, not necessarily because Schütz meant to repeat material. In the psalm, the parts of each choir, respectively, sing together but not necessarily using rhythmic homophony.

The *Gloria Patri* is distinctive both formally and structurally. Schütz used an additive construction while maintaining the echo between the choirs. The sopranos sing the first two phrases by themselves, and then altos, then tenors, and finally basses join. At that point, each choir sings in rhythmic homophony. Schütz used polyphony between all the voices and both choirs in the "Amen" section to make a formal and structural distinction with that word.

Text and Translation

(Psalm 100, Lesser Doxology)

Jauchzet dem Herren alle Welt!
Dienet dem Herrn mit Freuden;
kommt vor dein Angesicht mit Frohlocken!
Erkennet, daß der Herre Gott ist.
Er hat uns gemacht und nicht wir selbst,
zu seinem Volk und zu Schafen seiner Weide.
Gehet zu seinen Tore nein mit Danken,
zu seinen Vorhörfen mit Loben;
danket ihm lobet seinen Namen!
Denn der Herr ist freundlich,
und seine Gnade whäret ewig
und seine Wahrheit für und für.
Ehre se idem Vater und dem Son
und auch dem heiligen Geiste
wie es war im Anfang, jetzt, und immerdar
und von Ewigkeit zu Ewigkeit. Amen.

Shout for joy to the Lord, all the earth!
Serve the Lord with gladness;
come before his presence with rejoicing!
Know that the Lord is God.
He has made us and not we ourselves,
to be His people and the sheep of His pasture.
Enter into His gates with thanksgiving,
and into his courts with praise;
give thanks to Him; praise His name!
For the Lord is kind,
and His mercy is everlasting
and His truth endures for ever and ever.
Glory be to the Father and to the Son
and also to the Holy Spirit
as it was in the beginning, is now, and always,
world without end. Amen.

Suggested Listening

Schütz—The Christmas Story: Cantiones sacrae. Oxford Camerata.
    Jeremy Summerly, conductor. (Naxos 553514).

Masterpieces for Choir. Stockholm Motet Chor. Per Enevold, conductor.
    (Bis CD-148).

Schütz: Polychoral Sacred Concertos. Bernhard Klebel, conductor. (Entree CD 48).

Contributed by:

G. Mikael Lindström

Repertoire Resource Guide

Jubilate Deo

Mack Wilberg
(b. 1955)

SATB/brass and organ
Hinshaw Music, Inc.: Vocal score=HMC 1203,
Full score and parts=HMC 1203 A,
organ and percussion parts only=HMC 1203 B
Overall: 4
Vocal: 4
Tonal/Rhythm: 5

Composer

Mack Wilberg is an associate director of the Mormon Tabernacle Choir. He also conducts the Temple Square Chorale. Wilberg holds degrees from Brigham Young University and the University of Southern Califonia. He also performs as a pianist, chamber musician, clinician, and guest conductor.

Composition

"Jubilate Deo" and "Laudate Pueri" were commissioned and premiered by the Utah Symphony Chorus, Ed Thompson, conductor, in 1989. "Laudate Dominum," which completes the set of three in *Tres Cantus Laudendi*, was composed in 1990. The work was first performed in three-movement form by the Brigham Young University Concert Choir. The text is from Psalm 100:1–4.

An instrumental introduction with the last measure in 7/8 is followed by a choral statement of the main theme. Psalm verses are then set to interesting rhythms that capitalize on the syllables' abstract sounds, until measure 100.

There, the "Jubilate" theme repeats and is developed. The development draws to a close on the main theme and moves to a resounding and long-held final cadence, capped by an instrumental crash.

Historical Perspective

Sets of psalm texts have been assembled for musical worship for centuries, especially when celebrative music is called for. This work could easily be included in a church or performing hall dedication, to celebrate a major anniversary, or to laud an outstanding personage.

Technical Considerations

The required resources, melodic construction, difficult rhythms, and frequently dissonant areas suggest that this is a piece for an experienced choir. The instrumental parts are very difficult; be sure you have ample rehearsal time with the brass players, especially if you are using student players.

Begin by learning the alto and bass rhythms in measures 20 to 35 in little sections. Then do the same with the soprano and tenor rhythm. Let all voices learn both rhythms; this will help them to better mesh when singing their own parts. Rehearse these parts together, and introduce the pitches. Only later add the simple words.

The musical ideas correspond to the lines of psalm text (mm. 39–55, 58–66, 67–76, which elide into 76–80, 80–92, which elide into 92–99). Then, the extended "Jubilate" section ensues.

A further challenge resides in the hockets that punctuate the piece. Rearticulating the vowel will make them beautiful and clear. Practice measures 51 to 55 in the soprano, for example, and other such places.

There is no room for inappropriate dipthongs. So much goes on between the instrumental ensemble and the choir that text will simply be unintelligible unless you insist on accurate word stresses and pronunciation.

The changes in meter are simple if taken slowly at first. Finding one's pitch after tacet is not so easy. The conductor should point out where and how each part can find its note, then practice by having the accompaniment realized on piano and asking the choir enter and hold their opening pitches.

Stylistic Considerations

The notes in the extreme high and low ranges should be made to sound beautiful instead of forced. Rehearsing at a slow tempo, removing text, and reinforcing rhythms separately from pitches will help to quell panic in the difficult sections. There are many, but not an overage, of dynamic and expressive markings. Merely realizing those given will occupy both the conductor and the choir.

Form and Structure

Introduction–A (repeated)–B (repeated)–C (repeated).

Text and Translation

(Psalm 100: 1–4)

Jubilate Deo, omnis terra.
Servite Domino in laetititia!
Introite in conspectu ejus in exulatatione.
Scitote quoniam Dominus ipse est Deus:
Ipse fecit nos, et non ipse nos;
Populus ejus, et oves pascuae ejus.
Introite portas ejus in confessione,
Atria ejus in hymnis: confitemini illi.
Laudate nomen ejus.

Sing joyfully to God, all the earth,
Serve the Lord with gladness.
Enter into his presence with jubilation.
Know that the Lord alone is God;
He has made us, and not we ourselves;
We are his people, and sheep of his pasture.
Enter his gates with thanksgiving,
His courts with praise; give thanks to him.
Praise his name.

Suggested Listening

Sing Noel. Phoenix Chamber Choir. John Alexander, conductor.
    (DJ Records CC1.11.3) www.dj-records.com/orderform.html.

Additional References and Resources

Jeffers, Ron. Translation and Annotations of Choral Repetoire. Volume I:
    Sacred Latin Texts. Corvallis, Oregon: Earthsongs. 1988. 135.

Contributed by:

Lani Johnson

Repertoire Resource Guide

Komm, heil'ger Geist, Op. 52, No. 1

Georg Schumann
(1866–1952)

SATB divisi/a cappella
Earthsongs: R-07
Overall: 4
Vocal: 4
Tonal/Rhythm: 5

Composer

Georg Alfred Schumann was born in Königstein, Germany, on October 25, 1866. A composer, violinist, organist, and conductor, Schumann's early musical instruction was from his father and grandfather; he later studied at the Leipzig Conservatory. After various conducting jobs, Schumann became conductor of the *Singakademie* in Berlin in 1900, a position he retained for fifty years. With this organization, he completed extensive international tours and developed an idiosyncratic style of choral performance.

He was appointed professor of composition at the *Berline Akademie der Künste* in 1913 and was appointed president of the *Akademie* in 1934. In addition to his choral compositions, Schumann composed for orchestra, organ, and solo voice. He died in Berlin in 1952.

Composition/Historical Perspective

"Komm, heil'ger Geist" is the first of Schumann's *Drei Motetten*, Op. 52, written in 1910. The German motet is set for SSAATTBB *a cappella* and falls in a long tradition of pieces ranging from early composers (e.g., Schein, Isaac, Schütz, and, of course, J. S. Bach) to the late Romantic (e.g., Mendelssohn, Brahms, and Richard Strauss). These were works, often multi-movement, that set biblical and sacred texts in increasingly complex ways, often for double choir. Other Germanic composers active during the life of Georg Schumann include Gustav Mahler, Richard Strauss, and Johannes Brahms (who died in 1897).

Technical Considerations

The vocal ranges are not extreme for mature singers, but they do require musical and vocal independence. A good amount of vocal control is necessary to realize the many precise musical and dynamic instructions Schumann provides in the score. While the ranges of the parts are slightly different (e.g., soprano 1 is slightly higher overall than soprano 2), both parts make essentially identical technical and musical demands. The *a cappella* nature of the work requires that each vocal part be able to sing independently and securely. The harmonies are not as difficult to hear as they are deceptive; it could be challenging for less experienced singers to learn exactly where their parts fit into the lush, thick sonorities.

Stylistic Considerations

This eight-part motet features rich Romantic harmony. Despite sections of chordal writing, it could in no way be called homophonic. This motet features imitation and antiphonal effects, and these effects are what make the piece so stunning.

It will be important for the conductor to impart an image of the complete piece (not just individual parts) to every singer. Knowledge of how each fits into the whole will enable singers to take ownership in the whole piece. Imitative or accompanimental lines can seem confusing or dull when viewed in isolation, but when the singers understand their "role," their parts assume much more interest and excitement.

Musical Elements

Schumann makes rich use of musical material in this motet; dynamics are extremely important, and emotion is everywhere. Schumann composed during a time of great expressionism in music, and this motet is no exception. Crescendos and diminuendos are used liberally, along with such marks as *espr.* and *cantabile*. Small gradations of dynamic are common (e.g., *piu dim.*). Restraint is an important factor in constructing a successful performance because Schumann's use of soaring lines and thick textures can make the temptation to over-do it strong. It should be noted that although the dynamic *pp* appears many times, the loudest dynamic marking used is *f*.

The opening of the motet ("Komm") is calm and peaceful, and the voices "stack" to transform what at first is an A-flat major chord into an Fmm^7, which travels through various elevenths and ninths to eventually resolve into the A-flat major chord again (measure 3). He repeats that word with similar musical material before every major verb. The Holy Spirit is exhorted to "come" and then to "fill," "kindle," "enlighten," and "strengthen." In addition, Schumann uses the word and its musical material to end each of the piece's two major sections.

Form and Structure

Schumann's motet is in two parts. The first half (mm. 1–22) sets the beginning of the Lutheran hymn "Komm, heil'ger Geist," whose text is a virtual translation of the Latin hymn "Veni Sancte Spiritus." The second part (mm. 23–43) uses bits from the sequence "Veni Creator Spiritus" and the hymn "Veni Sancte Spiritus." Both textual sources are associated with the Christian Feast of Pentecost. It is interesting to note that Gustav Mahler used the hymn "Veni Creator Spiritus" just a few years before Schumann composed this motet in his Symphony No. 8.

Text and Translation

Komm, heil'ger Geist,
erfülle die Herzen deiner Gläubigen.
Komm, heil'ger Geist,
entzünde in ihnen das Feuer
deiner göttlichen Liebe, komm.
Komm, heil'ger Geist,
erleuchte uns, dass wir erkennen all unsre Sünde
und dem Tod entrinnen.
Komm, heil'ger Geist,
und stärke die Deinen, schenke Frieden und Trost,
komm, komm, komm.

Come, Holy Ghost
Fill the hearts of your faithful.
Come, Holy Ghost
kindle in them the fire
of your divine love, come.
Come, Holy Ghost
enlighten us, that we recognize all our sins
and escape from death.
Come, Holy Ghost
and strengthen yours, grant peace and comfort,
come, come, come.

Additional Reference and Resources

Jeffers, Ron and Gordon Paine. *Translations and Annotations of Choral Repertoire. Volume II: German Texts.* Corvallis, Oregon: Earthsongs. 2000.

Contributed by:

Matthew W. Mehaffey

Repertoire Resource Guide

Kyrie

Ludwig van Beethoven
(1770–1827)

SATB/keyboard
Plymouth: PCS 175
Overall: 4
Vocal: 4
Tonal/Rhythm: 4

Composer

Ludwig van Beethoven was born in 1770 in Bonn, Germany. His father, a tenor singer at the court in Bonn, seems to have been instrumental in obtaining lessons for the boy. By his eleventh birthday, Beethoven had developed a reputation as a child prodigy. In 1792, he left Bonn to pursue his musical career in Vienna, studying with Joseph Haydn for a time.

Beethoven's career was shaped by one of the great personal crises in his life, his encroaching deafness, which began to manifest itself around 1796. As a result, he developed an individual style that came to fruition in his last great works, the *Missa solemnis* and the Ninth Symphony. A tremendously influential composer, he is considered to be a transitional figure between the Classical and Romantic eras, embodying characteristics of both in his compositional output.

Composition

"Kyrie" from the Mass in C, Op. 86, was composed in 1807. As with Haydn's late masses, it was commissioned by Prince Nicholas II Esterhazy for the name day of his wife, the princess. This mass setting is clearly modeled after Haydn's masses, especially in the use of a quartet of soloists, which is woven into the texture of each movement. The work is also indebted to the Viennese Classical style of Haydn and Mozart in its harmonic clarity and balanced phrase structure. In contrast to his predecessors, Beethoven is concerned with creating a close relationship between the music and the ancient text of the Catholic mass, which is beautifully effected throughout the work.

Technical Considerations

The melodic and harmonic content of the "Kyrie" movement of the Mass in C is not challenging overall, but there are a few places in the piece to which the conductor must direct his or her attention. In measure 33, the conductor should check the intonation of the augmented sixth chord leading to the cadence on the dominant, a B major chord. The conductor should rehearse measures 29 to 33 slowly on a neutral sound, such as "doo," to tune this cadential approach. The conductor should also isolate the descending chain of suspensions between the soprano and alto in measures 108 to 112 so the expressive dissonances created between these two parts can be brought out. In addition, the director should ensure that the final unison of the piece from measure 123 to the end is well-blended, which can be accomplished by modeling the desired vowels for the word "eleison" and making sure that the singers conform to the director's interpretation. In the same measures, the director may have to work with the choir to effect a change from forte to *subito piano* so the piano dynamic remains vital and well-supported.

Stylistic Considerations

The "Kyrie" is recommended for collegiate choirs, community choruses, and even well-trained high school choirs as a stand-alone piece. However, the work's apparent simplicity can be deceiving. One of the challenges for the conductor is selecting the appropriate tempo. Beethoven's famous marking *Andante con moto assai vivace quasi Allegretto ma non troppo* seems very precise, but still leaves room for interpretation. It can be translated, "Andante with enough quick motion as if Allegretto, but not too much." The tempo indication seems to indicate that the movement should be midway between reverent and celebratory in tone. However the conductor chooses to interpret Beethoven's marking, it is necessary for him or her to practice the movement at the same tempo in every rehearsal so that the tempo becomes inculcated in the ensemble.

The conductor must make decisions concerning phrasing before the piece is rehearsed. There are many opportunities to breathe throughout the "Kyrie" during text repetition, but the conductor may not desire a breath after each comma. It is recommended that the conductor analyze the structure and harmonic syntax of each phrase to make informed decisions about ensemble breaths and to mark them in the music in advance to save rehearsal time. The conductor should also formulate some rules to help the singers in phrasing. This is particularly important for phrases in which a breath is not indicated. An example might be for the conductor to ask singers to produce a slight crescendo in measure 3 between the dotted quarter note and the ensuing eighth note in the soprano and alto and apply that as a general rule to all such examples in the music where a breath should not be taken. It is recommended for the conductor to have the choir speak the opening ten bars on the text in an energized, high-pitched manner to practice the phrasing and breaths independent of the pitches.

The choir should sing with a full, vibrant tone. Vibrato should be employed to add warmth to the tone but never to such a degree that the intonation is obscured.

Finally, the director must consider issues of diction in the work, particularly in terms of using ecclesiastical Latin or German Latin pronunciation. In general, German Latin is appropriate for any work with Latin text written by a German-speaking composer. Performing the movement in German Latin can provide a gentle introduction to the changes between the two pronunciation methods in that only two sounds differ from ecclesiastical Latin. (The "y" in "Kyrie" becomes an open German "ü" as in the word "Glück" and the "s" in "eleison" becomes a "z.") Whether German or ecclesiastical Latin is selected by the conductor, all vowels must be carefully produced with rounded tone. Also, consonants must be enunciated clearly and crisply, particularly the "k" in "Kyrie."

Form and Structure

The "Kyrie" movement is in ABA' form, following the tripartite division of the text. The key of the piece is C major, with a significant harmonic shift to E major in the B section.

Text and Translation

Kyrie eleison.
Christe eleison.
Kyrie eleison.

Lord, have mercy.
Christ, have mercy.
Lord, have mercy.

Suggested Listening

Beethoven Messe in C. Monteverdi Choir. John Eliot Gardiner, conductor.
(Archiv Produktion D 101485).

Contributed by:

Christopher Jackson

Repertoire Resource Guide

My Spirit Sang All Day

Gerald Finzi
(1901–1956)

SATB/a cappella
Boosey & Hawkes, Inc.: OCTB 5814
Overall: 4
Vocal: 3
Tonal/Rhythm: 4

Composer

Introspective twentieth-century English composer Gerald Finzi lived through two World Wars: one during his youth, the other after he had retired to the country, prompting him to return temporarily to London to work for the war effort. He taught at the Royal Academy of Music (1930–33); hobnobbed with contemporary composers like Rubbra, Holst, and Vaughan Williams; grew rare apple trees; lectured; and brought music to small country towns through the Newbury String Players, which he founded and his son continued.

Finzi possessed neither piano nor vocal prowess but worked extensively to revive eighteenth-century English compositions through published scholarly editions. Weakened by Hodgkin's Disease, he died of chickenpox. His library of music and literature was willed to libraries and is available to researchers. The Finzi Trust continues his legacy of performance and scholarship.

Composition

Text reigns supreme in "My Spirit Sang All Day." It has been set to show off the poetry, using traditional contrapuntal techniques with a vocabulary of moderate post-Romantic harmony, like a "love song." Dissonance abounds, but it can be analyzed and is satisfactorily resolved. The Robert Bridges poem comes from a set of three songs, all of which Finzi set. "My Spirit Sang All Day" is the third.

Historical Perspective

Finzi believed that no fine text, however difficult, was incapable of being set to music. He fully grasped the creative breadth of the English language and its imagery, transforming compositional influences—including Parry, Bach, Elgar, and Vaughan Williams—and literary giants—among them Hardy, Rossetti, Wordsworth, and Traherne—into personal and integrated works.

Several authors feel this paean of love was intended for Finzi's wife, Joyce. Notice the unusual capitalization in the fourth line of text ("My").

Technical Considerations

The music poses some difficulties but could be sung by most high school choirs. It is my experience that this piece is well-loved by high school students, and their enjoyment of the piece will encourage them to work diligently to overcome musical difficulties. It is most efficient to learn this work in small sections because Finzi uses motivic development throughout. Whet the choir's appetite by teaching a couple of phrases at a time and pointing out the close relationship between the excellent text and Finzi's music.

Inexperienced singers may feel anxious about the meter changes and chromaticism. The first challenge can be dealt with by teaching the words in rhythm (without pitch) one verse at a time. Soon after beginning work, on the second or third rehearsal, read or ask an ensemble member who has prepared the text to read it in its entirety. The second challenge can be met by calling attention to the predominantly stepwise motion by which Finzi accomplishes his unusual modulations and by the sense of "rightness" one feels stepping from one key to the next. Taking a moment to point out E-sharp and B-sharp may save time and fear because singers seldom see these pitches notated.

In your conducting, go beyond mere beating to a depiction of the line's progress as well as its tacti. The conductor must be more prepared to negotiate the meter shifts the less experienced his or her ensemble is with a piece in this style.

Stylistic Considerations

Even before introducing notes and certainly in note-teaching sectional rehearsals, aim for a joyous declamation. Insist on an ecstatic affect at every step: it will go some distance toward distracting anyone afraid of the notes from focusing on that aspect and provide less-skilled note readers with continual increments of success.

Choose an expressive emotion for each of the three strophes, have every singer record it in their music, and reinforce the differentiation by asking for these same affects in warm-up exercises.

The 44 measures are liberally strewn with expressive markings, leaving few decisions for the conductor.

Form and Structure

"My Spirit Sang All Day" is a through-composed work with similar phrase contours indicating the beginnings of strophes. The piece begins in the E minor on its way to G major (where it also ends) with significant excursions to C-sharp minor and C major. The meter changes to accommodate the text. Homophony and counterpoint—often imitative—alternate. There is a hocket in the tenor voice in measures 13 to 15. Motives are excised from the first section and altered in a number of ways during the remainder of the piece. Phrases and sections are of irregular length.

Text

My spirit sang all day
O my joy.
Nothing my tongue could say,
Only My joy.
My heart and echo caught—
O my joy
And spake, Tell me thy thought,
Hide not thy joy.

My eyes gan peer around,
O my joy—
What beauty hast thou found?
Show us thy joy.
My jealous ears grew whist;
O my joy.
Music from heaven is't,
Sent for our joy?

She also came and heard;
O my joy,
What, said she, is this word:
What is joy?
And I replied, O see,
O my joy,
'Tis thee, I cried, 'tis thee:
Thou art my joy.

—Robert Bridges

Note: whilst=hushed, gan=began

Suggested Listening

My Spirit Sang All Day. Simon Carrington and Robert Chilcott. (Angel Records 49765).

Contributed by:

Lani Johnson

Repertoire Resource Guide

Ngana

Stephen Leek
(b. 1959)

SATB divisi/a cappella
Morton Music: MM405
Overall: 4
Vocal: 4
Tonal/Rhythm: 4

Composer

Stephen Leek is one of Australia's best-known composers for choir. His music is often described as capturing the rhythms, colors, and ethos of Australia and Australians. He is equally adept at writing simple songs for young singers and demanding works for mature choirs. Yet whatever the technical difficulty, his music always utilizes a straightforward musical language that speaks directly to its audience.

In addition to composing, Leek is active as a conductor, educator, and publisher. He lives in Brisbane, where he is a founder, artistic director, and conductor of the acclaimed the Australian Voices, an ensemble of high school singers whose focus is to commission, perform, and record the music of Australian composers.

Composition

"Ngana" is an energetic, rhythmic piece using indigenous texts, which makes creative use of ostinatos, drones, and canons—sometimes only a beat apart. The inclusion of clapping and shouting in addition to the driving vocal rhythms gives "Ngana" an earthy, primitive quality. It was commissioned in

1994 by Graeme Morton for his high school choir in Brisbane, the St. Peter's Chorale.

Technical Considerations

Several factors contribute to this piece being fairly easy to learn. First, "Ngana" draws on a limited harmonic palate, primarily the first six notes of the C major scale (B is heard only six times in the four minute and thirty second work). In addition, the voice leading is always smooth and natural.

What may present some significant challenges to many ensembles is the rhythmic complexity—particularly the canons one beat apart at rehearsal letters B and C and the *mangana* theme in compound meter against the duple *lina* theme at rehearsal letters M and N. An effective way for the conductor to deal with these rhythmic challenges would be to introduce the piece by first teaching the thirty-six-measure canon at the end. Begin with the entire ensemble in unison, then have the choir sing the canon, in only two parts before doing all four. Once the choir knows this canon they will have all the building blocks they need to learn the entire piece. In terms of learning other difficult rhythmic passages, such as the canons at rehearsal letters B and C, the conductor may find in helpful to eliminate the notes temporarily and have the choir simply speak the rhythm, always observing the articulation markings and the correct durations.

On the whole, the vocal ranges are average except for the tenor line, which rests fairly high (more than half the piece sits between C4 and G4). Considering this high tessitura, it would be perfectly permissible to have some altos join the tenors on occasion (e.g., the soft, sustained E's and D's in the first page and a half.) The conductor may even want to consider having tenor and alto switch parts completely at rehearsal letters N and O. Here, Leek sets the tenors above the altos to create a nice change in texture and color, but his wishes may not be ideally realized by some young or inexperienced tenors!

Stylistic Considerations

A distinct change in musical character with each of the three main themes is crucial to a successful performance. Leek has carefully placed accents, staccatos, and tenuto markings throughout the score. Vigorous execution of the accents in particular will contribute to proper word stress and will enrich the rhythmic energy of the piece. Achieving varied vocal colors and characters for the different themes helps the audience realize Leek's vision for "Ngana." He writes that the text he has chosen tells a story, which "calls to the shark (*ngana*) and the fish (*mangana*) welcoming (*yah*) them to the translucent blue waters (*lina*) around the reef." The conductor and choir should work to imbue each phrase with the appropriate "personality."

It is also advisable to use a non-Western vocalism for this piece. Tone should be more nasal and bright than the traditional "choral blend" expected. For this reason, the piece can be vocally tiring; make sure you take this into account when designing your program order. "Ngana" would work best as a closer or an encore.

Form and Structure

Through-composed and highly economical, "Ngana" draws almost all of its musical material from three short phrases. The first half of the piece, using only the *ngana* theme, gradually builds in intensity and contrapuntal complexity to a quasi-homophonic climax. The second half begins with the slower, softer *lina* theme. Next, the *mangana* theme is introduced, then both the *mangana* and *lina* themes are presented simultaneously. The piece closes with a thirty-six-measure canon incorporating all three themes.

Text and Translation

Ngana=Shark
Mangana=Fish
Yah=Welcome
Lina=Water

Suggested Listening

Worthy to Be Praised. St. Olaf Choir. Anton Armstrong, conductor.
    (St. Olaf Records 6465).

Contributed by:

J. Aaron McDermid

Repertoire Resource Guide

O schöne Nacht, Op. 92, No.1

Johannes Brahms
(1933–1897)

SATB/piano
G. Schirmer, Inc.: 11800
Overall: 4
Vocal: 4
Tonal/Rhythm: 4

Composer

Johannes Brahms was born in Hamburg and received his earliest musical education from his father who played double bass in the Hamburg Opera. His early teachers were pianist Otto Cossel and Eduard Marxsen, and the latter introduced Brahms to the music of Bach, Haydn, and Mozart. Brahms came to know the poetry of the German Romanticists well, and he immersed himself in as much as he could find. He also collected folk poetry, songs, and tales in his early years, which he set and arranged for solo voice or choir.

After extensive travels to the United States and around Europe, Brahms came to know Robert and Clara Schumann, who were impressed with Brahms' skills as a composer and performer; Robert Schumann encouraged Brahms to present his works for publication. When Schumann died in 1856, Brahms wanted to carry on the legacy of his friend and champion as a gesture of thanks. Brahms remained a close friend to Clara and sought her counsel on his compositions, to which he did not always adhere.

Brahms applied his studies of the music of earlier periods to his compositions in Renaissance, Baroque, and Classical styles using the nineteenth-century harmonic practices. In 1862, Brahms traveled to Vienna and became well-accepted in the highest musical circles. He had the opportunity to meet Wagner, and although Wagner was critical toward Brahms' music, Brahms supported Wagner's musical endeavors. Financial difficulties forced him to undertake several extensive concert tours throughout Europe from 1865–69. Brahms wanted freedom from professional positions to compose; however, he accepted several professional engagements in the 1870s. He returned to concert touring for a while but concentrated on promoting the music C. P. E. Bach, W. F. Bach, François Couperin, Mozart, and the composers of the generation before such as Schubert, Schumann, and Chopin.

Brahms stopped composing in 1894 because the deaths of several of his friends left him devastated; however, he set his existential views to music in *Vier ernste Gesänge* in 1896 as Clara Schumann lay on her deathbed. He composed his final works after she died.

Composition

This piece is set for four voice parts and piano as are the other pieces in Op. 92. Brahms intended for soloists to sing "O schöne Nacht," not a choir. Choirs have sung and recorded this work with great success, in spite Brahms' intentions.

Historical Perspective

Brahms was a prolific song and quartet composer; however, he was often criticized for the mediocre quality of his texts. Besides setting poems by leading writers such as Eichendorff, Goethe, Heine, Ludwig Hölty, Mörike, Rückert, and Theodor Storm, he also settled upon lyrics by minor poets who were fashionable in his time, including Daumer, who wrote the poem "O schöne Nacht." Sometimes Brahms' choice of poetry was the result of external circumstances. According to the *New Grove's Dictionary of Music and Musicians*, he wrote the quartet "O schöne Nacht," Op. 92, No. 1 as a correction of Heinrich von Herzogenberg's setting of the same text, and he even borrowed his colleague's opening measures to make his point clear.

Technical Considerations

Because Brahms wrote this piece as a solo quartet, conductors must decide whether to maintain the illusion of the solo quartet (and if so how to accomplish that). These questions may not be pertinent because the piece may work just as well as a choral tutti; however, it is important to know Brahms' intentions.

Brahms' piano accompaniment is rhythmically intricate and truly functions as a separate musical part in its own right. It offers no doubling support for the singers but instead offers a commentary on the story related by the voices. The singers have to develop a strong sense of rhythmic independence to perform this work convincingly.

Brahms emphasizes the C major section in yet another way by adding another voice to the piano part. This fact may not change what happens in the voices; however, it is important to notice that Brahms makes sure to announce that this section is different.

Brahms instructs the singers to sing *mezza voce* (half voice) in the C major section. It is important that singers support this *mezza voce* correctly and that they not sing off the voice.

The two hemiola figures in the last six measures that appear in the three lower voices are characteristic devices Brahms uses at important cadences. This is a remnant from the early Baroque that creates a slowing effect in the tempo without actually slowing the tactus. Brahms studied the masters of earlier periods and paid homage to them by using their devices with a nineteenth-century flavor added—in this case the soprano part offset by one beat and the piano part that further obscures the rhythm. The hemiola should be brought out but not overly emphasized.

Musical Elements

The piece is centered on E major and its dominant until the tenor and bass duet, which centers on C major. The text shifts from describing nature to dealing with matters of love. However, when the main thematic material returns at the end, Brahms brings back the initial key. The chromatic mediant key relationships, such as E major to C major, are important in nineteenth-century harmonic practice and should be emphasized. Brahms creates this emphasis by almost understating the C major section as he asks for the tenor and bass to sing *mezza voce*, or half voice.

Form and Structure

The thematic material of this piece returns three times with some rearrangement of the voicing and rhythmic alteration of the text setting. The harmonic content is left virtually unchanged in the repeats. The thematic outline for the voices, A–B–A'–B'–C–A''–Coda (based on A material), is different from the piano outline, D–E–D–F–G–D'–Coda (based on D material). The voices sometimes overlap thematically with the piano to further obscure the form.

Text and Translation

O schöne Nacht!
Am Himmel märchenhaft
Erglänzt der Mond in seiner ganzen Pracht;
Um ihn der kleinen Sterne liebliche
Genossenschaft.

Es schimmert hell der Tau
Am grünen Halm; mit Macht
Im Fliederbusche schlägt die Nachtigall;
Der Knabe schleicht zu seiner Liebsten sacht—
O schöne Nacht!

O lovely night!
In the heavens,
The moon gleams magically in all its splendor;
About it, the sweet comradeship
Of tiny stars.

The dew glimmers brightly
On the green blades of grass; with great power,
The nightingale sings out in the elder-bush;
The young man steals quietly to his sweetheart—
O lovely night!

Suggested Listening

Johannes Brahms: Liebeslieder Waltzes. Robert Shaw Festival Singers.
    Robert Shaw, conductor. (Telarc CD-80326).

Westminster Choir at Spoleto Festival U.S.A. Westminster Choir.
    Joseph Flummerfelt, conductor. (Gothic Records CD 49078).

Monteverdi Choir. John Elliot Gardiner, conductor. (Polygram Records CD
    32152).

Contributed by:

G. Mikael Lindström

Repertoire Resource Guide

The Promise of Living

Aaron Copland
(1900–1990)

SATBB/piano four hands
Boosey & Hawkes, Inc.: M-051-45020-6
Overall: 4
Vocal: 5
Tonal/Rhythm: 4

Composer

Aaron Copland was born in Brooklyn, New York. After pursuing studies with Ruben Goldmark and Victor Wittgenstein, he studied in Paris with Nadia Boulanger between 1921–24, who is considered to be one of the formative influences on his compositional career. After initially experimenting with avant-garde styles in Paris, such as dodecaphony, he settled into a quintessentially American style in the 1930s, which contained elements of jazz and American folk music. It is this latter style, exemplified by such works as *Billy the Kid*, *Rodeo*, *Appalachian Spring*, and *The Tender Land* that defined his compositional output. In addition to composing, Copland was also known for his work as a writer, critic, music activist, pianist, and conductor.

Composition

"The Promise of Living" was originally a vocal quintet from Copland's opera *The Tender Land*, written 1952–54. The text is by Horace Everett. It has been arranged as a stand-alone composition for five voice chorus (SATBB) and four-hand piano, although two versions with orchestral accompaniment, one to match that of the original, can be used for performances. The vocal writing is mostly homophonic in the outer sections of the piece, while the central section contains some light polyphonic writing.

Technical Considerations

"The Promise of Living" is often performed by high school and collegiate choirs, but there are several challenges to both singers and conductors alike in this work. One of the challenging aspects of the work is the range of the voice parts. Although much of the work has a rather moderate range (usually not spanning more than an eleventh) and tessitura, the musical climax from measures 87 to 97 can provide difficulties for untrained singers. For example, the tessitura for the baritone and tenor lies rather high from measures 88 to 90 in particular.

Also, the climactic held note in all voices in measure 95 is in the extreme upper range for all the voices. This ending must be considered in the context of the piece's origin as a vocal quintet in a larger operatic work. If this piece is performed with an ensemble that contains a mixture of trained and untrained singers, it might be advisable to edit measure 95 so that the highest parts can be mixed in with the lowest parts for that measure (e.g., some second sopranos move down to sing the alto note, some altos move down to sing the tenor note, and some tenors sing the baritone note). The tessitura issues in measures 88 to 90 can be alleviated by asking the tenors and baritones to sing lightly in head voice.

Another challenge concerns the shifting meters in the work. This aspect becomes especially problematic in the half notes tied to dotted half notes that end each verse. The 4/4 and 3/4 measures alternate so that the positioning of the half notes as related to the dotted half notes shifts. Consider having all singers count-sing the first melodic statement in the tenor, so they are aware of how long they are to hold each of these tied notes. This will also serve the purpose of teaching the melody to the singers (the tenors and sopranos both get the melody, and the other parts need to be aware of it as they sing) and working the desired phrasings and breaths in one rehearsal package.

A third challenge is that of triple against duple meter between the voice parts and the piano accompaniment. In some cases, the accompaniment supports the singers when they must sing duplets in a compound meter. In measures 78 to 86, however, soprano and alto sing duplets against the predominant 9/8 meter in the lower voices and accompaniment. It is advisable to have the singers practice alternating between triplets and duplets out of context with the piece (such as: "One-and-uh, two-and-uh, one-and, two-and") until they become comfortable with the concept, then chant the rhythms in the context of the work *with* the text.

Finally, the voice crossing found throughout the piece can be problematic. This is especially evident in measures 23 to 33, in which the tenors sing a countermelody against the sopranos, who now sing the main tune from the opening of the piece. In several instances, the tenors cross above the sopranos, which can lead to intonation and balance problems. Simply point out the moments of voice crossing and the insecurity that leads to intonation problems should improve. It is important to make the singers aware that the sopranos have the melody, so the tenors can sing lightly when the voices cross and not overbalance the soprano part at those places in the music.

Stylistic Considerations

The second main section of "The Promise of Living" (mm. 44–69) is heavily informed by American folksong. As a result, it should have a completely different character from the opening. Copland clues us into this difference with the change of scoring from high voices (SAT) to men's voices (TBB) and with a change from simple to compound meter. The pentatonic-flavored, robust melody demands an incisiveness and rhythmic energy that contrasts the lyricism of the opening.

In the last section of the work (measures 70 to the end), the opening melody is initially presented in the soprano part, along with the rhythmic profile of the melody of the second section in the altos. The conductor should make the audience aware that Copland is intertwining the two melodic ideas by keeping the soprano line lyrical and the alto line incisive.

The choir should sing with a full-bodied sound throughout the work, which is in keeping with the original conception of the work for a quintet of soloists. Maintaining a full sound is especially tricky in the opening section, which is marked piano all the way to measure 48. It is incumbent upon the director to work with his or her choir to sing with a well-supported and vibrant tone at the piano dynamic.

Form and Structure

"The Promise of Living" is in three main sections (ABA' form) and in the key of F major.

Text

The promise of living with hope and thanksgiving
Is born of our loving our friends and our labor.
The promise of growing with faith and with knowing
Is born of our sharing our love with our neighbor.
The promise of living, the promise of growing
Is born of our singing in joy and thanksgiving.
For many a year we've known these fields
And known all the work that makes them yield,
Are you ready to lend a hand?
We're ready to work; we're ready to lend a hand...

Suggested Listening

Westminster Choir at Spoleto Festival U.S.A. Westminster Choir. Joseph
    Flummerfelt, conductor. (Gothic Records 0033490782).

Contributed by:

Christopher Jackson

Repertoire Resource Guide

Psalm 96

Jan Pieterszoon Sweelinck
(1562–1621)

SATB/a cappella
Theodore Presser Company: 352-00004
Overall: 4
Vocal: 4
Tonal/Rhythm: 4

Composer

Jan Pieterszoon Sweelinck was born in Devenster in 1562. Little is known about his early life; some sources report he studied in Venice with Zarlino, but no concrete evidence exists to substantiate that claim. We do know he had musical instruction from his father, from Jacob Buyck (an Amsterdam pastor), and from Jan Lossy (a countertenor and shawm player). Around 1580, Sweelinck became organist at Oude Kerk in Amsterdam, Buyck's church; he lived in Amsterdam the rest of his life.

Famous as a brilliant keyboard improviser and teacher, Sweelinck heavily influenced the North German organ school, which ultimately influenced the organ playing of J. S. Bach. His extant compositions include keyboard and vocal works (including 153 psalm settings).

Composition

"Psalm 96" is a psalm setting in the style of a motet published in 1621. Sweelinck wrote the setting for *a cappella* SATB choir, which is very typical of his psalm settings. The texture is polyphonic and basically syllabic with occasional short melismas.

Technical Considerations

"Psalm 96" offers numerous challenges to choir and conductor alike. The piece is heavily polyphonic, and each part has to function independently of the others. It is not, however, fugal; the choir will need to be able to read well, or the conductor can expect to spend considerable time drilling individual parts. The vocal ranges are reasonable (the basses sing from F2 to B3; the sopranos sing from A3 to D5), and the tessitura of each part should feel quite comfortable to the average singer. (Some editions exist that raise the music a whole step.)

The music seems to call for a brisk tempo, which can make finding places to breathe and executing the occasional melismatic passages challenging. The conductor is advised to assign specific rhythmic values to breaths (e.g., in measure 4, ask the altos to make their first note a sixteenth followed by a sixteenth note-long breath). The conductor should be careful that the final notes before breaths do not feel accented. The melismatic passages should be rehearsed on the neutral syllable "du," with each note being pronounced as "du." When this is secure, ask the choir to pronounce only one "d," at the beginning of the sixteenth note passage and gradually increase the tempo.

Although the tessitura is reasonable, the conductor should not hesitate to ask neighboring sections to "help out" when a particular part is in its extreme range or at an awkward place. For example, in measure 7, the altos sing a melismatic passage from the G-sharp below middle C to the E above; some tenors could be asked to support this to fortify the sound and to discourage the altos from forcing their way across an awkward vocal break. Tenors should also be encouraged to use *falsetto* freely when they have awkward leaps (e.g., measure 1).

Finally, the text is in French. The conductor should carefully prepare to coach the pronunciation or recruit someone qualified to do so. It is important to realize, however, that the diction rules for sung French differ in some ways from spoken French. The conductor is strongly encouraged to separate text from the music at the beginning of the learning process. Learn the notes and rhythms via count-singing and neutral syllables. Then, take the notes away from the words. Speak the text in rhythm, being extremely careful that the choir observes all articulations and breathing places. When this is mastered, the words, notes, and rhythms can be reunited.

Stylistic Considerations

Sweelinck's music lies on the cusp between the Renaissance and Baroque periods. Therefore, some stylistic elements from both periods need attention. Like Baroque music, "Psalm 96" tends to be rhythmically motoric; the choir simply jumps in and goes with no stops to the final cadence. This means the conductor needs to ensure that the choir understands the construction of the piece and which parts are most important when. Bringing the counterpoint to life in this way will make the music much more interesting for singers and listeners.

In the manner of Renaissance music, the phrases are extremely important and determined by text. Careful score study and teaching (as outlined above) builds in this component of the music without extra effort.

The choir should sing lightly but with much energy. Take care to ensure that phrases are well-shaped and that articulations are clean. It can be helpful to ask the choir to substitute a rest for a dot (e.g., soprano, measure 3), and to imagine skipping rather than marching. They will really need to listen carefully to one another to achieve the subtle musical effects and demands of this music.

Form and Structure

The piece is modal, mostly in Dorian, and through-composed with overlapping polyphonic sections.

Text and Translation

Chantez à Dieu chanson nouvelle,
Chantez, ô terr' universelle,
Chantez, ô terre et son Nom bénissez,
Et de jour en jour annoncez
Sa délivrance solemnelle.

Sing to God a new song,
Sing, all the earth,
Sing, o earth and bless God's name,
And from day to day tell of
His great deliverance.

Suggested Listening

Beyond Chant. Voices of Ascension. Dennis Keene, conductor.
    (Delos DE 3165).

Additional References and Resources

Cox, Richard. *The Singer's Manual of German and French Diction*. New York:
    Macmillan, 1970.

Contributed by:

Anthony Reeves

Repertoire Resource Guide

(Rejoice, O Virgin)
Bogoroditse Devo

Sergei Rachmaninoff
(1873–1943)

SATB divisi/a cappella
Musica Russica: RA028
Overall: 4
Vocal: 4
Tonal/Rhythm: 3

Composer

Sergei Rachmaninoff was a Russian composer, pianist, and conductor internationally recognized as one of the finest pianists of his day. He attended the conservatory in St. Petersburg as a child and later studied with Nikolay Zverev at the Moscow Conservatory. While there, he met Tchaikovsky and completed one of his earliest compositions, the six-part motet "Deus meus." After his first symphony failed to garner praise, he focused on conducting successes, not returning to composition until 1890. He composed more than 85 percent of his music at the beloved country estate of Ivanovka, including several operas.

In 1914, he toured southern Russia with Koussevitsky, giving concerts to support the war effort. Despite the outbreak of war, Rachmaninoff was able to compose the *All-Night Vigil*, the work from which this motet is taken, in the early months of 1915. He fled Russia in 1917, by which time Ivanovka had been looted and razed, and took up residency in New York City in 1918. He lived in the United States until his death and is buried in Valhalla, New York.

Composition

Rachmoninoff's *All-Night Vigil*, commonly also referred to as "Vespers," is a collection of fifteen hymn settings comprising the Ressurectional Vigil as celebrated by the Russian Orthodox Church. This Vigil is commonly observed on Saturday night and is a combination of the Ordinary of Vespers and the Ordinary of Matins. The entire work is set for choir with an occasional soloist and without any other accompaniment. This particular movement, the "Bogoroditse Devo," is a setting of the Russian Orthodox equivalent of the Ave Maria and forms the closure of the vesperal portion of the Vigil. The title is better translated "Rejoice, O Virgin."

Historical Perspective

Rachmaninoff composed this piece at a time of great awareness of the European influence on Russian classical composition and of renewed interest in native Russian sources of compositional inspiration. Rachmaninoff was interested in these issues and had great respect for Stepan Smolensky, who encouraged composers to look to traditional Russian Orthodox chants as a source of musical material for modern compositions. Smolensky was the director of the Synodal School from 1886 to 1901, and Rachmaninoff wrote the work for the Moscow Synodal Choir and dedicated it to Smolensky, as if answering his call for natively inspired music.

Several of the movements of this work are directly based on Russian Orthodox ecclesiastical chants while others, such as the movement presently considered, are based on what Rachmaninoff called "counterfeits." He deliberately composed these "counterfeit" movements to seem as though they were based on actual chants when, instead, they are simply infused with the style and inspiration of traditional chants.

Technical Considerations

While "Bogoroditse Devo" is a challenging piece, the difficulties do not lie in the technical aspects of the music. The rhythms are all based on flowing eighth notes that closely follow the natural rhythms of the spoken text. While the second half of the piece is in 6/4, the quarter note motion is slow enough that the rhythm is not difficult to follow. Ranges are not extreme, although there is one section of prolonged high G's in the soprano and tenor, and there are two measures of pedal low F's in bass 2. The piece is in F major throughout without any chromaticism. Every voice part splits into two parts at some point, but only the altos split for more than a few measures.

Though there are no awkward leaps, and almost all of the motion is stepwise, the melody lines are largely long and sustained, often through many measures. This may pose a problem without adequate support. Also, these long melodies must reflect the flexibility of the underlying text, which can be difficult with an inexperienced group.

The biggest challenge for an English-speaking choir will probably be the Church Slavonic text. The sounds of the language are very close to those of Russian, so some knowledge of Russian diction will help a conductor teach this piece.

Stylistic Considerations

This piece is constructed of several long, largely homophonic phrases, generally shaped into several small, arched shapes. The overall shape of the piece is a prolonged arch, crescendoing to a point of maximum dynamic about three-quarters of the way through the piece and quickly diminishing in volume to the close. Although the phrases are long, they are supple, often ending in flowing eighth-note motion.

The expression marking at the beginning of the work is *Andante moderato*, but the original marking in the autograph was *Andante, leggiero, molto dolce*. The entire piece has a feeling of tenderness about it, even at the crescendo to fortissimo. The central stylistic aspect of this piece is the careful marriage of tender devotion to the extended melodic phrases, which gently rise in volume and then quickly fall away.

Musical Elements

This work is solidly in F major. Any dissonance is carefully controlled and resolved. The work is largely homophonic, but there is an extended middle section with two independent melodies, one sung by the altos and basses and the other sung by the sopranos and tenors.

Form and Structure

The structure of this work closely follows the structure of the text. There are three four-measure or five-measure phrases that begin the work, mirroring the opening three short phrases of the prayer. What follows is a long melody line sung by the altos, which corresponds to almost all of the remaining text. While the altos sing their melody line in flowing eighth notes, the sopranos and tenors sing a complementary melody in slower moving quarter notes, restating the opening text. The basses join the altos as all parts crescendo to fortissimo, although the energy is quickly spent and dissipates as the dynamic returns to piano. Parts of the eighth note melody are heard in the alto and tenor part as the volume decreases, as though they were lost vestiges of the previous outpouring. Finally, the closing phrase is sung at a very low dynamic.

Text

Bogoroditse Devo, raduysia,
Blagodatnaya Mariye, Ghospod s Toboyu.
Blagoslovenna Ti v zhenah,
i blagosloven Plod chreva Tvoyego,
yako Spasa rodila yesi dush nashih.

Rejoice, O Virgin Mother of God,
Mary full of grace, the Lord is with You.
Blessed are You among women,
and blessed is the Fruit of Your womb,
for You have borne the savior of our souls.

Suggested Listening

Rachmaninoff Vespers. Robert Shaw Festival Singers.
    Robert Shaw, conductor. (Telarc CD-80172).

Contributed by:

Thomas Cunningham

Repertoire Resource Guide

Sicut locutus est

Johann Sebastian Bach
(1685–1750)

SSATB/continuo
Hal Leonard: 8596740
Level 4
Vocal: 4
Tonal/Rhythm: 3

Composer

J. S. Bach composed his *Magnificat* (BWV 243) in 1723. It was written soon after his move from Cöthen, where he held a position at the court of Prince Leopold of Anhalt, to Leipzig where he took up the position as *Kapellmeister* at the renowned St. Thomaskirche. Bach spent the rest of his life working in Leipzig, composing many of his greatest works, including the St. John and St. Matthew Passion, numerous cantatas, oratorios, and the great B Minor Mass. Bach wrote hundreds of sacred choral works in German; the *Magnificat* is one of only eleven Latin texts Bach set to music.

The *Magnificat* was one of the first large works Bach composed in Leipzig and was his largest composition to date. It was originally scored in E-flat major (BWV 243a) and included interpolated Christmas motets in German. Nearly a decade later, between 1728 and 1735, Bach substantially revised the piece; he removed Christmas interpolations (thereby neutralizing its liturgical function), changed the key to D major, and made minor changes to the instrumentation. This revised version made the *Magnificat* setting much more versatile, as it was now suitable for any festive occasion. Bach's

Magnificat in D continues to be one of his most widely known and most often performed pieces today.

Composition

"Sicut locutus est" is the eleventh movement of Bach's *Magnificat in D* whose text comes from the Luke 1:46–55 and is often referred to as the Canticle of the Blessed Virgin Mary. The *Magnificat* functions liturgically as the last movement in the Office of Vespers. "Sicut locutus est" comes at the end of the *Magnificat* text directly before the Gloria Patri. Bach sets "Sicut locutus est" as a permutation fugue for SSATB voices and continuo.

Technical Considerations

"Sicut locutus est" is a permutation fugue that is very objective and straight-forward. It is a bit unusual for Bach to begin the fugue in the lowest voice as he typically saved the lowest voice for the final entrance of the fugue subject. However, this decision could very well be a bit of word painting, representing "God's promise" moving from the patriarch (bass) to each of his generations as the fugue subject moves continually higher through the texture. The conductor could emphasize this idea by instructing each section to decrescendo at the end of the fugue subject on the word "nostros." This will enable the singers and the listeners to clearly hear "the promise" move to the next section or "generation" of voices as they enter with the fugue subject.

The continuous five-voice polyphonic texture requires each section of the choir to function independently of the other voice parts. The conductor would be well advised to have the entire choir learn the first thirteen measures of the bass line because this excerpt provides an opportunity for the conductor to shape and phrase the different parts of the fugue subject and countersubject. Then, when each voice enters with this music, the artic-ulation and phrasing will effectively contrast and complement each other. One way to differentiate the subject from the countersubject would be to decrescendo on the word "nostros," as mentioned earlier, then change the half note value to a quarter note on the final syllable ("stros") and insert a quarter rest before "Abraham." This would effectively separate the subject from the countersubject as well as emphasize the important dotted rhythm. The rhythmic "Abraham motive" unifies the work by culminating in a contrasting homophonic setting of the text "Abraham et semini ejus in secula." This dramatic contrast between the dense, polyphonic opening and the "contrapuntally enlivened" homophonic ending effectively emphasizes the joy of God's eternal promise to Abraham and his people.

The vocal ranges are comfortable for all voice parts. The alto tessitura is a bit low and requires a solid G3 and A3. Soprano 1 and 2 parts are equivalent in range, but the soprano 1 part includes an extended passage that descends stepwise in half notes from G5 to A4. The conductor would be wise to use the sopranos with the lightest voices on this part. The conductor should also note the difficult soprano 2 part in measures 34 to 36. This short passage contains some very difficult and unpredictable skips, which require some attention during the initial rehearsals. The tenor and bass parts sit comfortably between D3 and F-sharp4 and G2 and D4, respectively.

Stylistic Considerations

Bach's music is the pinnacle of Baroque writing. His music uses motoric melodies and rhythms that drive the fast harmonic rhythm forward. Therefore, it is essential that the singers understand the formal structure of the piece and how their parts function in the overall structure. As stated before, this will bring the dense counterpoint to life in a way that makes sense to singers and listeners alike.

The conductor must also make the decision whether to perform the piece *a cappella* or with a continuo group. It is important to remember that a continuo group insinuates at least three performers: the singers, a keyboard instrument, and a melodic instrument. If a harpsichord is available, the conductor should make all possible efforts to use it. In most cases, an organ will be the most practical choice, but the conductor should keep the sound of a Baroque organ in mind when deciding on organ registration. The conductor will also have to decide what realization the keyboard player should use. There are many published editions with different realizations. When deciding on a realization, one should consider the type of keyboard instrument being played and the skill of the keyboardist. As for the melody instrument, a cello, double bass, or bassoon would be appropriate. One should not be afraid to use multiple keyboard and melody instruments (harpsichord and organ, cello and bassoon, etc.). These complementary tone colors would wonderfully affect to the overall sound as well as provide firm harmonic support for the choir. (See Laurence Dreyfus' book for more information on continuo possibilities.)

Finally, the choir should sing this music with much conviction yet remain light and buoyant with their vocal production. One way to help attain this balance is to insist upon correct text declamation and syllabic accents. By combining the well-shaped phrases with light and clean articulations, the choir will be able to sing with vocally efficient production, resulting in a buoyant and joyous presentation of the text and music.

Form and Structure

"Sicut locutus est" is a five-voice permutation fugue in D major.

Text and Translation

Sicut locutus est ad patres nostros,
Abraham et semini ejus in secula.

As He promised to our forefathers,
Abraham and to his seed forever.

Additional References and Resources

Butt, John. *The Cambridge Companion to Bach*. Cambridge. New York: Cambridge University Press. 1997.

Dreyfus, Laurence. *Bach's Continuo Group: Players and Practices in his Vocal Works*. Cambridge, Massachusetts: Harvard University Press. 1987.

Contributed by:

Lee D. Nelson

Repertoire Resource Guide

Te Quiero

Alberto Favero
(b. 1944)

SATB/a cappella with alto and bass solos
or SSAA with alto solo
Earthsongs: SATB=S-49, SSAA=W-19
arranged by Liliana Cangiano
Overall: 4
Vocal: 4
Tonal/Rhythm: 3

Composer

Alberto Favero was born in La Plata, Buenos Aires, Argentina, in December 1944. He grew up in a home of musicians, where his father and teacher Fermín Valentin Favero gave him lessons in voice and multiple instruments.

In 1958, he entered the College of Fine Arts at the University of La Plata to study piano, and in 1963 he graduated from National University of Buenos Aires with a bachelor of music in piano performance. He became professor of piano in 1968 and professor of composition in 1973 at the National University of La Plata. His teachers included Luis Gianneo, Guillermo Graetzer, Nidia Berardi de Aragón, Carlos Berardi, Roberto Castro, Ljërko Spiller, Ernesto Epstein, Mariano Drago, Carlos Suffern, Alicia Terzián, Valdo Sciamarella, Enrique Gerardi, Edgard Willems, and Marguerite Croptier, among others.

Alberto Favero's work is multi-faceted. He is an active performer, songwriter, and a writer and producer of musical theater.

Composition

Alberto Favero is a well-known Argentinean composer of popular music. "Te Quiero" "I Love You" is a heartfelt rendering of a love poem by the Uruguayan master Mario Benedetti. Favero sets the text "Te Quiero" as a ballad that perfectly melds text and melody. Liliana Cangiano has arranged several pieces of Argentinean popular music for choir with great success.

Historical Perspective

Benedetti's works include poems, novels, and tales presented in a clear and expressive manner. He has won international recognition for sincerely dealing with the social, political, and economic problems of Latin America. By setting Mario Benedetti's poem "Te Quiero," Favero makes a bold statement in support of the causes that Benedetti cared and fought for.

Technical Considerations

The ranges for the choral parts encompass an octave and a fourth for both soprano and bass and an octave and a second for alto and tenor; the solos encompass an octave each. There is a textless, harmonically static introduction with smooth interplay in the voice parts. The choral refrains in 4/4 meter are slow, and the harmonic rhythm is slow as well. The solo sections are in 2/2 with a slower pulse; however, the tempo feels faster. The harmonic rhythm of the choral parts is still slow, and the phrases form arch shapes. In the bridges between the solo verses and the choral refrains, there are immediate harmonic climaxes followed by a slight taper to the next sections. The coda is an arch form that builds up and winds down both harmonically and rhythmically.

Stylistic Considerations

"Te Quiero" is a pop ballad later set for choir and soloists; thus, that should color your performance in some aspects, such as the ebb and flow of tempo within and between sections. Tone color and vocal production do not have to be sacrificed due to the skillfully crafted choral arrangement. It is important to consider whether to use standard Castilian Spanish pronunciation or Argentinean Spanish.

Musical Elements

The harmonic language is simple but elegant, and the rhythmic vocabulary contains some syncopation, but is basically simple. The tonality is C Major, and the few accidentals used in the arrangement are well placed for a dramatic effect. Accidentals are most often approached by step in this piece. The bass G-sharp in the bridge between the solo verses and the choral refrains may be problematic; however, it fits into a sequential pattern that eventually solves the problem. Most of the phrases in the 4/4 sections are two measures long. In the solo sections, the choral phrases are four measures long while the soloists sing in two-measure phrases.

Form and Structure

This piece is a strophic song with and introduction, refrains, verses, and a coda.

The introduction begins with four bars that are rhythmically stable divided by a tempo change. The choral refrain section pairs different voice parts from phrase to phrase. A setting of the choral refrain and a solo section join in a repeat to accommodate the text of the poem. The first solo section and the bridge following it are in 2/2. Neither the bridge nor the following choral refrain is repeated. A meter change back to 4/4 and a slower tempo signal the return of the choral refrain. Because the lines of the poem are different, the second solo section repeats with a slight variation in the rhythm and returns to 2/2. The coda is divided into two phrases that seem similar; however, the first phrase is in 4/4 and accelerates, and the second phrase is in 2/2 and slows down.

Text and Translation

Si te quiero es porque sos
mi amor, mi cómplice y todo
y en la calle, codo a codo,
somos mucho más que dos.

Tu manos son mi caricia,
Mis acordes cotidianos
te amo porque tus manos
trabajan por la justicia...

If I adore you it is because you are
my love, my intimate friend, my all;
and in the street, arm in arm,
we are so much more than two.

Your hands are my caress,
my daily affirmations.
I love you because your hands
work for justice...

         —translated by Maria Guinand

Suggested Listening

Musica de Latinoamerica. Schola Cantorum de Caracas. Maria Guinand and Alberto Grau, conductors. (Earthsongs CD-01).

Gala del Dia. The Americas Vocal Ensemble. Nelly Vuksic, conductor. (North South Recordings N/S R 1025).

Additional References and Resources

www.autores.org.ar/Afavero

Contributed by:

G. Mikael Lindström

Repertoire Resource Guide

There Will Be Rest

Frank Ticheli
(b. 1958)

SATB divisi/a cappella
Hinshaw Music, Inc.: HPC-7095
Overall: 4
Vocal: 4
Tonal/Rhythm: 4

Composer

A native of Monroe, Louisiana, Frank Ticheli is professor of composition at the University of Southern California's Thornton School of Music. He received his doctoral and master's degrees in composition from the University of Michigan, where he studied with William Albright, Leslie Bassett, William Bolcom, and George Wilson. From 1991–98, he was composer in residence of the Pacific Symphony Orchestra.

Ticheli may be best known for instrumental music, having had works performed by a number of major international orchestras and wind ensembles including the Philadelphia Orchestra and the Atlanta Symphony. He has received many prestigious awards, including the Charles Ives Scholarship and Goddard Lieberson Fellowship (both from the American Academy of Arts and Letters), First Prize in the Texas Sesquicentennial Orchestral Composition Competition, the Frances and William Schuman Fellowship, and the Ross Lee Finney Award as well as completing frequent summer residencies at the MacDowell Colony and Yaddo. He is also an active conductor and clinician.

Composition

"There Will Be Rest" is a contemporary setting of Sara Teasdale's (1884–1933) poem in which the composer creates a logical structure incorporating tonal and extended harmony, various contrapuntal devices, and lyrical melodies. The tonal and vocal degree of difficulty vary throughout the work. The music ranges from four part homophony in the middle register to sections of imitative polyphony in higher ranges.

The piece begins with the building of a tone cluster, a technique that becomes the work's main melodic motive. This motivic portion is harmonized with a diverging line that comes to rest on a four-note cluster. The melody begins in measure 7, coincident with the first unequivocal tonic and dominant chords. The A section phrases run six, four, and five measures in length with the melody usually in the soprano line. Altos and tenors sing an accompaniment, and basses sing slow chords, which sometimes carry the flavor of the tune.

One of several nice details is that when the tune climbs, the dynamic reaches from *pp* to *mp*. Next, the same verse is repeated with the voice parts inverted and set to much the same tune—but with different trappings. The development section (32–49) ends with two instances of word painting: measures 46 to 47, "holy and low," sound like an organ; and measures 48 to 49, repeating the same text, are low.

The "low" word elides into the B section, a three-voiced imitation over bass E-flat pedal, until measure 54. There, the imitation becomes tenor and bass against alto and soprano using the word "dream" on a cascading A-flat major chord. There are many A-flat major chords throughout under which the basses add a D.

After a slight lift, the tempo picks up, and an area of homophony propels the more hopeful, or perhaps only more resolute text to the words "above me." This word is painted several times in canonic planes of smooth sound before the phrase finishes. At the end, the key abruptly changes to G major.

Historical Perspective

The work is dedicated to the memory of Cole Carsan St. Clair, son of Pacific Symphony Music Director Carl St. Clair. Composer Frank Ticheli calls the dedication "an example of how we as composers can use our gifts to help heal our friends when they are enduring tough times."

"There Will Be Rest" was one of Sara Teasdale's last poems. The musical setting was commissioned by the Pacific Chorale, John Alexander, conductor, and first performed in 1999.

Technical Considerations

The tone clusters and dissonances are not difficult to achieve because Ticheli employs sensible voice leading throughout. Most dissonances are approached and resolved by step or from a consonant harmony. It should be noted that these are only "dissonances" in the theoretical sense of the term. Even the most dissonant chords remain true to the words and are serenely beautiful and colorful.

This piece must be so smooth throughout that articulations are considerable challenges. Consonants must be placed exactly the same way by everyone, or text will disappear and, with it, all sense of the music. Consider the first phrase, "There will be rest." How natural it would be to elongate the "r" and "l," to hiss the "s," and to drop the "t." From the beginning, ask for precise diction. Also, from the very start, instruct singers where and how to place these consonants. It seems counterintuitive, but unified vowels will take care of themselves if the consonants are exact. Practice saying the text a phrase or two at a time, with consonants and breaths precisely placed. It will be best if you demonstrate each phrase first.

The sopranos' F5 and G5 and the basses' A-flat2 and G-flat2 must not sound strained. The triple divisi for the basses and significant areas of divisi for other voices will help you decide whether this piece will work for your ensemble. At the B section, be sure the imitative rising lines emerge from the mix.

Stylistic Considerations

Tempo rubato is specified at the beginning, then further described (e.g., *meno mosso*) in several places. Ticheli advises singers to strive for heartfelt expressiveness.

For the repeat of the first verse, the changing note values provide an opportunity to vary articulations, keeping interest high. If voices singing eighths and dotted quarter notes execute the eighths with a bit of bounce, and use *messa di voce* on the dotted quarter notes, the phrases will never sound boring. Meanwhile, soprano 1 has an ornament, a rising line, and the melody at measure 28. They are the stars of this section; all others are supporting characters.

Use the excellent onomatopoeia in measure 59 to 64 to express the fragility and crystalline nature of that elusive commodity of peace. It would be hard to be too smooth in measures 65–74. Because the composer shifts to G major for the ending phrase, point to it by shifting to a much brighter color, adding breath to keep the diminuendo *al niente* alive through the last measure.

Form and Structure

The form of "There Will Be Rest" is AAB. The tonality shifts from E-flat major to G major.

Text

There will be rest, and sure stars shining
Over the roof-tops crowned with snow,
A reign of rest, serene forgetting,
The music of stillness holy and low.

I will make this world of my devising,
Out of a dream in my lonely mind,
I shall find the crystal of peace,—above me
Stars I shall find.

—Sara Teasdale

Suggested Listening

Nocturne. Pacific Chorale. www. PacificChorale.org.

Contributed by:

Lani Johnson

Repertoire Resource Guide

To Be Sung of a Summer Night on the Water

Frederick Delius
(1862–1934)

SATTBB/a cappella
Boosey & Hawkes, Inc.: 3249
Overall: 4
Vocal: 4
Tonal/Rhythm: 5

Composer

Frederick Delius was born in Bradford, Yorkshire, to a wealthy family. His father owned a wool company and hoped his son would join his business; unlike many composers' fathers, however, he did not attempt to forbid his son's pursuit of music and art.

In 1884, the young Delius persuaded his father to purchase an orange plantation in Florida, which he was to manage. While in Florida, Delius met American organist Thomas F. Ward, who gave him instruction in music theory. In 1885, having decided not to continue in the orange business, Delius moved to Danville, Virginia, to be a music teacher. In 1886, he moved back to Europe and enrolled in the Leipzig Conservatory. There, he learned the music of Richard Wagner; the continuous melodic lines and thematic development that characterize Wagner's works are prevalent in Delius' compositions. He moved to Paris in 1888 and remained in France for the rest of his life. Blindness and paralysis, the effects of a syphilitic infection he developed during his time in America, plagued the last decades of his life. The great conductor Sir Thomas Beecham championed Delius' music, but his works are not often performed today.

Composition

This composition falls into a select category of choral repertoire in that it has no words. However, this piece can be considered a madrigal—the effect of the "uh" syllable denoted in the performance notes is purely programmatic. This piece can be quite effective as a mood piece in concerts, or would fit very well into a program of "night music."

In 1932, Eric Fenby transcribed the two movements of this piece for string orchestra at the request of violinist Albert Sammons, who premiered Delius's Violin Concerto in 1919. By 1932, however, Delius was too ill to compose and asked his assistant Fenby to make an arrangement of this vocal piece for string orchestra. The transcription is entitled *Two Aquarelles* and preserves the tenderness and beauty of the original vocal work.

The music is in two movements, the first for SATTBB choir and the second for the same choir with a tenor solo.

Historical Perspective

Delius composed "To Be Sung of a Summer Night on the Water" in 1917 for the Oriana Madrigal Society, conducted by C. Kennedy Scott. The first performance was in London at the Aeolian Hall on June 28, 1921. Despite all the atonal music written in Europe at this time, Delius' harmonic practices never stretched beyond the practices of the late Romantics. It is more accurate to group Delius with his English contemporaries Holst, Vaughan Williams, and Walton than to compare him with Stravinsky, Schoenberg, or Webern.

Technical Considerations

The performance note at the bottom of the first page of the score indicates that the choir should "Sing on vowel 'uh' (as in "love") with a very loose mouth, almost closed in the pianissimo, but which should gradually be opened or shut according as more or less tone is wanted. Breath should be taken only at the sign ' ' ' if possible, and quietly and quickly to preserve the legato."

Choir directors should take this direction of "uh" (as in "love") with a grain of salt. It is important to remember that British vowels are quite different from American vowels. American singers, when told to sing "uh" will produce a sound that is dark and caught "back" in their jowls. Therefore, the conductor should feel free to explore the possibilities of mixing the sounds "oo" and "ah" into the prescribed "uh." The resultant sound of the choir will reflect a greater variance of color and sound more in tune.

Because this piece is essentially an exploration of sound, it is important to maintain the legato phrasings Delius indicated. This can be quite difficult if the singers are inexperienced in singing long musical lines or if the group is small in number. The lack of *sostenuto* will cause this piece to be unsuccessful in performances.

Stylistic Considerations

Because this is British music, one should take the sounds of British choirs into account. This is not to say that women in choirs need to sing with a "straight-tone" quality. (In fact, this would be counterproductive.) However, it is important to remember that British music requires "bright-high-forward" resonance for optimal success. These keywords will help the choir find the luscious colors of Delius' harmonies, and help with intonation in this highly chromatic *a cappella* piece.

Musical Elements

The music of "To Be Sung of a Summer Night on the Water" is extremely chromatic, and does present some vocally challenging parts (specifically for tenor 1 and soprano). Descending chromatic lines pervade the first movement of the piece; this may be challenging for a less mature choir. Singers should be encouraged to picture very small descending intervals and larger ascending ones. The second movement is equally as challenging.

Form and Structure

This is a two-movement, textless piece for choir and tenor solo.

Suggested Listening

The Complete Part Songs. Elysuan Singers. Matthew Greenall, conductor. (Continuum CCD 1054).

A Delius Farewell. Royal Choral Society. Sir Malcolm Sargeant. (EMI CDM 7 69534 2).

Contributed by:

Matthew W. Mehaffey
Anthony Reeves

Repertoire Resource Guide

Two Hymns to the Mother of God

John Tavener
(b. 1944)

SATB divisi/a cappella
Chester Music Ltd.: CH55776
Overall: 4
Vocal: 4
Tonal/Rhythm: 4

Composer

Twentieth-century composer John Tavener should be distinguished from the outset from English Renaissance composer John Taverner (ca. 1490–1545). Both are English composers who composed many religious works, but the similarities end there. Tavener is one of a handful of "mystical minimalist" composers who have come to the forefront of art music in the early twenty-first century. Tavener, along with Arvo Pärt, Henryk Górecki, and James MacMillan have found a niche, and many say their works soothe the spirit.

Tavener's early musical influence was Igor Stravinsky, but since 1970 he has developed a style that is truly his own. He is greatly influenced by his belief in the teachings of the Russian Orthodox Church, of which he became a member in 1977. Many of his compositions since this time owe a great deal to his faith.

Tavener often generates form via techniques such as canon or palindrome. His music was brought to the world stage when his "Song for Athene" was performed at the funeral of Princess Diana. He was knighted by Queen Elizabeth II at the 2000 New Year honours.

Composition

Two Hymns to the Mother of God is divided into two separate movements: "A Hymn to the Mother of God," and "Hymn for the Dormition of the Mother of God."

The two pieces can be performed as a set or individually. These pieces were written in 1985 in memory of the composer's mother, not commissioned, and were first performed by the Winchester Cathedral Choir under the direction of Martin Neary.

Historical Perspective

There is not much to be said about historical perspective as these pieces are relatively modern. However, it is interesting to note that Tavener composed these pieces after his conversion to Russian Orthodoxy. The composer's words provide a bit of pertinent insight: "These short pieces can be sung by cathedral choirs and amateur choirs everywhere, and although it is the Orthodox Church which has inspired them, the Western Church sings them. It is humbling for me and at the same time a great honour, to give what I am able to the Western Church, having drunk deeply from the eternal depths of the one true Orthodox Church."

The first of the two pieces, "A Hymn to the Mother of God," uses a text from the Liturgy of St. Basil (an ancient Byzantine Liturgy). The second movement, "Hymn for the Dormition of the Mother of God," is drawn from the source of the same name, which speaks of the death and assumption of Mary.

Stylistic Considerations

Both of these pieces were inspired by a religion that places great emphasis on mysticism and wonder. The singers need to understand a little bit about the deep convictions that Tavener has. These pieces should be approached will a very clear, simple mindset. Rubato and outward expressiveness could ruin the performance.

These pieces will work best with "live" acoustics. In both pieces, Tavener inserts rests with fermatas at the end of each section. These rests are meant to serve as aural clearings for the audience. If you perform this piece in a large cathedral, you will need to make these rests longer. Conversely, if you perform in a less resonant space, you should make the rests shorter.

Musical Elements

The music to "A Hymn to the Mother of God" employs the technique of canon. Tavener divides the performing forces into two choirs; the second choir follows the first in exact repetition at a distance of three beats. The combination of the two choirs yields very full, rich harmonies. It would be most efficient to have all of the singers learn the Choir I part together; the music is not very difficult. After they can sing the Choir I part perfectly, move on to having the two choirs sing in canon.

The music to "Hymn for the Dormition of the Mother of God" is based on Russian chant. The tenors present the melody in its entirety under a three-note chord sung by the basses. It is possible to have just tenor 1 sing the chant and have tenor 2 sing the top bass note. The second section uses the same text but in three part harmony (SAB). Again, it is possible to divide the tenors. Have tenor 1 sing with the alto and tenor 2 sing the bass part.

This section shows one of Tavener's favorite compositional devices: inversion. The bass part is an exact inversion of the soprano part; that is, if the soprano part ascends a whole step, the bass descends a whole step; if the soprano part goes down a minor third, the bass goes up a minor third. The alto part sings in parallel motion with the soprano part. Teach the soprano and alto parts together, and rehearse the basses separately until the parts have been mastered. The third section, again using the same text, is for full choir and features parallel motion. The *pp* marking is of paramount importance. The dynamic coupled with parallel motion makes for a stunning effect.

Form and Structure

The first piece is an exact canon with the two choirs singing at a distance of three beats and is in ABA form. The second movement is in AA'A" form. (The same melody is used in all three sections.) Tavener employs different compositional techniques in each section to provide variations on the same melody and text.

Suggested Listening

The John Tavener Collection. (Decca Classics 475 096-2 DH).

Sacred Music of John Tavener. Choir of St. George's Chapel. Windsor College. Christopher Robinson, conductor. (Hyperion Records CDA66464).

Additional Reference and Resources

Haydon, Geoffrey. *John Tavener: Glimpse of Paradise.* London: Victor Gollancz. 1995.

Tavener, John. *Music of Silence.* Brian Keeble, editor. London: Faber and Faber. 1999.

Contributed by:

Matthew W. Mehaffey

Repertoire Resource Guide

Va, pensiero
(Chorus of the Hebrew Slaves)

Giuseppe Verdi
(1813–1901)

SSATTB/keyboard
Warner Bros. Publications: LG 52493
Level: 4
Vocal: 5
Tonal/Rhythm: 3

Composer

Giuseppe Verdi was born in October 1813 near Parma (the same year as Richard Wagner). The son of tavern keepers, Verdi began to study music at age three with the village organist, and succeeded him in his job at age nine in 1822 when the older man died. In 1823, Verdi was sent to school in Busetto and eventually was patronized by a wealthy merchant, Antonio Barezzi. In 1832, Verdi moved to Milan but was denied admission to the Conservatory there; instead, he became a private pupil of Vincenzo Lavigna, an opera composer and former *maestro al cembalo* at La Scala. Verdi became the civic music teacher and orchestral conductor in Busseto in 1836 and married Barezzi's daughter, Margherita, the same year.

Verdi moved to Milan in 1839, the year his first opera (*Oberto*) was produced at La Scala. Verdi traveled widely in connection with his compositions, including trips to London, Brussels, and Paris. Verdi developed his own style, which contrasted greatly with that of his contemporary German counterpart, Wagner. As a composer, Verdi wrote operas (including *Nabucco*, the source of this chorus), choral works, songs and vocal trios, and a few instrumental pieces. He died in Milan on January 27, 1901.

Composition

"Va, Pensiero" is from Verdi's opera *Nabucco*, a four-act *drama lirico* composed between 1839 and 1841; its first performance was in Milan at La Scala on March 9, 1842.

Historical Perspective

In 1838 and 1839, Verdi's two children died, and his wife died during the composition of *Un giorno di regno*, which was premiered in September 1840. In desperate grief, Verdi decided to give up music. He soon began composing again, however, and went to work on Temistocle Solera's libretto, *Nabucodonosor*. Robert Donington writes that *Nabucco* is in the "international Parisian style" and was composed under the influence of Rosinni. *Nabucco* is a setting of the Old Testament story of the Babylonian captivity of the Jews, ca. 586 B.C.E. The Chorus of the Hebrew Slaves comes just before the end of Act III. It is a paraphrase of Psalm 137, sung by Israelites lamenting the loss of their homeland. The Italians saw political correlations with their own situation and adopted this chorus as "the anthem of Italian patriotism." The crowd at Verdi's funeral sang the chorus spontaneously.

Technical Considerations

One will need a good pianist to perform this chorus because it uses a piano reduction of Verdi's orchestration. The beginning of the chorus (through measure 28) calls for unison singing, but much of the singing from that point on is six-part. Typical of Verdi's music, this chorus calls for an enormous range of singing and emotion. His first marking for the choir, for example, is *cantabile*, and their first entrance is **pp**. Soon, however, they are singing at **ff**. In addition, Verdi marked in various accents and other articulations.

Healthy singing should be the aim for this chorus. High, forward resonance and ample breath support are absolute necessities. Be certain that, in the soft sections, the choir does not go "off the breath" (detach their tone from vocal support) and that in the loud sections they do not bellow. For the *sotto voce* sections in particular, ensure that the choir maintains all the components of good forte singing. Work on breath support exercises, and do much humming for forward resonance. (When humming, be sure the choir keeps open space between their back teeth!) Work on *martellato* technique for the accented sections.

Finally, do not underestimate the amount of time needed to work on the unison sections. Good unison singing can be hard to accomplish, but attention to it will help both the unison and multi-part sections of this piece. Insist on careful listening, work to match vowel sounds, and be sure the choir is watching the conductor.

Stylistic Considerations

This is operatic music—full of drama and emotion. As long as the choir sings properly, it would be hard to overdo the drama inherent in the piece. Work to explore the widest dynamic spectrum the choir can accomplish for long phrases, and to realize all the markings Verdi put in the score (including the articulatory rests found in several places, for example, in measures 30–31).

Musical Elements

The chorus opens with an eleven-measure chromatic instrumental fanfare leading to the C-sharp major chord in measure 10 that sets up the key of F-sharp major at the chorus entry in measure 12 (measure 11 is all rest). The tonality remains essentially F-sharp major for the rest of the piece. Section B uses the typical "boom-chick" accompaniment one associates with nineteenth-century opera arias. Section C sets a six-part choir over a more elaborate arpeggiated accompaniment figure, one also commonly found in opera of this era. Section D returns to unison choral singing and features a yet more complex accompaniment (but still in the same pattern). Section E returns to six-part choral texture for the coda. As the chorus ends, the instrumental figures are greatly simplified and feature a written-in *rallentando* to the end. Further slowing is not likely to be helpful.

Form and Structure

SECTION	MEASURE	EVENT AND SCORING
A	1–11	Introduction
B	12–28	Unison choir
C	29–40	Six-part chorus
D	41–48	Unison choir
E	48–51	Choral and instrumental coda

Text and Translation

Va, pensiero, sull'ali dorate'
Va, ti posa sui clivi, sui colli,
Ove olezzano tepide e molli
L'aure dolci del suolo natal!
Del Giordano le rive saluta,
Di Sionne le torri atterrate.
Oh, mia patria sì bella e perduta!
Oh, membranza sì cara e fatal!

Arpa d'or dei fatidici vati,
Perché muta dal salice pendi?
Le memorie nel petto raccendi,
Ci favella del tempo che fu!
O simile di Solima ai fati
Traggi un suono di crudo lamento,
O t'ispiri il Signore un concento
Che ne infonda al partire virtù!

Fly, thought, on wings of gold;
Go settle upon the slopes and the hills,
Where, soft and mild, the sweet airs
Of our native land smell fragrant!
Greet the banks of the Jordan
And Zion's toppled towers.
Oh, my country so lovely and lost!
Oh, remembrance so dear and fraught with despair!

Golden harp of the prophetic seers,
Why dost thou hang mute upon the willow?
Rekindle our bosom's memories,
And speak of times gone by!
Mindful of the fate of Jerusalem, either give forth an air of sad lamentation,
Or else let the Lord imbue us
With fortitude to bear our sufferings!

Additional Reference and Resources

Donington, Robert. *The Opera*. New York: Harcourt Brace Jovanovich, Inc.
    1978.

Contributed by:

Anthony Reeves

Repertoire Resource Guide

Ave Maria, Op. 12

Johannes Brahms
(1833–1897)

SSAA/keyboard
C F Peters Corporation: 66136
Overall: 4
Vocal: 4
Tonal/Rhythm: 4

Composer

Johannes Brahms was born in Hamburg, Germany, to a poor family. Brahms studied piano from a young age and began giving lessons at the age of twelve. At this point, he also began playing in taverns and seedy bars around Hamburg.

His renown as a composer came in 1852 when composer Robert Schumann wrote of Brahms' genius in his publication *Neue Zeitschrift für Musik*. Brahms' friendship with Schumann continued until Schumann's death in 1856. Brahms maintained a lifelong friendship with Clara Schumann; many scholars believe that Brahms felt his love for Clara was unrequited. Brahms never married.

In the 1860s Brahms traveled frequently between Hamburg and Vienna and finally settled in Vienna in 1868. Brahms's output for choir is prodigious. He wrote large choral orchestral pieces, choral pieces with piano accompaniment, *a cappella* choral part songs, and chamber-music style choral songs. He is also famous for his piano music and his symphonies. Brahms composed up through the last year of his life. He died in Vienna of liver cancer in 1897.

Composition

"Ave Maria" is a motet-like setting of the traditional Roman Catholic prayer. Brahms scored the piece for SSAA choir and orchestra or organ. Countless composers in every historical period have set "Ave Maria." Other Romantic composers who set the prayer include Verdi and Bruckner.

Historical Perspective

Brahms composed "Ave Maria" in 1858 and it was published 1860–61. The first performance was in Hamburg on December 2, 1859, the same year in which he founded an amateur women's choir, the Hamburger Frauenchor. Brahms conducted the group for three years, until his first trip to Vienna in 1862.

Technical Considerations

Brahms scored this piece for SSAA choir and orchestra or organ. The orchestra is traditional: two flutes, two oboes, two clarinets, two bassoons, two horns, and strings. Brahms supplied an organ part, which could be used instead of the orchestra. (His manuscript carries the direction, next to the organ part, *statt des Orchesters*.) In the absence of orchestra or organ, the piano does work well, but you will need a good pianist to play with the appropriate style and sensitivity.

The music calls for legato articulations, and the conductor should work for an extremely resonant, high, and forward tone. Brahms marked in specific dynamics, including crescendos and diminuendos, and the choir will need firm breath support as well as warm resonance to accomplish his directions.

Stylistic Considerations

"Ave Maria" is a setting of a traditional Catholic prayer of devotion to the Blessed Virgin Mary. Brahms' setting includes the entire text without extraneous additions and is a good choice for either liturgical or concert use. The use of rubato in this music is quite appropriate, especially when used discreetly to clarify the formal aspects of the music (e.g., a slight *rallentando* at measure 21 to emphasize the repeat of the A section beginning at measure 22, which should be *a tempo*). Remember, a little goes a long way, and less is more!

Musical Elements/Form and Structure

The form may be described as shown in the chart below, and it is clearly connected to the text. Brahms predictably used a rich, Romantic harmonic palate. The tonalities indicated are simply predominant harmonies within a section. It would be a gross oversimplification to say this piece is "in F major"; in fact, in every section Brahms used many accidentals, altering chords, tonalities, and modalities. This is a basic stylistic trait of his music.

Knowing this has an effect on the way the piece should be taught. Each individual section is not difficult to learn because the music is largely diatonic; it is the migration between tonal centers that will confuse singers. Locate where in phrases and sections the accidentals begin to change the tonality; focus on these sections, and be sure that the singers understand how Brahms alters the music from the prevailing tonality. This will make singers aware of where they need to listen more carefully.

SECTION	MEASURE	EVENT AND SCORING
A	1–21	"Ave Maria...Dominus tecum"; predominantly F major; opening, greeting Mary
A'	22–42	"Ave Maria...Dominus tecum"; F major; repeats opening, end transitions to A minor
B	43–59	"Benedicta...Jesus"; A minor; third relations, rich harmonies; C major for the first citation of the name "Jesus"
C	60–92	"Sancta Maria...nobis"; F major; *a capella* with octave C's leading into CMm^7 chord for return to F major at m. 68
Coda	92–101	"Sancta Maria, ora pro nobis"; F major; Cadence is dovetailed; m. 92 is the resolution of the dominant seventh chord that ends the previous section and also is the beginning of the coda; features theme from section A

Text and Translation

Ave Maria, gratia plena, Dominus tecum.
Benedicta tu in mulieribus,
et benedictus fructus ventris tui, Iesus.
Sancta Maria, ora pro nobis.
Amen.

Hail Mary, full of grace, the Lord is with thee.
Blessed art thou amongst women,
and blessed is the fruit of thy womb, Jesus.
Holy Mary, pray for us.
Amen.

Suggested Listening

Johannes Brahms' Works for Chorus and Orchestra. Danish National Choir. Gerd Albrecht, conductor. (Chandos CHAN 10165).

Brahms Motets. Corydon Singers. Matthew Best, conductor. (Hyperion CD66389).

Contributed by:

Anthony Reeves

Repertoire Resource Guide

Heaven-Haven
(A Nun Takes the Veil)

Samuel Barber
(1910–1981)

SSAA or SATB/a cappella
G. Schirmer, Inc.: SSAA=50308900, SATB=50308880
Overall: 4
Vocal: 4
Tonal/Rhythm: 4

Composer

Samuel Barber was born in West Chester, Pennsylvania, into a musical family. Barber began composing at the age of seven. He entered the Curtis Institute in 1924 as part of its first class, where he studied voice, composition, piano, and conducting. By the time Barber graduated from Curtis, he was already established as a composer, but it was the 1938 performance by Toscanini of his Adagio for Strings that brought him widespread fame. He won two Pulitzer Prizes (for the opera *Vanessa* in 1958 and his Piano Concerto in 1962), and although his music was never on the cutting edge, a high percentage of Barber's compositions have entered the standard repertoire, a remarkable feat for an American composer.

Composition

This work was published originally as part of *Four Songs*, Op. 13, for soprano and piano, which were all composed between 1937 and 1940. The musicality of the text is typical of the poet Gerald Manley Hopkins (1844–1889), who was a self-taught musician and composer. The successful reception of this song

430

and "Sure on This Shining Night" led Barber to compose choral settings of the two songs more than thirty years after their original publication.

Historical Perspective

Barber was an American composer who immersed himself in the art music of Europe. Composed in the first half of the twentieth century, his art is a synthesis of the expanded chromaticism of the late Romantic period and the restraint and balance of the Classical period. His interest in vocal music led him to be a part of the American quest for a truly native operatic language, and he made great contributions to the development of the American art song. "Heaven-Haven" contributed to his fame as a composer of lyrical songs.

Technical Considerations

There are few specific technical difficulties associated with this piece. The tempo is slow, so the dotted rhythms and the shifting meter should pose little difficulty. The low alto part has regular low G's, but the two low F's can be sung an octave higher. Otherwise, none of the vocal ranges is extreme. The most demanding technical challenge is found in the delicacy of the harmonies, which shift slowly and to sometimes remote locations. The emotive content of this work is carried almost entirely in these intimate harmonic shifts, which require the utmost sensitivity to be effective.

Stylistic Considerations

The text of the poem speaks in the first person of a request for a place of shelter from the harsh outside world. This intimate appeal is reflected in Barber's music by the directness of the setting and the sensitivity of the underlying harmonies. Rising to forte only briefly, the piece is largely quiet and intense, mirroring the private nature of the poetic utterance. Stylistically, the delicate harmonies and sustained melodic lines must evoke the intimacy and immediacy of the text for an effective performance.

Musical Elements

The work begins and ends on a D major chord, but it does not feel rooted in D major. The meanderings of the harmonies seem dictated entirely by the movements of the text, although the final resolution to D major feels like an arrival to a place of serenity, if not of final stability. The work is almost entirely homophonic, reinforcing the singular point of view of the poem. The melody lines are mostly stepwise with no awkward leaps or intervals. Though the meter shifts several times, the tempo is so slow that the overall pulse is not disrupted.

Form and Structure

The piece is quite brief and through-composed. A recurring harmonic dissonance ends the first half (measure 8) and closes the piece, and the final statement is resolved to a D major chord. Parts of the opening harmonic sequence reappear at the beginning of the second half of the piece, but there are no overt structural cues that divide the piece into sections or establish strong connections between parts.

Text

I have desired to go
Where springs not fail,
To fields where flies no sharp and sided hail
And a few lilies blow.

And I have asked to be
Where no storms come,
Where the green swell is in the havens dumb,
And out of the swing of the sea.

—Gerald Manley Hopkins

Suggested Listening

Samuel Barber Choral and Organ Works. Cambridge University Choir. Tim Brown, conductor. (Gild Music GMCD 7145).

Contributed by:

Thomas Cunningham

Repertoire Resource Guide

Rise Up, My Love, My Fair One

Imant Raminsh
(b. 1943)

SA divisi/viola and piano
Boosey & Hawkes, Inc.: OCTB7066
Overall: 4
Vocal: 4
Tonal/Rhythm: 4

Composer

Imant Raminsh was born in Ventspils, Latvia, but he has lived in Canada since 1948. He studied violin at the Royal Conservatory of Toronto and the University of Toronto and studied composition, violin, and conducting at the Akademie Mozarteum in Salzburg. The founding conductor of the Prince George Symphony, the Youth Symphony of the Okanagan, the NOVA Children's Choir, and the AURA Chamber Choir, Raminsh also established the music department at the College of New Caledonia in Prince George, British Columbia.

He is currently the principal violinist of the Okanagan Symphony Orchestra. During the summers, Raminsh pursues his interests in geology and biology as a naturalist in the provincial parks of British Columbia.

Composition

This work is a setting of a small section of the Song of Solomon for two-part treble voices, viola, and piano; the voices do divide into four parts on occasion. Written in 1997, it is one of Raminsh's most recent works, commissioned by the Lyons Township High School Treble Choir of La Grange, Illinois. The work does not fall easily into a particular genre; the text is biblical, but the sentiments are often interpreted in a secular manner. The sensuous nature of Raminsh's setting seems to support a reading of the text as a love poem rather than a solely religious utterance.

Historical Perspective

The Song of Solomon has long served as a source of inspiration for composers. Palestrina wrote more than thirty motets using various portions of this text, and settings of this particular verse continue to be popular. The poem itself, long considered a sacred allegory depicting the relationship of God and Israel or that of Christ and his church, is now usually interpreted in a secular setting as a love poem, at times highly erotic. This verse contains the words the woman of the poem imagines her lover to speak to her through her open window.

Technical Considerations

"Rise Up, My Love, My Fair One" offers a moderate amount of technical difficulty. There is frequent rhythmic independence of lines, often pitting four or two beats against three, either between two vocal lines or a vocal line and an instrumental line. There are shifts of meter, including long sections in 9/8, but the rhythms are otherwise straightforward, moving in flowing eighth notes. The piece calls for a wide range, including a B-flat5 in the highest treble part; the lowest treble part only descends to B-flat3. The extended melodic lines are well-suited to a natural text declamation. The work is somewhat chromatic, with several changes of key, and there is frequent division of the two treble parts into three and four parts, though the division is more frequent in the lower part.

Stylistic Considerations

The work is comprised principally of extended, flowing phrases with gentle crescendos and decrescendos. There is a subtle interplay between the voices and the instruments, especially with the solo viola, which often acts as another vocal line, carrying the same melodic material. The delicacy of the scoring and voicing (such as in the "turtledove" theme) and the careful tempo changes necessitate great attention to detail in the preparation of this piece. The sound is in general lush, full, and lyrical, with a dynamic range dominated by piano and mezzo piano.

Musical Elements

This work offers frequent shifts of key, some dramatic, but the musical material of each section never drifts too far from the home key. The harmony features frequent suspensions and added tones, with the viola frequently in the same range as the voices, adding further color to the harmony. There are several meter changes, but the pulse is fairly constant and without sudden changes. The work is largely two- and three-part, but there are some sections in four parts and one five-part chord.

Form and Structure

This piece breaks into clear sections based on the changing text. Each section also has its own key area.

MEASURE	EVENT AND SCORING
1–26	"Rise up, my love"; E-flat major
27–34	"For lo, the winter is past"; G-flat major
34–40	"The flowers appear on the earth"; A major
41–54	"And the voice of the turtle-dove"; B-flat major
55–65	"Arise my love"; E-flat major
65–79	"O my love"; B major
80–90	"For sweet is thy voice"; E-flat major
91–103	Instrumental interlude; E-flat major
104–117	Coda; E-flat major

The "Arise my love" section in E-flat recalls the opening bars, as do the instrumental interlude and the coda, providing points of articulated overall structure and marking returns to the original meter and texture. The two climaxes each occur just before these returns, the first at the end on the "And the voice of the turtle-dove" section and the second at the end of the "For sweet is thy voice" section.

Text

Rise up, my love, my fair one, and come away,
For lo, the winter is past, the rain is over and gone,
The flowers appear on the earth,
The time of the singing of birds has come,
And the voice of the turtle-dove is heard in our land.
Arise, my love, my fair one, and come away.
O my love, who art in the clefts of the rock,
O my love, in the secret places of the stairs,
Let me see thy countenance, let me hear thy voice,
For sweet is thy voice and thy countenance is comely.
O rise up, my love, my fair one, and come away.

Contributed by:

Thomas Cunningham

Repertoire Resource Guide

Vier Gesänge für Frauenchor, Op. 17

Johannes Brahms
(1833–1897)

SSA/two horns and harp
Peters Music Publishers: 6617
Overall: 4
Vocal: 4
Tonal/Rhythm: 4

Composer

Johannes Brahms was born in Hamburg, Germany, into a poor family. Brahms studied piano from a young age; he began giving lessons at the age of twelve. At this point, he also began playing in taverns and seedy bars around Hamburg.

His renown as a composer came in 1852 when composer Robert Schumann wrote of Brahms' genius in his publication *Neue Zeitschrift für Musik*. Brahms' friendship with Schumann continued until Schumann's death in 1856. Brahms maintained a lifelong friendship with Clara Schumann; many scholars believe that Brahms felt his love for Clara was unrequited. Brahms never married.

In the 1860s Brahms traveled frequently between Hamburg and Vienna and finally settled in Vienna in 1868. Brahms output for choir is prodigious. He wrote large choral-orchestral pieces, choral pieces with piano accompaniment, *a cappella* choral part songs, and chamber-music style choral songs. He is also famous for his piano music and his symphonies. Brahms composed up through the last year of his life. He died in Vienna in 1897.

Composition

Brahms conceived *Vier Gesänge für Frauenchor, zwei Hörner und Harfe* (Four Songs for Women's Chorus, Two Horns and Harp) while he was living in Detmold in 1859. It was composed in 1860 and finally published in 1862. The four movements are all settings of laments. The texts are by Friedrich Ruperti, William Shakespeare, Joseph von Eichendorff, and James MacPherson ("Ossian").

Historical Perspective

In 1859, Brahms settled in Hamburg, the city of his birth. Upon his arrival, he established a women's choir called the Hamburger Frauenchor. Brahms took this choir very seriously and held them to the highest standards. Members of this choir included Clara Schumann and her eldest daughter, Marie. The first three movements of *Vier Gesänge* were premiered by this group on May 2, 1860. The first complete performance came during a Clara Schumann concert on January 12, 1861.

Technical Considerations

This piece is not appropriate for very young singers because the music requires great range, grit, and power in all of the voices.

Rhythmic precision is very important for this piece to be successful. Brahms uses many different rhythms throughout; be sure that the singers perform the written rhythms exactly. Make a distinction between eighth note triplets and dotted eighth-sixteenth notes. The fourth movement contains sections that require the choir to perform duple rhythm against the triple rhythm of the harp.

Stylistic Considerations

Brahms was a master at weaving styles together. *Vier Gesänge* highlights his ability to fuse Classical and Romantic styles. The works are Classical in their use of form but reflect the Romantic ideals in the use of instrumentation and expressive considerations.

The music requires the singers to produce a wide range of dynamic shadings. It is important for singers to exaggerate the dynamics to achieve the desired effect.

The use of rubato is not only appropriate, but necessary. Subtle changes in tempo will augment the expressiveness of the texts and the voices. Despite its appropriateness, rubato can also destroy a piece; remember, whenever you slow the tempo, you must pay back the time you stole with a slight increase of tempo either before or after the slowing.

Musical Elements

The choice of accompanying instruments is based on the texts; movements 1 and 4 speak of horns and harps.

Form and Structure

The four movements of this piece are unrelated to each other. However, they all use the same accompanimental forces and are all settings of laments.

Movement 1 depicts mourning over the loss of a lover and the loss of all dreams and joy of which the resounding refrain of the harp is a reminder. This strophic movement is full of expansive phrases. The choral parts are very homophonic.

The second movement provides a nice contrast to the first movement. This strophic movement, a translated setting of a portion of Shakespeare's *Twelfth Night*, uses shorter motifs.

Brahms continues to use strophic form in the third movement. The homophonic texture of the choral parts is offset by running sixteenth notes in the harp. Mary Breden writes, "The unvaried accompaniment pattern played by the harp, perhaps portrays the urgency of emotion felt by the gardener who realizes the futile nature of loving one above him in class. Each verse concludes with a sudden outburst of vocal polyphonic activity as if the emotions are no longer restrainable."

The final movement is the most complex of the set. The long poem speaks of the heroes and heroines of ancient Ireland. Brahms abandons the strophic form for an A–B–A–Coda form. This movement sees the only expansion to four-part writing.

Text and Translation

No. 1, Es tönt ein voller Harfenklang
        —Friedrich Ruperti

Es tönt ein voller Harfenklang,
Den Lieb und Sehnsucht schwellen,
Er dringt zum Herzen tief und bang,
Und lässt das Auge quellen...

A full harp sound rings forth,
Increasing love and longing;
It pierces deep into the frightened heart
And makes the eyes overflow...

No. 2, Lied von Shakespeare
—Song from Shakespeare

Komm herbei, komm herbei, Tod!
Und versenk in Zypressen den Leib.
Lass mich frei, lass mich frei, Not!
Mich erschlägt ein holdseliges Weib.
Mit Rosmarin mein Leichenhemd,
O betellt es!
Ob Lieb ans Herz mir tödlich kommt,
Treu halt es…

Come away, come away death,
And in sad cypress let me be laid;
Fly away, fly away, breath;
I am slain by a fair cruel maid.
My shroud of white, stuck all with yew,
O prepare it!
My part of death, no one so true
Did share it…

No. 3, Der Gärtner (The Gardener)
—Joseph von Eichendorff

Wohin ich geh' und schaue,
In Feld und Wald und Tal,
Vom Berg hinab in die Aue:
Viel schöne, hohe Fraue,
Grüss ich dich tausendmal…

Wherever I go and look,
In field and forest and valley,
From the mountain down to the meadow,
Most beautiful, noble lady,
I greet you a thousand times…

No. 4, Gesang aus Fingal (Song from Fingal)
—James MacPherson

Wein an den Felsen der brausenden Winde,
Weine, o Mächen von Inistore!
Beug' über die Wogen dein shcönes Haupt,
Lieblicher du als der Geist der Berge,
Wenn er um mittag in einem Sonnenstrahl
Über das Scheigen von Morven fährt…

Weep on the rock of the raging winds,
O maid of Inistore!
Bend thy fair head over the waves,
Thou lovelier than the ghost of the hills,
When it moves, in a sunbeam at noon
Over the silence of the Morven...

—translations all by Ron Jeffers

Suggested Listening

Lieder und Gesange: Secular Choral Songs. RIAS-Kammerchor. Marcus Creed, director. (Harmonia Mundi 901592).

Additional Reference and Resources

Breden, Mary. "Classic Beauty and Romantic Flair in Brahms' *Vier Gesänge für Frauenchor, zwei Hörner und Harfe.*" *The Choral Journal.* Vol. 31, no 5. December 1990. 35–43.

Weidensaul, Jane B. "Notes on the *Four Songs for Women's Chorus, Two Horns, and Harp* (Op. 17) by Johannes Brahms." *American Harp Journal.* Winter 1983. Vol. 9, No. 2. 32–37.

Contributed by:

Matthew W. Mehaffey

Repertoire Resource Guide

Absalon, fili mi

Josquin Desprez
(ca. 1440–1521)

TTBB/a cappella
Broude Brothers Limited: CR 38
Overall: 4
Vocal: 4
Tonal/Rhythm: 4

Composer

Josquin Desprez was one of the most prolific composers of the Renaissance. Scholars believe he was born in Picardy, France, ca. 1440. Very little is known about his youth; the earliest primary evidence is a 1459 notice that lists Josquin as a singer at Milan Cathedral. In 1474, he was a singer in the chapel of Duke Galeazzo Maria Sforza in Milan. Josquin probably went to work for King René of Anjou in 1477 and was sent to the king's duchy of Bar in 1478.

Josquin traveled widely and worked in numerous places. He may have worked for King Louis XII from 1501 until 1503, and we know he was *maestro di cappella* at the Court of Ferrara in 1503. By 1508, Josquin was a cleric at Notre Dame Cathedral in Condé-sur-Escaut, Hainaut, France. Apparently he remained there the rest of his life. He died in Condé on August 27, 1521.

Josquin's musical output is impressive, including about twenty masses, more than one hundred motets, and around seventy-five secular works (mostly French *chansons*, but also pieces in Italian and a few instrumental works).

Composition

"Absalon, fili mi" is a motet. Motets originated at the end twelfth century at Notre Dame Cathedral in Paris; they were a "descendant" or embellishment of chant. Throughout the thirteenth and fourteenth centuries, the motet underwent considerable development. The early period of the motet is generally agreed to be ca. 1200–1450. Josquin was a pivotal figure in the development of the Renaissance motet of ca. 1450–1600; it is noteworthy that Josquin was born ca. 1440.

Renaissance motets are typically polyphonic settings of sacred Latin texts. While the medieval motet was almost always a setting of a liturgical text, Renaissance composers began to set biblical texts. "Absalon, fili mi," for example, is a setting of 2 Kings 18:33.

Historical Perspective

Absalon was King David's third son; his mother was Maacha. In his youth, Absalon was supposedly beautiful, and as he grew he became increasingly ambitious to become the heir to his father's throne. After killing one of his older brothers, he became increasingly alienated from King David. Eventually, he garnered enough support and followers that he declared himself King of Hebron (David's kingdom), resulting in the flight of David and his followers. A great battle that supposedly resulted in the deaths of 20,000 men was eventually fought in the forest of Ephraim, with David's army being victorious. Although David had ordered that Absalon be spared, he was killed during the battle. "Absalon, fili mi" is a setting of King David's lament upon hearing of the death of his son.

We believe Josquin wrote this motet upon the death of one of his patron's sons ca. 1500. Three manuscripts from the time exist, of which the best is arguably the one in the British library.

Technical Considerations

In this motet for four voices, Josquin used low tessituras, perhaps to reflect David's grief. The highest note sung by the superius is A-flat4; the lowest note sung by the bassus is B-flat1. Although some editions raise the notes by a step or so, the tessitura is nonetheless low, and the conductor should be careful to ensure that his singers can sing the piece well. In contemporary choirs, the piece probably would work best with a four-part male choir with the superius sung by men using a mixed *falsetto*.

Long, flowing vocal lines are essential in this music, so careful breath management will be necessary. Also, as the parts all tend to be low in the singers' ranges, the conductor should insist on a bright tone quality; dark or rear-focused tones, combined with the low tessitura, will result in poor intonation and singing that is muddy and unclear.

Josquin is famous for his use of "points of imitation," which are segments of the music in which the vocal parts enter imitatively in succession. While the points of imitation in this motet overlap, the conductor should carefully analyze the piece to ensure that the singers know where each new point of imitation begins, which part has new melodic material, and which parts are imitating. It will be a great help to know exactly the articulations and phrase shapes desired for each point and to teach them from the beginning; as in any imitative music, it might be helpful to have all the parts sing one line that is in a reasonable range and/or to rehearse each part separately to build in the desired musical effects.

Musica ficta is an issue with almost any Renaissance music, and this motet is no exception. Essentially, *musica ficta* is a chromatic alteration to notes written by the composer (with the alterations, of course, unnotated in the music) to provide sensible voice leading. Most good editions suggest alterations, often with an accidental symbol placed above the note instead of in front of the note on the staff. If the editor is reliable, it is simpler to adopt the suggestions, although it can be interesting to research the issue and come to one's own conclusions.

Stylistic Considerations

Forward motion is important in this style of music. Throughout the piece, longer note values should move musically (i.e., slightly grow or diminish in tone), not be allowed to remain static. It can assist singers to encourage them to have all accented syllables diminuendo and all unaccented syllables crescendo. This may seem illogical, but it is the diminuendo of an accented syllable that makes an unaccented syllable *sound* unaccented to the listener's ear; the converse is true as well. This does not mean long dramatic crescendos and diminuendos, but small, tasteful gestures of a beat or two that help to clarify the text and to create phrasing.

It is useful to help the singers imagine the kind of resonant performance space in which this music was originally performed and to understand the kind of phrase shapes required by imitative text-based music.

Musical Elements

In "Absalon, fili mi," Josquin uses low tessituras and rich harmonic language to reflect the grief-like quality of the text. While Josquin lived and worked in an era in which the music was still modal, he does anticipate some interesting tonal considerations in this motet. A downward harmonic sequence following the circle of fifths moves from B-flat "harmonies" down to G-flat and concludes with the bassus' descent to low B-flat at the end of the piece. One might reasonably speculate that Josquin was reflecting the text in the overall construction of the music, (The text concludes: "That I might live no longer, but go down into hell weeping.")

Form and Structure

This motet is a sequence of overlapping points of imitation.

Text and Translation

Absalon, fili mi, fili mi, Absalon!
Quis det ut moriar pro te,
fli mi, Absalon?
Non vivam ultra,
sed descendam in infernum plorans.

Absalon, my son, my son, Absalon!
Who grants that I may die for you,
my son, Absalon?
That I might live no longer,
but go down into hell weeping.

Additional Reference and Resources

Charles, Sydney Robinson. *Josquin des Prez: A Guide to Research*. New York: Garland Publishing, Inc. 1983.

Sherr, R., editor. *The Josquin Companion*. Oxford: Oxford University Press. 2001.

Contributed by:

Matthew W. Mehaffey
Anthony Reeves

Repertoire Resource Guide

Ave Maria (Angelus Domini)

Franz Biebl
(1906–2001)

TTB/TTBB or SAT/SATB or SAATTBB
Hinshaw Music, Inc.: TTB/TTBB=1253, SAT/SATB=HMC 1255,
SAATTBB=HMC1251
Overall: 4
Vocal: 4
Tonal/Rhythm: 3

Composer

Franz Biebl was born September 1, 1906, in Germany. He studied at the Musikhochschule in Munich and was later employed as a theory teacher and choral conductor at the Musikhochschule in Salzburg, Austria. Biebl was drafted into the German Army in 1943, and was captured by the Americans in Italy in 1944; his POW internment was at Fort Custer, Michigan. After World War II, Biebl returned to Austria and later to Germany, working as a church musician and choral conductor until the Bavarian Radio Broadcast Company appointed him their first head of choral music programming. Biebl has numerous compositions, but is best-known (at least in America) for his "Ave Maria." Biebl died in 2001.

Composition

"Ave Maria" may be classified as a motet. Biebl composed it in 1964 for a firemen's choir near Munich, but it did not become internationally popular until it was recorded in the 1990s by the professional ensemble Chanticleer.

Technical Considerations

"Ave Maria" is set for two male choirs, one TTB and one TTBB, and several soloists. (It is also available for SAATTBB and for SAB/SATB.) It would be possible to use one on a part for the TTB chorus, but the director should consider overall balance when making this decision. The soloists may be members of either group.

This music calls for *sostenuto* singing, which will be difficult for many singers. Much attention to breath support and clear, smooth note-to-note transitions will be necessary. In addition, the piece requires a good deal of attention to forward motion for its successful performance. The *sostenuto* singing, the coordination of two choirs and several soloists, and the lushness of the harmony all contribute to a tendency for the piece to "bog down." Count-singing can be a useful tool to acquire rhythmic accuracy as well as forward momentum.

The ranges of the individual parts are reasonable for experienced singers, but this is not a piece for beginners. The first tenor parts, in particular, call for several A's and travel frequently back and forth across the *passagio*. It is very appropriate for the tenor parts to switch between *falsetto* and chest voice. Intonation may also be a problem. Careful listening and count-singing will help with this, but it may be advisable (providing the singers can handle the range) to try raising the piece a half-step.

Stylistic Considerations

The music calls for two different kinds of singing: choral and chant. Although *sostenuto*, the choral parts have to be rhythmically vital and accurate. The solo chant parts, however, should be sung with considerable rhythmic freedom, featuring forward motion and natural temporal cadences.

Musical Elements

"Ave Maria" is in C major with predictable emphasis on the F and G triads. Biebl used chromaticism somewhat freely, often resulting in extended (or added-note) chords. These contribute to the lush, Romantic feeling of the music. He also uses accidentals to alter the mode (e.g., F minor chord instead of F major at measures 6 to 8) and to create secondary dominants (e.g., measure 28). Extra care will have to be exercised to tune these "out-of-key" chords.

Form and Structure

See Text and Translation.

Text and Translation

The text combines two ancient liturgical texts: the Angelus and the Ave Maria. The Angelus, a short devotional liturgy, consists of three repetitions of "Ave Maria, Sancta Maria," preceded each time by its own introductory versicle. The liturgy concludes with a final versicle and prayer. Biebl used part of the Angelus text but substituted the first part of the famous prayer, Ave Maria, for the words "Ave Maria, Sancta Maria." In place of the concluding versicle and prayer, Biebl used the second part of the Ave Maria prayer.

VERSICLE 1:
Angelus Domini nuntiavit Mariae
et concepit de Spiritu sancto.

Ave Maria, gratia plena, Dominus tecum.
benedicta tu in mulieribus
et benedictus fructus ventris tui, Jesus.

The angel of the Lord announced to Mary
and she conceived by the Holy Spirit.

Hail Mary, full of grace, the Lord is with thee;
blessed art thou amongst women,
and blessed is the fruit of thy womb, Jesus.

VERSICLE 2:
Maria dixit: Ecce ancilla Domini
fiat mihi secundum verbum tuum.

Mary said: Behold the handmaiden of the Lord
do to me according to your word.

VERSICLE 3:
Et verbum caro factum est
et habitavit in nobis.

And the Word was made flesh
and dwelt among us.

Sancta Maria, ora pro nobis.
Amen.

Holy Mary, pray for us.
Amen.

Contributed by:

Andrew Reeves

Repertoire Resource Guide

De profundis

Arvo Pärt
(b. 1935)

TTBB/organ and percussion
Universal Edition: UE 32974
Overall: 4
Vocal: 5
Tonal/Rhythm: 4

Composer

Arvo Pärt is one of the best known Estonian composers outside of Estonia. After graduating from Tallinn Conservatory in 1963, Pärt made a living as a recording engineer and a composer of film and theater music. His early serious compositions were officially criticized by the Soviet authorities for their serialist leanings. A growing fascination with the music of J. S. Bach lead him to compose works in imitation of Baroque style, even basing tone rows on the notes B-A-C-H. (In German notation, H stands for B-natural and B stands for B-flat.) His *Credo* is a combination of the famous C major prelude from Bach's *Well-Tempered Clavier* and serial techniques. This work earned censure not only for its serial compositional content, but for its Christian subject matter.

Pärt composed very little between 1968 and 1976. He spent his time studying early music, especially Gregorian chant, and creating a new style of composition, which would become the hallmark of his later works. Called *tintinnabuli*, the name of the style makes reference to the sounds of bells, which Pärt feels his technique evokes. Most of Pärt's works since the evolution of this new style have been choral, including the St. John Passion from 1982, which makes rigorous use of the *tintinnabuli* style.

Composition

This setting of Psalm 130 is a motet for four-voice men's choir, organist, and percussionist lasting approximately seven minutes. The piece is an example of *tintinnabuli* technique, exhibiting the concentration of limited compositional resources common in Pärt's music. In its essence, *tintinnabuli* involves a pair of voices, one carrying a melody, typically stepwise, and the other sounding only the notes of a particular major or minor triad. The relationship between the melodic voice and the *tintinnabuli* voice remains constant; typically, the tintinnabuli voice is either the closest available note to the melodic voice or the next-to-closest available note (either above or below the melodic voice).

In this work, the compositional technique can be seen clearly in measure 21 where bass 2 carries the melody and the bass 1 is the *tintinnabuli* line. The melodic voice is largely stepwise, but the *tintinnabuli* line always sounds the notes of an E minor triad, always using the next-to-closest note to the melodic line. Once the melody moves to low G in measure 22, the *tintinnabuli* voice is forced to jump from a B to an E, because the B would no longer be the next-to-closest note of an E minor triad, but becomes the closest note. This pattern is observed, either above or below the melody from measures 21 to 40. At measure 42, a voice parallel to the melody enters, and at measure 65 a second *tintinnabuli* voice enters.

Other aspects of this work are also governed by such compositional rules. The length of each measure is entirely dictated by the length of each word of the text. The melody line always uses E as its central note, sometimes rising to E, sometimes rising from E, sometimes falling to E, and sometimes falling from E. The distance the melody rises or falls is determined by the number of syllables in each word of the text. For instance, in the phrase beginning at measure 21, "iniquitates" and "observaveris" have five syllables and the melody rises five notes from low E. The word "Domine" has only three syllables, so the melody rises only three notes. "Si" is a single syllable, so it is sung on the note E. The organ part also follows these rules. The strictness of the technique and economy of compositional material have led to descriptions of Pärt's music as spartan, meditative, and spiritual.

Historical Perspective

Estonia has a long tradition of choral singing, traced back to the early days of the nineteenth century when the German church established schools in Estonia with singing as an important part of the curriculum. This led to the growth of well-trained parish choirs, small orchestras, and brass bands. More important, the suppression of political freedoms by first the Germans and then the Russians made choral singing an essential component of national identity and patriotic pride. The first Estonian song festival drew 1,000 singers and established itself as an important social and patriotic event. It has been held every five years from 1869 to the present day.

The advent of the twentieth century brought the first Estonian graduates of the St. Petersburg Conservatory. In 1918, Estonia gained its independence, and in 1919, the Tallinn Conservatory was established. Estonia fell under Russian rule in the aftermath of World War II but became independent again in 1991.

This work was written in 1980. It comes from the early years of Pärt's experimentation with his *tintinnabuli* style and is a concentrated application of that style. It is, as are many of his choral works, a setting of a sacred text, demonstrating Pärt's commitment to his faith despite the enforced secularism of Soviet rule.

Technical Considerations

The rhythms in this work are simple; the choir sings entirely in half notes. The range extends from a low E in bass 2 to two high A's and one high B for tenor 1. The vocal lines are always slowly moving and sustained. There is no chromaticism in this piece because the work uses only the notes of an E natural minor scale, although there are parallel seconds between the voices and the organ. This work requires an organist and a percussionist who can play tam tam, bass drum, and bell.

Stylistic Considerations

The piece is certainly spartan, with strictly controlled lines and sharply defined phrases. The dynamics change only at the start of a new phrase, although there is a dynamic arc over the entire piece that slowly builds to forte at measure 65 and subsides to mezzo piano by measure 79. The mood of this work is that of kaleidoscopic shifting within a larger stasis.

Musical Elements

This work uses only the notes of an E natural minor scale, so there is a solid sense of E as the central tone throughout. The harmonies in this work are always constructed of a melodic line and its parallel harmonizations paired with various members of the E minor triad. Dissonance is created either between the melody and a static member of the E minor triad or between two parallel melodic lines, which sound a dissonant interval.

There are no harmonic progressions, and the texture is always homophonic. Every motive is built from a mathematical variant of the basic premise: melody lines that descend or ascend away from or toward E over varying distances depending on the number of syllables in each word.

Melodies are almost exclusively stepwise except for leaps at the end of each word to the starting pitch for that phrase. Meter constantly shifts depending on the number of syllables in each word, but the half-note pulse remains constant.

Form and Structure

The form of this piece depends upon the lengths of the phrases of text and is composed of a slow accumulation of compositional density.

MEASURE	EVENT AND SCORING
1–19	One voice; melody only (*p*)
20	Bell
21–40	Melody; *tintinnabuli* voice (*mp*)
41	Bell
42–63	Melody, parallel voice (tenth); *tintinnabuli* voice (*mf*)
64	Bell
65–82	Melody, parallel voice (third); two *tintinnabuli* voices (*f*, *mf*, *mp*)
83	Bell

Text and Translation

(Psalm 130)

De profundis clamavi ad te Domine:
Domine exaudi vocem meam
Fiant aures tuae intendentes
in vocem deprecationis meae.

Si iniquitates observaveris Domine:
Domine quis sustinebit?
Quia apud te propitiatio est:
et propter legem tuam sustinui te Domine.

Sustinuit anima mea in verbo ejus:
speravit anima mea in Domino.
A custodia matutina usque ad noctem,
speret Israel in Domino.

Quia apud Dominum misericordia:
et copiosa apud eum redemptio.
Et ipse redimet Israel
ex omnibus iniquitatibus ejus.

Out of the depths I cry to you, O Lord:
O Lord, hear my voice.
Let your ears be attentive
to my cry for mercy.

If you, O Lord, kept a record of sins,
O Lord, who could stand?
But with you there is forgiveness:
therefore you are feared.

I wait for the Lord, my soul waits,
in his word I put my hope.
More than watchmen wait for the morning,
O Israel, put your hope in the Lord.

For with the Lord is unfailing love
and with him is full redemption.
He himself will redeem Israel
from all their sins.

Contributed by:

Thomas Cunningham

Repertoire Resource Guide

Hvalite imia Ghospodne (Praise the Name of the Lord)

Piotr Tchaikovsky
(1840–1893)

arr. Pavel Chesnokov
(1877–1944)

TTBB or SATB/a cappella
Musica Russica: TTBB=TA 023MC, SATB=TA 023
Overall: 4
Vocal: 4
Tonal/Rhythm: 3

Composers

Piotr Tchaikovsky was born in Votkinsk, Russia, on May 7, 1840. He was a member of the St. Petersburg Conservatory's first class, matriculating in 1862. When he graduated in 1866, Tchaikovsky became a professor of harmony at the Moscow Conservatory, a post he retained until 1878. Tchaikovsky's musical output is most impressive, including operas, ballets, orchestral works, solo pieces and concerti, chamber music, piano music, and vocal music. Tchaikovsky died in St. Petersburg on November 6, 1893.

Pavel Chesnokov was born in 1877 and graduated from the Moscow Synodal School in 1895. Until 1905, he taught chant, and there he taught music in several other Moscow schools as well as working as a church musician. In 1913, Chesnokov enrolled in the Moscow Conservatory and joined their faculty in 1920. He remained a significant choral conductor in post-Revolutionary Russia. Chesnokov was an influential figure in Russian and early Soviet choral music and wrote the book *The Choir and How to Direct It*. Chesnokov died in 1944.

Composition

This arrangement is from one of the movements of Tchaikovsky's *All-Night Vigil* (1882). The arrangement for male chorus, made by Chesnokov, actually omits some of Tchaikovsky's musical material (the *All-Night Vigil* was originally scored for mixed choir). The text, from Psalms 134 and 135, is known as the *polyeleion* (from the Greek for "many mercies") and is a hymn sung at festal Matins (the first of the church's eight canonical hours). In the liturgy, the singing of the *polyeleion* occurs during the clergy's procession to the middle of the church, as all the lights are lit in preparation for the reading of the Gospel.

Technical Considerations

"Hvalite imia Ghospodne" calls for an interesting set of singing styles. The psalm verses need to be legato and somewhat in the manner of chant, while the "Alleluias" need to have more "swing." This "swing" will be easier to accomplish (especially in a resonant space) if the choir thinks of a less legato articulation for the "Alleluia" sections.

Tchaikovsky's metronome marking of quarter note = 108 gives a good idea of the basic tempo, but the conductor must realize that inherent in the Russian style (especially in the psalm sections of this text) is some tasteful use of rubato. Tchaikovsky also marked dynamics, and Chesnokov retained these markings.

Phrasing is quite important in this music, and Tchaikovsky did a good job of tying it to the next—not surprising, as the music is *a cappella* and text-based. The conductor must ascertain the correct Slavonic (the language of the Russian church) pronunciation and be able to demonstrate it clearly. It would be better to recruit an outside expert to do the diction coaching (assuming they realize that Church Slavonic is pronounced somewhat differently from ordinary Russian) than to "wing it." The text is too important, and the pronunciations are too tricky for people who do not know Slavic languages.

Stylistic Considerations

Tchaikovsky used a standard Russian liturgical melody from the *Obihod* (a collection of hymns) as a *cantus firmus* in this piece. In the psalm verse sections of the piece, the chant melody is in the top voice (tenor 1). However, Tchaikovsky did not adhere to the chant for the "Alleluia," writing his own lilting music instead. It will be important, then, for the singers to realize that the tenor 1 part is the melody during the verses and allow it to be heard. The "Alleluias" are almost antiphonal in nature and can be sung with more abandon to portray the text.

Musical Elements

"Hvalite imia Ghospodne" is mostly homophonic during the psalm verses, and becomes responsorial (with voice pairing) in the "Alleluias." The harmonies are straightforward G major progressions. The only accidentals occur to form secondary dominant chords for half cadences.

Form and Structure

The form is based upon the text, which consists of the first and last verses of Psalms 134 and 135 with each verse followed by an Alleluia refrain. The resultant musical form could be described as ABCD.

Text and Translation

Hvalite imia Ghospodne,
Havalite, rabi Ghospoda. Alliluya.
Blagosloven Ghospod ot Siona,
zhïvïy vo Ierusalime. Alliluya.
Ispovedaytesia Ghospodevi, yako blag,
yako v vek milost Yego. Alliluya.
Ispovedaytesia Bogu nebesnomu,
Yako v vek milost Yego. Alliluya.

Praise the name of the Lord;
praise the Lord, O you His servants. Alleluia.
Blessed be the Lord from Zion,
He who dwells in Jerusalem. Alleluia.
O give thanks unto the Lord, for He is good,
for His mercy endures forever. Alleluia.
O give thanks unto the God of Heaven,
for His mercy endures forever. Amen.

Additional References and Resources

Morosan, Vladimir. *Choral Performance in Pre-Revolutionary Russia.* Ann Arbor, Michigan: UMI Research Press. 1986.

See Musica Russica (www.musicarussica.com) for materials to assist in Russian pronunciation.

Contributed by:

Matthew W. Mehaffey
Anthony Reeves

Level Five

Repertoire Resource Guide

Os justi

Anton Bruckner
(1824–1896)

SATB divisi/a cappella
C F Peters Corporation: 6315
Overall: 5
Vocal: 5
Tonal/Rhythm: 4

Composer

Anton Bruckner was born near Linz, Austria, into a musical family. By the age of ten, he was deputy organist to his father, and on his father's death he moved near the monastery of St. Florian, where he became a chorister. Bruckner returned to St. Florian in 1845 and taught there until he left to become the cathedral organist at Linz. He became the conductor of the principal choral society of Linz and soon after composed his Mass in D Minor, his first mature work.

Influenced strongly by the music of Wagner, Bruckner continued to compose masses until 1868, when he moved to Vienna to become provisional organist at the imperial chapel and concentrated principally on symphonic works, though several choral miniatures also come from his time in Vienna. Among them are two other graduals, "Locus Iste" and "Christus Factus Est."

Composition

The Gradual was originally a piece of chant which followed the lessons of the Roman Catholic Mass, especially the Epistles. It is mentioned in the oldest sources for the liturgy of the Roman Mass, and nearly all of them were psalm texts. "Os Justi" is a setting of Psalm 37:30–31, and though it does not seem to quote plainchant, the influence of chant is felt strongly throughout the work. Bruckner wrote the piece while he was living in Vienna.

Historical Perspective

Bruckner lived during the time of the Cecilian movement, which was composed of a group of Roman Catholics who felt that music should abandon the excesses of the Romantics and focus instead on reviving the styles of the Renaissance, especially the music of Palestrina. "Os Justi" displays many of the characteristics of Cecilian influenced music, including the use of an old church mode (lydian), chant-like vocal lines, relatively equal weight between the voices, and a sense of balance and restraint. The work itself is dedicated to a prominent Cecilianist Ignaz Traumihler of St. Florian, to whom Bruckner wrote, "I should be very pleased if you found pleasure in the piece. It is written without sharps and flats, without the chord of the seventh, without a six-four chord, and without chordal combinations of four and five simultaneous notes."

Technical Considerations

The piece is a slow-moving, evenly flowing work without dramatic rhythmic contrast. The sopranos must sing a high A, and the basses have forte low F. There is a small section of eight-part voicing, but most of the piece uses only four parts. The most difficult aspect of a performance of "Os Justi" is sustaining the extremely extended phrases to their inevitable climaxes, which are often followed by moments of silence. The dramatic importance of these pauses is negated without the appropriate long term build-up of musical tension. The relaxation of the tension of the climaxes is also often prolonged, and it can be very difficult to maintain a slow, even dissipation.

Stylistic Considerations

The general style of this work is similar to a Renaissance motet, although the dynamic range is very large and the overall scope of the sound varies from a single (piano) melodic line in the alto to an eight-part climax (fortissimo). These dynamic changes are almost all achieved gradually, with an even build-up and dissipation of tension and volume. The middle section of the piece is largely equal-voiced polyphony, necessitating careful attention to the entrances of the principal imitative idea. Bruckner often makes use of dramatic pauses in his choral writing to take full advantage of the resonance of the cathedrals in which he worked. The notated lengths of the rests which comprise these pauses should not necessarily be taken literally.

Musical Elements

The work is written entirely in the lydian mode (raised fourth scale degree), so there is no dominant seventh chord. Bruckner maintains a sense of tonal closure by preceding the final tonic with a long dominant pedal and establishing the return of the tonic with a largely static phrase entirely on the tonic to close the piece. The central section is imitative, though not strictly fugal. The work is bookended by two slower moving sections without any motion faster than the quarter note, while the middle section moves in flowing, step-wise eighth notes.

Form and Structure

"Os Justi" is in three short sections divided both texturally and textually. The first portion begins with piano F major chords, which slowly expand outward to an eight-part climax. This musical peak falls away as the tension dissipates, coming to rest on a quiet, four-part G major chord.

The second section begins with the words "et lingua ejus" and establishes a flowing eighth note melody line in the alto, which is imitated first by the soprano and then bass and tenor. The imitation is not strict, although fragments of the principal idea return throughout the section. There is another longer build-up, this time to a widely voiced, fortissimo G major chord, which is followed by a large pause.

After the dramatic silence, the closely voiced chorus reenters with the same sonority (piano), beginning the third and final section. The opening material returns, shifting subtlely back to F major and leading again to the eight-voice climax. The descent from this musical summit is a slow diminuendo to a long dominant pedal on C in the bass, leading to the final phrase, a soft, slow gesture on a resonant F major chord. There is an "Alleluia" appended to the end of the piece, which is simply a short piece of unison plainchant. The Gradual would have typically been followed by an Alleluia in the Roman Mass.

Text and Translation

Psalm 37:30–31

The mouth of the righteous speaketh wisdom, and his tongue talketh
    of judgment.
The law of his God is in his heart: none of his steps shall slide.

Suggested Listening

Mysteries Beyond. Voices of Ascension. Dennis Keene, conductor. (Delos DE 3138).

Bruckner Motets. Corydon Singers. Matthew Best, conductor. (Hyperion Records 66062).

Like as the Hart: Psalms and Spiritual Songs. Westminster Choir. Jospeh, Flummerfelt, conductor. (Chesky Records CD138).

Contributed by:

Thomas Cunningham

Repertoire Resource Guide

A Procession Winding Around Me

Jeffrey Van
(b. 1944)

SATB/guitar
Hal Leonard Corporation: 08500277
Overall: 5
Vocal: 4
Tonal/Rhythm: 5

Composer

Guitarist and composer Jeffrey Van has premiered more than fifty works for guitar, including four concertos and a broad variety of chamber music, and his compositions include works for guitar, violin, flute, chorus, chamber ensemble, and organ. He has performed in Carnegie Hall, London's Wigmore Hall, and the Kennedy Center, and he has premiered commissioned works by Stephen Paulus, Katherine Hoover, Roberto Sierra, Andrew Waggoner, Tania Leon, Michael Daugherty, Libby Larsen, Frank Ferko, and Robert Rodriquez as part of Duologue with flutist Susan Morris De Jong.

Van has been featured on many National Public Radio broadcasts, including St. Paul Sunday, and has made several solo and ensemble recordings. He appears on eight recordings with the Dale Warland Singers. Van has taught master classes throughout the United States, and he earned a master of fine arts from the University of Minnesota School of Music, where he is a lecturer on classical guitar. Former students include Sharon Isbin, John Holmquist, and members of the Minneapolis Guitar Quartet.

Composition

A Procession Winding Around Me is a dramatic cantata setting of four of Walt Whitman's (1819–1892) *Drum Taps* (from *Leaves of Grass*) of 1865. This four movement, twenty-minute work examines the Civil War from a variety of perspectives. The first movement, "By the Bivouac's Fitful Flame," offers a first-person account of a soldier who has settled down at the campfire for the night. The listener can sense fear, paranoia, loneliness, and the loss of innocence. The second movement, "Beat! Beat! Drums!", tells how war disrupts the lives of everyone in society, not just those fighting. In this movement, the war "bursts" through a town and consumes it, affecting all in its path.

The third movement, "Look Down Fair Moon," chillingly depicts a soldier encountering dead bodies, asking the moon to provide warmth and comfort, to no avail. The fourth movement, "Reconciliation," pleads for the healing of all wounds. This movement features a beautiful men's chorus in which a man comes face to face with his dead enemy at a funeral. This emotional meeting highlights the absurdity of all that has come before. The work ends by reminding all that time and death will heal all wounds society has suffered: "The hands of the sisters Death and Night incessantly softly wash again, and ever again, this soil'd world."

Historical Perspective

Many of the *Drum-Taps* poems resulted from Whitman's years in Washington, D.C., spent as a psychological nurse to sick and wounded soldiers. Whitman was in his forties during the time of the Civil War, so he did not participate as a soldier. These poems are a result of his experiences as a nurse and the stories he heard from soldiers he treated. Despite their age, these poems still resonate in today's society. They can be valuable teaching aids for high school students. Singers of all ages and backgrounds can easily understand the imagery and emotion used in the poetry.

Van tells of the background of his piece in the liner notes to *Music of Jeffrey Van* in his own words:

> The unwitting genesis of this work was an unexpected visit to the battlefield at Gettysburg in the summer of 1989. The richness and depth of that experience can only be hinted at in words. A year later, when the Lancaster Chorale commissioned me to write a work for the Lancaster Festival, I was drawn to Whitman's poems and selected these four from his *Drum-Taps* of 1865. The percussive qualities of the guitar figure prominently throughout this work, evoking the ever-present drums of war: the call to attention of the field drums, the rattle of the snare, and the ominous pulse of the bass drum. While the Civil War was always present in my mind as the context for these poems,

there is nothing in these texts which specifically identifies that war, and Whitman's powerful and timeless words ring true for any war in any age. Choose your war: there will always be the waiting in readiness, surrounded by the procession of thoughts of home and those who are far away; there will always be the fury of the battle, sweeping all areas of personal and corporate life before it; there will always be a field littered with dead, where we whistle fearfully in the brittle stillness, and there will always be the possibility of reconciliation, the washing again and again of this soiled world. Walk out onto the fields of Gettysburg; you will never be the same.

Technical Considerations

The guitar part for this work is very difficult; it is necessary to have a virtuoso player. The part must be played on a classical gut string guitar, not a steel-stringed acoustic. The guitar serves as a character in this drama. Through extended performance techniques, the guitar sounds like a snare drum, insects, and gunshots to heighten the meaning of the text through sound. If the choir is larger than forty, or the performance hall's acoustic is less than desirable, it may be wise to amplify the guitar. Leave the method for this up to the player, as he or she probably has the necessary equipment.

This piece sounds extremely different when rehearsing with piano than with the guitar. The thickness of the piano's sound can make many of the dissonances in the work sound very unpleasant. Encourage your singers to overlook the sound of the piece with piano; the addition of the guitar makes it superb.

Stylistic Considerations

The style of each movement is very different. Strive to have the sound of the choir change with the character of each movement. There are times when loneliness, terror, horror, and even hope must be present in the sound. The sound must change with each of these emotions, or else the emotional content of the poetry will be lost. Encourage your singers to be actors and actresses when singing this piece. They are telling a story to the audience in the way they sing. A *Procession Winding Around Me* is a wonderful vehicle for getting better emotional expressions from your singers.

Musical Elements

The harmony of this piece ranges from passages of extreme dissonance to beautiful, rich consonance. The use of dissonance always mirrors the meaning of the text and aids in heightening the drama of the poetry. Don't be afraid of the dissonance in this piece, because the composer almost always approaches and leaves it by stepwise motion. This makes the lines far more singable and easy to learn. Once your singers get used to Van's harmonic language, they will pick up the music very quickly.

The rhythm of the second movement, "Beat! Beat! Drums!", can be difficult to master because the meter switches very often. The words are the most important part of this piece, so it is useful to speak the words in rhythm before learning the pitches.

It is also important that the singers understand the concept of macrobeat. The meter often switches from simple time to compound time (e.g., 3/4 to 6/8); the singers must feel the change between the quarter note getting the beat and the dotted quarter note getting the beat. All this must happen while maintaining the tempo of the microbeat (in this case, the eighth note). The singers' rhythm will be most secure if they understand both layers of rhythm constantly occur under the rhythm of the text.

Form and Structure

This work is divided into four movements; each movement uses a different Walt Whitman poem as the text. The music for each movement follows the form of the poetry. When textual ideas recur, the music usually repeats. The scoring is very logogenic, meaning that the melodies and rhythms follow the natural flow of the words.

Text

No. 1: By the bivouac's fitful flame,
A procession winding around me, solemn and sweet and slow—but first I
    note,
The tents of the sleeping army, the fields' and woods' dim outline,
The darkness lit by spots of kindled fire, the silence
Like a phantom far or near an occasional figure moving,
The shrubs and trees, (as I lift my eyes they seem to be stealthily
    watching me,)
While wind in procession thoughts, O tender and wondrous thoughts,
Of life and death, of home and the past and love, and of those that
    are far away;
A solemn and slow procession there as I sit on the ground,

No. 2: Beat! Beat! Drums!—Blow! Bugles! Blow!
Through the windows—through doors—burst like a ruthless force,
Into the solemn church, and scatter the congregation,
Into the school where the scholar is studying;
Leave not the bridegroom quiet—no happiness must he have now
    with his bride,
Nor the peaceful farmer any peace, ploughing his fields or gathering his
    grain,

So fierce you whirr and pound you drums—so shrill you bugles blow.

Beat! Beat! Drums!—Blow! Bugles! Blow!
Over the traffic of cities—over the rumble of wheels in the streets;
Are beds prepared for sleepers at night in the houses? No sleepers must sleep
    in those beds,
No bargainers' bargain by day—no brokers or speculators—would they
    continue?
Would the talkers be talking? Would the singer attempt to sing?
Would the lawyer rise in the court to state his case before the judge?
Then rattle quicker, heavier drums—you bugles wilder blow.

Beat! Beat! Drums!—Blow! Bugles! Blow!
Make no parley—stop for no expostulation,
Mind not the timid—mind not the weeper or prayer,
Mind not the old man beseeching the young man,
Let not the child's voice be heard, nor the mother's entreaties,
Make even the trestles to shake the dead where they lie awaiting
    the hearses,
So strong you thump, O terrible drums—so loud you bugles blow.

No. 3: Look down fair moon and bathe this scene,
Pour softly down night's nimbus floods on faces ghastly, swollen, purple,
On the dead on their backs with arms toss'd wide,
Pour down your unstinted nimbus, sacred moon.

No. 4: "Reconciliation"
Word over all, beautiful as the sky,
Beautiful that war and all its deeds of carnage must in time be utterly lost,
That the hands of the sisters Death and Night incessantly softly wash again,
and ever again, and ever again, this soil'd world;
For my enemy is dead, a man divine as myself is dead,
I look where he lies white-faced and still in the coffin—I draw near,
Bend down and touch lightly with my lips the white face in the coffin.

Suggested Listening

Music of Jeffrey Van. (Centaur Records CRC 2687).

Contributed by:

Matthew W. Mehaffey

Repertoire Resource Guide

Water Night

Eric Whitacre
(b. 1970)

SATB divisi/a cappella
Hal Leonard Corporation: 08500040
Overall: 5
Vocal: 5
Tonal/Rhythm: 5

Composer

An accomplished composer, conductor, and lecturer, Eric Whitacre is one of the bright stars in contemporary concert music. Regularly commissioned and published, Whitacre has received composition awards from ASCAP, the Barlow International Composition Competition, the American Choral Directors Association, and the American Composers Forum.

Born in 1970, Whitacre has already achieved substantial critical and popular acclaim. The *American Record Guide* named his first recording, *The Music of Eric Whitacre*, one of the top ten classical albums of 1997, and the Los Angeles Times praised his music as "electric, chilling harmonies; works of unearthly beauty and imagination." His "Water Night" has become one of the most popular choral works of the last decade and is one of the top selling choral publications in the last five years. His music has been the subject of several recent scholarly works and doctoral dissertations, and his twenty-eight published works have sold well over 100,000 copies worldwide.

Composition

"Water Night" may be described as a twentieth-century secular motet. The texture, while filled with luxurious harmonies and subtle, shimmering dissonances, is basically homophonic throughout. Whitacre's rhythmic choices always allow the text to unfold as naturally as possible. This simple homophony and natural rhythm cause the words to stand out in relief from the music that supports them. Perhaps this is why Whitacre likens "Water Night" to a simple pop song.

Technical Considerations

Most conductors and singers would agree that "Water Night" possesses an intangible quality that makes it a joy to rehearse. This is fortunate because many of the elements involved in bringing it to a high level of performance require great patience! First of all, while each singer must always sing their line musically and expressively, the proper execution of the many chord clusters requires them to pay particular attention to the vertical sonorities.

The voice leading is always stepwise, making it easy for the singers to find their notes, but the singers and conductor must pay particular attention to balance and fine-tune intonation. One way for the conductor to focus the singers' ears within these thick vertical sonorities is by isolating the perfect fifths within them. For instance, to balance the chord in measure 48, the conductor could have only the sopranos on G-flat and D-flat sing—listening carefully to balance and intonation. Next, let the sopranos on C and the altos on F sing their fifth alone, followed by the other two perfect fifths in the women's voices. Once these have all been sung individually, have the sets of fifths enter one at a time until all eight pitches are present. This will help the singers to be sensitive to how their single pitch fits into to greater whole.

Stylistic Considerations

When trying to achieve the smooth legato this piece calls for, the conductor may find that certain percussive consonants are disrupting the line. To prevent this, the conductor may wish to make some out-of-the-ordinary requests of the choir regarding diction, such as asking to soften the "t" in "water" by pronouncing it like a "d" instead.

Also, because the notes and rhythms are so clearly guided by the natural flow of the text, the conductor should allow some flexibility of tempo. This will further heighten the expressive delivery of the poem.

Form and Structure

"Water Night" is through-composed and closely follows the form of the poem. It is interesting to note that Whitacre added a small portion of text, "a silent and beautiful current."

Text

Night with the eyes of a horse that trembles in the night,
night with eyes of water in the field asleep
is in your eyes, a horse that trembles,
is in your eyes of secret water.

Eyes of shadow-water,
eyes of well-water,
eyes of dream-water...

—Octavio Paz, translation by Muriel Rukeyser

Suggested Listening

Eric Whitacre: The Complete A Cappella Works: 1991–2001. The Brigham
    Young University Singers. Ronald Staheli, conductor. (Arsis CD 147).

Additional References and Resources

www.ericwhitacre.com

Contributed by:

J. Aaron McDermid

Repertoire Resource Guide

Wie lieblich sind deine Wohnungen

Johannes Brahms
(1833–1897)

SATB/keyboard
G. Schirmer, Inc.
Overall: 5
Vocal: 5
Tonal/Rhythm: 4

Composer

Johannes Brahms was born in Hamburg in 1833 and died in Vienna in 1897. Much has been said about his backward-looking tendencies and his opposition to the newer music of his contemporaries. Brahms was a lover of the music of the Renaissance and Baroque, as evidenced by his vast library of scores and writings from those periods. However, he viewed himself as a forward-looking composer whose musical inheritance from Bach, Mozart and the other masters, allowed him to chart the future of the musical art form in a unique manner. Regardless of the debate, his choral works remain eloquent testaments to mid-nineteenth-century Austro-German Romantic ideals and artistic expressions.

Composition

The details surrounding the genesis of Brahms's *Deutsches Requiem*, Op. 45, from which "Wie lieblich sind deine Wohnungen" is taken, cannot be precisely determined. The work was not commissioned, nor was it composed for use at a special occasion. This fact, together with Brahms' statement in correspondence that the *Requiem* should be called a requiem for "humanity," rather than a "German" requiem, suggest that he composed the work for artistic purposes. Brahms had completed assembly of the German texts by 1861, and the score was composed between the years 1865 and 1868. The initial version of the work, consisting of movements 1–4 and 6–7, received its first performance in Bremen on Good Friday, April 10, 1868, with Brahms conducting. Movement 5 was composed a month after the Bremen premiere, and the first performance of the work as we know it today took place in Leipzig in February 1869.

Technical Considerations

"Wie lieblich sind deine Wohnungen" is suitable for choirs of varying sizes, as long as all sections are strongly represented. Each voice part carries an equal amount of melodic and harmonic importance throughout the work. As is typical of most Brahms works, the melodic lines encompass a fairly large range and might provide challenges to untrained and younger singers. Phrases are primarily eight measures long, and, considering the tempo indication of *mässig bewegt* in 3/4 meter, present minimal difficulty for most singers to sustain. A conductor may, however, find that the choir is tempted to drag the tempo during the sweeping legato phrases, thereby making sustained phrases more difficult.

The text might present some diction problems, especially for untrained singers not used to singing in German, particularly the fugal section on the text "die loben dich immerdar," set syllabically on paired eighth notes. To facilitate the diction and articulation of these phrases, conductors may wish to slow the tempo considerably, rehearsing the paired eighths on the neutral syllable "doh." This will solidify the notes, as well as get the singers used to articulating the "d" consonant where it often falls in this particular textual phrase.

Finally, the keyboard reduction in most octavos, consisting of nearly constant arpeggiations over an extended range, requires a proficient pianist or organist. The conductor might wish to schedule a separate rehearsal to prepare the accompanist.

Form and Structure

"Wie lieblich sind deine Wohnungen" (How Lovely Are Your Dwellings) is the fourth and center movement of the *Deutsches Requiem*. Extracted from the major work, it is suitable for isolated performance, for use as concert literature, or during worship services. A variety of choral octavos are available. Originally composed for SATB choir and orchestra, this work is now published in a number of editions arranged for various voicings with keyboard reductions of the orchestral parts.

The text from Psalm 84 is through-composed, with a repeat of the opening melody (varied somewhat) for verse 1 ("Wie leiblich sind deine Wohnungen, Herr Zebaoth!") occurring between each successive verse and as the final phrase. Verses 2 and 4 are set to music using a mixture of polyphonic and legato homophonic statements. Verse 4 contains a thirty-bar fugato setting of the text "Die loben dich immerdar."

Text and Translation

The source for "Wie lieblich sind deine Wohnungen" is Psalm 84:1–2, 4. Unfortunately for those wishing to perform the work in its original language, many octavos incorporate only an English translation.

Wie lieblich sind deine Wohnungen, Herr Zebaoth!
Meine Seele verlanget und sehnet sich nach den Vorhöfen des Herrn;
Mein Leib und Seele freuen sich in dem lebendigen Gott.
Wohl denen, die in deinem Hause wohnen,
Die loben dich immerdar.

How lovely are your dwellings, Lord Sabaoth!
My soul desires and longs for the courts of the Lord;
My body and soul rejoice in the living God.
Blessed are they that dwell in your house,
Who praise you there forever.

Suggested Listening

Brahms Requiem. Atlanta Symphony Chorus. Robert Shaw, conductor. (Telarc CD 80092).

Choral Masterpieces. Atlanta Symphony Chorus. Robert Shaw, conductor. (Telarc 80119).

Contributed by:

Wayne Glass

Repertoire Resource Guide

Ave Maria

Gustav Holst
(1874–1934)

SSAA double choir/a cappella
Collegium Music Publications: CCS401
Overall: 5
Vocal: 5
Tonal/Rhythm: 4

Composer

English composer Gustav Holst is best known for his widely popular symphonic work *The Planets*. Though an idiosyncratic composer, Holst's early works, such as this one, were in traditional forms and set to traditional texts. He studied piano, violin, and trombone as a child, the last as a cure for his asthma.

Holst began composing in his early teens, and after an unsuccessful application to Trinity College of Music, he studied counterpoint with the organist at Merton College, Oxford. In 1893, he was accepted into the Royal College of Music where he studied with Charley Stanford and Parry and eventually won a scholarship in composition. It was at the College that Holst became a close friend to Vaughan Williams, a fellow folklorist.

In 1896, Holst was named the conductor of the Hammersmith Socialist Choir. Not only did the choir afford Holst the opportunity to work closely with choral music, it was also the setting where he met Isobel Harrison, his future wife. Holst composed "Ave Maria" shortly after he completed his studies.

Composition

This motet is written for two women's choirs and is evocative of the style of Holst's teacher Charles Stanford. Holst's first published work, "Ave Maria" is *a cappella* and appropriate for the high church style of turn-of-the-century England, although the conservative harmonies do move through unusual modulations in places.

Historical Perspective

Though Holst is known both for his interest in Hindu mysticism and native folksong, this early work is strongly rooted in the styles of the past. Stanford's craftsmanship and delicate feel for counterpoint are in evidence here, and this piece was said to have gained his approval. "Ave Maria" is an early foray into serious composition for Holst and demonstrates his considerable skill in traditional practices.

Technical Considerations

The rhythms of this piece are straightforward, moving mostly in flowing quarter notes in an *Adagio* 6/4. The range is considerable, however, extending to a high B-flat in the top soprano voice of Choir I and descending to several low G's and F's in the low alto voice in both choirs. The melodic contour is comprised of extremely extended lines in all voice parts, and there are several moments of somewhat distant chromaticism, including moves from the home key of E-flat major to sections in A and D major.

Stylistic Considerations

This work evokes a large, late-Romantic sound, replete with soaring melodies, long arched phrases, and lush harmonies. The piece is at a slow tempo, but it features a wide range of dynamics that build and relax over large stretches. The most difficult aspect of the style is sustaining the breadth of sound both in the large dynamic range and the extended melodic structure.

Musical Elements

The piece is largely in E-flat major with a great deal of flat-side coloration. The chord structural is mostly triadic, although there is often passing motion through sustained triads, creating large chord clusters. Dissonance is rare; the counterpoint instead moves through suspensions and passing notes, which are carefully resolved. The texture is polychoral, with each choir presenting either homophonic blocks of sound or gentle counterpoint. The two choirs often trade musical material.

Form and Structure

Measure	Event and Scoring
1–9	Opening phrase in E-flat major
9–16	Similar to the opening phrase, but moving to B-flat major
17–28	Beginning of modulatory central section (D minor and G minor)
29–44	Widely modulatory (D minor, F major, F minor, A-flat major)
44–57	Return to opening, again in E-flat major
58–63	"Amen" in E-flat major

Text and Translation

Ave Maria, gratia plena, Dominus tecum.
Benedicta tu in mulieribus,
et benedictus fructus ventris tui, Iesus.
Sancta Maria, ora pro nobis
Amen.

Hail Mary, full of grace, the Lord is with thee;
blessed art thou amongst women,
and blessed is the fruit of thy womb, Jesus.
Holy Mary, pray for us.
Amen.

Suggested Listening

This Have I Done for My True Love. The Holst Singers. Stephen Layton, conductor. (Hyperion CDH55171).

Essential Holst. Purcell Singers. Imogen Holst, conductor. (Decca Classics 444549).

Contributed by:

Thomas Cunningham

Repertoire Resource Guide

Ave verum corpus

Francis Poulenc
(1899–1963)

SSA/a cappella
Editions Salabert: R.L.12532
Overall: 5
Vocal: 5
Tonal/Rhythm: 5

Composer

Francis Poulenc was a French composer and pianist born into a wealthy family in Paris. His father was from rural France, and it was from his father that Poulenc felt he took his strong connection to his Roman Catholic faith. He inherited his artistic inclinations from his Parisian mother; it was this combination of primary forces that he believed shaped him as an artist. Early in his career, he was associated with the controversial avant-garde group of composers critically known as *Les six*, though he quickly achieved fame as a collaborator with the baritone Pierre Bernac, establishing him as a first-rate composer of melodies and a successful touring pianist.

An important turning point for Poulenc came in the form of a pilgrimage in 1936 to the Notre Dame de Rocamadour, which reawakened his Catholic faith. Immediately following this religious rebirth, Poulenc began the composition of sacred vocal works, a practice he would continue for the rest of his life. Some of his major choral works include the *Litanies à la vierge noire* (1936), Mass in G (1937), "Stabat mater" (1951), "Gloria" (1960), and *Sept répons des ténèbres* (1962). After achieving international success as a performer of his melodies and a composer of piano music, orchestral music, and opera, he died of a sudden heart attack in 1963.

Composition

"Ave verum corpus" was composed in 1952 and is a setting for women's voices in three parts. It is a motet, and although it strongly suggests the atmosphere of plainchant in the opening bars, its modern genesis is quickly betrayed with the entrance of strong, angular block chords and rhythmic sixteenth note phrases. The work is dedicated to "la chorale féminine de Pittsburgh," possibly inspired by his many visits to the United States for both concert tours and performances of his works.

Historical Perspective

The motet is an ancient form of sacred music, and in the twentieth century it became a historically aware genre. The connection between the modern and the ancient is felt especially strongly in choral music because it carries associations with the ancient church more than any other type of music except, perhaps, organ music. Poulenc here makes very conscious references to the older style of music, using both chant-like melodies and ancient, imitative polyphony in the opening bars. The tension between this style and the more modern style of the rest of the work is particularly strong in the phrases that mark the transitions from the modern language back to the ancient style, and it underscores the strong contrast between the meditative associations of the ancient prayer and the immediacy of the suffering of Jesus Christ to a modern believer.

Technical Considerations

This piece presents a variety of technical challenges. While the tempo is slow (quarter note = 60), the shifts between quarter note motion and sixteenth note motion make apparently simple rhythms difficult. The changing time signatures also complicate an understanding of the rhythm. Ranges are not extreme, with high G's in the soprano part and momentary low G's in the alto part. The most difficult aspect of this work is the advanced harmonic language, which involves a large degree of chromaticism. Frequent voice crossings further complicate the harmonic language of this piece for the singer. While the work suggests an opening and closing tonality of modally inflected A minor, the harmony moves into and out of foreign key areas fluidly. Although the quarter note pulse is slow, the sixteenth note runs may present difficulties to some singers.

Stylistic Considerations

The opening phrase is a stepwise melody reminiscent of Gregorian chant and marked *très doux et très lié* ("very sweet and very connected"). The style implied by the expression marking and by the association with chant governs both the opening six bars and occasional brief returns to this mode of expression later in the piece. Contrasted with this style is a suddenly forte, harmonically and melodically angular section that comprises the bulk of the work. The broad, flowing melodies of the opening are replaced in measure seven with strong quarter note chords and running sixteenth note phrases. The articulation of this contrast, highlighted several times in this piece, is central to the overall style of this work. These two seemingly opposing ideas resonate with the contrast of the prayerfulness of the contemplation of Christ and the violence and suffering of the events referenced in the text.

Musical Elements

While the opening stays solidly within a modal A minor, this simplicity is quickly undermined, first by a sudden change of mood and melodic contour, then by the entrance of increasingly distant harmonic elements. Chords are often triadic, especially at cadences, but the relationships between sequential chords are often harmonically complicated. Dissonance tends to enter this piece more through the juxtaposition of distantly related chords and harmonies rather than through the simultaneous sounding of unrelated pitches.

Texturally, the work begins in simple, imitative polyphony, but the bulk of the piece is set in alternating sections of homophonic chords and nearly homophonic melody lines. The meter changes frequently, but the quarter note is constant.

Form and Structure

The form of this work is determined by its focus on sharp contrast. The work opens with a plainchant-like melody intoning the opening text of the prayer. The words "corpus Christi" are repeated in a sudden forte, marking the first real statement of contrast. Two phrases within which chordal statements are contrasted with running sixteenth note phrases are followed by a two-measure phrase that returns to the opening mood. Two measures of pianissimo chant are followed again by phrases of forte chords and sixteenth notes, although there is again a transition to the earlier texture. The opening melody returns in the lowest voice, this time forte, and the piece closes with strong chordal utterances and sixteenth note runs, transitioning again in its final moment to the opening texture.

The forte explosions seem strongly motivated by the text, occurring on the words "corpus Christi" and "immolatum," words clearly connected by the imagery of suffering central to the text.

Text and Translation

This text is only the first part of the prayer "Ave verum corpus," probably written in the thirteenth century.

Ave verum corpus Christi,
natum ex Maria Virgine
vere possum immolatum
in cruce pro homine.

Hail, true Body of Christ
born of the Virgin Mary
who has truly suffered,
was sacrificed on the cross for mortals.

Suggested Listening

Poulenc: Sacred and Secular Vocal Works. Groupe Vocal de France.
John Alldis, conductor. (EMI Classics 7243 5 85776 2 4).

Poulenc. Sacred Music. The Cambridge Singers. John Rutter, conductor.
(Collegium CD CSCD 506).

Contributed by:

Thomas Cunningham

Repertoire Resource Guide

Give Us

Mark Winges
(b. 1951)

SSAA with soloists/a cappella
Alliance Music Publications: AMP-0252
Overall: 5
Vocal: 5
Tonal/Rhythm: 4

Composer

Mark Winges was born in 1951 in Louisville, Kentucky, and currently lives in San Francisco, California, where he is composer-in-residence for the San Francisco Chamber Singers. He studied at the College-Conservatory of Music at the University of Cincinnati, at San Francisco State University, and at the Musikhögskolan in Stockholm, Sweden. Other recent choral works include *Symphonia Spiritus* (based on the texts of Hildegard von Bingen). and "Freed from Words." He has also written several arrangements of early American shape-note tunes.

Composition

This work is a modernist piece for four women soloists and four-part women's choir. It is based on a text from the *Popol Vuh*, the Quiché Mayan creation story. Incorporating unusual vocal techniques, including glissandos, unspecified extreme pitches, and speaking during inhalation, this piece's rich sound palate pushes the boundaries of what is traditionally understood as choral music.

Historical Perspective

The work is part of a modern effort to expand the range of possible sounds produced by traditional instruments, such as the voice. Most of the pitches are defined, but the piece makes little use of traditional tonal resources and instead produces clusters of often dissonant notes, inspired more by the text than by motivic transformation or harmonic goals.

The text connects this work to a modern trend of cultural exploration in composition. Making free use of the Mayan creation myth, Winges explores the roots of another culture through the Western idiom of choral music. Originally written in Mayan hieroglyphs, the *Popol Vuh* was transcribed into the Roman alphabet in the sixteenth century and only made accessible to the public ten years ago. The work is considered among the most important of the texts in the native languages of the Americas, and the translation used in this piece, that of Dennis Tedlock, is considered definitive.

Technical Considerations

This piece is of high technical difficulty. The rhythms are varied and difficult, including frequent triplets in eighth notes and quarter notes. There are several places in which quarter note triplets are sounded against straight eighth notes at a brisk tempo. The time signature shifts frequently, but the quarter note remains constant. There is one section of three independent vocal lines, which are not rhythmically coordinated, either between the lines or between individual voices.

The range of the voice parts is extreme, including notated high A's for one of the soloists and high G's for the top choral part. The altos descend only to low A, but the solo parts include requests for the highest possible note and the lowest possible note.

The parts are melodically difficult because the piece carries no real tonal center aside from a tentative resting E in the opening section, which makes occasional appearances later in the piece as an implied tonic. The lines are often chromatic and occasionally extremely so, as in the parallel movement of a close pair of minor seconds up a minor third. Sometimes the melodic lines are instrumental in shape, as in the chromatic counterpoint at measure 63 where the repeated descent from E to E passes through D, C-sharp, C-natural, A-flat, G, and F-sharp, forming a palindromic interval pattern against independently chromatic countermelodies using different scales in competing rhythmic patterns.

The unusual notational aspects of the piece are not difficult, however, and involve controlled glissandi, rhythmic speech, highest and lowest possible notes, whispering, and speaking during inhalation.

Stylistic Considerations

The interpretation of this piece relies heavily on an understanding of the text. The articulations and phrasings are strongly connected to the sounds of the spoken text, and the angular melodic shapes and sharp rhythms communicate the sense of the text in an immediate way that still preserves the sense of awe that comes from the invocation of the deity. The first expressive mark is "Energetic," suggesting an excitement that quickly becomes nervous energy in the piano entrances of the first melodic lines.

The dynamics are widely ranging and varied, often changing abruptly. The tempo is quite fast at the beginning and end, framing a more relaxed central section. The overall mood is one of excited evocation of the Maker in the outer sections and one of anxious uncertainty in the slower middle section.

Musical Elements

This piece is comprised of disparate musical elements, which are combined to create a soundscape of unusual variety. The only clear moments of rest are at the end of each section marking a tempo change. There are no formal cadences; instead there are dissipations of energy on static, held pitches. There is no clear sense of tonality, but E plays the role of a resting pitch, sounded or implied, to a greater or lesser degree throughout much of the work. The interval of a minor third plays an important role in the melodic construction of many vocal lines in this piece, and the movement from the opening octave E's to the closing octave G's could be seen as a structurally important instance of this generative interval.

The piece is at times homophonic, but it is more often contrapuntal, sometimes passing melodic control from one voice to another while the background voices sustain their pitches. The soloists almost always form a backdrop against which the choral vocal lines sound. In the beginning, the soloists create a texture of sung and spoken eighth notes with the word "wait" and humming on glissando octaves between E's. In the closing section, the soloists reiterate the opening melodic fragments of the choir and then return to the octave glissandi, this time on vowels.

Aside from the generative use of the minor third, there is little repetition of motivic units or harmonic structures.

Form and Structure

This work can be divided into three large sections: a fast opening section, a slower central section, and a fast closing section. The first section is characterized by high E's, which descend through an octave glissando, the word "wait," which is spoken and sung on indeterminate pitches, and a tentative opening duet. This resolves into a strongly contrapuntal choral statement, which is followed by a rhythmic homophonic statement in a fast crescendo.

The section closes with three independent vocal lines, which are repeated a specified number of times without coordination between the vocal lines or between individual singers.

The second section is at a relaxed tempo. The text asks nervously about the coming growing season, first with unharmonized melodic lines in individual voice parts and then with a largely homophonic statement and a strong crescendo.

The closing section returns to the original tempo and completes the invocation of the creator. The soloists return, first with a restatement of the original choral melody and then with a return of the glissandi on octave E's, this time with an accompanying crescendo. The chromatic counterpoint in the chorus on the word "plumed" is parallel to a similar section in the first part on the word "sky," but only in general rhythmic and melodic shape. The work closes with a homophonic statement and a final expansion from octave C's to double-octave G's on an open vowel.

Text and Translation

Wait!
Maker, Modeler,
look at us, listen to us,
don't let us fall, don't leave us aside,
god in the sky, heart of earth,
give us our sign, our word,
as long as there is day, as long as there is light...

—translated by Dennis Tedlock

Contributed by:

Thomas Cunningham

Repertoire Resource Guide

Benedicamus, Domino

Krzysztof Penderecki
(b. 1933)

TTTBB/a cappella
Schott: C 47592
Overall: 5
Vocal: 5
Tonal/Rhythm: 5

Composer

Polish composer Krzysztof Penderecki was once the leading representative of the Polish avant-garde. Later in his career, he began to incorporate stylistic allusions to earlier music, especially that of the eighteenth and nineteenth centuries, creating a fusion of genres and styles across historical eras. After graduating from the State Higher School of Music in Kraków, he immediately joined the faculty as a composition teacher. In 1959, Penderecki won the top three prizes of a Union of Polish Composers competition and attracted the interest of a publisher and the director of the music division of German radio. He quickly earned a reputation as one of the most innovative composers of his generation, winning many composition awards and acting as visiting professor at universities around the world. He taught at Yale University between 1973 and 1978, and he eventually returned to the Kraków Academy (renamed School of Music) as rector.

Penderecki's output includes many choral works, especially in the genre of oratorio. His St. Luke's Passion brought him critical and popular acclaim in the 1960s, and he followed this work with *Utrenia*, which was a sequel to the Passion, and a setting of the Magnificat in 1974. His oratorios use old Polish hymns as compositional material several times, and his Passion includes references to plainchant.

Composition and Genre

This work is a motet for five-voice men's chorus based on a two-voice antiphon from the archives of the Engelberg monastery. The text is from the first words of the antiphon coupled with Psalm 117 (*Laudate Dominum*). The compositional technique of using plainchant as the basis for a work is a very old one, connecting this work with the earliest polyphonic compositions.

Historical Perspective

This work was written in 1992, when his conception of style had expanded to include a large number of historical genres and styles. Especially in his sacred music, Penderecki makes use of very early musical material, such as hymns and plainchant. This work not only quotes the two-voice antiphon directly several times, but many of the other melodies closely resemble those of plainchant. Despite these ties to the past, Penderecki's modernist bent is clearly heard in the sextuplet rhythmic figures scattered throughout and the tone cluster harmonies formed between the independent contrapuntal voices.

Technical Considerations

The rhythms of this work are straightforward with the exception of one repeated figure that shifts between triple and duple feeling. There is a great deal of syncopation, but the tempo is slow. The voice parts range from a low F in the bass to a high F in the baritone and a high A-flat in the top tenor part. The work is composed of long, extended chromatic lines, which produce sustained major and minor seconds and other difficult intervals. The independence of the five vocal parts sometimes leads to dissonant tone clusters and unusual interval patterns.

Stylistic Considerations

This is a modern work with five strongly independent vocal lines. Much like Renaissance polyphonic compositions, the most important vocal line shifts between voice parts, and each voice part receives almost equal weight. When the two-voice antiphon is quoted directly, the voices are paired. There are very few dynamic indications, but those that are present are significant, serving to highlight the plainchant quotations. The tempo is slow, but there is often a large amount of contrapuntal activity.

Musical Elements

The sense of key center in this work is somewhat sporadic, though most of the work has a tonal center of F, either major or minor. The harmonies tend to be linearly motivated, resulting in complex sonorities. There is frequent strong dissonance, although the phrases typically end with a sense of resolution and a relaxing of tension. The texture is largely contrapuntal with occasional groups of voices moving together. The plainchant is quoted clearly twice, once at measure 15 and once at measure 55. The meter is a slow 3/2 or 2/2.

Form and Structure

MEASURE	EVENT AND SCORING
1–14	Opening section of rising lines over repeated rhythmic figure
15–18	Plainchant antiphon quoted and imitated
19–35	Contrapuntal imitation on the text "Quoniam"
36–47	Return of opening material
48–54	Completion of text on mostly homophonic phrases
55–61	Plainchant quoted and imitated, paired with melismatic "Alleluia"

Unit 8: Text and Translation

ANTIPHON:
Benedicamus Domino.

Let us give praise to the Lord.

PSALM 117:
Laudate Dominum omnes gentes,
laudate eum omnes populi,
quoniam confirmata est super nos
misericordia eius,
et veritas Domini manet in aeternum.

O praise the Lord, all ye nations,
praise him, all ye peoples,
for his loving kindness has been bestowed upon us,
and the truth of the Lord endures forever.

Contributed by:

Thomas Cunningham

Masterwork

Masterwork

Requiem

Gabriel Urbain Fauré
(1845–1924)

SATB divisi/organ and orchestra
Hinshaw Music, Inc.: full score=HMB147A;
vocal score=HMB147; orchestral parts=HMB147b
Edited by John Rutter

Prepared by: Bruce Chamberlain, Matthew W. Mehaffey,
and Anthony Reeves

GABRIEL FAURÉ—BIOGRAPHY

Gabriel Urbain Fauré was born in Pamiers, France, May 12, 1845, the youngest of six children born to a schoolteacher and his wife. In 1854, Fauré won a scholarship to study at the newly-founded École Niedermeyer in Paris, a school established to train church musicians. The young Fauré remained at the École for eleven years; his studies included organ, piano, voice, counterpoint, harmony, and plainsong.

The fact that the curriculum at the École placed much emphasis on plainsong undoubtedly influenced Fauré's concept of music. Characteristics of plainsong pervade Fauré's melodies and harmonies—his melodies tend to be long and flowing, and his harmonies are heavily influenced by modality.

In 1861, following Niedermeyer's death, Fauré began piano studies with Camille Saint-Saëns, another instructor at the École who was to become a close friend and advocate. Saint-Saëns introduced his students, to the contemporary music of the day, including works by Robert Schumann, Franz Liszt, and Richard Wagner. Fauré's first known compositions date from his time at

the École, and upon his graduation in 1865, he was awarded the *premiers prix* in composition for his famous choral piece *Cantique de Jean Racine*.

From 1866 until 1870, Fauré worked as organist at the Church of St. Sauveur in Rennes; in March 1870, he returned to Paris and was appointed organist at Notre Dame de Clignancourt (not the famous Notre Dame Cathedral in Paris).

The breakout of the Franco-Prussian War inspired Fauré to enlist in the infantry; upon his discharge in March 1871, he resumed his church music career. He was assistant organist at St. Sulpice, working under renowned organist Charles Widor, from 1871 to 1874; in 1874, he left St. Sulpice to assume a similar position at the Madeleine, where he assisted his former teacher Saint-Saëns. Upon Saint-Saëns' resignation in 1877, Théodore Dubois, famous for his *Seven Last Words of Christ on the Cross*, became organist at the Madeleine, and Fauré was appointed choirmaster.

Church of the Madeleine, Paris

The Madeleine is one of Paris's great churches, built on the classical temple model. Dedicated to Mary Magdalene, it has a very interesting history. The church was originally designed in 1764 by Constant d'Ivry, under commission from King Louis XV. Work on the structure was erratic, however, and ceased completely during the French Revolution. In 1806, after the Battle of Iéna, Napoleon commissioned Barthélemy Vignon to redesign and finish the building as a Temple of Glory to his *Grande Armée* (Great Army). Work on the structure continued, even after Napoleon's rule ended. After suggestions that it be everything from a railway station to a bank, the building was finally consecrated as a church in 1845. It remains a well-established church with regularly scheduled services attended by Paris' high society and is a popular concert venue because of its size and acoustics.

During this time, Fauré traveled a great deal, especially to Germany and England. During his travels, he met numerous significant musicians of the day (including Franz Liszt) and heard various productions of Wagner's operas. He also continued to compose; his First Piano Quartet, Op. 15, dates from this period. In 1883, Fauré married Marie Fremiet, who bore two sons, Emmanuel (b. 1883) and Philippe (b. 1889). He worked hard to support his family by continuing his position at the Madeleine, teaching privately, and composing (mainly during the summer months). It was also during this period that the *Requiem* had its genesis; it is believed that Fauré began composing the piece around 1877.

Fauré's family was important to him; however, despite his love for his wife, he had several relationships with other women, which was not unusual in Europe. In 1891, one of his patrons, the Princesse Edmond de Polignac (an American heiress), took Fauré on vacation to Venice. Other important women in his life included Emma Bardac and Marguérite Hasselmans. Bardac, who later married Claude Debussy, inspired Fauré to compose *La bonne chanson*, his most significant song cycle. Hasselmans, a pianist, was Fauré's mistress for the last twenty-odd years of his life.

By the 1890s, Fauré was achieving wider recognition as an important musician. He became the inspector of the provincial conservatories in 1892, and, finally, in June 1896, became organist at the Madeleine. In October of the same year, Fauré succeeded Jules Massenet as professor of composition at the Conservatoire Paris. His pupils at the Conservatoire included Maurice Ravel, Florent Schmitt, and Nadia Boulanger. During this period, Fauré traveled frequently across the English Channel to visit Britain, where he had numerous supporters; these included John Singer Sargent, who painted Fauré's portrait and drew several sketches of him.

Sargent's portrait of Fauré (1889).   **Sargent: Fauré (1896).**

In 1901, Fauré returned to his roots when he became, in addition to his work at the Conservatoire, professor of composition at the École Niedermeyer. Sadly, a slight deafness (which increased through the years) began to afflict Fauré in 1903; nevertheless, he worked as music critic for the daily *Le Figaro* from 1903 until 1921. In 1905, Fauré was appointed to succeed Dubois as director of the Conservatoire. Angry because of the Conservatoire's repeated poor treatment of his pupil Ravel, Fauré instituted many reforms,

eventually resulting in the resignations of several professors. Increasingly vocal in his views, Fauré broke with the conservative *Société nationale de musique* in 1909, helping establish and lead a new rival organization, the *Société musicale indépendente*.

Very busy with his many jobs, Fauré continued to have precious little time to compose. As always, most of his writing took place during the summer months; it took him five years (1907–12) to compose his only opera, *Pénélope*. Fauré traveled when he could, visiting England, Germany, and Russia.

Despite the outbreak of World War I in 1914, Fauré remained in Paris as director of the Conservatoire. The war years were actually quite productive for him as a composer, and his output during this period included the Second Violin Sonata (Op. 108), the First Cello Sonata (Op. 109), and the Fantasie for Piano and Orchestra (Op. 111).

In 1920, at age seventy-five, Fauré was awarded the *Grand-Croix* of the *Légion d'Honneur* (most unusual for a musician) and resigned as director of the Conservatoire to spend his time on other projects. In 1921, he revised the complete piano works of Robert Schumann for his publisher, Durand; he also collaborated with Joseph Bonnet on editions of J. S. Bach's organ works. Despite his declining health, he continued to compose his own music. In 1922, his friend Fernand Maillot organized a national tribute to Fauré at the Sorbonne, at which well-known performers played Fauré's music to an audience that included the president of France. Fauré died in Paris on November 4, 1924.

Today, we remember Fauré as a composer who was successful in many genres, as witnessed by the continuing popularity of his music. Choirs around the world sing his *Requiem*, singers perform his solo songs, and chamber music concerts frequently include his music for small ensembles. A serene beauty characterizes his music, which is usually very gentle and unassuming, much like its composer.

The Requiem Mass

A Requiem Mass is a mass for the dead (*Missa pro defunctis*) celebrated in the Roman Catholic Church. Although it has other uses (e.g., it may be offered for the dead in purgatory, or celebrated in memory of the faithful departed on All Soul's Day on November 2). Its historic function in the Roman Catholic Church would equate to what most Protestants call a funeral. Many of the traditions carry over into the contemporary Roman Catholic Funeral Mass. A Requiem is a specialized kind of mass, but follows the same basic structure as any other mass. It gets its name because the word *requiem* is the first word of the Introit. (*Requiem aeternam* is Latin for "rest eternal.")

The liturgy of the mass for the dead actually has Judaic origins: even before Christ, the Jews prayed for the souls of the departed to have *requiem aeternam*.

Christian writings mention a Eucharistic celebration for the dead within the first two centuries of the Church, but the Roman Catholic Church did not standardize the liturgy until after the Council of Trent. The basic purpose of the Council was to deal with the problems caused by the Protestant Reformation. The decrees of the Council of Trent were many, and they dealt with virtually every facet of the church; many have said it marked the birth of the modern Roman Church. In addressing church music, the Council directed that dignity should be restored to the services, forbade the use of secular melodies in church music, and mandated that the texts in liturgical music had to be intelligible.*

Considerable variations in the liturgy were common prior to its codification, and latitude in the liturgy continued to surround the celebration of Requiem Masses even after the Council of Trent. A Requiem Mass, as any other mass, consists of Ordinary (included every day) and Proper (seasonal or occasional) elements. In a Requiem Mass, however, some parts of the liturgy normally expected in a common Mass are omitted, and the Propers of the Requiem are those *proper to* the Mass for the Dead. A comparison of the 1570 Common and Requiem Mass follows.

---

* The liturgy was prescribed in the *Missal* of Pius V, 1570. Pius writes:

By these presents [this law], in virtue of Our Apostolic authority, We grant and concede in perpetuity that, for the chanting or reading of the Mass in any church whatsoever, this Missal is hereafter to be followed absolutely, without any scruple of conscience or fear of incurring any penalty, judgment, or censure, and may freely and lawfully be used.

The Requiem Liturgy of 1570

The following chart compares the common and Requiem Mass liturgies from the 1570 Missal.

COMMON MASS (TRIDENTINE MASS)	REQUIEM MASS
Pre-Mass rites • Psalm 42 "Judica me" • Psalm 110 "Confiteor"	
Introit (Proper) (The Introit is sung as the celebrant enters the church and approaches the altar. Formally, it is comprised of an antiphon sung with one or more verses of a psalm.)	**Introit** "Requiem aeternam …" The antiphon ("Requiem aeternam…luceat eis") is based on a passage from one of the books of the Apocrypha: 4 Esdras 2:34b–35: "Wait for your shepherd; he will give you everlasting rest, because he who will come at the end of the age is close at hand. Be ready for the rewards of the kingdom, because perpetual light will shine on you forevermore." (This translation is from the *New Revised Standard Version*, hereafter referred to as *NRSV*.) The psalm verse is from Psalm 64:1–2: "Praise is due to you, O God, in Zion; and to you shall vows be performed, O you who answer prayer! To you all flesh shall come." (*NRSV*; this is Psalm 65 in any Protestant bible.) Zion is the citadel of Jerusalem, seized by David from the Jebusites (2 Samuel 5:6–7). The name came to signify God's holy hill at Jerusalem or the city itself (Psalm 2: 6; Isaiah 1: 27), as well as the symbol of contact between God and man.

Common Mass (Tridentine Mass)	Requiem Mass
Kyrie	**Kyrie** See Psalm 6:3 and 40 [41]:5, 11; found in ancient Christian rites. The nine-fold form ("Kyrie" three times; "Christe" three times; and "Kyrie" three times) appears to have its origins in the eighth century.
Gloria	Omitted
Collect (Proper)	**Collect** "Deus, cui proprium"
Epistle Reading (Proper)	Epistle Reading (Proper)
Gradual (Proper)	**Gradual** "Requiem aeternam …"
Alleluia-Verse or Tract (Proper)	**Tract** "Absolve Domine…"
Sequence (Proper) (standard until the Council of Trent)	**Sequence** *Dies Irae* The *Dies Irae* did not become a part of Requiem liturgies until the fourteenth century. It is actually a poem common scholarship has attributed it to Thomas of Celano, a thirteenth-century Franciscan who was also a biographer of St. Francis. However, the text has been found in twelfth-centuy manuscripts, so the author is unknown.

Common Mass (Tridentine Mass)	Requiem Mass
	Many scholars believe the original *Dies Irae* consisted of seventeen stanzas of three lines each, and that the last six lines were added sometime later. Those lines are based on two sources: a twelfth-century trope (textual addition) on Libera Me, a responsory sung at the Absolution following the mass, which in turn derives from Zephaniah 1:14–16; and an anonymous concluding prayer.

Hence, structure of the text is:

- Seventeen stanzas, three lines each, eight syllables per line, with the last two syllables of each line rhyming *followed by*
- two stanzas, two lines each, eight syllables per line, with the last two syllables of each line rhyming *followed by*
- one stanza of two lines, six syllables each with no rhyming

The text is syllabic, as are other sequences.

The *Dies Irae* is a meditation on the gospel for the First Sunday of Advent, Luke 21: 25–36, and its first liturgical use was possibly for that Sunday. Its liturgical use is unusual in that it is very personal and liturgy ("the work of the people") is normally communal. This probably explains the addition of the last six lines.

Common Mass (Tridentine Mass)	Requiem Mass
	The first six stanzas of the poem describe the terror of Judgment Day. In the seventh stanza, the poet speaks in first person, wondering who his protector will be. He prays to Christ, the "King of fearful majesty" who is also a "fount of pity." He then gives grounds for his request for mercy: Christ's incarnation, work, and suffering and the sinner's (poet's) repentance.
Gospel Reading (Proper)	Gospel Reading (Proper)
Credo	Omitted
Offertory (Proper)	Offertory "Domine Jesu Christe" This text originated as a prayer for those who were ill and in danger of death. It is problematic, theologically, because Michael is not the archangel God sends to lead souls "into holy light." Biblically, he is portrayed in more vigorous, battle-related roles, and as the helper of the chosen people (e.g., Revelation 12:7–9; Daniel 10:13 and 12:1). It is possible that this text derives from a Coptic rite that references St. Michael in accordance with what is known of Egyptian iconographical art, which does depict Michael as weighing the merits of the dead.
Secret Prayer	Secret Prayer
Preface	Preface

Common Mass (Tridentine Mass)	Requiem Mass
Sanctus and Benedictus	**Sanctus and Benedictus** The Sanctus is also called the *Trisagion* ("Thrice Holy"). It comes at the end of the Preface, and, with the Benedictus, forms a bridge into the Canon, or Eucharistic Prayer with the Benedictus. The text of the *Sanctus* is related to Isaiah 6:3b ("Holy, holy, holy is the Lord of hosts; the whole earth is full of his glory") and Revelation 4:8 ("Holy, holy, holy, the Lord God the Almighty, who was and is and is to come.") Both translations are from the *NSRV*. This text originated in the Jewish liturgy and became a part of the Catholic rite around the seventh century. "Sabaoth" is derived from the Hebrew word for "armies" or "hosts," and is a biblical title ascribing glory or majesty. The Benedictus immediately follows the Sanctus and is based on Matthew 21:9b: "Hosanna to the Son of David! Blessed is the one who comes in the name of the Lord! Hosanna in the highest heaven!" This verse is itself related to Psalm 117 [118]:26a: "Blessed is the one who comes in the name of the Lord" (*NRSV*). The word "Hosanna" was a Hebrew cry to God: "O save!"
Canon (including Pater Noster)	**Canon (including Pater Noster)**

Common Mass (Tridentine Mass)	Requiem Mass
Agnus Dei	**Agnus Dei** (including "Dona eis Requiem" and "Dona eis Requiem sempiternam" instead of the usual "Miserere nobis" and "Dona nobis pacem.") The Agnus Dei text is derived from the *Gloria in excelsis* and the words of John the Baptist: "Here is the Lamb of God who takes away the sin of the world!" (John 1:29b, *NRSV*) In the liturgy of the mass, its tripartite form, coming near the end of the mass, balances that of the Kyrie, which comes near the beginning. In the celebration of the Mass, the Agnus Dei comes at the end of the Eucharistic Prayer, between the Fraction and the Communion antiphon.
Communion (Proper)	**Communion** "Lux aeterna…" The Communion balances the Introit; it is another "processional" movement, featuring an antiphon (this one quotes the antiphon of the Introit) and a verse. The procession here is of the assembled faithful approaching the altar to receive the host.
Ite missa est	**Ite missa est**

COMMON MASS (TRIDENTINE MASS)	REQUIEM MASS
	Absolution Responsory "Libera me" Prescribed as a part of the liturgy, this responsory is not actually sung at the mass but during the Burial Rite. It contains two excerpts from previous movements ("Dies illa…" and "Requiem aeternam…"). The responsory is sung as the coffin is sprinkled with holy water. It has often been included in musical settings of the Requiem.
	Antiphon "In paradisum…" This antiphon is a part of the Burial Rite and is sung as the coffin is borne to the grave. The text hearkens back to the Proper gospel for the Requiem when it is sung on the day of death or burial, and it concerns Lazarus, whom Jesus raised from the dead (see John 11). It has often been included in musical settings of the Requiem.

COMPOSITION: THE FAURÉ REQUIEM, OP. 48

The history and evolution of Gabriel Fauré's setting of the Requiem Mass is somewhat convoluted. Many scholars have speculated that the deaths of Fauré's father (1885) and/or mother (1887) were his inspiration to compose anew, but, in 1910, Fauré wrote in a letter to his friend and fellow composer Maurice Emmanuel that he had begun work on the *Requiem* in 1887 "for the pleasure of it." While there is no reason to question Fauré's words in this regard, it would be shortsighted to believe that the composer's life events did not affect his creative output. On the other hand, Fauré was choirmaster at the Church of the Madeleine as well as a composer interested in new music; it is not unreasonable, therefore, to believe he had non-personal reasons to compose his own setting of the Requiem Mass.

Many people have speculated that Fauré's *Requiem* reflects his own feelings and attitudes about death. In 1902, Fauré said, "I see death . . . as a joyful deliverance, an aspiration towards a happiness beyond the grave, rather than as a painful experience." The *Requiem* does seem to communicate much of that feeling with its emphasis on lyricism and beautiful melody. Fauré's fusion of traditional Requiem texts with texts from the Burial Rite coupled with the way he chose to set them musically highlights his feelings.

The Different Versions

The first version of Fauré's *Requiem* was premiered January 16, 1888, at the funeral services of architect Joseph Le Soufaché. Fauré expanded this original composition twice, in 1893 and 1900. For a January 1893 performance, he added two movements to the original version and expanded the orchestration. The 1900 version features a larger orchestral complement; this is the version that became most familiar with twentieth-century performers and audiences. It is unclear exactly why this third version was produced and whether Fauré himself made the larger orchestration. Furthermore, many changes of markings and notes alter the music substantially from earlier versions. The manuscript of the 1900 version apparently no longer exists, and scholars have increasingly debated Fauré's intentions and the reliability of this version. In the accompanying chart, one can see the development of each movement from version to version. The instrumental additions or changes are indicated in italics.

In 1984, John Rutter published a new edition of Fauré's *Requiem* (Hinshaw Music, Inc.) in which he attempted to sift through the three versions to establish one he felt was true to Fauré's intentions. Rutter writes in the Editor's Preface that he reached two basic conclusions in preparing his edition of the work:

1. The two movements added in 1893 should be included.
2. The accompaniment should essentially be that of the 1888 version with the addition of horns (per Fauré's 1893 version) mandatory and some other changes optional.

Comparison of the Three Fauré Versions Plus Rutter's Edition

	1888	1893	1900	Rutter Complete	Rutter Essential
No. 1: Introit and Kyrie	SATTBB choir viola (divisi) cello (divisi) bass timpani organ	SATTBB choir viola (divisi) cello (divisi) bass timpani organ *horn (2)* *trumpet (2)*	SATTBB choir viola (divisi) cello (divisi) bass timpani organ *horn (4)* trumpet (2) *bassoon (2)*	SATTBB choir viola (divisi) cello (divisi) bass timpani organ horn (2) trumpet (2)	SATTBB choir viola (divisi) cello (divisi) bass timpani organ
No. 2: Offertory	None	baritone solo SATB choir viola (divisi) cello (divisi) bass organ	baritone solo SATB choir viola (divisi) cello (divisi) bass organ	baritone solo SATB choir viola (divisi) cello (divisi) bass organ	baritone solo SATB choir viola (divisi) cello (divisi) bass organ
No. 3: Sanctus	SATTBB choir solo violin viola (divisi) cello (divisi) bass harp organ	SATTBB choir solo violin viola (divisi) cello (divisi) bass harp organ *bassoon (2)* *horn (4)* *trumpet (2)*	SATTBB choir solo violin viola (divisi) cello (divisi) bass harp organ bassoon (2) horn (4) trumpet (2)	SATTBB choir solo violin viola (divisi) cello (divisi) bass harp organ bassoon (2) horn (4) trumpet (2)	SATTBB choir solo violin viola (divisi) cello (divisi) bass harp organ horn (2)
No. 4: Pie Jesu	soprano solo viola (divisi) cello (divisi) bass organ *(This is assumed by Rutter as no manuscript exists.)*	soprano solo viola (divisi) cello (divisi) bass organ *(This is assumed by Rutter as no manuscript exists.)*	soprano solo viola (divisi) cello (divisi) bass organ *harp* *flute (2)* *clarinet (2)* *bassoon (2)*	soprano solo viola (divisi) cello (divisi) bass organ	soprano solo viola (divisi) cello (divisi) bass organ harp

	1888	1893	1900	Rutter Complete	Rutter Essential
No. 5: **Agnus Dei**	SATTBB choir viola (divisi) cello (divisi) bass organ	SATTBB choir viola (divisi) cello (divisi) bass organ *bassoon (2)* *horn (4)*	SATTBB choir viola (divisi) cello (divisi) bass organ bassoon (2) horn (4)	SATTBB choir viola (divisi) cello (divisi) bass organ bassoon (2) horn (4) *violin*	SATTBB choir viola (divisi) cello (divisi) bass organ
No. 6: **Libera Me**	None	baritone solo SATTBB choir viola (divisi) cello (divisi) bass organ horn (4) trombone (3) timpani	baritone solo SATTBB choir viola (divisi) cello (divisi) bass organ horn (4) trombone (3) timpani *violin*	baritone solo SATTBB choir viola (divisi) cello (divisi) bass organ horn (4) timpani	baritone solo SATTBB choir viola (divisi) cello (divisi) bass organ horn (4)
No. 7: **In Paradisum**	SATTBB choir viola solo viola (divisi) cello (divisi) bass harp organ	SATTBB choir viola solo viola (divisi) cello (divisi) bass harp organ *bassoon (2)* *horn (4)*	SATTBB choir viola solo viola (divisi) cello (divisi) bass harp organ bassoon (2) horn (4)	SATTBB choir viola solo viola (divisi) cello (divisi) bass harp organ bassoon (2) *horn (2)*	SATTBB choir viola solo viola (divisi) cello (divisi) bass organ

The Manuscript and the 1893 Version

The 1888 version is the only extant manuscript, and it contains only four of the five movements. The "Pie Jesu" apparently has been lost; however, the movement is listed on the title page of the manuscript. The manuscript is actually cataloged as four different entries at the Bibliothèque Nationale in Paris (numbers 410–13).

According to this manuscript, the organ plays almost continuously, always containing the essence of the harmonic structure, while the other instruments double, elaborate, and decorate the melodies sung by the choir and reinforced by the organ. The horn, trumpet, and bassoon parts appear in the manuscript in Fauré's hand, but most scholars believe they were added at a later date.

Jean-Michel Nectoux, for example, believes the horns and trumpets were added for a January 1893 performance, but the bassoons were used at some other undetermined performance.

The "Offertory" and "Libera me" were added for the 1893 version. Fauré composed the "Offertory" in 1889 but he may have composed the "Libera me" somewhat earlier.

The 1900 (Published) Version

John Rutter relates that some believe Fauré's publisher, Hamelle, asked him to arrange a "version symphonique" sometime in the 1890s. In fact, in 1898, Fauré did tell his publisher he would prepare the score of the *Requiem* for publication but did not mention expanding the orchestra. He asked permission for his pupil Roger-Ducasse to prepare the piano reduction. Rutter believes Fauré actually had someone (perhaps Roger-Ducasse) reorchestrate the piece and cites three good pieces of evidence to support his theory:

1. Fauré had some of his other compositions rescored;
2. Fauré was especially busy during this time; and
3. The score is replete with misprints and inaccuracies of the kind the meticulous Fauré would never have allowed.

Rutter's theory seems quite plausible; in fact, in a letter to Eugène Ysaÿe, the conductor of the Brussels premiere of the 1900 version, Fauré expresses dismay over all the misprints in the score. Rutter used educated speculation to support the need for his own edition. Lamenting the 1900 version's "ineptitude and slipshod preparation," he feels the large orchestra called for in the 1900 version is alien to Fauré's original vision of a "petit Requiem." As further evidence, he cites the size of the Madeleine's choir of no more than thirty voices, which clearly would have been terribly overbalanced by the orchestration of the 1900 version. Rutter's orchestration remains true to the peaceful and reflective nature of Fauré's setting.

Rutter's Edition

In our opinion, Rutter's edition of the Fauré *Requiem* is the best one available today, and the analyses and details (i.e., rehearsal letters, orchestral seating, etc.) refer to that edition. Rutter's scholarship appears solid, and his editorial procedures are clear. His additions or changes are generally obvious (e.g., the use of square brackets to indicate changed or added dynamic markings).

However, the conductor does need to be aware of some places where Rutter's editorial procedures are unclear—for example, his failure to clearly distinguish his editorial changes in the instrumentation. In his preface, Rutter says: "The accompaniment should follow the 1888 version, but with two

or (preferably) four horns as added for the 1893 version...[and] trumpets and bassoons may also be used if players happen to be conveniently available, but they...can well be omitted. The timpani in the 1888 version can also be omitted." An outline of the instrumentation is provided on page five of Rutter's preface, which distinguishes between "essential" and "dispensable" instruments; this outline is reflected in our chart above under the columns "Rutter Complete" (which shows all available instrumentation in his edition) and "Rutter Essential" (which omits those instruments Rutter deems dispensable).

Rutter suggests the possible omission of the trumpets and bassoons because they double other parts. We surmise that he considers the horns necessary because they were always part of "Libera Me," which was not present in the 1888 version; it seems logical that if they are hired for that movement, it would be wasteful not to use them in other movements. Less clear is the reason Rutter feels that timpani could be omitted; while Fauré only wrote timpani parts for the first movement in 1888, he added them for the "Libera Me" in 1893. The same logic for including the horns would seem to strengthen the case for using timpani instead of omitting them; furthermore, timpani were a part of Fauré's orchestration from the beginning, and it is worth noting that the orchestration of the 1888 and 1893 versions is by Fauré himself.

Also interesting is Rutter's decision to eliminate the trombone parts in the "Libera Me." The trombones were part of the 1893 version of the *Requiem*, which was the first to include trombones. Granted, they play only in this movement, and only in the "Dies Irae" section of the "Libera me"; trombones, however, have traditionally been a part of the "Dies Irae." While considerations of economy may dictate a conductor's decision to omit trombones, it is curious that Rutter chose to eliminate them from his score altogether. Other instruments from the 1900 version eliminated by Rutter include the flute, clarinet, and violin sections. (He maintained the solo violin in movements 3 and 7.) These omissions are more understandable because they involve instruments added only for the 1900 version to movements that always lacked them before.

Finally, one must remember that Fauré's 1888 and 1893 versions were performed at the Madeleine under his direction. No evidence seems to exist that Fauré preferred the 1900 version for performance by his church choir; it was, in fact, performed at the Paris World Exhibition in 1900. It is entirely conceivable that Fauré desired two versions of his piece, one for concert use and one for more intimate performances.

Fauré's Setting: Texts

In his *Requiem,* Fauré changed portions of the text from the official texts prescribed for the Requiem Mass. For example, in the "Libera Me" and

"Offertory" he omitted certain words and repeated others, so that the movement became more musically balanced and the words could be more clearly understood. The *Dies Irae* is only partially present (within the "Libera Me" and the "Pie Jesu"), and the Benedictus is completely absent. The final two movements, "Libera Me" and "In Paradisum," are prayers said over the coffin at the graveside, not part of the liturgy of the Mass of for the Dead.

No one knows why Fauré made the textual decisions he did. It is worth bearing in mind, however, that Fauré composed his *Requiem* within a very large shadow. Well-versed in plainchant and liturgical music, he knew the older settings; with his education, training, and work in the Parisian churches, he certainly knew the older settings of the Requiem. In addition to the older settings, however, he knew the nineteenth-century Requiems. Beginning with Mozart (1791), composers had been increasingly adventurous in their settings of the Requiem. This, combined with the facts that Requiem Masses have always been subject to variation and that Fauré was himself an adventureous composer who liked to write "different" music, would make it surprising if he had strictly followed the codified liturgy.

Fauré's Composition within the Nineteenth Century Context

The following chart shows four well-known Requiem settings from 1791–1874 and some salient points about each.

Mozart (1791)	• Soloists (four part) • Chorus (four part) • Unusual orchestration • Mozart died before the work was completed, and various versions exist • Fourteen sections constitute Süssmayr's completion, setting the Introit, Kyrie, Sequence, Offertory, Sanctus, Benedictus, Agnus Dei, and Communion
Berlioz (first performance, December 1837)	• Tenor soloist • Choir of sopranos, tenor, and basses (divisi)—altos only specified in Sanctus • Large orchestra with four brass bands • Ten movements, setting the Introit, Kyrie, Sequence, Offertory, Sanctus, and Agnus Dei

	• Words often repeated out of order • Quite dramatic, but with great melodic sense
Brahms **(first performance, April 1868)**	• Soprano and baritone soloists • Chorus (four part) • Standard orchestra • Seven movements, none liturgical • German biblical texts chosen by Brahms • Symmetry within movements
Verdi **(first performance, May 1874)**	• Soloists (four part) • Chorus (four part, divisi) • Large orchestra • Very dramatic and operatic, lyrical arias, and aria-like melodies • Seven movements, setting the Introit, Kyrie, Sequence, Offertory, Sanctus, Benedictus, Agnus Dei, and Libera Me

Examination of the above chart reveals that Fauré drew ideas from each of the cited Requiems. For example, Fauré's orchestration is remarkable because of its emphasis on the lower strings. Mozart's setting eschewed the higher woodwind instruments and called for basset horns, presumably to obtain a dark and somber tone quality. The opening of Brahms' *Ein Deutsches Requiem* features an orchestration quite similar to Fauré's with no violins with *divisi* in the lower strings.

Furthermore, none of the cited composers sets the entire liturgical Requiem texts; they all picked and chose to some degree. Although Fauré used liturgical texts, they were not all from the mass for the dead, and he did rearrange and repeat words, presumably to match his musical forms. In this sense, he may have taken inspiration from Berlioz, Brahms, and Verdi. Berlioz used texts from the Requiem Mass, but treated the texts rather freely. Brahms ignored the liturgical texts completely, setting biblical texts that reassured the living more than they prayed for the dead. Verdi set the Libera Me in his Requiem. Fauré omitted the Sequence in its entirety, save the small portions quoted in the "Libera Me" and "Pie Jesu." It seems Fauré may have been more interested in music and texts that served to comfort the living while praying for the dead than in using texts to portray the plight of the dead facing judgment. The following chart shows Fauré's text selections:

MOVEMENT	TEXT MISSING
"Introit and Kyrie"	None.
"Offertory"	Mm. 1–30 omit some words ("omnium fidelium") and rearrange the text.
	Some text is skipped ("sed signifer…semini ejus.")
	Mm. 34–76 present the entirety of the last portion of the text.
	Mm. 77–93 reprise the text of Fauré's opening section with further omissions.
"Sanctus"	Text complete, but no Benedictus.
"Pie Jesu"	Only the final two lines of the *Dies Irae* are used.
"Agnus Dei" (including Communion)	None. This movement also contains the text "Lux aeterna."
"Libera Me"	Text complete but highly rearranged.
"In Paradisum"	None.

While Fauré's *Requiem* could hardly be described as operatic, his long-breathed melodies accompanied by strings outlining the salient harmonies certainly bear some resemblance to operatic techniques. While he knew the music of Wagner, he was not a Wagner disciple, and his melodic ideas bear far more resemblance to Verdi's.

Fauré's *Requiem* stands alone in the gamut of nineteenth-century Requiems in that it focuses (through liturgical texts) on the peaceful side of death. The piece seeks to console those remaining in this world, rather than painting a fearful picture of death and the journey of the soul. While Brahms certainly did the same, his Requiem made no use of the traditional liturgical texts. Fauré's *Requiem* inspired many composers of the twentieth century to follow in this vein; Maurice Duruflé and John Rutter, for example, both found a model in Fauré's *Requiem* for delivering a message of peace and hopefulness to both the departed soul and the listener.

ANALYSIS

Deciphering the Analysis Charts

Score analysis is one of the conductor's most important activities. The creation of analysis charts assists conductors in unraveling complicated choral and orchestral scores. Such charts enable the conductor to see, hear, and ultimately digest the musical form in the abstract, yielding an understanding of the composer's musical syntax from the perspective of an aural expectation rather than a visual cue.

Each chart appearing below (one for each movement) delineates the large sections of the musical forms (i.e., Introduction, A section, B section, A' section, Coda, etc.). These larger formal designations are then reduced into moderate subset bar groupings (usually based upon the text distribution) and are further reduced into combinations of smaller bar groupings. It might be helpful to think of these levels of division as being roughly analogous to the prose designations of paragraphs (e.g., A section), sentences (e.g., seventeen measures, 1–17), clauses [e.g., 6(3+3) +11 (8+3)], and so forth. This process capitalizes on the notion that music is a language and each composer has a unique and recognizable syntax, harmonic usage, and structure. In order to allow the choir and orchestra to speak fluently in the composer's language during performances, the conductor must fully understand the inherent characteristics of the language. Each chart also indicates meter, tempo, significant key areas and/or harmonic uses, and text. The narrative analysis following each chart explains the markings on the charts in more detail; the narrative also highlights important harmonic motion and resolutions. A chart of the overall musical structure appears near the end of the chapter after all the movement charts and narrative analyses.

Understanding the structural aspects of music helps a conductor assimilate a score much more quickly. Devising and studying analysis charts and placing pertinent information in the score helps a conductor design rehearsal strategies based upon the musical structure and the composer's intentions. In this way, a conductor can function much more effectively as the composer's advocate in music making.

Judiciously give the singers information about form to help them make sense of seemingly complex forms. Do not burden singers with too much information. Give them only the information you feel will hasten their learning and assimilation of the music.

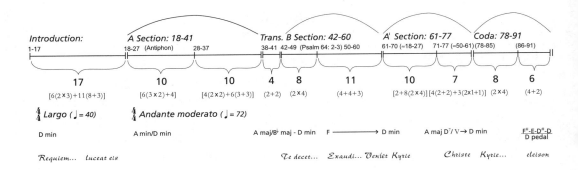

Movement No. 1—Introit and Kyrie

The first movement of Fauré's *Requiem* employs two liturgical texts: the Introit, Proper to the Requiem Mass; and the Kyrie, part of the mass Ordinary. The Introit is comprised of Psalm 64 (65):2–3 and an antiphon. Textually, the first movement has a tripartite formal design of antiphon, psalm verse, and Kyrie. The above chart reflects this by dividing the movement into three large sections: A (mm. 18–41), setting the antiphon text; B (mm. 42–60), setting the psalm verses; and A' (mm. 61–77), setting the Kyrie. The tonal design is also tripartite; the keys move from the tonic (D minor) to its flatted submediant (B-flat major) back to tonic.

This third relation (harmonic motion by thirds) is a significant feature of Fauré's compositional language and is visible throughout the *Requiem*. Surrounding the internal tripartite form are an Introduction (mm. 1–17) and a Coda (mm. 78–91). The seventeen-measure Introduction is organized into groups of 6(2x3)+ 11(8+3)* measures over a bass line that gradually descends stepwise from D to C before reaching a half cadence in D minor (m. 17). Employing a rich harmonic language laced with modal colors, this seventeen-measure introduction typifies the concepts of "the Fauré style." The chant-like quality and slow tempo (quarter note = 40) must be unfaltering while the music explores the dynamic extremes. Be sure the choir is secure in measures 9–17 because the chord progression following the E-flat Neapolitan chord is very challenging with its cross-relations and distantly related harmonies.

The twenty-four-measure A section, following the grand pause and tempo change to *Moderato* (quarter note = 72, not quite twice as fast), can be organized into two ten-measure subsets (mm. 18–27 and 28–37), with a four-measure transition (mm. 38–41). Both ten-measure groups use the entire antiphon text sung in unison by the tenors over an orchestral texture of divided strings supported by the organ. Fauré's musical economy is striking.

---

* Read this as "a group of six measures, comprised of two subsets of three measures each, plus a group of eleven measures, comprised of a subset of eight measures, followed by a subset of three measures."

For example, the orchestra plays a two-measure ostinato pattern, while the tenors' chant-like melody employs only five pitches. In measures 28–29, the horns and trumpets play the chant-like motive. Harmonically, the motion toward A minor begins in measure 33 and is completed at the downbeat of measure 38; this harmonic completion begins the four-bar transition that modulates to B-flat major at the beginning of the B section (m. 42).

The B section (mm. 42–60) is a nineteen-measure unit, divisible into two phrases: 8(2x4) + 11(4+4+3), corresponding with the two verses from Psalm 64. Only sopranos sing the very important antecedent/consequent melody, modulating to D minor in the first phrase while the orchestra again plays a rhythmic ostinato pattern. The second phrase's urgent cry, "Hear us Lord," is set for the entire choir, alternating between forte and piano. Also interesting is Fauré's use of brass instruments for color in the soft measures, and the setting of the string section in unison.

The A' section (mm. 61–77) is (like the A and B sections) divided into two smaller phrases: 10[2+8(2x4)] and 7[4(2+2)+3(2x1+1)]. The first phrase (mm. 61–77) is equal to the first phrase of the A section (mm. 18–27), while the second phrase (mm. 71–77) is only roughly similar to the B section's second phrase (mm. 50–60). This creates musical and textual links between the Introit and the Kyrie.

The fourteen-measure Coda (mm. 78–85) completes the movement's symmetry. The Coda is divisible into two phrases, 8(2x4) + 6(4+2). Be sure the E-natural of measure 81 is high and the E-flat of measure 85 is low; it is also important to cue the first horn for the countermelody. Note that the bass line in the final six bars descends by step over the timpani pedal point, an obvious reference to the Introduction's descent.

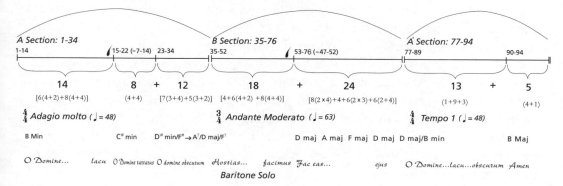

Movement No. 2—Offertory

The "Offertory" is possibly the most problematic movement of the Fauré *Requiem*. Fauré composed the movement in 1889 and added it to the *Requiem* in 1893. This movement is the only real example of imitative writing in the *Requiem* and features the most ambiguous harmonic language of any movement. Fauré's ambivalence regarding tonality or modality, coupled with his unusual arrangement of the Proper liturgical text, yields a complicated musical puzzle.

Analysis of this movement yields an ABA' structure based upon the changes of tempo and meter and the introduction of the baritone soloist. These changes mark the beginning of the B section; their negation marks the beginning of the A' section. Section A (mm. 1–34) is divisible into three smaller sub-groups: fourteen measures [6(4+2) + 8(4+4)]; eight measures (4+4); and twelve measures [7(3+4)+5(3+2)].

The meter is 4/4 with a tempo indication of *Adagio Molto* (quarter note = 48). The key scheme, however, is not extremely clear; it is not until measure 5 (and the arrival of F-sharp major) that we fully understand the music is in B minor. Fauré inverts the opening instrumental music to derive the musical material for the canonic imitation of the altos and tenors (mm. 6–10). Measures 15–22 are a structural repeat of measures 7–14 transposed up a whole step to C-sharp minor. Measures 23–34 begin in D-sharp minor, continuing the sequence from measures 7–14 to 15–22. Fauré now pairs the altos and baritones in imitation while the tenors sing a new countermelody. This section can be troublesome for choirs as there are momentary arrival points of F-sharp major (m. 26) and F-sharp minor (m. 30) while the orchestra moves from A-sharp minor to A^7 in measures 33–34, signaling the beginning of the B section. (**Conducting tip:** Be sure to cue the *pizzicato* of the double basses in measure 34 because a clean ensemble attack for this significant harmonic shift is crucial.)

Fauré omitted the words "omnium fidelium" and "libera eas" from the Offertory, and used "O Domine Jesu Christe, rex gloriae, libera animas defuctorum" as a kind of refrain. He also subsequently omitted "sed signifer sanctus Michael repraesentet eas in lucem sanctam: Quam olim Abrahae promisisti et semini ejus," for unknown reasons.

The B section (mm. 35–76) features changes of key, meter, and tempo (D major, 3/4, and *Andante moderato*, quarter note = 63). The baritone soloist's first entrance sets Revelation 8:3-4, the internal Biblical text that is surrounded by the antiphon. (**Conducting tip:** It is important that the conducting gesture be very clear to enable the double basses to play their *pizzi-cato* notes with rhythmic accuracy. Also, a slight *rallentando* is appropriate in measure 44.)

Section B divides into two smaller groups of measures, eighteen measures [4+6(4+2) + 8(4+4)] + twenty-four measures [8(2x4)+4+6(2x3)+6(2+4)]. In the first grouping, the orchestra plays another two-bar ostinato pattern based upon a rhythmic figure from measure 5 under the baritone melody. The second grouping of the B section (mm. 53–76) begins with a reference in the organ part to the "Te decet" melody from Movement I; the baritone's melody at measure 57 ("fac eas") recalls the same melody. Through a literal repeat of

measures 47–52, the second grouping in the B section closes in the same way as the first, cadencing to D major in measure 77; this cadence overlaps the beginning of the A' section.

The A' section (mm. 77–94) features the return of the opening's imitative texture, 4/4 meter, and tempo, all supported only by organ. The harmonic language is again convoluted, moving through several tonalities. By measure 87, the B minor tonality is firmly established, but the final five-measure "Amen" features a mutated B major tonality.

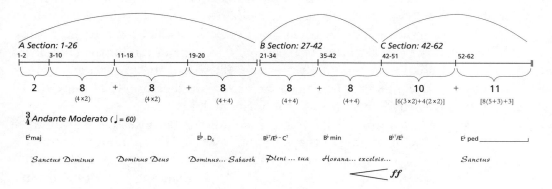

Movement No. 3—Sanctus

The third movement sets the Sanctus text from the mass Ordinary, without the customary Benedictus. This movement again employs divided violas and cellos with contrabass and organ; it makes sparing use of horn and trumpet, and adds—for the first time—bassoon, harp, and solo violin. The *Andante moderato* tempo indication (quarter note = 60) and 3/4 meter remain constant throughout the movement.

The text has a three-phrase structure that defines the movement. As indicated in the chart, the A section (mm. 1–26) is twenty-six measures long (2+8+8+8); the B section (mm. 27–42) is sixteen measures long (8+8); and the C section (mm. 42–62) is twenty-one measures long (10+11). The three-part form in this movement is rather arbitrary, but these sectional divisions will help the conductor organize the music.

The "Sanctus" begins with a two-measure orchestral introduction. The running sixteenth notes of the violas create a hemiola pattern set in two-measure groups, which is expandable into larger four- and eight-measure phrases. The entire A section features this hemiola, but the measures are best organized as 2 + 8(4x2) + 8(4x2) + 8(4+4). Fauré sets the text in the same manner by alternating the text "Sanctus, Sanctus, Sanctus, Dominus Deus Sabaoth" between sopranos and tenor/baritones as a textual hemiola: "Sanctus" (mm. 3–6), "Sanctus Dominus" (mm. 7–10), "Dominus Deus" (mm. 11–14), "Deus Sabaoth" (mm. 15–18). The economy of melodic material is impressive here as well; the first phrase uses only B-flat, C, and A-flat, and the second phrase uses only B-flat, C, D-flat, D-natural, and A-flat. The third phrase, however, expands the musical process by introducing a momentary modulation to D major (m. 22), which shifts to B-flat^7 in measure 26; this B-flat^7 functions as a dominant seventh chord in E-flat, reestablishing E-flat major as tonic in the B section. The solo violin, marked *con sordino* ("with mute"), sounds above the tenor/baritone response to the sopranos, playing the "Te decet" melody from the first movement.

The B section (mm. 27–42) is a sixteen-measure complex, quite similar to the A section except that the text here consists of the second and third phrases of the "Sanctus." The sixteen measures are divisible into two 8-bar phrases, each grouped (4+4) instead of (4x2). It is important to note the thickening of the orchestration in measure 30 in preparation for the *crescendo* to forte and change of texture at measure 42, where the C section begins. (**Conducting tip:** The trumpets need a clear cue in measure 42 because they have not played since measure 74 of movement 1.)

Measure 42 is a critical bar for the conductor because the end of the B section and the beginning of the C section overlap. The conductor must be sure the gesture does not interrupt the conclusion of one phrase even while giving the cue to begin the new phrase. The concluding C section (mm. 42–62) can be divided into two groups, 10 [6(3x2)+4(2x2)] + 11[8(5+3)+3]. Measures 42–47 employ a two-measure unit in the orchestra, which is repeated three times, while the tenor and baritone reiterate the "Hosanna" twice. Measures 48–51 are a four-bar unit, featuring a *diminuendo* to **pp** while the strings play *pizzicato* (plucked). Measures 52–53 feature another phrase overlap as the sopranos conclude and the tenor/baritone begin, while the orchestra reestablishes the hemiola pattern of the opening of the movement. The final three measures, 60–62, are a written out *ritardando* as the violas' sixteenth-note figure mutates into eighth notes; it is, therefore, important not to allow any additional slowing. It would be advisable, however, to ask the harpist to roll the final chord, making the six-note chord sound like six eighth notes.

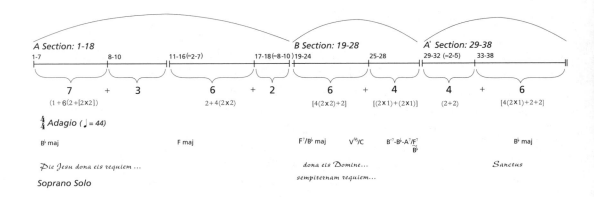

Movement No. 4—Pie Jesu

It is almost certainly by design that the central movement of Fauré's *Requiem* is a prayer for mercy and eternal rest on behalf of the dead. Interestingly, Fauré did not include the dramatic, horrible scene of judgment found in the *Dies Irae* sequence, which so many other composers have set. Instead, Fauré extracted the concluding two lines of the *Dies Irae* to use as the central movement and theme for the entire work.

This thirty-eight-measure prayer is cast in an ABA' form, set for muted strings, harp, organ, and solo soprano. The *Adagio* tempo indication (quarter note = 44) and 4/4 meter remain constant throughout the movement, as does the primary tonic of B-flat major. The analysis of movement 1 demonstrates the harmonic motion from D minor to B-flat major, back to D minor. It is significant that the *Requiem* as a whole moves from D minor (movement 1) to B-flat major (movement 4) back to D minor/major (movements 6 and 7).

The A section (mm. 1–18) can be organized 10[7(1+2+2+2)+3]+ 8 [6(2+2+2)+2]. The B section (mm. 19–28) is a ten-measure complex, organized 6[2+4(2x2)]+4[(2x1)+(2x1)]. The first four bars firmly reestablish B-flat major while the next two bars move through G$^{6/5}$, C major, and D minor on the way to A major. It would be appropriate to allow a slight *rallentando* in measure 28 beats 3 and 4 to facilitate the *crescendo* and enable the soprano and orchestra to poise for the arrival of the A' section.

Organ provides the sole accompaniment in the A section, but in the B section muted strings play as well. The text underlay is quite interesting; Fauré rearranged the second phrase of text and combined it with one additional phrase, "sempiternam requiem."

The A' section (mm. 29–38) is a ten-measure structure, similar to the opening phrase of the A section, but instead of being 7+3, the grouping is 4(2+2) + 6[4(2x1)+2+2]. Measures 29–32 are identical to measures 2–5; it is worth noting the subtle change of text underlay here as well.

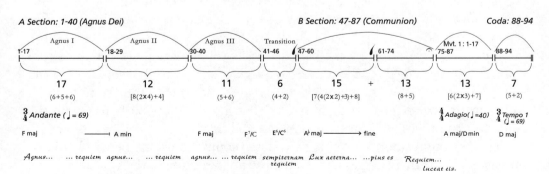

Movement No. 5—Agnus Dei

The fifth movement of the *Requiem*, the "Agnus Dei," combines two liturgical texts, the Ordinary Agnus Dei and the Proper Communion. The text of an Agnus Dei in a Requiem Mass differs slightly from that of the Tridentine Mass (see page 503). The A section (mm. 1–40) divides into three smaller subsections: Agnus I, mm. 1–17; Agnus II, mm. 18–29; and Agnus III, mm. 30–40. A six-bar transition to the Communion (mm. 41–46) follows section A.

The Communion text, like the Introit and Offertory, consists of an antiphon and a verse; the B section (mm. 47–87) reflects the two-part text structure: measures 47–74 set the antiphon text, and measures 75–87 set the verse. The movement concludes with a seven- measure Coda (mm. 88–94) that reprises measures 1–6. This combination of texts, including phrases such as "Lux aeterna luceat eis," and "Requiem aeternam dona eis, Domine," has inspired numerous composers to "recapitulate" music from earlier in their Requiem settings, just as Fauré did. (**Conductor's note:** The conductor should strictly observe the dramatic dynamic shifts from forte to piano, etc., as these shifts add to the unsettling quality of the Agnus II.)

As noted in three of the four previous movements, Fauré began with an orchestral introduction (F major, 3/4, *Andante*, quarter note = 69), employing a rhythmic/melodic ostinato motive that sets the musical environment for the vocal material. The opening seventeen-measure structure of the A section typifies this procedure, as the 6+5+6 sub-groups employ the same five measures three times (1–5 = 7–11 = 12–16; measure 6 = measure 17; they serve as transitional measures). The organ plays with the divided viola and cello parts, and the double basses play the bass line *pizzicato*. The second incantation of the Agnus text (mm. 18–29) is a twelve-measure complex grouped [8(2x4)+4]. Note the harmonic shift to A minor (up a third) from the F major of the opening, as well as the bassoon entrance (in unison with the strings) and the role of the horn (harmonic support for the choir). The third setting of the Agnus text (mm. 30–40) is an eleven-measure structure grouped (5+6), structurally quite similar to measures 7–17, but modulating to C major. The organ and divided strings do not, however, play *colla parte* here, but are in a quasi-canonic relationship two bars apart. The undulating six-bar transition (mm. 41–46), grouped (4+2), comes to a point of stasis with the soprano C5 (m. 45). In a gesture of pure romantic genius, Fauré uses the soprano note to pivot to the warm (third-related) tonality of A-flat; he simultaneously ushers in the B section and highlights the arrival of "eternal light."

The B section (mm. 47–87) has two large components, measures 47–74 and measures 75–87; these correspond to the overall structure of the verse text. The first component is a twenty-eight-measure complex, grouped 15(7+8) + 13(8+5). Measures 47–53 are repeated in measures 55–60, with a deceptive cadence into F minor (m. 60); the substructure here is [4(2x2)+3]. Measures 61–74 begin in F minor and arrive at a half-close to D minor at measure 69. The

B section uses only strings and organ, the divided violas playing constantly moving eighth notes while the cello/double bass provide the bass line. The organ, while not exactly *colla parte* with the choir, provides harmonic and melodic support. Fauré indicates both crescendo and decrescendo in measure 53, and the authors would suggest a slight *rallentando* in this measure and in measure 73, before the Grand Pause of measure 74.

As mentioned earlier, the Communion text lends itself quite readily to musical recapitulation, and Fauré has seized upon this opportunity; measures 75–87 are a virtual repeat of the opening segment of movement 1. With an *Adagio* tempo indication (quarter note = 40), in 4/4 meter, this thirteen-measure "recapitulation" is very effective, but can pose some musical problems for both choir and orchestra. Grouped [6(2x3)+7], this thirteen-measure complex is truncated by four measures and culminates in a full close on D major in measure 88 (as opposed to the half close in movement 1). Other differences include the A-flat in measure 82, which leads to D-flat major in measure 84, as opposed to the E-flat major of movement 1. In addition, the bassoons assume the function filled by the horns in movement 1. Precise and solid pitch accuracy and careful attention to intonation in both places are crucial to a satisfactory result.

The final seven-measure Coda (mm. 88–94) is a literal repeat of measures 1–6, this time in D major, the parallel key to the recapitulated material from movement 1.

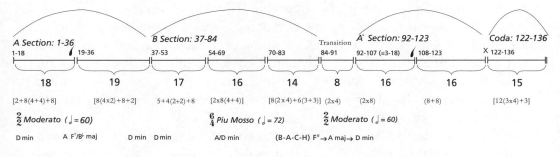

Movement No. 6—Libera Me

The Responsory text, "Libera Me," is not part of the liturgical Requiem Mass, but part of the Burial Rite. (See page 504.) A Responsory, which functions as a musical postlude, consists of a respond and verse. Like the Communion text Fauré included as part of the Agnus Dei, the Responsory contains textual reprises from previous movements that are innate to a Requiem Mass (the Sequence *Dies Irae* and the Introit, "Requiem aeternam." Often, the "Libera Me" is intoned in procession, while the bier is moved from the church to the cemetery where the antiphon "In Paradisum" is intoned at the graveside.

Evidence exists that Fauré composed the "Libera Me" as early as 1877 as an independent piece for baritone solo and organ. He added the movement to his *Requiem* in 1893, when he also added horn and trumpet parts.

The movement is cast in a tripartite form (A, mm. 1–36; B mm. 37–83; and A', mm. 92–121) plus a Coda (mm. 122–136). It contains the most dramatic music of the *Requiem*. The 2/2 meter and *Moderato* tempo indication (half note = 60), along with the opening two-measure rhythmic pattern in the organ pedals and pizzicato lower strings, seem to portray the solemn procession from the church to the gravesite. The A section consists of two smaller subsections: 18[2+8(4x2)+8] + 19[8(2+2+2+2)+8+2]. The baritone soloist sings a hauntingly beautiful melody as the music moves from D minor to A major, shifts to F^7/B-flat major, and then goes back to D minor in antecedent/consequent phrase structures. Note the progression by step in the bass line that also serves to heighten the processional quality of this music (measures 3–8 = D, E, F, F-sharp, G, A; and measures 11–16 = G, A, B-natural, C, D). This stepwise progression appears in the baritone melody in measures 19–25 (A, B-flat, C, D, E), uniting the two phrases of the A section in a very significant way.

The B section (mm. 37–83) incorporates the verse text, which is sung by the choir. It is structured in three subgroups of 17[5+4(2+2)+8] + 16[2x8(4+4)] + 14[8(2x4)+6(3+3)]. Note that the first subgroup (mm. 37–53) moves into the tempo/meter change, *Piu mosso* (half note = 72) 6/4; the horns create the new tempo and feeling in measures 52–53 as they complete the previous eight-measure group. (**Conducting tip:** A very clear yet rounded preparatory beat is needed on beat two of measure 52 to prepare the horns to establish the new tempo and compound meter. Be sure the horns do not sustain long notes at a fortissimo dynamic but only initiate the tone at that dynamic and then diminish, sustaining at forte or even mezzo forte. Encourage the choir to use crisp and articulate diction to balance the dramatic orchestral texture.)

The new subgroup (mm. 54–69), with its 2x8-measure structure, does not really begin until measure 54. Some balance problems may surface in this subgroup as the choir progresses quickly from unison to two-part to four-part textures as the horns sound the accented, rhythmic hammer blows of the last judgment's gavel. The third subgroup (mm. 70–83) reprises the opening Introit text in a harmonic sequence that moves over a chromatically rising bass line in measures 70–74 (D-flat, D-natural, E-flat, E-natural, F, F-sharp, G, G-sharp), arriving at F-sharp major in measure 78. Simultaneously, the melodic sequence in the sopranos features the B-A-C-H motive (B-natural–A–C–B-flat), but begins on A-flat in measure 70 and on C in measure 74. The final six bars of this subgroup move deftly to a cadence on A major, creating the transition (mm. 84–91) back to the *Moderato* tempo (half note = 60) and 2/2 meter. This eight-measure transition is actually a long dominant pedal point on A, preparing the return of the A' section and D minor tonic tonality.

The A' section (mm. 92–123) is a literal repeat of measures 3–34, again using the respond text, now sung by the choir in unison. The orchestration is enhanced subtly as the timpani joins the horns for the critical harmonic conclusions, the entire string section plays *pizzicato*, and the organ provides harmonic support. (**Conducting tip:** Be careful to cue the second viola's D pedal point in measure 123. The fermata in the last measure can be quite long, allowing for a careful crescendo/decrescendo in the orchestra.)

The Coda (mm. 122–136) is a fifteen-measure complex grouped [12(3x4) + 3]. Note that the Coda, beginning in measure 122 with a four-measure ostinato pattern, overlaps the conclusion of the A' section by two bars.

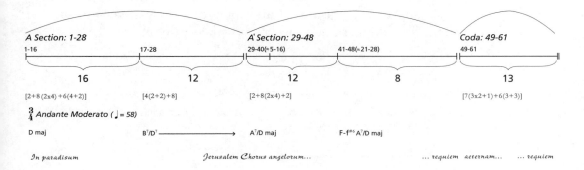

Movement No. 7—In Paradisum

The transcendent final movement of Fauré's *Requiem* is an antiphon used following the mass while the coffin is transported to the grave site. (See page **504.**) The calm, still peacefulness of this music helps those living picture eternal rest. Fauré's use of this text gives the *Requiem* a subtle and interesting textual symmetry, as his is the first Requiem that begins and ends with the word "requiem." This movement is very similar in style, form, tempo (quarter note = 58), and meter to the "Sanctus." For example, its through-composed structure, running sixteenth note figures, and economy of material are reminiscent of the third movement. The bipartite musical structure reflects the two-part text, A A' Coda, shown in the analysis chart.

The A section (mm. 1-28) divides into a two-part complex of 16 + 12 measures. It begins with a two-measure introduction that sets the atmosphere for the entire movement. Fauré marked the divided violas and cellos *con sordino*; the basses play *pizzicato*. Although the rhythmic figure appears to be a two-bar ostinato pattern, closer inspection reveals it to be a little more complicated. The addition of the *pizzicato* double bass every four measures influences the musical texture. Understanding the groupings of the opening sixteen measures as [2+8(2x4) + 6(4+2)] can help the conductor organize the music's evolution. Measures 17–28 are a twelve-measure passage divisible as [4(2+2) + 8], reflecting the third-related harmonic motion (B^7 to D^7) and the entrance of the tenor, bass, and, finally, the alto and bassoon. This section overlaps with the beginning of the A' section in measure 29.

The A' section (mm. 29–48) parallels the A section closely, but with some modification. Measures 29–40 are congruent with measures 5–16, and measures 41–48 are similar to measures 21–28; in the A' section, Fauré eliminated the A section's measures 17–20. The addition of the violin and harp (m. 29) and the horns (m. 44) enrich the orchestration as well. The basses should be marked *arco* ("bowed") in measures 47–48, and revert to *pizzicato* in measure 49. Once again, an overlap is present; the A' section overlaps the beginning of the Coda in measure 49.

The Coda (mm. 49–61) is thirteen measures long, grouped [7(3x2+1) + 6(3+3)]. D major arrives in measure 49 and remains in first inversion until measure 56 where the double basses and organ pedal settle on D.

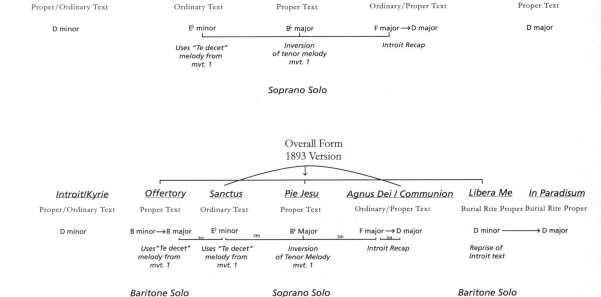

The Overall Structure

After achieving a full understanding of the form and structure of the individual movements, it is necessary to step back and observe the overall structure of the *Requiem*. Knowing the order, key relationships, text progression,

and musical relationships of the movements allows a conductor to pace the performance and create a unified whole from the individual movements.

There are two Overall Structure Charts; the first shows Fauré's original five-movement version of 1888, and the second includes the two movements added for the 1893 version. The inclusion of the two additional movements strengthens the overall structure of the work in a significant way.

Analysis of the original five-movement structure reveals symmetrical construction revolving around the interior three movements, which form the essence of a Requiem Mass for Fauré. Note that the texts for the "Sanctus," "Pie Jesu," and "Agnus Dei" alternate from Ordinary to Proper to Ordinary/Proper and have a key scheme that ascends by fifths, from E-flat major to B-flat major to F major. The strong bond uniting these movements allows the conductor to proceed from one movement to the next during performances without undue delay. The two exterior movements (in D minor/D major) form the structural bookends and highlight the ultimate key movement by third: from D minor to the middle movement in B-flat major back to D minor/major. The central movement, "Pie Jesu," with its theme of mercy and rest, seems to portray Fauré's view of death. He said, "Death is a happy deliverance, a reaching for eternal happiness, rather than a mournful passing." It is also important to note that the "Sanctus," "Pie Jesu," and "Agnus Dei/Communion" all use certain musical components of the "Introit and Kyrie." Thus, the ideas found in the opening movement provide much of the musical material for the entire *Requiem*, excluding the movement traditionally used in the Burial Rite ("In Paradisum").

The seven-movement version of 1893 inserts two additional movements, the "Offertory" and "Libera Me," both of which call for a baritone soloist. Fauré thus preserved the work's symmetry by employing soloists in movements 2, 4, and 6. Additionally, the rather abrupt tonal change from the "Introit and Kyrie" (D minor) to the "Sanctus" (E-flat major) present in the 1888 version is negated by the insertion of the "Offertory" for the 1893 version. The second version (with the insertion) forms a descending-third key relationship from the "Introit and Kyrie" (D minor) to the "Offertory" (B minor/B major) and an ascending-third key relationship from the "Offertory" (B minor/B major) to the "Sanctus" (E-flat major). This key relationship by thirds is mirrored by the key movement of the "Agnus Dei/Communion" (F major) to the "Libera Me" (D minor). Furthermore, the texts inherent in the Requiem liturgy conclude with the "Agnus Dei/Communion." Fauré created a self-contained Burial Rite with parallel key motion from D minor to D major.

A conductor who understands and digests this seven-movement structure can design the performances and rehearsals with a greater degree of understanding. Thus, the conductor will truly function as Fauré's advocate on the podium.

WORKING WITH THE CHOIR: A CONDUCTOR'S GUIDE

Rehearsal Rubric

Conducting teachers usually spend considerable time on the physical aspects of the art, and the rehearsal technique is often neglected or not addressed at all. Knowing what to rehearse, when, and how to do it, comes from years of experience, knowledge of your ensemble, and a knack for good timing. The following list outlines a basic rehearsal method the authors believe can be useful for every piece of music.

1. *Know the score.* A conductor has no greater responsibility than this. You must spend time learning the music before you enter a choral rehearsal because it is unrealistic to expect singers to be able to sing anything you cannot. If you have never spent time doing score study, start with learning to sing each part; simply doing this will teach you a great deal about the music. You will learn which passages are difficult and will be better able to teach your choir the music. Much more is written about score study in the chapter on Analysis.

2. *In the first rehearsal of a piece, begin by having the accompanist play some (or all) of the music.* Be sure your singers look at their scores and listen attentively. From this initial exposure, the singers can learn much about the harmonic environment into which they are about to enter and will hasten note learning.

3. *At first, give the singers general markings for their score.* (See the section below on marking the score.)

4. *Start with the music only—the notes and rhythms.* It is completely unreasonable to expect singers, even professionals, to sight read music with all of the correct language, phrasing, dynamics, expression, and so forth. Simply put, do not sight sing using the text. The following list details several advantages to this methodology.

   - Singers will be unable to apply poor diction habits to singing.
   - Singers will be forced to deal with the notes and the rhythms. Many singers say they read music while they actually read words. They will complain they are unable to sing music without words, but this will strengthen their skills and require them to learn to read music.
   - The conductor can focus on proper pronunciations of words when the time comes to work on text. It is nearly impossible for any conductor to evaluate dozens of things at the same time; if you are trying to discern whether the text is pronounced correctly while you are trying to detect wrong notes, you will probably miss a good half of

both errors. Singing without text will enable you to hear more and to diagnose problems more quickly.

5. *When reading without text, choose appropriate neutral syllables.* While you are teaching notes and rhythms devoid of text, you can do a great deal to shape the final sound of the piece. The proper neutral syllable will help you teach tone (vowel) and articulation (consonant). Choose a vowel based on the color of sound you would like to achieve for that section; for example, an [i] will yield brighter sound than a [u]. After choosing a vowel, choose a consonant based on the articulation required by the passage you are rehearsing. For example, [t] will produce a much crisper articulation than [n]. Be sure to choose these syllables wisely as they can greatly hasten the group's learning. (**Conducting tip:** As a rule of thumb, use closed vowels for the neutral syllables. The vowels [u] or [i] often work well; when the volume is louder or the range is extended, use a pure [o] vowel.)

6. *Be sure the singers perform the correct notes and rhythms.* Notes and rhythms are the foundation of every musical composition; without them, the piece is unrecognizable. Wrong notes and rhythms are unacceptable. Most conductors hear wrong notes and assume the choir can't hear the pitches. While this is sometimes correct, many conductors ignore the fact that wrong notes may be a result of poor rhythmic understanding. A wise conductor once said, "A right note at the wrong time is still a wrong note!" Therefore, when working on pitches, ensure that the rhythms are secure.

It is easy to blame the choir, but if wrong notes are sung in performances it is usually the conductor's fault. One of our conducting teachers often said, "Little ever happens on the concert stage that didn't happen numerous times in the rehearsal room." Providing you have chosen appropriate repertoire for the ensemble, teaching notes should not be a huge problem, but when a troublesome passage does arise, the conductor must find a way to teach the choir the notes. The bottom line is, do not move on to any other aspect of the music until the notes are secure, even if important aspects of the music have to be ignored.

7. *Once the notes and rhythms are secure, it is time to add the more "interesting" parts of the music: dynamics, phrasing, rubato, and so forth.* Adding these essential elements before the notes and rhythms are solidified in the singers' ears yields unsatisfying performances. It is important to understand your role as teacher and conductor; the more time you devote to teaching your ensemble, the more benefits you will reap from your rehearsal time.

- *Add the text.* Text should be the final element added to the music. Diction, especially in a foreign language, contains so many pitfalls that it requires its own space. After everything else is in good shape, you can devote your undivided attention to teaching proper diction. Teaching diction should consists of the steps outlined in the following list.

    - Demonstrate! Speak a small selection of the words out of rhythm and slowly, in a high, forward speaking voice.
    - Have the choir repeat the selection of text in a similar high, forward speaking voice. Do not allow them to speak back in their jowls or in their lower registers; this will affect the way they produce the sounds when they sing.
    - Have the choir speak the words very slowly. Be sure, as they sustain vowels, that the composite sound does not change. If they change the vowel while speaking, they will *certainly* do so while singing.
    - Have the choir speak the text in rhythm, without pitch. (If rhythmic problems arise at this point, eliminate the text and rehearse just the rhythm on a neutral syllable.)
    - Add pitch to the rhythmic text.

For specific information about diction for the Fauré *Requiem*, refer to page 556.

Following the above method is not a panacea, but it *is* a good starting point for every piece you teach. It is always best to work from the most general aspects of music (notes and rhythms) to the most specific (diction). This practice will ensure that your singers do not become confused or frustrated by the learning process. Using the same basic method with every piece will enable singers to feel more comfortable in rehearsals; they will know what to expect. As a bonus, any departure from the method will cause the singers to pay close attention because something different will happen. Remember that if you always do things differently, variety itself turns into a routine! Give the singers structure by using a rehearsal method, not just a series of random techniques.

Marking the Score

Do not assume choir members know how to mark their scores. We find it helpful and efficient to distribute a sheet of standardized score markings to all singers, regardless of experience. Every conductor should make his own chart, as everyone has different training and preferences. Devise a chart that makes sense to you and communicates what you want to communicate. For an example of such a chart, see Lloyd Pfautsch's chapter in *Choral Conducting Symposium*, Second Edition, 1988. 89–91.)

Singers should be taught to mark cut-off information very clearly. We recommend giving choirs rhythmic cut-off markings; that is, shorten or lengthen notes by an exact rhythmic value so the cut-offs become simpler to understand and easier to accomplish. For example, in the Fauré *Requiem*, examine rehearsal letter D of the first movement. In this measure, have the choir mark an eighth note rest on the second half of beat four. (In other words, the syllable "di" will become an eighth note, followed by an eighth rest.) All singers should observe this precise rhythmic value.

Another example comes in measure 57; in this case, nothing is altered, but it is important that the choir realizes not to sound the [t] until precisely on the downbeat of measure 58. The *Sanctus* provides a clear example that is repeated several times. In measure 5, the sopranos have a quarter note tied to an eighth note, but putting an [s] on an upbeat can be tricky, especially for a large or inexperienced ensemble. In this case, it is perfectly acceptable to instruct the singers to mark through the tied-over eighth note, replace it with an eighth rest, and pronounce the [s] exactly on beat two. (The same should then happen for the men in their analogous passages.) Mark these things carefully in the conductor's score before rehearsals and before sight reading a movement, give the choir all the markings they will need to create a rhythmically accurate performance during the process. Save expressive markings for later, after the notes and rhythms are solidified.

Seating Plans

Many successful methods of seating a choir exist, but we believe the ones determined empirically are the most effective. Ideal seating arrangements should not be created in silence while the choral director sits at his or her desk and decides where people stand based on a perception of singers' voices. (Even worse are the arrangements based solely on the heights of the singers.) Certainly, good choral directors can remember their singers' sounds; however, to know how two people will sound standing next to one another requires actually hearing them sing together. Even in cases in which you have the same singers for long periods, their voices will change, causing their combined sound to change.

For a good seating plan, line up singers in front of rows of chairs. To do this, choose a simple song everyone knows well, like "My Country, 'Tis of Thee." Work with only one section at a time, and have each member of the section, in turn, sing the first line as a solo (just the words, "My Country, 'Tis of Thee."). Select the singer whose sound you like best for the repertoire you are singing (choosing a light voice will yield a sectional sound lighter in color, and choosing a heavy, dark voice will yield a heavier and darker sectional sound). The person you choose does not have to be the best singer or musician but *should* be someone whose voice is pleasant and who can sing in tune.

Next, with your chosen singer remaining stationary, have each of the other members of the section sing next to him or her, in turn; instruct the singers not to try to blend, but to sing with their natural voices—the ones they use in the heat of rehearsals and performances. (The "non-chosen" singers at this point simply rotate, moving so that each of them takes a turn beside the "chosen one.") Listen to each combination of two singers as each member of the section sings with the person you chose first, and choose for your second singer in the line the one who combines with your first singer to produce the sound closest to your internal sound model for the music. Now you have the first two members of the line.

Have all the remaining singers sing with the two "chosen" singers, and select a third member of the line; repeat the process for a fourth, fifth, etc. Continue until you have all the members of the section standing in line in the order that sounds best.

Once you have your singers lined up this way, it is important to keep them in the proper order when you seat them. The specifics of this process depend, of course, upon the seating possibilities of your rehearsal and performance spaces. After you have selected the first singer, form the line to his or her right or left. When placing the singers into chairs, be sure the line retains its integrity of right and left. To accomplish this, give each singer a number, starting with the first singer. Next, avoid the "snake" method of seating and use the "typewriter" method.

Explain to the singers that being one of the last to be placed in the line does not mean they are less desirable as singers but simply means that their voices work best at a different place in the line for the music being rehearsed. In addition to providing a desirable standing order, this acoustically grounded method of seating will help singers become aware of how much each voice adds to the sound of a section. Highlight this fact as you do these standings: no singer can argue that his or her voice will not be missed if they decide to skip a rehearsal! This procedure does take time, but the authors have found it to be time very well spent. If you conduct an inexperienced choir, you will have to repeat the process often as the singers develop vocally; as they progress, the overtones they produce change, and their voices will stick out of the texture. When this happens, it is time to reseat the section. You can also create different standings for different styles of repertoire, completely changing the sound of the choir without saying a word about tone. Remember, it is in no way undesirable to have the choir change formation even several times during a concert.

Achieving Results Via the Conducting Gesture

Developing a wide vocabulary of conducting gestures is important to any conductor, and can be a daunting prospect for a less-experienced conductor.

Young conductors always worry about how they look when they conduct, but self-conscious conductors tend to be ineffective and uninspiring in performances. The important concept to remember is that a conductor must, through movement, send a clear and informative message to the ensemble. The information contained in the message should allow performers to feel confident and comfortable; the better your performers feel, the more beautifully they will sing.

The question then becomes, what gestures will evoke the sounds in the conductor's inner ear? Human beings are moving creatures. We perceive so much about people from the way they move, walk, and carry themselves; body language can sometimes tell us everything we need to know about a situation. Because conductors are all "professional movers," the powerful subliminal movements they use should form the nucleus of their conducting techniques.

Some people think conducting is simply knowing various beat patterns. Of course, beat patterns are necessary; without them, ensembles become lost, and precious rehearsal time is wasted. However, while many conducting books write extremely well about the ABC's of conducting, it is more difficult to find books that clearly discuss conducting *beyond* the patterns. Conducting gestures can be improved through movements that are commonplace in our lives. If you use your imagination to engage such descriptions, they can prove very helpful in developing a larger gestural vocabulary. Incorporating the suggested motions into a beat pattern (be careful that you do not replace the beat pattern with another gesture, especially if you are conducting orchestral instruments) opens a whole new world of sound possibilities to you and your choir.

Conducting Gestures Specific to the Fauré Requiem

Fauré's music requires the ability to conduct a free-flowing musical line. When conducting such a line, remember that the speed and weight of one's gesture generates forward motion of sound. Weight can be added to or removed from conducting gestures, and even very subtle weight changes effect drastic color changes.

Obviously, one does not strap weights to one's arms when conducting, but it is easy to imagine weight in the arms and to alter the weight imagined. Think, for example, of swimming through a pool of molasses, and then imagine petting the softest dog in the world. Your arm works at different "weights" in these situations. These same ideas can be applied to conducting; practice by conducting a pattern in four using the two different weights you experienced, and you should immediately sense these gestures to be appropriate for different styles of music.

The following charts of each movement of Fauré's *Requiem* suggest gestures based on real life movements for each segment of the piece. These suggestions work for us, but they may not work for you; if one does not work,

use your imagination to come up with a new idea. Remember, each conductor is built differently; the same gestures look different performed by different people, and their success will vary according to the way they look.

Possible Problems and Their Solutions for Each Movement of the Requiem

Movement No. 1: Introit and Kyrie

PROBLEM | REMEDY

The slow tempo in the Introduction

It is vitally important that the choir sense the rhythmic subdivisions in the opening section. The opening seventeen measures (marked *Molto Largo*) are probably best conducted in a subdivided four pattern; the choir always needs to have an active awareness of at least one subdivision below what you are conducting (e.g., if you are conducting eighth notes, they need to feel sixteenths).

- Have the choir count-sing the underlying sixteenth note pulse. (They would sing: one-ee-and-ah, two-ee-and-ah, tee-ee-and-ah, four-ee-and-ah.[*])

- When count-singing, be sure to maintain a consistent tempo or the exercise is useless. Count-singing should be rehearsed with maximum energy. If the choir can energize the micro level of subdivision (in this case, sixteenth notes) they will be able to sing the long, slow moving introduction with great clarity and precision.

Achieving line

In measure 18, a new section marked *Andante moderato* begins. This new section requires more sweep and forward motion than the opening of the movement.

- Try using a gesture that is slightly larger and moves faster. There are many points in this work in which an exact, precise beat pattern must be employed, but this section is not one of them.

Conducting gestures

The first section of this piece requires a very exact, even, (probably) subdivided beat pattern.

---

* The syllable "tee" is used in place of "three" to allow singers to "spring the vowel." The "thr" consonant combination takes too much time to be useful as a rhythmic teaching tool.

PROBLEM	REMEDY

Conducting gestures (continued)

• Imagine you are playing "Duck, Duck, Goose" with some of your friends. Your subdivided gesture should be similar to the gentle tapping of a head in this children's game.

The fourth beat of measures three and six may have a *ritardando* to highlight the orchestral crescendo.

• To create the *ritardando*, imagine your hands are pulling taffy; they must move a little further and a little more slowly.

At rehearsal letter A, the texture of the music completely changes.

• At bar 18, the gesture needs to be free flowing. A good example for the gesture needed in this section would be "using a bubble wand." When one uses a bubble wand, speed is necessary to create larger bubbles, but too much speed will cause the bubbles to break. Too heavy a motion will prevent the bubbles from forming; a motion that is too light will have the same result.

Poor tenor tone

All of the beautiful line in the world will not overcome poor singing. The tenor line at rehearsal letter A is actually much trickier than it looks. First, this section lies in an awkward place in the tenor voice. (Almost the entire passage lies in the lower *passagio* of the tenor voice.) Singing in the *passagio* can often cause out-of-tune, usually flat singing.

Instruct the tenors to sing with high, forward resonance. To achieve this, try the following :

• Have the singers put the heel of their hands on their forehead; instruct them to send all of the sound into their hands.
• Ask the singers to sing a descending 5–4–3–2–1 scale on [nu] Have the singers point on each note change and move their hands upward as they descend.

PROBLEM	REMEDY
Poor tenor tone (continued)	• Have the singers sigh on [u] from the top of the voice to the bottom, pointing upward during the descent. Make sure the voice doesn't "change gears" on they way down. In other words, stay in head voice as long as possible.
	• The sound of this section is similar to chant, and well-performed chant is usually sung in head voice. Try to get the tenors to sing from the top down, meaning they mix as much of their *falsetto* or head voice as possible into the lower notes; if they succeed, intonation and evenness of sound will not be a problem.
Soprano at C	• The sopranos must continue the flowing line tenors established as they sing the psalm verse of the Introit. The range here is low for sopranos. Like the tenors, the sopranos should bring as much of the head voice as possible to the lower regions of their voices.
	If they start their first pitch, F, in a low position, they will not sing a pleasant E-flat in the next measure. A good rule of thumb is to breathe "for" the highest note of a phrase (i.e., make sure the singers realize what they must do during that breath). Another way of getting at this is to ask the sopranos to sing a high F well and then ask them to sing the low F in the same space and continue with the phrase.
	Fauré puts many of the accented syllables on unusual beats in this section. We believe that these instances (e.g., "Deus" in measure 43, and "tibi" in measure 46) combine to make one of the strongest arguments for using French Latin Pronunciation when performing the Fauré *Requiem*. (See page **557**.)
Tenor/Bass divisi	The two male voice sections must divide to cover three parts in this section. They then alternate between singing in two and three parts. The stem placement in Rutter's edition indicates the tenors should divide, but we believe it is better to have an even three-part divisi in which some baritones and second tenors have the middle part. Organize this before you rehearse this section, or it will waste valuable rehearsal time. Take the time to assign each singer to a specific part.

535

PROBLEM	REMEDY
Juxtaposition of fofrte and piano	This appears to be an easy concept: sing loudly, and then sing softly. However, very few choirs perform this task successfully. Most choirs associate loud with strong and soft with weak, but this is not always the case. Piano singing requires just as much—if not more—energy than forte singing. Piano singing that maintains rhythmic and vocal vitality can be exhilarating.
	This concept is most effectively taught in warm-ups. Have the choir sing an exercise forte, and immediately follow the forte by singing the same exercise piano. Tell them that they should keep the same mental attitude and support, only sing more softly.
When to breathe	Achieving appropriate phrasing is easy if you ask the singers to follow the punctuation in the text.
	For example, at rehearsal letter E, the choir sings "Kyrie" three times. A comma follows the first two occurrences. A slight lift between the first and second and the second and third repetitions of "Kyrie" will provide a much more interesting phrase and will solve the breathing problem. There should be no lift after the third "Kyrie" as there is no punctuation, and the sentence continues on to the word "eleison."

Movement No. 2: Offertory

PROBLEM	REMEDY
Choral rhythms	The rhythms of the choral parts in this movement appear to be very exact and rigid. However, because the tempo is slow, you may conduct in a subdivided four pattern, and the dotted rhythms should be slightly softened, not performed in an over-dotted style.
Alto/tenor duet	Having the first tenors sing the alto part in *falsetto* and the second altos sing the tenor part might help to achieve a uniform sound. This would help the voice parts sound more ethereal and less distinct. This will work until measure 22, when all voices should sing their parts as written.

PROBLEM	REMEDY
Bass entrance	When the basses enter in measure 23, they sing the same melody assigned to the altos at the beginning of the movement. Make sure this part is audible and slightly more prominent than the tenor and alto parts.
Baritone solo	Coach the baritone soloist to sing a weightless line. In other words, the soloist should not make a "big deal" of every downbeat of a measure, or, worse, of each individual beat. The line should go to the end of the phrase.
	If you hire a soloist, he probably will not assume that you are performing the piece using French Latin pronunciations; it would be helpful and time-saving to send the soloist the pronunciation guide ahead of time. (Any soloist worth the price you are paying should be familiar with the IPA, or International Phonetic Alphabet.) In addition, it will be your responsibility to meet with the soloist before the dress rehearsal so you can coach his diction and other aspects of his performance. Remember, you probably know more than he does about this "new" style of diction, so do not be afraid to correct them.
Prosody/choral parts	Prosody is the rhythmical and intonational aspect of language. Prosody in music usually refers to correct textual accentuation. Proper pronunciations enable considerable nuance within a phrase; to assist in this, singers should make every attempt to diminuendo through all accented syllables of words and crescendo through all unaccented syllables. This may at first seem illogical, but it is the diminuendo of an accented syllable that makes the following unaccented syllable sound unaccented to the ear. The converse is true as well.
	Keep in mind that the accentuation of French Latin will be slightly different from the standard-liturgical Latin we all know. Using French Latin pronunciation for this movement, many of the seemingly misplaced accents fall right into place. For example, the downbeat of measure 81 contains all unaccented syllables of

PROBLEM	REMEDY
Prosody/choral parts (continued)	words; many critics would argue that a good composer would never have done such a thing. However, when one considers that French Latin tends to place the accent on the final syllable of a word, it is clear that Fauré set this text perfectly.
Conducting gestures	Finding the right gesture for this movement is difficult. The best advice is to find a neutral, easy to follow stock gesture. In the choral sections of this movement, your primary responsibility is to provide a clear, unwavering tempo. To do this, conduct a subdivided four pattern. Less is more here! Be a timekeeper and no more.
	In the solo section, your gesture needs to be more expressive. The orchestra plays what is essentially a rhythmic ostinato; the baritone soloist must sing very legato while the undulating orchestral rhythm remains energized. Imagine you are an astronaut, floating weightlessly in the space shuttle. Your friend needs you to pass some food across the vessel; to do this you need use only the slightest impulse to send the food floating all the way across the ship. Your gesture in this section can be very similar—slight impulses on every beat to keep the orchestra together, followed by the weightless motion of your arm to the next impulse. This kind of gesture will inspire clarity and legato.
"Amen"	It is challenging to sing the "Amen" section beautifully. The biggest problem is with the [a] vowel. Make sure it is very bright and has high, forward resonance. It may be useful to rehearse the pitches on a bright [i] vowel. In rehearsals, have the choir use pointing or lifting gestures to help keep the sound high and forward. The second syllable of the word should be sung as a schwa—an unaccented neutral syllable. Singers can accomplish this by "wrapping their lips around the vowel." Choirs will probably tend to sing a vowel that is too open, yielding both an undesirable sound and a misplaced syllabic accent.

Movement No. 3: Sanctus

PROBLEM	REMEDY
Achieving line	Flow of line is an important element of the "Sanctus." Two primary things can make this movement challenging; first, the harp and viola play a constant sixteenth note figure through most of the movement.

- To enable the instrumentalists to do their jobs correctly, the conductor should maintain a consistent tempo and a clear beat pattern.

  In the implied hemiola of the voice parts can be problematic; the voices sing in two-note groups within a 3/4 metric scheme. This can obfuscate the shape and linear direction for the singers.

- Therefore, the singers must learn to sing with the proper line in rehearsals. Ask them to pulse-sing sixteenth notes. (Pulse-singing is similar to count-singing but does not use numbers; the choir should sing on a neutral syllable—[du] works well.) This will help the singers understand that their rhythm is not the basic rhythmic level in this movement; that occurs, in fact, in the harp and viola parts.

- Be sure the choir sings all the sixteenth notes with the same weight (i.e., do not put stress on each beat or on the downbeat of each measure). In this section, the line is not a slave to the meter but moves independently. Singing every sixteenth note with the same weight will eliminate any confusion about the hemiola. Singing all the sixteenth notes with the same weight will help the choir internalize the motoric rhythm underlying their line and perform a rhythmically accurate line that is seemingly weightless.

Conducting gesture	The conducting gesture from the beginning of this piece through rehearsal letter C should be similar to the dotting of an "i" with your pencil: an initial dab that is a direct motion with a weightless release. This gesture should ensure rhythmic security for the orchestra and simultaneously provide the supple, weightless gesture the choir needs to see.

PROBLEM	REMEDY
Conducting gesture (continued)	At reheaersal letter C, the gesture must change because the texture of the music changes. Here, to help the singers remain centered in their body for the required forte singing, the conducting gesture should be centered lower on your body. The gesture should also have more weight and sustenance than the dotting of an "i." A non-violent, downward punching gesture can accomplish all of this quite nicely. Imagine the kind of gesture used to punch down dough after it rises.
Sopranos at rehearsal letter A	Before rehearsal letter A, the sopranos perform the same pattern four times. At A, they break the pattern and sing a higher note. The conductor can help them reach their F beautifully.

• A slight increase in the gestural speed (not tempo) at rehearsal letter A will inspire the singers to use more energy to place the top note properly. When they reach the top note, do not allow your gesture to become dramatic, but do keep the speed of your gesture moving forward, encouraging them to sing *through* the top pitch. As they descend, return to a normal gesture.

| Men at rehearsal letter C | Fauré requires all men to sing at rehearsal letter C. The E-flats can be high for basses. |

• As before, instruct the men to mix as much head voice or *falsetto* into the lower register as they can. Basses, especially, will often try to push the high notes out, using their chest voice—exactly what you don't want them to do. Instead, ask them to sing with a lot of internal space to close all the vowels and to "wrap their lips around the sound." This is very similar to a fish-mouth technique. Wrapping their lips around the sound can enable the men to sing into their head voice and maximize their resonance. Singing with open vowels and without wrapping their lips around the sound will result in a brassy, out-of-tune, unpleasant sound.

PROBLEM	REMEDY
The altos?	The altos do not sing until the very end of this movement. Because the range of the soprano part is not prohibitive, the altos will remain more involved if they double the soprano part throughout the movement. This will also bolster and enrich the soprano sound.

Movement No. 4: Pie Jesu

PROBLEM	REMEDY
Soprano solo	If at all possible, hire a professional singer for this movement; it will definitely be worth your time and money. Another wonderful option is to employ a very good boy soprano. Although it appears simple, this movement is difficult to sing. The lines are long and the tempo is rather slow. Consult with your soloist about a good tempo for the piece; each singer has different capabilities when it comes to singing long lines.
	If at all possible for her, encourage the soloist to sing some four-measure phrases instead of breathing every two measures. For example, singing measures 11–14 in one breath is quite beautiful and provides a variation from the first setting of the same words. No breath before measure 29 is ideal, but do not insist on this unless the soloist is comfortable with it. Also, ensure that the singer does not breathe between measures 34 and 35; have her carry the sentence through to completion.
	As with the baritone soloist, realize that the soprano is not likely to assume you are performing this piece with French Latin pronunciation. Send her a pronunciation guide before your first rehearsal and set up a time to coach her. Singers appreciate coaching times before dress rehearsals because the conductor does not have to correct them in front of the larger ensemble.
	The performance of this movement should be simple. Do not allow the singer to add *portamento* between pitches; it is stylistically inappropriate. Pitch changes should be clean and quick.

PROBLEM	REMEDY
Tempo/organ	Your job as the conductor is to establish and maintain a tempo enabling the soloist to sing long lines without impeding on her artistic freedom. The organ can be very helpful in this regard. If the registration is too muddy (meaning it doesn't speak quickly or seems heavy and dark), the tempo will invariably slow down. Consult the chapter on the organ for ideas.
Conducting gesture	Stay out of the way in this movement; keep your pattern very small and unobtrusive. Be sure to give the strings a cue each time that they enter. When only the soloist and organ are playing, relegate yourself to the background. Listen attentively, and be sure the tempo remains consistent. The more subtle your gesture, the greater influence you will have on dynamics in this movement. Be sure to follow Fauré's dynamic markings exactly.

Movement No. 5: Agnus Dei

PROBLEM	REMEDY
Tenor sound	The tenor line that opens the "Agnus Dei" is one of the most beautiful sections of the *Requiem*. Be sure the tenors envision this sectional solo more as plainchant than opera. The line must be sung lightly, yet with fullness of tone.
	To achieve these ideals, begin by having the tenors sing from the top of the register down. As mentioned in the sections on other movements, teach the singers to anticipate all the notes they must sing on a given breath. For instance, when the tenors enter on C, they must be able to sing F on the same breath. This is not easy if they breathe for the phrase as though C were the only note they had to sing. Have the tenors sing the F; instruct them to use as much head voice and high, forward resonance as possible. Once they can sing the F beautifully, have them sing the C in the same "house" as F. If they can bring the head resonance necessary for the F down into the C, they will be able to sing this phrase effortlessly. Remind the tenors of this every time they sing the phrase; after many repetitions, they will assimilate it into their

PROBLEM	REMEDY
Tenor sound (continued)	singing habitually. The same applies to the tenor line after rehearsal letter B.
Rehearsal letter A	At rehearsal letter A, the choral music becomes quite chromatic; soprano and tenor sing essentially in sixths. Rehearse their parts together, and then rehearse the alto and bass together. Hearing the parts this way will make the dissonances less jarring to the singers and hasten the learning process.
Tenors before C	The notes immediately before rehearsal letter C are usually difficult for tenors to sing in tune. Instruct them to bring as much high, forward resonance as possible into the B-naturals, close all vowels, and wrap their lips around the sound.
Rehearsal letter C	The tonal transition at rehearsal letter C is Fauré's depiction of "eternal light," another magical moment in the piece. Notice the tonality immediately preceding rehearsal letter C is C major. The sopranos then enter on a C, the root of the previous chord. Fauré takes the listener by surprise by inserting an A-flat major chord under the lone soprano note, making C the third of the chord. Thirds must always be imagined high to be perceived as "in tune." While it might be impossible to measure how much sharper the C must be to sound in tune as the top note of a major third, calling this phenomenon to singers' attention can be enough to do the trick. Play the transition at the keyboard so the singers to understand the deceptive harmony employed by Fauré. Telling the sopranos it needs to be higher might be all you have to do, but some repetition will probably be necessary to achieve optimal results. One thing is sure: you don't want this section to sound out of tune because "lux aeterna" is one of the aspects of the afterlife Fauré tried to portray vividly—and who would want to think of living eternal life with bad intonation?

PROBLEM	REMEDY
Rehearsal letter C (continued)	Once again, the choir sings in sonorous, dense homophonic chords. Count-singing will help the choir move this section along. A slight *ritardando* in measure 53 will highlight the repetition of the phrase at measure 54.
Rehearsal letter E	See the section on first movement, as the music is essentially repeated.
Conducting gesture	The beginning of this movement is another section not requiring great gestural precision. An easy-flowing gesture with lots of sweep (pulling motion) and increased speed will help the tenors achieve a weightless, flowing line. Imagine running your hand through bath water; sometimes you will skim, and sometimes you will pull deeper. Examine the phrases to discover where a deeper gesture is needed (e.g., measure 14). Above all, do not be afraid to play!

At rehearsal letter A, imagine the bath water is a little more viscous; that will help your hand (and entire arm) to feel more resistance. Fauré's harmonic language in this section tells the conductor more "tension" is needed in the phrase. Adding more weight, or tension, into your gesture for this section will provide a greater sense of stress and release as the choir sings through the very chromatic passage.

At rehearsal letter C, be very still as the two measures of rest pass. Of course, you need to keep the beat going but excess motion will disturb the tranquil sound expected from the sopranos.

At measure 47, when choir and orchestra return, you must still maintain some sweep in your gesture, but it should have a bit more clarity and point to help the voice parts move cleanly and in tempo from pitch to pitch. Imagine whisking eggs in a bowl; the motion needs to be somewhat circular but requires regular impulses to beat the eggs.

At rehearsal letter E, use the instructions given above in movement 1.

PROBLEM	REMEDY
Conducting gesture (continued)	To make the tempo transition at letter F, make the last two subdivided eighth notes of the previous tempo equal the tempo of a quarter note at rehearsal letter F.

Movement No. 6: Libera Me

PROBLEM	REMEDY
Rhythm	In this movement, it is essential that both conductor and choir thoroughly understand the difference between simple and compound meter. The movement opens in 2/2—a simple meter; the half note receives the beat so the conductor should beat half notes. (The subdivision is the quarter note—thus simple meter.)

At rehearsal letter C, the music switches to 6/4. There are still two beats in a bar, but now the dotted half note gets one beat. The subdivision is still the quarter note, but there are now three quarter notes per beat—compound meter.

Of course, most of us know the theoretical differences between simple and compound meter, but sometimes performers do not apply theoretical understanding to actual performance. Compound meters need more swing or lilt, and simple meters must be more exact and square. Understanding the difference here is crucial, as the choir must sing with lilt in the 6/4 section while the orchestra accompanying them plays a squarer rhythm.

Conducting gesture　　Refer to the analytical charts found in this volume to decide how to group the 2/2 bars into larger beat patterns (showing the "macrobeat") in the opening and closing sections of this movement (rehearsal letters A, C, and E to the end). For example, one can conduct a two bar phrase in 2/2 using a 4/2 pattern instead of the up and down of the 2/2 pattern. The only caveat is to be sure the orchestra players know what you are doing because they will see only one downbeat over the space of two measures.

PROBLEM	REMEDY
Conducting gesture (continued)	The gesture for these sections needs to be weighty but buoyant to portray the long lines. Imagine pushing down on a spring mattress on the first beat of each bar. This gesture will provide depth and weight to each beat but will cause your arms to release upward to assist in the legato line.

Your tactile sense must be awake as you conduct this section; imagine you are touching the sound as though you were pushing into a wall of tightly stretched spandex. By imagining the texture of the sound, you will connect more deeply to the ensemble and the sound.

From rehearsal letters C through E, where the time signature is 6/4, the conducting gesture should be stronger and more violent. Imagine the following activities for help in finding the appropriate gesture:

- An athlete pumping his or her fist in celebration
- Snapping a wet towel
- Shaking a can of spray paint (once)
- Cracking a whip

For help in finding the appropriate gesture for this section, go to your local music store and buy a percussion egg or make one of your own. The more sound you can get out of the egg as you practice the above activities, the better your gesture will be for this music. If no sound comes out of the egg, you are locking your gesture and preventing the transfer of energy from your body.

To release your gesture, work with the egg until you get a very solid sound on each beat. A sound on the upbeat shows you are locking the release of your beat and performing subdivisions in tempo. All releases of beats should be out of tempo unless you are consciously subdividing for clarity (which you should not be doing here). Work with the egg to remove subdivisions.

PROBLEM	REMEDY
Choral sound	The sound of the choir in this movement must be darker and rounder than in any other movement. To achieve this, make sure all sections "wrap their lips around the sound."

A good exercise to help monitor this is to have the choir make the "OK" sign with their thumb and pointer finger, and put the "OK" sign around their lips as they sing (with text) in this position. This will ensure that all of the vowels are rounded and none of them is too spread.

As they sing with "OK" sound, instruct the choir to sing with a very tall space inside their mouths; they should not close down inside just because their lips are rounded. (Also, be sure they do not think you want them to be louder.) Ask them to imagine a large capital A inside their mouths; the top of it is very sharp and could puncture their soft palate if it gets too low. If this is unsuccessful, ask them to imagine singing with cotton pads between their rear molars.

Style	This movement is the most outwardly dramatic and romantic part of the entire *Requiem*. The juxtaposition of this movement between the "Agnus Dei" and the "In Paradisum" is startling.

Make every effort to have this movement be dramatic. Fauré gives you many guides with his dynamic markings and phrase indications; be sure to follow all of them exactly.

Movement No. 7: In Paradisum

PROBLEM	REMEDY
Texture	The texture of this movement can be challenging because two articulations must occur simultaneously. First, the pattern in the organ part must be very crisp. But, above the organ, the choir must sing and sustain a *sostenuto* line Fauré marks piano/*dolce*. The juxtaposition of these two articulations can be difficult to achieve; however, when rehearsing the choir,

PROBLEM	REMEDY
Texture (continued)	the rhythmic pattern in the organ will become your best friend.
	As with the "Sanctus," have the choir pulse-sing sixteenth notes. This will enliven the rhythm of their *sostenuto* singing and will make pitch changes cleaner and quicker, producing a *sostenuto* line.
Conducting gesture	The same gesture is required throughout this movement, and it must communicate both the above-mentioned articulations, crisp and *sostenuto*.
	• To achieve this, imagine dotting an "i" with a pencil, trying to thread a needle, or doing petit-point embroidery. All these activities require a gesture that is direct and quick, yet which has a gentle, relaxed release. If you can achieve this gesture, you will portray a crisp, light articulation on your downbeats, but the release of your gesture will show the flow of line that the choir needs.
Style	Both choir and conductor must sense peace in this movement. Although this is the music of a late nineteenth-century composer, its performance should not be overly dramatic or Romantic. Remember, Fauré did not include many of the traditional Requiem texts so beloved by Romantic composers but added more peaceful, reassuring texts. The simpler the conductor can make this piece, the more effective and beautiful it will be.
Soprano sound	The sound of the choir should be angelic because the text speaks of a chorus of angels. Vibrato should be minimized, but asking for straight-tone is not the best answer. Straight-tone singing lacks tone color and vibrancy, both of which are qualities one wants from a chorus of angels! So the question becomes: how can one maintain color and vibrancy in the sound without having vibrato overwhelm it?

PROBLEM	REMEDY
Soprano sound (continued)	First, make sure you have completed a seating plan as described earlier in this chapter.

When singers listen to themselves, they tend to not listen to the pitch. When they abandon pitch to evaluate their vocal sounds, their vibrato will creep into the texture and become noticeable.

Begin with the first phrase; inexperienced singers never sing this phrase beautifully because they prepare for it incorrectly. Most prepare to sing the first note, the F-sharp, and fail to consider the D that must hover effortlessly above the texture.

To help your sopranos with this passage, have them sing the D with a sound that is spacious, high and forward. Once they have achieved a beautiful sound on the D, ask them to sing the F-sharp in the same "house" as the D. (This sound might be a bit airy, as the sopranos must bring a lot of head voice down to sing the F-sharp in the same position as D.) Once they have accomplished that, ask the sopranos to breathe for the F-sharp as though they were going to sing the D and then perform the whole phrase. Apply this technique throughout the movement.

| Alto, tenor, bass | The singers on the lower three parts must realize that their music in this movement is purely accompanimental—their lines should be less prominent than that of the soprano. It is very easy for altos, tenors, and basses to become bored in this role, but work hard not to allow that in this movement. Rehearse them with pulse- or count-singing, to ensure rhythmic accuracy. When you add the diction, be sure they use quick and light consonants, so they do not disturb the serenity of the soprano line. |

WORKING WITH THE ORCHESTRA:
A CONDUCTOR'S GUIDE

Dealing with and conducting the orchestra can be one of the most daunting aspects of performing major choral/orchestral works. For a choral conductor this is quite understandable because orchestral players' needs, working relationships, and conventions are quite different from choral singers' experiences. While it is true that everyone wants the performance to be as good as it can be, attention to these differences will help ensure the performance is of high quality.

1. Remember that orchestral players only have their parts in front of them; chorus members usually have piano/vocal scores with a lot of information. To negotiate their way through the music, therefore, orchestral players depend upon the conductor for clear, accurate beats and for help with entrances. For example, the conductor must account for the downbeat of every measure so a horn player (who may have had 137 measures of rest) will know exactly when to play. In a case such as this, a reassuring glance just prior to a significant entrance can make the player much more confident.

2. Most orchestral players have spent years developing proficient technique on their instruments and have considerable music reading skills. This is quite different from choral singers, many of whom have little if any professional musical training. In addition, most orchestral players expect to be paid, but most choral singers participate for the love of the music and the experience without pay. Thus, an orchestral rehearsal can and should move much more quickly; they usually prefer to play through entire movements without stopping and then hear clear and precise instructions and corrections.

3. You do not need to conduct the orchestral warm-up; they will do this on their own and be ready to play at the appointed time. They will also be ready to leave at the time designated for the end of the rehearsal. If your rehearsal runs overtime, they will leave unless you pay them extra. Poor organization will cost you money.

4. The orchestra must tune before they begin to rehearse or perform; this is something the concertmaster (in this case the principal violist) will handle. Because the Fauré *Requiem* uses organ, the other instruments must tune to the organ. You should be sure that the concertmaster knows where the organ console is located and advise the organist (before the rehearsal) to play A–440 on a clear, non-mixture stop.

5. It is absolutely crucial to know the orchestra's language. If you encounter terminology or markings unfamiliar to you as you study the score, look them up in a music dictionary. Using terms the instrumentalists understand will save a great deal of rehearsal time.

6. The conducting gesture for the orchestra should be very efficient and clear. Instrumentalists often dislike playing for choral conductors because they say they "can't see the beat." Unlike choirs, where all of the instruments (voices) speak the same way, orchestras are made of instruments that must articulate differently (e.g., a tuba player must use air differently than a piccolo player). Choral conductors spend a great deal of time developing gestures that enable singers to sing on the breath and produce a gentle onset of tone; these gestures are often useless to an orchestra. Therefore, when conducting a choral/orchestral work, your gesture needs to be much clearer and more precise. Remember, you have probably had many hours of rehearsal with the choir; tell the singers you must spend your energy during orchestral rehearsals ensuring ensemble and clarity within the entire ensemble—especially within the orchestra. Place responsibilities such as counting and reliability for accurate entrances on you singers. They may resist at first, but once they see all you have to do, they will understand the necessity of assuming responsibility.

The Rehearsals

The number and length of orchestral rehearsals will vary with the scope of the work, the size of the orchestra, and the budget. A standard orchestral rehearsal is two and one half hours including a fifteen-minute break in the middle, meaning a contracted rehearsal period of 150 minutes yields only one hundred and thirty-five minutes of rehearsal. This time is precious, so use it wisely. A competent professional orchestra can prepare a work such as the Fauré *Requiem* in two rehearsals; the first rehearsal should focus mostly on the orchestra and the second (or dress rehearsal) should involve cleaning up details from the first rehearsal and running the work straight through.

The first rehearsal will set the tone for subsequent rehearsals and for the performance itself. It is unnecessary to rehearse the movements in order; in fact, it is probably counterproductive. Rather, with a work such as Fauré's *Requiem*—with substantially different orchestral complements in every movement—it is preferable to begin with the movements employing the most instruments and end with the movements requiring the least. Be sure to excuse the instrumentalists when you have rehearsed all movements in which they are involved; this will show you value their time, and ensure they will play for your performances again.

Time	Minutes	Mvt.	Org	Stgs	Bssn	Hn	Tpt	Timp	Harp	Violin	Chorus	
7:00	(15)	3	X	X	X	X	X	—	X	X	X	
7:15	(15)	7	X	X	X	X	\	—	X	X	X	
7:30	(20)	1	X	X	\	X	X	X	\	O	X	
7:50	(25)	6	X	X	\	X	O	X	\	O	X	+ Baritone
8:30	(25)	5	X	X	X	X	O	O	\	O	X	
8:55	(25)	2	X	X	O	O	O	O	\	O	X	+ Baritone
9:20	(10)	4	X	X	O	O	O	O	X	O	O	+ Soprano

(135) Minutes	X = plays	O = excused
	\ = waits	— = not called yet

The orchestra rehearsal chart details which instruments play in which movements, gives a suggested rehearsal order to maximize players' time, and offers a suggested time allotment for each movement (based on the standard two-hour rehearsal beginning at a hypothetical 7:00 p.m. and ending at 9:30 p.m.). Because the rehearsal is only 135 minutes long, the conductor must constantly be aware of the time devoted (*versus* the time allocated) to each movement and of the time remaining. While this chart provides suggestions, some variation in timings is inevitable, and depends upon the performers, venue, and other factors. Some additional observations and suggestions are:

1. Call the timpanist for 7:15 and excuse him by 8:15. (This may allow for a smaller fee).

2. Inform the bassoons that they will have one hour free (forty-five minutes and the fifteen-minute break).

3. Inform the harpist that he or she will have one hour and fifty minutes free, from 7:30 until 9:20.

4. Be sure to excuse the violin, trumpet, bassoon, and horn sections when they are finished.

5. If the baritone soloist is not part of the choir, call him for 7:30 and excuse him at 9:20. Inform him that he will have free time during the rehearsal.

6. If the soprano soloist is not part of the choir, call her for 9:10.

7. Excuse the choir at 9:20.

In this initial rehearsal, adopt a three-fold hierarchy of rehearsal priorities. When you stop, correct problems in the following order:

1. *Ensemble and articulation*—Ensure that everyone is playing/singing together at the right time and using the same note lengths (i.e., articulation).

2. *Balance*—Listen carefully to all aspects of the texture, checking that what should be heard is actually being heard. Remember, the choir is not always the most important feature; at times an orchestral voice may need to predominate.

3. *Details of musical insight*—Neither the players nor the singers will achieve a high level of music making until they feel confident they are together and balanced. Once the basics of ensemble are there, it is then appropriate (and desirable) to provide insightful comments about the music to capture the group's artistic imagination and provide a deeper understanding of the music.

At the first rehearsal, be sure to focus your attention on the orchestra's needs (even at the expense of the choir). Begin by playing completely through a movement before stopping to rehearse small sections. When you do stop, give no more (or fewer) than three corrections at a time; giving only one correction will frustrate the players and is an inefficient use of rehearsal time. Be sure to address whatever problems you hear in the orchestra; ignoring problems in the orchestra to address a choral problem will frustrate an orchestra very quickly. (Remember, you have had numerous choral rehearsals without the orchestra.) Be certain to thank all the players, soloists, and chorus when their contributions to the rehearsal have been made.

The second (or dress) rehearsal can be in two parts. Use the first portion for attention to problems that plagued the first rehearsal. It will be necessary to hire all players for the entire rehearsal this time (do not let anyone go early). Orchestral players are accustomed to this and will expect to wait during the dress rehearsal "spot checks." If the conductor follows the tempo indications from Rutter's version of the Fauré *Requiem*, the running time of the entire work will be approximately thirty-five minutes. Therefore, the second portion of the dress rehearsal can include a "run" of the work in order. Be sure to allow some time at the end of the rehearsal to give any final corrections and discuss details such as attire, call times for the performance, and warm-up and gathering spaces at the performance venue.

What to Do About the Orchestra Parts

When arranging for the purchase or rental of performance materials, make sure that all of the music (i.e., full-score, set of orchestral parts, and the chorus/piano/vocal scores) are the same edition or compatible. We recommend the edition by John Rutter published by Hinshaw. If it becomes absolutely necessary for any of the performance materials to come from another edition or publisher (which is unnecessary if you use the Rutter edition), you must reconcile all the rehearsal numbering/lettering systems in both scores to avoid wasting valuable rehearsal time telling the performers where to begin. You should also do a note for note check to make sure the editions are compatible.

Never distribute unmarked parts to a string section; nothing wastes valuable rehearsal time more than bowing discussions amongst the strings. Bowing procedures can be perplexing and even intimidating to the choral conductor; it is strongly advisable to hire the concertmaster for an additional hour well before the first rehearsal to go over the bowings, taking into account the tempi, articulations, dynamics, size of the section, and the complete orchestration. As with the organ, you must have ideas, but unless you are an expert, it is wise to defer to the concertmaster's expertise. Write the bowings into each string part and into the full score.

It is also advisable to photocopy all the orchestral parts after having purchased or rented the set. This allows you to distribute the copied parts instead of the originals to the players. Lost rental parts can be expensive to replace, and if a player were to lose a part or forget to bring it with them to the rehearsal or performance, you can simply provide the original and avert disaster. Following the performance(s), you must destroy all photocopied materials.

Hiring the Players

Most cities with a symphony orchestra have an established musician's union that will prescribe a fee schedule for rehearsals and performances. Most fees are based on the standard two and one half-hour rehearsal, with a slightly higher fee for the performance. Unfortunately, it will be your budget (or lack of it!) that determines how many players you can hire and how much rehearsal time you can have. Based upon the Rutter edition of Fauré's *Requiem*, we recommend an orchestra ranging from a minimum of eighteen players (two horns, harp, organ, one violin, six violas, six celli and one double bass) to a maximum of twenty-six (two bassoons, four horns, two trumpets, timpani, harp, organ, one violin, six violas, six celli, and two double basses).

Hiring a contractor can save a great deal of time and effort (not to mention your sanity!). A contractor is usually a member of the local orchestra who is familiar with all the players; this person uses his connections to

contact and hire your entire orchestra. Contractor fees vary and may be as much as double the single player fee. If the contractor also plays for your performance, you should certainly expect to pay him at least double the fee of the other orchestral players. To find a contractor, contact the local symphony office, other conductors, or instrumentalists for referrals. Do not hire a contractor without a written contract. Procedures vary, but it will be easiest if the contractor agrees to take care of all details involved in hiring instrumentalists, including all payments. (You simply give the contractor a check for the total amount.)

Whether or not the contractor plays for your performances, he should definitely be at the first orchestral rehearsal; if possible, he should attend the beginning of all orchestral rehearsals. You need to contact and reach agreement with the contractor well in advance of your rehearsal/performance schedule. (In large cities or for performances at busy times of the year, even a year ahead is not too much.) Do not expect the contractor to perform miracles on short notice!

Seating the Orchestra

The conductor should expect to spend considerable time devising a carefully thought out orchestral seating plan. The set-up of the orchestra will largely depend upon the size of the orchestral complement and the configuration of the rehearsal/performance venue. Because of the importance of the organ part and the fact that many organ consoles in churches do not move, the placement of the orchestra will depend in large part upon the location of the organ. The organist and conductor must have unobstructed eye contact, and the harp must be placed near the organ because these two orchestral voices play together most of the time. Do not hesitate to use a closed-circuit video setup if any doubt exists as to whether the organist will be able to see the conductor and/or other players.

Also, consult with the management of your performance space well in advance to determine their rules and procedures for setup and to learn other details, such as whether the organ console is moveable. Notice on the orchestral seating plan that the violin soloist is not in the traditional concertmaster location; in Fauré's *Requiem* that duty falls to the principal violist. Place the bassoons close to the lower strings and the trumpets near the timpani because these instruments play together most often. You will be well advised to arrange for a setup crew (not including you or any ensemble members) to work all rehearsals and performances if the concert venue management does not provide such a crew.

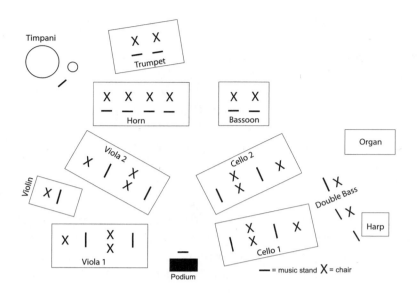

PRONUNCIATION OF TEXTS IN FAURÉ'S REQUIEM

Diction is an important aspect of presenting a stylistically authentic performance of Fauré's *Requiem*. Certainly, clear and uniform pronunciation of the text is always important, but using pronunciations the composer knew and used in his lifetime can produce vigorous and exciting performances of historical works and make singing them easier. We have often found that the use of historically appropriate diction solves vocal problems. The best vocal composers have always considered vocal ranges and singing technique when setting texts. Pronunciation changes over time, however, and modern pronunciations can change vowel sounds, making a passage much more challenging to sing. Restoring the sounds the composer intended can ease such vocal difficulties. (For more on the topic of French Latin pronunciations in general, the reader may consult Anthony Reeves's article in the October 2001 issue of *Choral Journal*, which is cited in the bibliography at the end of this chapter.)

Included below are pronunciation charts for the Fauré *Requiem*. These French Latin pronunciations represent the Latin Fauré knew and used. The charts use the International Phonetic Alphabet (IPA), the standardized alphabet of phonetic sounds, and its universality makes it useful to choral conductors and singers. Essentially, the IPA codifies every sound produced in language, enabling those who read it to pronounce words in any language, no matter how unfamiliar. The chapter bibliography lists some useful IPA resources.

It is worth any conductor's time to teach his or her choir the IPA symbols for basic vowel sounds. Most consonants are obvious, and one can teach special symbols as the need arises. If a choir understands these symbols, you

can communicate precisely the sounds you wish them to sing in every instance. Using made up phonetic sounds (e.g., "ee" for [i], or "oo" for [u]) can lead to confusion and consternation because different people often pronounce identical spellings with some variation.

In the following pronunciation chart, the left column shows the vowels and consonants as they are spelled in Latin texts, and the right column provides the appropriate IPA transliteration for each sound.

Nineteenth-century French Latin Pronunciation Chart

Vowels Spelling	Pronunciation Notes/IPA
a	[a], more forward than Italian or German
ae	[e]; [ɛ] in a closed syllable
am, an	[am] or [an], *but* if a consonant follows, [ã] followed by the consonant
au	[o] no diphthong; not [ɔ]
e	[e]; [ɛ] in a closed syllable
em, en	[ɛm], [ɛn]
emp, ent	[ɛ̃mp], [ɛ̃nt]
eu	generally as [ɛy] because (unlike French) these letter almost always belong to different syllables
i	[i]
im, in	as an initial sound or alone as [ɛ̃]; otherwise as [im], [in]
o	open syllable [o]; closed syllable [ɔ]
oe	[e]; [ɛ] in a closed syllable
om, on	[ɔ̃]
non	[nɔn]
u	[y]
um, un	[œ̃m], [œ̃n]
unc, unt	[œ̃t], [õt]
y	[i]

Consonants:

Spelling	Pronunciation Notes/IPA
c	
before e, ae, oe, i, or y	[s]
otherwise	[k]
cc	
before e, ae, oe, i, or y	[s]
otherwise	[ks]
ch	
before e, ae, oe, i, or y	[ʃ]
otherwise	[k]
d	[d]
g	[ʒ]
gn	[ɲ] or [gn] in certain words, e.g., Agnus
h	mute
j	[ʒ]
m, n (initial sounds)	[m], [n]
qu	[kw]
quo	[ko]
r	flipped, not the uvular r used in spoken French
s	usually [s], but [z] between vowels or voiced consonants
s, t (final)	not dropped at ends of words
sc	[s]
ti	[si]
x, xc	[ks] before consonant; [gs] before vowel
z	[z]

Pronunciation for the Fauré Requiem

We now turn to the application of these guidelines to the Fauré *Requiem*. The following chart shows the text of the entire work and its IPA transliteration. Excellent literal translations of the Latin Mass are available in Ron Jeffers's

book *Translations and Annotations of Choral Repertoire: Sacred Latin Texts* (see Bibliography). A few important notes:

- Accentuation in French Latin follows the lead of spoken French, in which the syllables of each word receive very little special accent; instead, the words are spoken evenly with a slight accent on the final syllable.

- The chart shows instances in which liaison (the attachment of a word's final consonant to the initial vowel or sound of the word following) is appropriate.

- In determining French Latin pronunciations, one must consider the context of the sounds. For example, many pronunciations are determined by whether a syllable is open or closed. In instances where the pronunciations below do not seem to follow the pronunciation chart above, the reason is usually contextual.

- Another point of potential confusion is that French Latin pronunciations tend to avoid having too many distinct consonant sounds in a row, necessitating the omission of one of the sounds. We have done this a few times in the chart; it is generally a matter of taste and a conductor bothered by this may certainly reinstate the omitted sounds.

Texts of the Fauré Requiem

Text	Pronunciation/IPA
Requiem aeternam dona eis, Domine,	rekwiɛ metɛrnam dona ei sdɔ̃mine
et lux perpetua luceat eis.	ɛ tly kspɛrpetya lysea teis
Te decet hymnus, Deus, in Sion,	te desɛ timnys dey sin siɔ̃
et tibi reddetur votum in Jerusalem.	e tibi redetyr voty min ʒerysalɛm
Exaudi orationem meam;	ekzodi orasionɛmeam
ad te omnis caro veniet.	ad te ɔ̃ni skaro veniɛt
Kyrie eleison.	kirie elɛizɔ̃
Christe eleison.	kriste elɛizɔ̃
Kyrie eleison.	kirie elɛizɔ̃
Domine Jesu Christe, rex gloriae,	dɔ̃mine ʒezy kriste rɛks glorie
libera animas defunctorum	libera anima sdefœ̃torœ̃m
de poenis inferni,	de peni sinfɛrni
et de profundo lacu.	e de profœ̃ndo laky

Text	Pronunciation/IPA
Libera eas de ore leonis,	libera ea sde ore leɔnis
ne absorbeat eas Tartarus,	ne abzɔrbea tea startarys
ne cadant in obscurum.	ne kadã tin ɔbskyrœm
Hostias et preces tibi,	ostia se presɛstibi
Domine, laudis offerimus,	dɔ̃mine lodi soferimys
tu suscipe pro animabus illis	ty sysipe pro animaby silis
quarum hodie memoriam facimus.	kwarœ̃ modie memoriam fasimys
Fac eas, Domine,	fa seas dɔ̃mine
de morte transire ad vitam.	de mɔrte tranzire ad vitam
Quam olim Abrahae promisisti,	kwa molimabrae promisiti
et semini ejus.	e tsemini eys
Sanctus, sanctus, sanctus,	sãty sãty sãtys
Dominus Deus Sabaoth.	dɔ̃miny sdey zabaɔt
Pleni sunt coeli et terra	pleni sɔ̃ tseli e tɛra
gloria tua.	gloria tya
Hosanna in excelsis.	ozana inɛksɛlsis
Pie Jesu Domine,	pieʒezy dɔ̃mine
dona eis requiem,	dɔ̃na ei srekwiɛm
requiem sempiternam.	rekwiɛm sɛ̃mpitɛrnam
Agnus Dei,	agny sdei
qui tollis peccata mundi:	kwi toli spesata mœ̃ndi
dona eis requiem,	dona ei srekwiɛm
requiem sempiternam.	rekwiɛm sɛ̃mpitɛrnam
Lux aeterna luceat eis, Domine:	ly ksetɛrna lysea teis dɔ̃mine
cum sanctis tuis in aeternum,	kœ̃ msãkti styi si netɛrnœ̃m
quia pius es.	kwia piy sɛs
Requiem aeternam dona eis, Domine,	rekwiɛ metɛrnam dona ei sdɔ̃mine
et lux perpetua luceat eis.	ɛ tly kspɛrpetya lysea teis
Libera me Domine,	libera me dɔ̃mine
de morte aeterna,	de mɔrte etɛterna
in die illa tremenda:	in die ila tremɛnda
quando coeli movendi sunt et terra.	kwãdo seli movɛndi sɔ̃ te tɛra
Dum veneris judicare	dœ̃m veneri ʒydikare
saeculum per ignem.	sekylœ̃m pɛ riɲem
Tremens factus sum ego, et timeo	tremɛnz faty sy mego e timeo
dum discussio venerit,	dœ̃m diskysio venerit
atque ventura ira.	atkwe vɛntyra ira

Text

Dies illa, dies irae,
calamitatis et miseriae,
dies magna et amara valde.
Requiem aeternam, dona eis, Domine:
et lux perpetua luceat eis.

In paradisum deducant te Angeli,
in tuo adventu suscipiant te Martyres,

et perducant te in civitatem sanctam Jerusalem.
Chorus angelorum te suscipiat,
et cum Lazaro quondam paupere
aeternam habeas requiem.

Pronunciation/IPA

diε sila diε sire
kalamitati sεt misεrie
die smaɲa etamara valde
rekwiε metεrnam dona ei sdɔ̃mine
e tlyk spεrpetya lysea teis

in paradisiœ̃m dedykã te ã ʒeli
i ntyo advεnty sysipiã te martirεs

e tpεrdysã te i nsivitatεm sãtam ʒerysalεm
kory sãʒeloroe mte sysipiat
e tkœ̃m lazaro kondam popere
etεrna mabea srekwiεm

Bibliography

The following sources provide good reference materials about the IPA system and French Latin pronunciation. Although French Latin follows different rules of pronunciation than modern French, diction books can be useful in understanding the IPA symbols common to all French language.

Adams, David. *A Handbook of Diction for Singers: Italian, German, French.* New York: Oxford University Press. 1999.

Cox, Richard. *A Singer's Manual of French and German Diction.* New York: Schirmer Books. 1970.

Grubb, Thomas. *Singing in French: A Manual of French Diction and French Vocal Repertoire.* New York: Schirmer Books. 1979.

International Phonetic Alphabet Association Handbook: A Guide to the Use of the International Phonetic Alphabet. New York: Cambridge University Press. 1999.

Jeffers, Ron. *Translations and Annotations of Choral Repertoire: Sacred Latin Texts.* Corvallis, Oregon: Earthsongs. 1988.

Ranum, Patricia. *Méthode de la prononciation latine dite vulgaire ou à la française : petite méthode à l'usage des chanteurs et des récitants d'après le manuscrit de dom Jacques Le Clerc.* Paris: Actes sud. 1991.

Reeves, Anthony R. "The Use of French Latin for Choral Music." *The Choral Journal* 42 (October 2001): 9–16.

Wall, Joan and Robert Caldwell, editors. *Diction for Singers: A Concise Reference for English, Italian, Latin, German, French, and Spanish Pronunciation.* Dallas: Caldwell Publishing. 1990.

——. *International Phonetic Alphabet for Singers: A Manual for English and Foreign Language Diction.* Dallas: Caldwell Publishing. 1989.

The Organ

This short introduction to the organ acquaints the conductor with basic information needed to communicate intelligently with an organist. A glossary of terms is included at the end of this chapter. For more extensive information, the reader may consult one of the sources listed in the bibliography.

What Is a Pipe Organ?

The pipe organ consists of complex rows of pipes that produce sound when air, forced by a wind mechanism, passes through the pipes. A set of valves controls the airflow, and one or more manuals (keyboards), as well as other mechanisms (such as drawknobs) control the valves. An organ includes any number of divisions (sets of ranks of pipes), and each division generally corresponds to a different manual. Some of the more common names for divisions are great, swell, choir, positiv, and pedal. Divisions tend to differ in the overall character of their sound, and these sound characteristics have changed through different historical eras and according to geographical areas.

Each division is located in a different place or cabinet, and while they are usually close together, they do not have to be. It is quite common, for example, for an organ located at the front of a church to have a division at the rear (often called an antiphonal division), controlled from the console at the front. The pipes of each division stand in a windchest that includes the mechanism to open and close the valves controlling the flow of air into each pipe. An electric blower (or, before the advent of electricity, a person or people coerced into the task) produces air and sends it into a reservoir where it is regulated at a constant pressure. From the reservoir, the wind flows into whichever pipes have open valves.

Stops

A stop is a set of pipes, generally one for each note on the keyboard. The pipes of an organ are made of metal or wood, depending upon the stop, and fall into one of several categories, the two most common being flues and reeds. Flue pipes, which allow the wind to pass through a flue (opening) in the pipe, are more common. Reed pipes have a thin metal tongue, or reed, that vibrates and produces a distinctive "reedy" sound. The organist controls which stops are

enabled to sound at any given time by mechanical means, usually by pulling drawknobs located on either side of the console or by flipping tabs, which may be located above the manuals.

Both a name and numeral identify individual stops. The name indicates the family of pipes to which a stop belongs, and the numeral indicates the pitch level of the stop. The numeral roughly corresponds to the length of the lowest (and longest) pipe of the stop.

NUMERAL	PITCH LEVEL AT WHICH PIPES SOUND
2'	Two octaves higher than written pitch
4'	One octave higher than written pitch
8'	At written pitch
16'	One octave lower than written pitch
32'	Two octaves lower than written pitch

For example, an 8' rohrflöte stop is a member of the flute family and sounds at written pitch; a 4' diapason belongs to the principal family and sounds one octave higher than written. Two kinds of stops have unusual numbers on their drawknobs: mutations and mixtures. Mutations have numbers that include fractions (e.g., 2 2/3). These stops actually sound pitches other than (or in addition to) those corresponding to the keys played; the pitches correspond to the natural non-octave overtones. Mixtures have Roman numerals (e.g., Mixtur IV). Mixtures are stops including more than one rank of pipes and usually result in increased brightness of the sound.

Using the Organ in Fauré's Requiem

Fauré included an organ part as an integral component of every movement of every version of the *Requiem*. He carefully notated the organ part, reproduced exactly in the Rutter edition's vocal score. It is a substantial organ part and not easy to play. From his markings, it is clear that Fauré intended the organ to be heard and sometimes even to dominate the sound. The single most important thing a conductor can do regarding the organ part, therefore, is to hire the most competent organist available.

Still, as with any other instrument or voice, the conductor must have definite ideas about how the organ should sound and what its role in the performance should be. The fact that every organ is different complicates this task. Violins certainly vary somewhat, but a violin is still a violin, and conductors may rightfully expect a particular set of tone qualities and sounds. Each organ is unique, however, and the tonal design of organs varies enormously. The wise conductor, therefore, will develop ideas about the role of the organ in the *Requiem* but keep an open mind and consult thoroughly with the organist about using the individual instrument in the performance space.

Organs have developed individual characteristics based largely on their country of origin and the organ repertoire of that country's composers. Many organs built today are modeled after such "nationalistic" instruments. To form basic conclusions about the potential role of the organ in the Fauré *Requiem* requires one to have a basic understanding of French organs, and, in particular, of the French organs Fauré would have known.

La Madeleine, Fauré's church, has two organs: a choir organ (1843) and a main organ (1846), both by Aristide Cavaillé-Coll (1811–99), the greatest French organ builder of the nineteenth century. A native of southern France, Cavaillé-Coll utilized various technical innovations to build organs that were revolutionary in their tonal design. He is regarded as the father of the French Romantic organ—the instrument that inspired such organists as Franck, Saint-Saëns, Widor, and Duruflé. The organs at La Madeleine are large, powerful instruments that offer great diversity in sound. An enormous variety of sounds are possible there, and if one seeks any kind of "stylistically correct" performance of the *Requiem* today, it is mandatory that both the conductor and organist agree on a clear sound concept informed by French Romantic organs.

Working with the Organist

Your first decision must be what your accompanimental forces will be. An organist will likely play Fauré's organ part very differently if he or she is accompanying the choir alone than if part of a larger ensemble. For our purposes, let us assume you are hiring an orchestra. You must then decide how authentic you wish to have the sound be. Music from the late nineteenth century is usually easier to deal with in this respect than that from earlier eras as most of the instruments used were at least similar to those in use today.

John Rutter, in his edition of Fauré's *Requiem*, has sought to find a "happy medium" between the earlier, chamber-like versions and the later "symphonic" version. We suggest that a similar approach to the conductor's internal sound model would prove productive. While it would be virtually impossible to reproduce the acoustical environment of La Madeleine, it is invaluable to consider what the organs Fauré played were like and how music sounds in the church. It would certainly be ideal to travel to Paris and visit La Madeleine to hear the organs there. As that is prohibitive for most people, begin by talking with organists (including, of course, your performance organist), and listen to recordings they recommend. Make notes about how the organ sounds, and about what you like and dislike. Then have another conversation with the performance organist and discuss your conclusions.

Listen carefully to the organist and give his or her ideas very heavy weight. He or she is the expert on the instrument and probably knows a great deal about what will be possible with the organ you will use. As a group, French organists have been—since at least the seventeenth century—extremely par-

ticular about their registrations. In fact, countless French composers have given very precise instructions for registering their organ pieces. Fauré did not do this with the organ part for the *Requiem*, so trust the organist you have hired to do the most possible within your jointly agreed sound goals.

While suggesting registrations would be futile, we can list some things a conductor might consider when preparing performances of the Fauré *Requiem*.

1. Try to discern and realize Fauré's intentions regarding the organ at every moment. Is it supportive, accompanimental, or does it play a larger role in the orchestration?

2. When change seems called for (e.g., when a new dynamic mark is introduced) does the music seem to call for a change of loudness, texture, or tone color?

3. When the loudness itself is to change by means of a crescendo or diminuendo, should the basic sound remain the same, or does the sound quality need to change?

4. How quickly does the organ "speak?" Does the organist need to play ahead of the conductor's beat to have the sound arrive on the beat?

5. Always know what you want the sound to be from all performers and instruments. Realize, however, that—unless you are an organist—you probably know considerably more about the voice (or your own instrument) than you do about any of the other instruments, including the organ. Consultation is important; if you can express what sound you desire, a good instrumentalist can usually find ways to produce it. If you are an organist, why would you hire someone you do not trust? Allow him or her to be creative with her own ideas.

6. If you are familiar with a particular organ or with organs in general, feel free to suggest stops, but always leave the final decision to the organist.

7. Ensure a good sight line between the organist and the conductor. Use a video camera and monitor if necessary.

8. Be certain the organist can hear the rest of the ensemble, but clarify that he or she must play with your beat, even if it seems wrong from the organ's location; you must be the timekeeper for the entire ensemble.

9. Know when the organist will need time to change registrations and how much time is needed.

10. Allow time for the sound to clear at pauses and between movements. (Listen to the entire ensemble for this.)

Glossary

Box: An enclosure containing pipes with shutters on one side controlled by a pedal on the console.

Chiff: An audible edge to the sound at the moment a pipe begins to speak.

Choir organ, *organe de choeur, Chororgel*: A division, often enclosed, traditionally located near where the choir is seated.

Combination action: The device allowing organists to turn on numerous stops at once by way of pistons.

Console, "the desk," *Spielschrank*, or *Spieltisch*: The piece of furniture to which the manuals, pedalboard, and other organ controls are attached.

Coupler, *accouplement, tirasse*, or *Koppel*: A mechanism, usually controlled by a tab on the console, that allows pipes in one division to be operated by the keys of another manual.

Drawknob, drawstop, stop-knob, *tyrant, tyrant de register, Registerknopf, Registerzug*, or *tiro*: A knob on the console that, when pulled out, enables a stop to sound.

Flue, *lumière, saillie, Kernspalte*, or *anima*: An opening in a pipe through which wind passes to produce sound.

Foundation stops, *fonds d'orgue, Grundstimmen*: Stops whose pipes sound the note of the key being played with a strong fundamental harmonic.

Great organ, *grande orgue, Hauptwerk, Oberwerk*, or *organo primo*: The largest or main division (its manual is called "the great") of an organ. On a two-manual organ, it is usually the bottom manual.

Manual: A keyboard played by the hands. An organ console may have as few as one, or may have several.

Mixture, *Mixtur, mixtura*: a stop consisting of more than one rank of pipes. Playing a single key plays more than one note.

Mutation, "overtone stops": A rank of pipes that sounds pitches other than those notated and played.

Pedal, *pédale, Pedal*, or *pedale*: an organ console usually includes several different kinds of pedals. The more common ones include: pedals of the pedalboard, which play the pipes of the pedal organ; swell pedals, which control the volume of enclosed divisions by opening and closing the shutters; and other pedals, possibly including controls for couplers, pistons, or individual stops.

Pedalboard, *pédalier*, *Pedalklavier*: The keyboard played by the feet.

Pédale de combinaison: A combination action pedal; that is, a pedal operating a device allowing the organist to turn on a group of stops simultaneously.

Piston, *Druckknopf*, *Druckschalter*: A button on the console between the manuals or on the pedalboard that turns on pre-set combinations of stops.

Rank: The set of pipes comprising a stop.

Reed pipe, *anche*, *tuyau à anche*, *Zungenpfeife*, *Zungenstimme*, *ancia*, or *canna ad ancia*: A pipe featuring a metal tongue that vibrates to produce the sound.

Solo organ: The division (and its manual) featuring many colorful solo stops. It is often the fourth manual.

Solo stop: A colorful stop usually pulled alone on its manual, used to play the melody and accompanied on another manual by softer stops.

Stop, *register*, *Register*, *registro*: A set of pipes, one for each note on the keyboard (except for mixtures and mutations). Stops differ individually and dramatically as to their tone and volume (and sometimes even their pitch) based primarily on the shape and size of the pipes and their mouths.

Suboctave: A coupler that adds notes an octave below those played.

Superoctave: A coupler that adds notes an octave above those played.

Swell organ, *récit expressif*, *Schwellwerk*: A division of an organ enclosed all around by a box, one side of which is comprised of shutters that open and close when the organist operates a pedal on the console. On a two-manual organ, it is usually the top manual.

Swell-box, "the box," *Schwellkasten*: An enclosed space with movable shutters on the side opening into the room. These shutters are controlled from the console to manage the loudness of the pipes inside the box.

Tirasse: A coupler, especially a pedal coupler. For example, "*Tirasse du Grand Orgue*" means "*Grand Orgue* to Pedal."

Bibliography

Audsley, George Ashdown. *Organ-Stops and Their Artistic Registration: Names, Forms, Construction, Tonalities, and Offices in Scientific Combination.* New York: Warner Brothers. 2000. (originally 1921).

Stiven, Frederic B. *In the Organ Lofts of Paris.* Boston: The Stratford Company. 1923. (out of print).

Sumner, William Leslie. *The Organ: Its Evolution, Principles of Construction and Use.* New York: St. Martin's Press. 1962.

The Harvard Dictionary of Music, s.v. "Organ."

The New Harvard Dictionary of Music, s.v. "Organ."

Bruce Chamberlain is Professor of Music and Director of Choral Activities at the University of Arizona. He has conducted collegiate and festival choirs in nineteen states, Canada, Hungary, China, and the Czech Republic and has appeared with numerous orchestras around the world. His career has focused upon the major choral/orchestral repertoire. A summa cum laude graduate of the Indiana University School of Music with BME, MM and DMus degrees, Chamberlain studied conducting with Julius Herford, Margaret Hillis, and John Nelson, piano with Menachem Pressler, Wallace Hornibrook, and Nicholas Zumbro, and has continued choral/orchestral conducting studies with Helmut Rilling, Andrew Davis, Dale Warland, and Robert Page.

Matthew W. Mehaffey is Assistant Professor of Music and Director of Choral Activities at The George Washington University in Washington, DC.

Anthony Reeves is Assistant Professor of Music and Director of Choral Studies at the University of North Dakota where he conducts the Concert Choir and Varsity Bards, and teaches graduate and undergraduate courses in conducting, choral methodology, and history and literature. Formerly on faculty at Hamilton College, he has also taught middle and high school and worked as a church musician. Reeves completed the Doctor of Musical Arts degree in Choral Conducting and Historical Musicology at the University of Arizona; his dissertation detailed French Baroque performance practice for the choral idiom and included a modern transcription of one of Jean-Philippe Rameau's grand motets. Dr. Reeves is especially interested in conducting techniques, editing choral music, and rehearsal psychology. Active as a clinician, adjudicator, and author, his article, "The Use of French Latin for Choral Music," was the cover article for the October 2001 issue of the Choral Journal.

Bibliography

Diction Resources, Language Dictionaries, and Texts and Translations

General

Collison, Robert L. *Dictionary of English and Foreign Languages: A Bibliographical Guide to both General and Technical Dictionaries.* Second edition. New York: Hafner. 1971.

McGee, Timothy J., et al. *Singing Early Music: The Pronunciation of European Languages in the Late Middle Ages and Renaissance.* Bloomington, Indiana: Indiana University Press. 1996. (includes CD).

Moriarty, John. *Diction.* Boston: E. C. Schirmer. 1975.

Wall, Joan. *International Phonetic Alphabet for Singers: A Manual for English and Foreign Language Diction.* Redmond, Washington: Caldwell Publishing. 1989.

Wall, Joan, et al. *Diction for Singers: a concise reference for English, Italian, Latin, German, French, and Spanish pronunciation.* Redmond, Washington: Caldwell Publishing, 1990.

English

Marshall, Madeleine. *The Singer's Manual of English Diction.* New York: Schirmer Books, 1953.

Merriam-Webster's Collegiate Dictionary, tenth edition. Springfield, Massachusetts: Merriam Webster, Inc. 1993.

Oxford American Dictionary. Eugene Erlich, editor, et al. New York: Oxford University Press. 1980.

Oxford English Dictionary. Second edition. Prepared by J.A. Simson and E.S.C. Weiner. Oxford: Clarendon. 1989. 20v.

A Pronouncing Dictionary of American English. John Samuel Kenyon and Thomas Albert Knott, editors. Springfield, Massachusetts: Merriam-Webster, Inc. 1987.

Webster's Third New International Dictionary of the English Language, Unabridged. Philip Babcock Gove, editor. Springfield, Massachusetts: Merriam-Webster. 1961.

French

Adams, David. *A Handbook of Diction for Singers: Italian, German, French.* New York: Oxford University Press. 1999.

Cox, Richard G. *The Singer's Manual of German and French Diction.* New York: Schirmer Books. 1970.

Greimas, A.J. *Dictionnaire de l'ancien français jusgu'au milieu du XIV siècle.* Second edition. [revue et corrigèe] Paris: Larousse. 1977.

Grubb, Thomas. *Singing in French: a Manual of French Diction and French Vocal Repertoire.* New York: Schirmer Books. 1979.

Pocket French-English/English-French Dictionary. Paris: Larousse. 1999. (This is an inexpensive, paperback dictionary of modern French.)

A Short Old French Dictionary for Students. Kenneth Urwin, editor, with a foreword John Orr. Oxford: Blackwell. 1972. (This dictionary deals with Old French, not the modern version of the language. Consult this dictionary when performing Medieval and Renaissance Music with French texts.)

German

Adams, David. *A Handbook of Diction for Singers: Italian, German, French.* New York: Oxford University Press. 1999.

Cox, Richard G. *The Singer's Manual of German and French Diction.* New York: Schirmer Books. 1970.

Grimm, Jacob and Wilhelm Grimm. *Deutsches Wörterbuch.* Leipzig: Hirzel, 1854–1960.

Jeffers, Ron and Gordon Paine. *Translations and Annotations of Choral Repertoire: Volume II, German Texts.* Corvallis, Oregon: Earthsongs. 2000.

Langenscheidt's German-English/English-German Dictionary. The Langenscheidt Editorial Staff, editors. New York: Pocket Books. 1976. (This is an inexpensive, paperback dictionary of modern German.)

Italian

Adams, David. *A Handbook of Diction for Singers: Italian, German, French.* New York: Oxford University Press. 1999.

Colorni, Evelina. *Singers' Italian: A Manual of Diction and Phonetics*. New York: Schirmer Books. 1970.

HarperCollins Italian Dictionary: Italian-English, English-Italian. New York: Harper Collins, 2000.

Latin

Angelis, Michael de, editor. Nicola A. Montani. *The Correct Pronunciation of Latin According to Roman Usage*. Chicago: GIA Publications, Inc. 1965.

Cassell's Latin and English Dictionary. D. P. Simpson, compiler. New York: Collier Books. 1987. (This is an inexpensive, paperback dictionary of Latin.)

Copeman, Harold. *Singing in Latin*. Oxford: Harold Copeman. 1990.

Harper's Latin Dictionary: A New Latin Dictionary Founded on the Translation of Freund's Latin-German Lexicon. E.A. Andrews, editor. Revised, enlarged, and in great part rewritten by Charlton T. Lewis and Charles Short. New York: American Book Company. 1907. R/Oxford: Clarendon Press. 1965.

Jeffers, Ron. *Translations and Annotations of Choral Repertoire: Volume I, Sacred Latin Texts*. Corvallis, Oregon: Earthsongs. 1988.

Russian

Auty, Robert. *Handbook of Old Church Slavonic: Texts and Glossary, Vol. 2*. Third edition. London: Athlone Press. 1968.

Bobrinskoy, Tania and Irina Gsovskaya. *How to Pronounce Russian Correctly*. Lincolnwood, Illinois: Passport Books. 1988.

The Pocket Oxford Russian Dictionary. Second edition. Coulson, et al, compilers. Oxford: Oxford University Press. 2000. (This is an inexpensive, paperback dictionary of modern Russian.)

Spanish

Castel, Nico. *A Singer's Manual of Spanish Lyric Diction*. New York: Excalibur Publishing. 1994.

The University of Chicago Spanish-English, English-Spanish Dictionary. Carlos Castillo and Otto F. Bond, compilers. Rev. D. Lincoln Canfield. New York: Washington Square Press, Inc. 1991. (This is an inexpensive, paperback dictionary of modern Spanish.)

History and Literature

General

Grout, Donald J. and Claude V. Palisca. *A History of Western Music*, sixth edition. New York: W. W. Norton & Company, Inc. 2000.

Routley, Erik. *The English Carol*. New York: Greenwood Publishing Group. 1973.

Medieval

Hoppin, Richard H. *Medieval Music*. New York: W. W. Norton & Company. 1978. (Norton also publishes an anthology in conjunction with this book.)

Reese, Gustave. *Music in the Middle Ages*. New York: W. W. Norton & Company, Inc. 1940. (Although old, this book contains much valuable information.)

Seay, Albert. *Music in the Medieval World*, second edition. Englewood Cliffs, New Jersey: Prentice-Hall. 1991.

Renaissance

Brown, Howard Mayer and Louise K. Stein. *Music in the Renaissance*, second edition. Englewood Cliffs, New Jersey: Prentice-Hall, Inc. 1998.

Perkins, Leeman. *Music in the Age of the Renaissance*. New York: W. W. Norton & Company, Inc. 1999.

Reese, Gustave. *Music in the Renaissance*, revised edition. New York: W. W. Norton & Company, Inc. 1959. (Although old, this book contains much valuable information.)

Baroque

Anthony, James R. *French Baroque Music: From Beaujoyeulx to Rameau*, rev. ed. Portland, Oregon: Amadeus Press. 1977.

Bukofzer, Manfred F. *Music in the Baroque Era: From Monteverdi to Bach*. New York: W. W. Norton & Company, Inc. 1947. (Although old, this book contains much valuable information.)

Palisca, Claude V. *Baroque Music*, third edition. Englewood Cliffs, New Jersey: Prentice-Hall. 1990.

Sadie, Julie Anne, editor. *Companion to Baroque Music*. Berkeley, California: University of California Press. 1998.

Classic/Romantic

Pauly, Reinhard G. *Music in the Classic Period*, fourth edition. Englewood Cliffs, New Jersey: Prentice-Hall. 1999.

Plantinga, Leon. *Romantic Music: A History of Musical Style in Nineteenth Century Europe*. New York: W. W. Norton & Company, Inc. 1984. (Norton also publishes an anthology in conjunction with this book.)

Contemporary

Salzman, Eric. *Twentieth Century Music: An Introduction*, third edition. Englewood Cliffs, New Jersey: Prentice-Hall, Inc. 1987.

Watkins, Glenn. *Soundings: Music in the Twentieth Century*. New York: Schirmer Books. 1995.

Choral Music History

Jacobs, Arthur, editor. *Choral Music: A Symposium*. Baltimore, Maryland: Penguin Books. 1963.

Smither, Howard E. *A History of the Oratorio: Volume I, The Oratorio in the Baroque Era, Italy, Vienna, and Paris*. Chapel Hill, North Carolina: University of North Carolina Press. 1977.

——. *A History of the Oratorio: Volume II, The Oratorio in the Baroque Era, Protestant Germany and England*. Chapel Hill, North Carolina: University of North Carolina Press. 1977.

——. *A History of the Oratorio: Volume III, The Oratorio in the Classical Era*. Chapel Hill, North Carolina: University of North Carolina Press. 1987.

——. *A History of the Oratorio: Volume IV, The Oratorio in the Nineteenth and Twentieth Centuries*. Chapel Hill, North Carolina: University of North Carolina Press. 2000.

Ulrich, Homer. *A Survey of Choral Music*. New York: Harcourt Brace Jovanovich, Inc. 1973.

Young, Percy M. *The Choral Tradition*. New York: W. W. Norton & Company, Inc. 1962.

Music Dictionaries

ASCAP Biographical Dictionary, fourth edition. Compiled for the American Society of Composers, Authors, and Publishers by Jacques Cattell Press. New York: Boker. 1980.

Baker's Biographical Dictionary of Musicians, eighth edition. Nicolas Slonimsky, editor. New York: Schirmer. 1992.

The Concise Edition of Baker's Biographical Dictionary of Musicians, eighth edition. Rev. Nicolas Slonimsky. New York: Schirmer Books. 1994.

The Garland Encyclopedia of World Music. 10v. Bruno Nettl, et al, editors. Hamden, Connecticut: Garland. 1997–99. (Each volume includes CD).

The Harvard Biographical Dictionary of Music. Don Michael Randel, editor. Cambridge, Massachusetts: Belknap, Harvard University Press. 1996.

The Harvard Dictionary of Music, second edition. Wili Apel, editor. Cambridge, Massachusetts: The Belknap Press of Harvard University Press, 1978.

The New Grove Dictionary of Music and Musicians, second edition. 29v. Stanley Sadie, editor. London: Macmillan. 2001.

The New Grove Dictionary of Musical Instruments. Stanley Sadie, editor. London: Macmillan. 1984.

The New Harvard Dictionary of Music. Don Michael Randel, editor. Cambridge, Massachusetts: Belknap, Harvard University Press. 1986.

Indexes

Heyer, Anna Harriet, editor. *Historical Sets, Collected Editions, and Monuments of Music: A Guide to Their Contents*, third edition. Chicago: American Library Association. 1980. 2v.

Hill, George and Norris L. Stephens. *Collected Editions, Historical Series, & Sets & Monuments of Music: A Bibliography*. Berkeley, California: Fallen Leaf Press. 1997.

Original Sources

Census-Catalogue of Manuscript Sources of Polyphonic Music: 1400–1550. Compiled by the University of Illinois Musicological Archives for Renaissance Manuscript Studies. Neuhausen-Stuttgart: Hänssler-Verlag/American Institute of Musicology, 1979–. [In progress.]

Répertoire International des Sources Musicales (International Inventory of Musical Sources). [RISM]. Various editors. **Series A**: Cassel: Bärenreiter. 1971–. **Series B**: München: Henle, 1960–. **Series C**: Cassel: Bärenreiter. 1976– (see above).

Weiss, Piero and Richard Taruskin, editors. *Music in the Western World: A History of Documents*. New York: Schirmer Books. 1984.

Performance Practice

Brown, Howard Mayer and Stanley Sadie, editors. *Performance Practice: Music Before 1600*. New York: W. W. Norton & Company. 1989.

——. *Performance Practice: Music After 1600*. New York: W. W. Norton & Company. 1990.

Cyr, Mary. *Performing Baroque Music*. Portland, Oregon: Amadeus Press. 1998.

Dart, Thurston. *The Interpretation of Music*. New York: Harper and Row. 1991.

Donington, Robert. *Baroque Music: Style and Performance, A Handbook*. New York: W. W. Norton & Company. 1982.

Donington, Robert. *The Interpretation of Early Music*, new revised edition. New York: W. W. Norton & Company, Inc. 1997.

Dreyfus, Laurence. *Bach's Continuo Group: Players and Practices in His Vocal Works*. Cambridge, Massachusetts: Harvard University Press. 1987. (Although this book focuses on J. S. Bach's music, much of the information can be applied to Baroque music in general.)

Harnoncourt, Nikolaus, translator. Mary O'Neill. *Thoughts on Monteverdi, Bach, and Mozart*.

Leinsdorf, Erich. *The Composer's Advocate: A Radical Orthodoxy for Musicians*. New Haven, Connecticut: Yale University Press. 1981.

McGee, Timothy J. *Medieval and Renaissance Music: A Performer's Guide*. Toronto: University of Toronto Press. 1991.

McGee, Timothy J., et al. *Singing Early Music: The Pronunciation of European Languages in the Late Middle Ages and Renaissance*. Bloomington, Indiana: Indiana University Press. 1996. (includes CD).

Mehaffey, Matthew W. "Considerations of Editorial Procedures in Preparing Performances of Renaissance Music." DMA document, University of Arizona. 2001. wwwlib.umi.com/dissertations.

Phillips, Elizabeth V. and John-Paul Christopher Jackson. *Performing Medieval and Renaissance Music: An Introductory Guide*. New York: Schirmer Books. 1986.

Reeves, Anthony R. "Understanding French Baroque Performance Practice via a Modern Edition of Jean-Philippe Rameau's *In convetendo*." DMA document, University of Arizona. 2001. (Available through UMI at wwwlib.umi.com/disserations.)

Sadie, Julie Anne, editor. *Companion to Baroque Music.* Berkeley, California: University of California Press. 1998.

Sherman, Bernard D. *Inside Early Music: Conversations with Performers.* New York: Oxford Univeristy Press. 1997.

Strunk, Oliver. *Source Readings in Music History.* New York: W. W. Norton & Co. 1950.

Thurmond, James Morgan. *Note Grouping: a Method for Achieving Expression and Style in Musical Performance.* Camp Hill, Pennsylvania: JMT Publications. 1982.

Choral Anthologies and Collections

Dakers, Lionel, compiler and editor. *The New Church Anthem Book: One Hundred Anthems.* New York: Oxford University Press. 1994. (The pieces contained in this book represent sacred choral masterworks from every historical period; the book would be useful to any choral conductor.)

Davies, Walford and Henry G. Ley, editors. *The Church Anthem Book.* London: Oxford University Press. 1933. (The pieces contained in this book represent sacred choral masterworks from every historical period; the book would be useful to any choral conductor.)

Dunn, Thomas, ed. *The Renaissance Singer.* Boston: E.C. Schirmer. 1976.

Greenberg, Noah, editor. *An Anthology of English Medieval and Renaissance Vocal Music: Part Songs for One to Six Voices.* New York: W. W. Norton & Company, Inc. 1961.

Harman, Alec, editor. *The Oxford Book of Italian Madrigals.* Oxford: Oxford University Press. 1983.

Hogan, Moses, editor. *The Oxford Books of Spirituals.* Oxford: Oxford University Press. 2001.

Keyte, Hugh and Andrew Parrott, editors. *The New Oxford Book of Carols.* New York: Oxford University Press. 1998.

Ledger, Philip, editor. *The Oxford Book of English Madrigals.* New York: Oxford University Press. 1978.

Morris, Christopher, compiler. *The Oxford Book of Tudor Anthems.* London: Oxford University Press. 1978.

Parker, Alice and Robert Shaw, arrangers. *The Shaw-Parker Book of Christmas Carols: Twenty-four Collected Carols for Unaccompanied Mixed Chorus.* New York: G. Schirmer, Inc. 1991. (This book contains many of the "classic" Shaw/Parker arrangements of Christmas Carols, along with three new arrangements by Alice Parker.)

Parrish, Carl. *A Treasury of Early Music: An Anthology of Masterworks of the Middle Ages, The Renaissance, and the Baroque Era.* New York: W. W. Norton & Company, Inc. 1958.

Rutter, John, editor. *European Sacred Music.* New York: Oxford University Press. 1996. (This contains fifty-four sacred masterpieces from every historical period, along with valuable notes, commentary, and translations. All of the pieces in this volume are available in single copies from Oxford University Press.)

Willcocks, David and John Rutter, editor and arranger. *100 Carols for Choirs.* New York: Oxford University Press. 1987.

Conducting and Rehearsal Techniques

Davison, Archibald T. *Choral Conducting.* Cambridge, Massachusetts: Harvard University Press. 1940.

Decker, Harold A. and Colleen J. Kirk. *Choral Conducting: Focus on Communication.* Prospect Heights, Ilinois: Waveland Press, Inc. 1988.

Decker, Harold A. and Julius Herford, editors. *Choral Conducting Symposium,* second edition. Englewood Cliffs, New Jersey: Prentice Hall. 1988.

Demaree, Robert W. and Don V. Moses. *The Complete Conductor.* Englewood Cliffs, North Carolina: Prentice Hall. 1995.

Durrant, Colin. *Choral conducting: philosophy and practice.* New York: Routledge. 2003.

Ehmann, Wilhelm, translator. George D. Wiede. *Choral Directing.* Minneapolis, Minnesota: Augsburg Publishing House. 1968.

Garretson, Robert L. *Conducting Choral Music,* eighth edition. Upper Saddle River, New Jersey: Prentice Hall. 1998.

Glenn, Carole, ed. *In Quest of Answers: Interviews with American Choral Conductors.* Chapel Hill, North Carolina: Hinshaw Music, Inc. 1991.

Green, Elizabeth A. H. and Nicolai Malko. *The Conductor and His Score.* Englewood Cliffs, New Jersey: Prentice Hall, Inc. 1975

Green, Elizabeth A. H. *The Modern Conductor,* sixth edition. Upper Saddle River, New Jersey: Prentice Hall, Inc. 1997.

Jordan, James. *Evoking Sound: Fundamentals of Choral Conducting and Rehearsing.* Chircago: GIA Publications, Inc. 1996.

McElheran, Brock. *Conducting Technique: For Beginners and Professionals.* New York: Oxford University Press. 1989.

Moses, Don V., Robert W. Demaree, Jr., and Allen F. Ohmes. *Face to Face with an Orchestra.* Princeton, New Jersey: Prestige Publications, Inc. 1987.

Pfautsch, Lloyd. *Choral Therapy: Techniques and Exercises for the Church Choir.* Nashville, Tennessee: Abingdon Press. 1994. (Excellent information for any choir, not just church choirs.)

Phillips, Kenneth H., *Directing the Choral Music Program.* New York: Oxford University Press. 2004.

Robinson, Ray and Allen Winold. *The Choral Experience: Literature, Materials, and Methods.* Prospect Heights, Illinois: Waveland Press, Inc. 1992. Originally published in 1976 by HarperCollins Publishers.

Rudolf, Max. *The Grammar of Conducting: A Comprehensive Guide to Baton Technique and Interpretation,* third edition. London: Macmillan. 1993.

Webb, Guy B. *Up Front!: Becoming the Complete Choral Conductor.* Boston, Massachusetts: E. C. Schirmer. 1993.

Vocal Techniques

Conable, Barbara. *The Structures and Movement of Breathing: A Primer for Choirs and Choruses.* Chircago: GIA Publications, Inc. 2000.

Ehmann, Wilhelm and Frauke Haasemann. *Voice Building for Choirs.* Chapel Hill, North Carolina: Hinshaw Music. 1982.

Haasemann, Frauke and James M. Jordan. *Group Vocal Technique.* Chapel Hill, North Carolina: Hinshaw Music. 1991. (This series also includes a video and set of exercise cards, available from Hinshaw.)

Horstmann, Sabine. *Chorische Stimmbildung.* Berlin: Verlag Merseburger. 1996. (in German).

McKinney, James C. *The Diagnosis & Correction of Vocal Faults.* Nashville, Tennessee: Broadman Press. 1982.

Miller, Richard. *The Structure of Singing*. New York: Schirmer Books. 1986.

Vennard, William. *Singing: The Mechanism and the Technic*, revised edition. Chicago: Carl Fischer, Inc. 1990.

Journals
American Choral Review. 1958–1991.
American Musicological Society Journal (JAMS). 1948–.
The American Organist. 1918–.
Bach Jahrbuch. 1904–.
The Choral Journal. 1959–.
Current Musicologist. 1965–.
Early Music. 1973–.
Ethnomusicology. 1956–.
Journal of Music Theory. 1957–.
Journal of Musicology. 1982–.
Journal of Research in Music Education. 1953–.
Journal of Research in Singing. 1977–.
Journal of Singing. 1945–. Formerly *The NATS Journal* and *The NATS Bulletin*.
NZ. Neue Zeitschrift für Musik. 1979–.
Neue Zeitschrift für Musik. 1834–.
Journal of Muscological Research. 1979–.
Music and Letters. 1920–.
Music Educators Journal. 1914–.
The Music Review. 1940–.
Musica Disciplina: A Journal of the History of Music. v2 1948–. See *Journal of Renaissance and Baroque Music*. v1 1946/47.
Musical Quarterly. 1915–.
The Musical Times. 1844–. Formerly *Musical Times and Singing Class Circular*.
Perspectives of New Music. 1962–.

Biblical/Liturgical Reference Materials
The Anchor Bible Dictionary. David Noel, et al, editors. New York: Doubleday. 1992. 6v.

Anderson, A.A. *The New Century Bible Commentary: The Book of Psalms*. (Volume I, Psalms 1–72; Volume II, 73–150). Grand Rapids, Michigan: Wm. B. Eerdmans Publishing Company, 1972. (These volumes provide excellent and intelligible information about the psalms, and can be useful in understanding pieces that use psalm texts.)

Cardine, Dom Eugene, translator and editor. William Tortolano. *Beginning Studies in Gregorian Chant*. Chicago: GIA Publications, Inc. 1988. (This book contains valuable information about the notation and performance of Gregorian chant. Dom Cardine was a Benedictine monk at Solesmes.)

Graduale Romanum. The Benedictines of Solesmes, editors. Available from GIA Publications, Inc. (This book contains many of the Proper chants not included in the *Liber Usualis* as well as additional Ordinary chants.)

Liber Usualis. The Benedictines of Solesmes, editors. (This book contains all of the standard chants for the Mass Ordinary, the Divine Offices, and Proper Antiphons, as well as The Requiem Mass, and other often used liturgical chants. It is available from St. Bonaventure Publications, P.O. Box 2750, Great Falls, Montana 59403-2750; or on the Web at www.ncn.net/~relbooks/liber.html.

The New Oxford Annotated Bible with the Apocryphal/Deuterocanonical Books (New Revised Standard Version). Bruce M. Metzger and Roland E. Murphy, editors. New York: Oxford University Press. 1994. (This volume contains the entire biblical text along with valuable notes, historical background, information about Hebrew poetry, literary forms, a concordance, maps, etc.)

Strong, James. *The Exhaustive Concordance of the Bible*. Nashville: Abingdon. 1990.

Theory and Analysis

Fux, Johann Joseph and Alfred Mann, editor. *The Study of Counterpoint*. New York: W. W. Norton & Company. 1990. (This was composed by an eighteenth-century musician but describes sixteenth-century counterpoint.)

Jeppesen, Knud. *Counterpoint: The Polyphonic Style of the Sixteenth Century*. New York: Dover Publications, Inc. 1992.

Kennan, Kent. *Counterpoint*, fourth edition. Englewood Cliffs, New Jersey: Prentice-Hall. 1998. (This book deals with eighteenth-century counterpoint.)

Kennan, Kent Wheeler and Donald Grantham. *The Technique of Orchestration*, fifth edition. New York: Simon & Schuster. 1996. (Contains excellent information about the various instruments of the orchestra, their transpositions, etc., with helpful charts and tables.)

Kostka, Stefan M. *Materials and Techniques of Twentieth-Century Music*. Englewood Cliffs, New Jersey: Prentice-Hall. 1990.

Kostka, Stefan and Dorothy Payne. *Tonal Harmony, with an Introduction to Twentieth-Century Music*, fourth revision. New York: McGraw-Hill. 2000.

Ottman, Robert W. *Elementary Harmony: Theory and Practice*, fifth edition. Englewood Cliffs, New Jersey: Prentice-Hall. 1998.

Music Reference

Daugherty, F. Mark and Susan H. Simon, eds. *Secular Choral Music in Print*, second edition. Philadelphia: Musicdata, 1987–96. 2v. plus supplements.

Eslinger, Gary S. and F. Mark Daugherty, editors. *Sacred Choral Music in Print*, second edition. Philadelphia: Musicdata, 1985. 2v. plus supplements.

Foster, Myles Birket. *Anthems and Anthem Composers: An Essay upon the Development of the Anthem from the Time of the Reformation to the End of the Nineteenth Century*. London: Novello. 1901. R/New York: Da Capo. 1970.

Hovland, Michael, editor. *Musical Settings of American Poetry: A Bibliography*. New York: Greenwood Press. 1986.

Music in Print: Annual Supplement 1986. Philadelphia: Musicdata. 1986.

Music in Print: Master Composer Index 1988. Philadelphia: Musicdata. 1989.

Music in Print: Master Title Index 1988. Philadelphia: Musicdata. 1990.

Répertoire International de Littérature Musicale (RILM). International Inventory of Music Literature. RILM abstracts of music literature. New York: International RILM Center. 1967. Available through OCLC First Search.

Sacred Choral Music in Print, second edition. *Arranger Index*. Philadelphia: Musicdata. 1987.

Secular Choral Music in Print. Second edition. *Arranger Index*. Philadelphia: Musicdata. 1987.

Index by Title

Index by Composer, Arranger

About the Editors

Australian born conductor **Heather J. Buchanan** is Director of Choral Activities and Assistant Professor of Music at Montclair State University, Upper Montclair, New Jersey, where she conducts the 135-voice Chorale and 36-voice Chamber Singers. Prior to Montclair she was on the conducting faculty at Westminster Choir College of Rider University. A certified Andover Educator, Buchanan specializes in the teaching of Body Mapping and somatic pedagogy for choral musicians. She is also a Ph.D. Candidate with the University of New England (Australia) researching the impact of Body Mapping on musicians. Buchanan serves as chair of Repertoire & Standards for Youth & Student Activities for NJ-ACDA. She earned her degrees from the Queensland Conservatorium of Music (Australia - BME) and Westminster Choir College of Rider University (MM). Her publications include the Video (2002) and DVD (2004) *Evoking Sound: Body Mapping & Gesture Fundamentals* (GIA Publications, Inc.). A vibrant musician and dynamic pedagogue, Buchanan is an experienced choral director and music educator and is in demand as a guest conductor, clinician, and adjudicator for choral and educational events in the United States and Australia.

Matthew W. Mehaffey is Assistant Professor of Music and Director of Choral Activities at The George Washington University in Washington, D.C. A native of Pittsburgh, Pennsylvania, he holds degrees from Bucknell University (BME), Westminster Choir College (MM in Choral Conducting), and the University of Arizona (DMA in Choral Conducting and Historical Musicology). As an author, Mehaffey has coauthored the GIA Music series *Choral Ensemble Intonation: Method, Procedures, and Exercises* with James Jordan of Westminster Choir College. In addition to his university duties, he serves as the President-Elect of The Maryland/D.C. Chapter of the American Choral Directors Association, and is a founding member of Viri Animarum, a professional men's vocal ensemble. He and his GWU colleague, Douglas Boyce, have been awarded two of the university's most competitive research grants for the development of interactive on-line software for teaching music fundamentals. He lives in downtown Washington, D.C. with his wife, Libby.